D#

P9-AGA-053

8-2-91

WITHDRAWN

28

DAVID O. McKAY LIBRARY
BYU-IDAHO
RICKS COLLEGE
DAVID O. McKAY LIBRARY
REXBURG, IDAHO 83440

The Life
of
Maxwell
Anderson

BOOKS BY ALFRED S. SHIVERS
Jessamyn West
Maxwell Anderson

The Life of Maxwell Anderson

Alfred S. Shivers, Ph.D.

𝔰𝔡

STEIN AND DAY/*Publishers*/New York

Permissions for quotations will be
found in the Acknowledgments.

First published in 1983
Copyright © 1983 by Alfred S. Shivers
All rights reserved, Stein and Day, Incorporated
Designed by Judith E. Dalzell
Printed in the United States of America
STEIN AND DAY/*Publishers*
Scarborough House
Briarcliff Manor, N.Y. 10510

Library of Congress Cataloging in Publication Data

Shivers, Alfred S.
   The life of Maxwell Anderson.
Bibliography: p.
Includes index.
   1. Anderson, Maxwell, 1888-1959—Biography.
2. Dramatists, American—20th century—Biography.
I. Title.
PS3501.N256Z89   1983   812'.52 [B]   80-5721
ISBN 0-8128-2789-9

to
my mother-in-law,
CLARE INTEMANN SAMMIS,
whose resourcefulness and devotion and generosity
for over twenty years
this dedication can never repay

    and

my friend since childhood,
RALPH DENVER OLIVE,
an enthusiast for the purple pageantry of the stage
who by being what he was long ago
and opening his library to me
helped change my life

CONTENTS

ACKNOWLEDGMENTS

This biography is based on miscellaneous items published in periodicals and books; on many letters included in Dr. Laurence G. Avery's volume of the Anderson correspondence titled *Dramatist in America* as well as on many not included there; on diaries; on business papers, such as those of The Playwrights Producing Company; on notes; on legal documents; on important oral and unpublished written reminiscences from Maxwell Anderson's relatives and friends (most such accounts generated especially for this book); on a memoir that Anderson left with the Oral History Research Office at Columbia University; on family genealogical records; and on hitherto unpublished photographs owned by the family.

In preparing for this biography I read literally everything that Anderson ever published, along with every letter and diary and playscript available to me; traveled to the two main archives of Andersonia, namely the Humanities Research Center at the University of Texas and the State Historical Society of Wisconsin at Madison; and also visited the Western Reserve Historical Society at Cleveland, O. By correspondence I was able to check the holdings at the University of North Dakota, Stanford University, and the Library and Museum of the Performing Arts at the New York Public Library. I am grateful to all these institutions for their help.

During my research at the University of Texas, however, I was denied access to a small group of letters and diaries that his widow, the third Mrs. Maxwell Anderson, had deposited there in 1973 under the provision that, except with her express permission, they cannot be read until her death. Nevertheless, I obtained from her copies of a few pages from the otherwise sealed 1952 diary and managed to supplement such information as they provide with firsthand studies of the other diaries on deposit there; with letters and questionnaires from her and other family members and friends; and with the interviews (see later). All evidence indicates that the restricted letters and diaries deal with the events surrounding Mab Maynard's death and with the playwright's relationship to his daughter Hesper. Not quite all the other correspondents allowed me to see Maxwell Anderson letters in their possession—for instance, those owned by Kenneth Anderson and Ralph Chambers (son of Maxwell's sister Ethel); and those written to Josephine Herbst and filed at Yale University under terms of the Herbst estate. The contents of all these restricted holdings, however, are sufficiently clear from examining the other end of the correspondence. In spite of such handicaps, I am confident that the record given here in *The Life of Maxwell Anderson* is reasonably complete and accurate.

Of special value for my work is the mail to me from several Anderson relatives, ten of whom read and commented on early drafts of the book, ranging from a few chapters to the entire text. Among these is the playwright's sister Lela Blanch Chambers, who was an accurate and ready source of information about Anderson's early years. I received more than sixty-six letters from her alone, not counting an extensive chronology of the family's movements in the Midwest as well as her lengthy, unpublished "Life" typescript. I was pleased to spend several days living in her household at Olean, N.Y., while interviewing her and her son Avery and his wife, Blanche, along with Maxwell's brother Kenneth, a large and formidable-looking gentleman in his seventies, who was at first reluctant to see me but who upon further acquaintance proved to be one of the friendliest and most helpful of all my informants. Kenneth's son, Dr. Donald Anderson, supplied me with a good deal of important genealogical material; although I never met him, he was so courteous and precise in his communications that I regret not having used his services more than I did. Even more valuable in my work are the extensive communications to me from the playwright's son Alan Haskett Anderson, who was formerly a Broadway stage manager and director as well as a confidant of his father. Alan was especially useful in helping me with the professional years, supplying material about his father's political and philosophical views, writing habits, recreations, hobbies, tastes, and dress, along with numerous bits of information about the marriages and children as well as the neighbors in New City, N.Y. Like Mrs. Maxwell Anderson (Gilda), he studied the entire text of this biography and offered numerous corrections and additions, most of which I was able to use in my revision. (Nevertheless, there were some instances in which I could not accept Alan and Gilda's views.) For a week I was privileged to be a guest in Alan's household at 170 South Mountain Road in New City, in the very farmhouse once owned and occupied by his father. Alan and his wife, Nancy, went far out of their way to put me in touch with other knowledgeable people in the region, such as the playwright's friends Lotte Lenya and Julie Sloane, and Alan's former sister-in-law Meg Anderson. I had several fruitful sessions with his brother Terence, and with Terence's wife, Lulu, occupants of the "studio house" built by the father next door. In New York City it was part of my continuing good luck to locate the third son, Quentin, and have a long talk with him. In Ledyard, Conn., I spent all of an afternoon at the apartment of Anderson's youngest brother, Lawrence, who with his wife, Lillian, assisted me in divers ways. One of my most eagerly anticipated visits was with Gilda Anderson (the third Mrs. Maxwell Anderson) at her home in Stamford, Conn.; she granted me a very long visit and then answered numerous queries by mail and telephone, even though it pained her to recall some experiences that my research touched upon. Like Lela, Lawrence, Alan, and Hesper, she supplied me with some unpublished photographs to use in this book. On the trip back home from these meetings in 1978 I stopped off at Chapel Hill, N.C., and talked with two of the playwright's friends, Paul Green (*The Lost Colony*) and his wife, Elizabeth. Two years later, in California, it was my privilege to interview the playwright's daughter Hesper as well as his friend and protégé Marion Hargrove (*See Here, Private Hargrove*).

I freely acknowledge my indebtedness to Dr. Avery's scholarship as represented in his *Dramatist in America* and *A Catalogue of the Maxwell Anderson Collection at the University of Texas*, and I feel most fortunate that the first-named book arrived on the market at about the time when I decided to resume Anderson studies and do the biography.

Not only am I indebted to the staffs of the libraries already named but also to Cleo B. Kelly, Elizabeth Jane Logan, and David Eugene Vancil of the Ralph W. Steen Library at Stephen F. Austin State University, where I received valuable interlibrary loan and reference services.

I wish to thank the following private individuals for their various types of assistance (usually letters).

Anderson's schoolmates and childhood acquaintances: Frederick J. Brockhoff (Park Ridge, Ill.), Hallie Loomis Craytor (Bloomington, Ind.), Melvin I. Orms (Zephyrhills, Fla.), Dr. C. L. Robertson (Jamestown, N.D.), and Mrs. George F. Shafer (Bismarck, N.D.).

Anderson's friends and acquaintances from adult life: Robert Woodruff Anderson (New York City), Milton Caniff (Palm Springs, Calif.), Phoebe Brand Carnovsky (Easton, Conn.), Lynn Fontanne (Genessee Depot, Wisc.), Marion Hargrove (Santa Monica, Calif.), Kathryn Hulme (Kapaa Kauai, Hawaii), Thomas James Montgomery Mulvehill (Arlington, Va.), Dr. Lee Norvelle (Bloomington, Ind.), Victor Samrock (New York City), and John F. Wharton (New York City).

Relatives outside the immediate family, exclusive of those already mentioned: Libbe Higger Axlrod (Miami, Fla.), Mrs. Olive Benson (Bottineau, N.D.), Lloyd R. Hamilton (Fontana, Calif.), Mrs. Laurel Hon (Redding, Conn.), Mrs. Esther Reagan (Savanna, Ill.), Ovid B. Romano (Lincoln, R.I.), Janet Sheldon (Yucca Valley, Calif.), Mr. and Mrs. J. Forest Wood (Atlantic, Pa.), and Mrs. Margaret Zimmer (Birmingham, Mich.).

Other people: Jane McDill Anderson (Nyack, N.Y.), Dr. Arthur F. Camp (Lake Alfred, Fla.), Jan Christopherson (Jamestown, N.D.), Dr. Charles W. Cooper (Santa Barbara, Calif.), Frank N. Fischer (Jamestown, N.D.), Dr. Louis G. Geiger (Colorado Springs, Colo.), Mrs. Helena Phillis Goodmote (Atlantic, Pa.), Dr. John P. Hagan (Houston, Tex.), Gertrude Hintz (New Hampton, Ia.), Hilliary Hunt (Haverstraw, N.Y.), Mrs. Robert Kenyon (Jefferson, O.), Dr. Thomas J. King and his son Rufus C. King (New City, N.Y.), Louis L'Amour (Los Angeles, Calif.), Dr. Henry G. Lee (Philadelphia, Pa.), Louis J. Lefkowitz (Albany, N.Y.), Sylvia Stallings Lowe (Alexandria, Va.), Thomas McGrath (Moorhead, Minn.), Dr. Elizabeth Dianne Malpass (Nacogdoches, Tex.), Helen Mohlberg, (Bottineau, N.D.), Shirley D. Naismith (Grand Forks, N.D.), Dave Peters (Cambridge, Mass.), Robert Ricci (Providence, R.I.), Cora W. Russell, (Bottineau, N.D.), Robert G. Smith and his widow, Ellen (Hartford, Conn.), Mrs. Perry W. Snyder (New Hampton, Ia.), J. Lloyd Stone (Palm Desert, Calif.), Carl E. S. Strem (Laguna Hills, Calif.), Earl S. Strinden (Grand Forks, N.D.), Mrs. Edna LaMoore Waldo (Castro Valley, Calif.), the Reverend Arthur Yeagy (Harrisburg, Pa.), and Thomas L. Yoset (Meadville, Pa.).

My gratitude also goes to my wife, Clare Ann, for her comments on the work-in-progress and for the patience with which she has borne my numerous absences from the family circle.

And to my colleagues Drs. Neal B. Houston and William Reed Cozart for giving the first half of the biography and the final chapter their scrutiny. Their encouragement meant a great deal to me.

And to my department chairman, Dr. Roy E. Cain, for his ready cooperation in providing telephone, postal, and duplication services.

And to Stephen F. Austin State University for the 1978 and 1979 Faculty Research Grants that made all the difference in whether this book would ever be researched and written.

And last but certainly not least, to my editor, Miss Patricia Day (of Stein and Day Publishers), for the faith she had in this book from the beginning and for her meticulous corrections and suggestions for improvement.

Selections from *Dramatist in America: Letters of Maxwell Anderson, 1912-1958* by Laurence Avery, The University of North Carolina Press. Copyright © 1977 by The University of North Carolina Press. Reprinted by permission of Gilda Anderson.

Selection from *Lela's Life* reprinted by permission of Lela A. Chambers.

Selections of letters and conversations with Alan Haskett Anderson and a selection from a letter by Margaret H. Anderson to Kenneth Anderson, reprinted by permission of Alan Haskett Anderson.

Selections from the memorial address by Quentin Anderson reprinted by permission of Quentin Anderson.

Selection from a letter from Dr. Lee Norvelle reprinted by permission of Dr. Lee Norvelle.

Selections from Lawrence Anderson reprinted by permission of Lawrence Anderson.

Selections from *Key Largo,* Copyright © 1939 by Maxwell Anderson, Copyright © renewed 1967 by Gilda Anderson, All rights reserved, reprinted by permission of J. Kenneth Anderson, Anderson House.

Selections from *Winterset,* Copyright © 1935 by Anderson House, Copyright © renewed 1963 by Gilda Anderson, all rights reserved, reprinted by permission of J. Kenneth Anderson, Anderson House.

Selections from *High Tor,* copyright © 1937 by Maxwell Anderson, Copyright © renewed 1964 by Gilda Anderson, all rights reserved, reprinted by permission of J. Kenneth Anderson, Anderson House.

Selections from Frederick J. Brockhoff reprinted by permission of Frederick J. Brockhoff.

Selections from the letters of Marion Hargrove and from his book *See Here, Private Hargrove* reprinted by permission of Marion Hargrove.

Selections from "The Masque of Pedagogues," from the Spring 1957 edition of the *North Dakota Quarterly,* University of North Dakota, reprinted by permission of the *North Dakota Quarterly.*

Selections from letters of Kenneth Anderson reprinted by permission of Kenneth Anderson.

Selections from the memoirs of Maxwell Anderson and Frank Ernest Hill on file in the Oral History Research Office. Copyright © 1972 by The Trustees of Columbia University in the City of New York. Reprinted by permission of Columbia University.

Selections from *The Tower of Jewels* by Robert L. Duffus, W. W. Norton & Company, Inc., reprinted by permission of W. W. Norton.

Selections from the letters of Libbe H. Axlrod reprinted by permission of Libbe H. Axlrod.

Selections from the letters of Kathryn Hulme and her book *Undiscovered Country* reprinted by permission of Kathryn Hulme.

Selections from Paul Green reprinted by permission of Paul Green.

Selections from the eulogy on Maxwell Anderson reprinted by permission of Robert W. Anderson.

Selections from *Magic Curtain* by Lawrence Langner reprinted by permission of Armina M. Langner, The Theatre Guild.

Selections from Melvin I. Orms reprinted by permission of Melvin I. Orms.

Selections from the letters of Dr. Donald Anderson reprinted by permission of Dr. Donald Anderson.

Selections from an article in the *North Dakota Alumni Review,* December 5, 1958, reprinted by permission of Earl S. Strinden, University of North Dakota Alumni Association and Foundation.

Selections from *Life Among the Playwrights* by John F. Wharton, published by Quadrangle/The New York Times Book Co., copyright © 1974 by John F. Wharton, reprinted by permission of Times Books.

Selection from the letter of R. Graeme Smith to Maxwell Anderson reprinted by permission of Ellen Smith.

Selections of letters, poems, and unpublished material of both Maxwell Anderson and Gilda Anderson reprinted by permission of Gilda Anderson.

INTRODUCTION

This is the story of James Maxwell Anderson (1888-1959), one of America's most distinguished dramatists, responsible for that remarkable parade of *Elizabeth the Queen, Mary of Scotland, Valley Forge, Winterset, The Wingless Victory, High Tor, Key Largo, Anne of the Thousand Days,* and other attractions so numerous as to suggest the achievement of two or three authors instead of one. It is also about his dream of trying to bring back poetic drama to the theater.

In his day, some critics considered Anderson second only to Eugene O'Neill in the annals of the American theater. Others (maybe including Anderson himself) thought that he ranked at least as an equal because, though he fell short in bold originality, he was obviously more versatile and had a far more graceful and melodious command of language.

My research into the life of this reclusive figure goes back more than a decade, to when I was preparing a book of dramatic criticism called *Maxwell Anderson,*[1] at which time I planned to use as much biography as my editor would tolerate because it was distressingly clear to me that the public knew all too little about the man behind the plays. But getting to know him well enough to write the full life story represented an awesome challenge to me even at that early date. It was after the foregoing book was published that I had the privilege of interviewing some of his close relatives and friends for the first time in my research and of examining in detail the Anderson papers and other numerous and miscellaneous types of memorabilia. On the one hand I encountered no lack of documentary source material and kinsmen willing to be interviewed (once they learned the seriousness of the project), but on the other some delicate problems, such as when his daughter Hesper told me that her father was indirectly responsible for her mother's death—an allegation that I doubted but, as a conscientious researcher, I had to investigate as well as I could. Various surprises awaited me in other quarters as well. Soon it was clear that only the most thorough inquiry and evaluation would resolve the conflicting pieces of information that early began to accumulate; moreover, I was to learn anew the old truth that any biographer who dares to write about the living or the recently dead is going to face formidable handicaps. I recognized early that some of my findings were not going to sit well with family sensibilities even though I was and still am one of the dramatist's devoted admirers.

In obtaining memoirs from people who had known Anderson more than casually, I found that pretty often a given informant was knowledgeable about one period in the life but understandably in the dark about all earlier and later ones. This circumstance suggests not merely that Anderson had extremely few intimates—even members of The Playwrights Producing Company rarely saw each other socially, at least in its last years[2]—but also that he seldom reminisced with anyone outside his immediate family, and sparingly even there.

In *The Life of Maxwell Anderson* I have tried to give an objective account of the whole man, replete with cinders and stardust. Putting it together has been the single most exciting experience that I ever had in research and writing, not merely because Anderson is so eminently worthy of study but also because there comes to some of us an indescribable feeling of triumph when we have outraced mortality and finally located, after long searching, the childhood sweetheart and the classmate and the colleague still alive and willing to send us a memoir through the mail; or, while leafing through the archives of some library, found that yellowing piece of paper whose faded ink still leaves it more reliable than the best memory.

Just as the 1920s in the American theater had belonged to Eugene O'Neill, so the 1930s belonged to Maxwell Anderson. But Anderson's productive period is much longer than that; in fact, there were few seasons from 1923 to the year before he died when he didn't have a new play readied for the New York stage, the most difficult of all places in which a writer can achieve sustained commercial success. During one season alone, three of his works—*The Wingless Victory, High Tor,* and *The Masque of Kings*—opened to popular acclaim on Broadway. In many a review he was the darling of discerning critics. University students studied his plays. In a city where promising playwrights come in droves, and most of even the better ones lose speed and droop after perhaps a spectacular mile or two, this rebel son of a preacher was indeed a long-distance runner. I wrote in my earlier book that Anderson the poetic dramatist is to the American theater what Johann Schiller is to the German, what Edmond Rostand is to the French, and what Sean O'Casey is to the Irish.

There never lived another American dramatist so confoundedly hidden from his public than this Anderson. But if there is one thing that most informants agree upon, it is that up until late middle age he was an out-and-out radical. One of his early newspaper editor friends, Bruce Bliven, called him with justice a "philosophical anarchist, with the utter pessimism about reform and reformers appropriate to that attitude."[3] To his eldest son, Quentin, he seemed nothing less than a "classical libertarian," fit company for the likes of John Stuart Mill.[4] John Wharton, his lawyer friend in The Playwrights Producing Company, wrote some complimentary things about him but also some unpleasant ones too, namely that he was a suspicious, argumentative, mercurial artist capable of sometimes explosive anger.[5] Later in the book we will see some examples of this anger. But when I told Anderson's daughter Hesper about the lawyer's appraisal, she was genuinely surprised at his use of the word "mercurial," asserting that, on the contrary, her father was steady in temperament and most predictable.[6] Like other complex personalities, he struck different acquaintances in different ways. For instance, theatrical director Dr. Lee Norvelle apparently never saw a flare-up of temper—or anything unpleasant at all—in his famous friend of many years. "I never knew a more humble man nor one with greater integrity," he wrote to me. And, "In all of my dealings with him he was kind, considerate, cooperative and trustworthy."[7]

To his brother Kenneth and to his third wife, Gilda, he was above all a romantic in temperament.[8] And the same goes for actor-playwright George Abbott, who had worked closely with Anderson in connection with two plays: "On the surface Maxwell was a stolid, scholarly man, but inside he was all romance: he wished to ride a white steed over the mountains and carry off a beautiful maiden as much as the next fellow."[9]

Maxwell Anderson granted but eight known interviews to the press, and in these gave tantalizingly few details about his personal life. When Burns Mantle was preparing his book *American Playwrights of Today,* he sent Anderson a questionnaire soliciting biographical data and got back little more than the scant reply: "When a man starts peddling personal stuff about himself they should send a squad of strong-arm worms after him, because he is dead."[10] Some years later Barrett H. Clark, wanting to do a whole book about this new author, applied for his *vita* also and received from him a note which began:

> I hope you won't think me discourteous if I am niggardly of information about myself. This modern craze for biographical information leaves me cold for many reasons. For one thing it's always inaccurate. … For another it's so bound up with publicity and other varieties of idiocy that it gags a person of any sensibility. For another, to be heralded is to become a candidate for the newest list of "the busted geniuses of yesteryear" of whom I hope never to be one.[11]

This was no pose. Consequently, Clark's *Maxwell Anderson: The Man and His Plays,* interesting mainly as a pioneering effort, was surely one of the thinnest books to come out in 1933, the biographical part consisting of just six tiny pages. The mystery playwright of Broadway had won again! Anderson's colleague in The Playwrights Producing Company, S. N. Behrman, wrote in *Tribulations and Laughter* that he had received from a reputable publisher the enviable offer of thirty thousand dollars as advance bounty to capture his friend in a book, but for some undisclosed reason he turned down the offer.[12] Possibly Behrman allowed his friend to talk him out of the project. Nor was our playwright secretly saving himself for the big autobiography that he would write and spring upon the world someday, for that never happened. No unpublished memoir, fragmentary or otherwise, remains. The closest he came to such a work was the interview he gave to Columbia University in his last years,[13] and a letter of reminiscence that he sent to his alma mater, the University of North Dakota, shortly before he died.[14]

For even more reasons than those already mentioned, it is clear that the full story of Maxwell Anderson could not have been written during his lifetime. Today the warring factions of his family would seem to prevent an objective biography coming from within the family circle; this necessarily leaves the task in the hands of an outsider. Eleven years of work went into this book, but whether it is definitive is more than I can say. I would feel satisfied if my book chances to win new friends and readers for the plays of Maxwell Anderson.

THE RESTLESS YEARS

There is no mystery more incalculable, more tantalizing, than the emergence of genius from an ordinary, even coarse, social texture.
    —S. N. Behrman, *People in a Diary*

Maxwell Anderson, whose wide-ranging sympathies as a dramatist made him at home in his art with the eminent and powerful of the earth, was himself of common origin in people only recently from the soil. He had not a single known ancestor with any kind of fame or fortune, and his sister Lela tells us that he believed without question that he had lifted himself up the ladder of success by his own bootstraps.

When Queen Anne elevated one of England's greatest generals, John Churchill, to become the first Duke of Marlborough, some members of the established nobility would not accept the newcomer socially because of his humble parentage, and they taunted him whenever the opportunity arose. On one such occasion an aristocrat said to him mockingly, "Tell me, whose descendant are you?" To which the new Duke replied: "Sir, I am not a descendant, I am an ancestor." This witty rejoinder by the victor of the Battle of Blenheim describes Anderson's situation in his family tree today.

In the summer of 1935, when his name was known from Boston to Bombay as the daring innovator of verse plays that were actually successful on the commercial stage—a feat common in the seventeenth century but quite an anomaly in the twentieth—Anderson took his companion Mab and his sisters Lela and Ethel on a sentimental journey to western Pennsylvania to the fly speck of a village called Atlantic, where he and Ethel had been born late in the last century; and then a few miles on to Geneva, near which his paternal ancestors had tilled the soil since right after the Revolutionary War. Dressed in shirt sleeves and felt hat, burly Anderson drove his Packard along narrow country roads and gazed through the mists of memory at the rustic scenes of his childhood. He may have been unconsciously refreshing himself on features of farm life, of terrain, of speech, and of dress that he would one day employ in his novel *Morning Winter and Night*.

Apparently it was his first visit to Atlantic since he was a teenager, and he was surprised to find some Mennonite families in the neighborhood. When the four rolled up to the site of what had been his Grandmother Shepard's farm, a half mile east of the railroad track that runs through the village, the primitive little house he so dearly remembered was gone and in its stead a small new one was being hammered together. Gone too was the nearby one-and-a-half-story clapboard structure in which he was born.

Surviving photographs and recollections from Lela show that the traveling group finally found, possibly at "Henry's Corners," the next crossing a mile east on the same road, what was left of his house of birth, which had been hauled there from its original site. To see it was a humbling experience. Although it had been given a coat of white paint in recent years, it was run-down and empty, yet not nearly as depressing a sight as it would become some years hence when he came back for still another visit, this time with his Uncle Frank as guide, and found the house reduced to serving as a chicken coop![1]

That same day Maxwell Anderson and the women drove over to Geneva and visited the grave of his mother, who had died the year before, and also the old Anderson farmhouse, where they were disappointed to find no one at home. His great-great-grandfather Samuel Anderson had lived here in Geneva, and later his son named after him. The first Samuel was a Scot who in the late eighteenth century is thought to have sailed to America by way of Ireland.[2] Later we find him serving in the Cumberland County militia during the Revolutionary War,[3] after which he moved here to Crawford County, bought a large acreage a few miles south of Geneva, and settled down to farming and blacksmithing. This ancestor of one of America's greatest men of letters was probably illiterate, like his offspring the second Samuel: The latter bore arms at Erie with the Pennsylvania militia during the War of 1812 and in a codicil to his will directed that "the Grave Yard on my land be . . . left for the benefit of the neighborhood for a Bering [sic] Ground . . .,"[4] and he affixed his mark of "X." His act of generosity created the present Anderson cemetery, where lie so many of Maxwell Anderson's forebears.[5] One of the second Samuel's grandsons was William Lincoln, father of the dramatist.

Among all of Maxwell's known predecessors on the father's side, there has been no discovery of writing skill or artistic talent. What we do find are plain folk of sturdy, pioneer stock who had a hand in carving an empire out of the American wilderness, the gene pool from which rare civilizing talents might emerge in more settled conditions.[6]

Anderson's mother, Charlotte Perrimela (Premma) Stephenson, had a somewhat more distinguished background. One of her paternal uncles was a physician, another a parson. Her father, William, was both a veterinarian and a maker of prosthetic devices for injured or crippled people. Premma, who had grown into a young woman in that same region of Pennsylvania, could trace her descent both to the Scots and to the Irish—and with less certainty to the French, too, according to a romantic story traditional among the Stephensons. The story goes that back in the eighteenth century a young, titled French girl, the original Perrimela, was getting ready to travel to America alone and had the pleasant problem of figuring out how to keep her fortune in gold pieces secure while she made the crossing. Being resourceful, she sewed the coins into a beautiful, quilted, satin petticoat. Just how this laden, aureate creature managed to board the ship—whether the crew had to hoist her over the rail in a cargo net or trundle her up the gangplank in a handcart—is not recorded. Had weighty Perrimela fallen overboard just once wearing that golden petticoat, some of the glory of the future American theater might have gone down in that same splash. But she managed to land safely in Philadelphia, made some friends there, and married a man said to be related to William Penn, a Mr. Fell, who no doubt thought her to be a lady of substance. Two of their descendants were Maxwell Anderson's mother and her sister, Emma, who grew up on a fifty-acre farm just east of Atlantic.[7] Emma stayed on the farm long after Premma married and moved on, for Emma was disfigured at birth by a clubbed hand on which three of the fingers were grown together.[8] Her younger and more favored sister, Premma, painted before marrying William Lincoln (Linc) Anderson; on the application for the marriage license, she listed her occupation as "artist."[9]

At the time he was courting Premma, curly-haired and brown-eyed Linc was a husky young backwoodsman with a forceful personality and an inquiring mind. One early photograph shows him as decidedly plain-featured, but later ones show him growing increasingly handsome even into old age (a snare for female hearts!). Handy with an ax, young Linc had labored as a woodcutter in the forests of Michigan, but at the time he met Premma he was living at home and helping to run his father's farm. After he and Premma married, they moved to Espyville, Pennsylvania, and rented a house there until their firstborn, Ethel, developed an ailment that called for the tender, loving offices of the maternal grandmother, Charlotte Shepard, whereupon they returned to tiny Atlantic. There, Linc sold the Shepards' timber for them and built for himself a small house a short distance to the east and somewhat to the south of the present Wesley J. Phillis house. In this little building James Maxwell was born on December 15, 1888, the second child and eldest son in a brood that was to number eight.[10] Little Maxwell, afflicted with what was thought to be a heart murmur, was ill for a long time; he was especially susceptible to colds and was kept indoors much.

Within three years Linc had moved his family to Andover, Ohio, where he got a job on the railroad. While he was at Andover the pulpit of the local Baptist Church fell vacant, and the parishioners asked him to fill it. No licensing was required for this position, but he found it necessary to prepare himself by studying at night.[11] His educational background was scanty and owed much to his own initiative as a reader of books; in spite of his later claim to having attended certain institutions of higher learning, his actual formal schooling seems to have been limited to little more than what he had already received at Meadville Academy.[12] With his excellent memory he learned quickly, and in due time he came to know the Bible from Genesis to Revelation. Moreover, he developed into an outstanding storyteller who could breathe new life into the old biblical accounts. "He would play all the different parts of the people. An actor. But you couldn't have told him he was an actor. He didn't think of it from that point of view," was his son Lawrence's recollection.[13] If any of this dramatic skill passed on to Maxwell, it did so not in the form of acting ability (of which he had not a jot and knew it) but in the much more enviable power to write graceful and affecting dialogue for plays. Unfortunately, the Reverend Anderson had such a flair for "passionate periods" as to give his son Max an abiding aversion to oratory and to any opportunities to make speeches.[14] (This is illustrated in *Valley Forge*, where Lafayette does not trust himself to use florid rhetoric when addressing General Washington.) Max reportedly said of the minister that he was "a good mixer, and a wonderful orator. . . . and in the pulpit was the most persuasive man I ever heard. But I knew it was all put on. I've never been able to stand anything affected since."[15] This was the evaluation that Max intended for public consumption; perhaps he was too kind to tell the whole truth. His last wife, Gilda, explained the problem this way:

> It troubled Max . . . how easily his father could turn on all that charm and persuasiveness for the congregation and switch it off at home. That would instill a feeling of distrust for what his father was selling.[16]

Max saw his father's personality as a mask deliberately worn to sway congregations to his Bible-thumping, Fundamentalist, fire-and-brimstone beliefs; and Max saw these methods as deceptive and fraudulent. But one suspects that there is a deeper cause for the dislike than a mere distrust of rhetoric.

Was the parson's apparent womanizing at the root of Max's resentment? Interviews with all four of the playwright's children, his widow, his brother Lawrence, and his onetime daughter-in-law Margaret (Meg) Anderson indicate that the preacher had a more than pastoral intimacy with some women in the congregations that he served. Premma, not being well and burdened with far more children than she could comfortably take care of on his salary, and being a retiring person, did not play the piano or sing in the choir or plan church dinners or supervise the missionary society; and yet all these things had to be done if the new and ambitious pastor were going to make the church flourish. Poor Premma must have been tired much of the time just keeping the ever-enlarging household running. At any rate, in her absence he turned often to the other women for help, and they in turn were more responsive and accommodating than Premma could have wished. As a handsome, charming, and thickly built six-footer, with arms like iron and with the lusty blood of a backwoodsman in his veins, he was surrounded by numerous temptations of the flesh wherever he moved in parishes about Pennsylvania and the states of the Middle West. Often he would be away from home for months on end when he was out spreading the gospel—or charm—and such absences were hardly conducive to fidelity. Lawrence tells us that his mother endured all the flirtations with admirable patience.

Lela, however, denies that any sexual infidelity ever took place *while she was living at home;* it was simply that some women told the Reverend Anderson their troubles and wept on his shoulders.[17] But it appears certain that Max thought otherwise.

It is possible that some of the Reverend Anderson's frequent "calls" to distant pulpits had their origin in amatory difficulties, but certainly there were other causes too. He had a temperament that often got him into hot water with parishioners soon after he settled into a town—at least this is the explanation Maxwell is said to have given to his son Quentin.[18]

Moreover, the pastor smarted under a series of frustrations when he tried to wrest what he considered a decent salary from tightfisted church deacons so that he could keep his ever-enlarging family in groceries and clothes.[19] The picture is of a man well aware of his value as a crowd-getter and impatient to be rewarded accordingly. So popular was this underpaid man, so "smooth" a speaker (as reported by one informant outside the family who heard him preach), that people would drive for forty or fifty miles down country roads to hear him; and, if the church happened to be packed, as it often was, someone would open the windows so that the overflow crowd left sitting outside could listen.[20]

Because various published accounts speak of Maxwell's father as being a poor parson, it is well to check on the evidence for this claim, keeping in mind that the tendency of the Anderson children now is to deny the suffering of those hard years. The parson's beginning salary was low and, despite all his moves, never rose high enough to provide the family with anything more than mere subsistence. Not all the salary figures are available, but in Richmond Center, Ohio, the Anderson residence next after Andover, the Reverend Anderson drew $250 a year plus "donations" and the use of the parsonage. The "donations" included apples, potatoes, and other vegetables.[21] It was lucky for him that he usually laid out his own vegetable garden, for a financial depression hit the country the next year, 1893. Several moves later, in McKeesport, Pennsylvania, it was $800; in New Brighton, Pennsylvania, $1,000; and in Jamestown, North Dakota, $1,200.[22] No doubt his lack of a divinity school diploma kept him in the low-salaried circuit. But money went far in those days.

The reader can get a good idea of how relatively inexpensive food was in 1906 at the time Max was living in New Hampton, Iowa, by noting the prices for that year in Washington, D.C., where a pound of beef stew meat cost five cents, a pound loaf of wheat bread five cents, a quart of milk seven cents, and a dozen eggs twenty-four cents. Offsetting these low prices, however, was the Reverend Anderson's skimpy pay. If he was earning about $1,000 a year then, which was likely, that figure seem dangerously close to the poverty level described in a U.S. Government survey in 1906 for Washington, D.C., which shows that the average annual income for fifteen "visibly, palpably, actually poor" white families in that city, supported by a single wage-earning parent in each instance, amounted to $535.60—a total more than twice what the Reverend Anderson had made during his second year of preaching.

In that day when fathers were *supposed* to rule the roost and would consider themselves failures if they did not—rather a universal rule among ministers' families—the Reverend Anderson was a stern, domineering, uncompromising parent who would call a child down for saying even innocuous things at the dinner table. At least this was the way the gentle Max saw him. The mother and the children were usually silent when the preacher held forth at mealtime. Still, he never punished any of the children much, save for Harold, who was a rambunctious young colt, often disobeying the parson's rules.

Until they were in their teens all of the children were forced to set a good example as members of a clergyman's family and attend a total of five church activities a week,[23] quite enough to kill off any love of church that someone not a fanatic might have—and it finally did precisely that. Two things characteristic of most of the minister's eight offspring can be traced to this upbringing: All of them became soft-voiced and mild of manner.[24] And very few of them in adult life ever took a strong interest in religion, certainly not Max—neither he nor his wives nor his children.[25]

When Max was two months old and dreadfully ill with pneumonia, the attending doctor declared him dead, but Linc could not accept such medical defeatism—an Anderson male is not *that* easily killed off, not *his* son, anyway! He carried the infant into another room where they could be by themselves and prayed to God for a recovery, promising to give his suffering child to the service of the church if God would only pull him through. And it worked.

It is true, however, that the act of throwing the burden of repayment upon the son was a trifle underhanded, and the sacred dedication did not take well. Max's daughter, Hesper, told me that when her father was eight and was asked to be baptized, he absolutely refused to go along with the ceremony; and this refusal seems to have marked the beginning of a lifelong rebellion against practically everything the father stood for. Some years after this incident the minister reminded him of the holy promise given when the boy was an infant. But the horse was fled from the barn by then, for agnostic Max declared that as far as he could see, there was no evidence whatsoever that God even existed. The preacher was aghast! He tried in vain to smash down Max's intellectual defenses.[26] Yet from that time onward the son never belonged to any church, nor even went to services except for a few times at a Unitarian chapel at Stanford and when he was obliged to do so as a professor at Whittier College. Rebellious though he was, and deeply distrustful of all institutional authorities, he nevertheless remained such a thoroughgoing idealist with a profound faith in the human spirit that he would one day write several plays about great Christian leaders.

Certainly the descriptions of the father as they come down to us from most family sources agree in representing him as an often harsh and severe man, the burden seemingly falling harder upon the sons than upon the daughters,[27] which might account for Lela's partiality toward the man. But rhetoric and theology alienated Max when he was still very young. By the time he was in his twenties and attending Stanford, the schism had deepened considerably. Frank Ernest Hill, an instructor at Stanford, recalls that he met the father,

> who was all you would not like an enlightened minister to be, although he had a very benign quality. When his father was around, Max said nothing and the father held forth and there was peace. But when the father wasn't there, Max believed in nothing. His belief had been completely shattered.[28]

However, there was another side to this preacher-father. Lela, the third child in the family and just two years younger than Max, recalls that her father was "capable of great tenderness and affection."[29] For instance,

> . . . Dad was the one who got up at night to comfort a scared or sick small one, he walked the floor with us when we had our frequent earaches. In the summer he put up our rope swings and [,] when he could [,] he took us for boatrides. He knew that I was far too shy and he talked to me about learning to carry on an interesting conversation. There were lots of things like these and they should be mentioned too.[30]

And what was the playwright's mother like? One suspects that she had a far greater beneficial influence upon Max than will ever come to light. Not being drawn into the public eye and not having had any recorded conflicts with her famous son, this gentle and patient woman slips too easily into that retiring background which it was thought in that day proper for a minister's helpmeet. When I asked Lawrence Anderson about her, I received a smiling reply that was loaded with a world of meaning: *"Mother was always there!"* Reliable, reassuring, comforting, lovable, she went her quiet way as the parson's loyal and long-suffering mate. With a total of eight children to bear and raise—and to feed and clothe on a tight budget—she must have always been hard-pressed to make ends meet. Lela wrote to me about this Premma Anderson:

> I can tell you how she looked. She was fairly tall for a woman [thus disproving the notion that Anderson's preference for short wives must reflect a fixation for his mother], and was very slim when she was

young. She had very dark brown hair and near-sighted dark brown eyes so she always wore thick glasses. . . . She had no very great variety of clothes but she knew how to wear what she did have and she took care of them so she always looked well dressed.

She was reserved and quiet but like many such people she had a knack for making herself listened to wherever she was. She didn't nag us nor complain; just expected the best of us so quietly that she usually got it.

How Max felt about her is probably best indicated by the fact that when she suffered a stroke in early 1933, he spent a small fortune trying to find some help or cure for her paralyzed condition.[31]

Anderson inherited from her his quiet, modest personality.

During his boyhood, the family moved about so frequently that they practically lived out of packing boxes. But the report that they lived in seventeen hamlets in Pennsylvania[32] is an exaggeration—the actual number was six. One of the most difficult problems of his biography is tracing the periods of his residence in that stream of faceless one-horse towns, starting with Andover, Ohio, where the minister had his first pastorate and where the third child, Lela, was born, and then after almost a decade of moves about Pennsylvania going back across the border to Jefferson, Ohio, in 1902 and thence to other points in a steadily westward direction. Had Lela, the unofficial "family historian," not kept some careful records, much of this whole period would be dark to us. Even so, anecdotes about Max's childhood are still uncommon.

After Andover, and then Richmond Center, they moved to Townville, Pennsylvania, where little Harold was born. Riding into Townville with the other children in a bobsled, Lela saw in a hardware store window a child's red wagon for sale, and she turned and said to Max: "I'm going to have a wagon like that when I'm grown up." The seven-year-old Max showed himself already something of a philosopher when he replied: "You won't want it when you're grown up." They were both wrong, for she continued to want it with the hunger that only a deprived child can know but never satisfy. He himself must have longed in vain for many a store window toy.

Following a year in Townville they moved to Edinboro, Pennsylvania, where at Christmastime he learned there was no Santa Claus when he joined his sisters in peering down a hole by the stovepipe and watching his parents fill the stockings. Another time, having found a garter snake, he took it to his mother, who was dreadfully afraid of all snakes, and insisted that she look at his "big worm." At Edinboro came his first contact with school, and likewise began the recurring ordeal of being the "new boy" at school, the one the bullies teased and taunted and fought with. His daughter Hesper, to whom he may have confided these things in order to make more bearable her unhappy schooldays, tells us that he considered his childhood to have been emotionally deprived, partly owing to his alienation from his father and partly to these unpleasant experiences at school. It didn't seem wise to cultivate any lasting friendships wherever he moved because he knew he would soon leave such friends behind. The pattern made for insecurity and loneliness. On the other hand, his third wife, Gilda, writes that he never spoke to *her* about being deprived in those days; he had had difficulties with his father but adored his mother and always had plenty of music and books as well as his brothers and sisters to play with.[33]

McKeesport came next, and some twelve months later, New Brighton. The mother, pregnant again, came down with a severe case of typhoid pneumonia, and the family had to scrape enough money together to hire a servant girl to do the housework. Then, as if to make matters worse, little Max developed what was probably a mastoid infection, so severe that he was kept indoors from play and missed so much school that he finally had to repeat a grade. But being shut up so much might have been a blessing in disguise, for he "read more than ever," Lela says. "He sent away for books, and read some of them to me. . . . *Kidnapped* and *The Last of the Mohicans* and *The Hound of the Baskervilles* are the ones I remember best. . . ." The Anderson children were avid readers.

In the spring of this crisis year of 1898 little Ruth was born, and luckily for the distraught family, Grandmother Shepard invited them to come to Atlantic to live with her during the summer so that she could provide help for the new baby. It would mean a needed period of recovery for Max and his mother and a vacation for all but the father. The Andersons had been to Atlantic several times already for visits lasting a week or two but never for a whole glorious summer! In their memoirs and letters, the three oldest children, having been so rootless in their nearly annual migration from parish to parish, regard the Shepard place as their only real home; the warmth was almost a tangible thing as they came to the door; and it is therefore not surprising that they always pictured Atlantic with a special fondness reserved for no other place. Thanks to a detailed sketch written by Ethel in her old age, to a letter to her from Max after he read the sketch, and to miscellaneous information from Lela, we have a good record of what that long-ago visit was like.[34] In part it is a record of a vanished idyllic era in rural Pennsylvania as seen through the golden glow of remembrance, depicting the charm and simplicity of a rural America that seems peculiarly attractive to those of us who live in a land of superhighways, crowded suburbias, crime-infested cities, and polluted air. Max's visit is the first long one of several that he would use a half century later in his hauntingly nostalgic novel, *Morning Winter and Night*.[35] It is also the first of two that brought him into prolonged, close contact with his maternal aunt, Emma, whose influence was to mark a turning point in his intellectual life.

In imagination we can accompany the Andersons in June of that year, when school is out, and recapture this childhood visit. Up the narrow, unnamed (even today!), and deeply rutted dirt road that runs eastward from the railroad tracks at Atlantic—just a whistle-stop cluster of low buildings nestled among rolling farmlands; past Henry Ross's store, Mrs. Isaac's millinery shop, and the doctor's house; on up the gentle rise past Otis Ransom's bee farm on the right-hand side of the road, just across from the McGranahans'; at last we top a rise from which we can see ahead the Harshman farm and Ungar's hatchery on the right and just beyond them the place so special in the hearts of the minister's children, the fifty-acre Shepard farm, marked by the tall willows bending by the road. The main dwelling is an ordinary, unpainted, clapboard affair of five rooms and a long attic, severely simple in design; a modest place by rural standards even then but sufficiently big and homey for Mrs. Shepard's eager grandchildren.

Inside the broken rail fence the path divides at a clump of yellow Maiden's Blush roses, the shorter route leading straight to the shaded stone steps at the front door, the other curving around the east side past scarlet geraniums and flowering currants, hollyhocks, and peonies to the kitchen door and the family vegetable garden, where the grandmother raises produce for home canning. Farther east still is the cow barn, where the children are free to play their raucous games and balance on the loose boards high up on the crossbeams and burrow in the fragrant hay to hunt for the elusive hens' eggs. Away on the other side of the house, built directly over the spring run, stands a common but important feature of farm life in days before modern refrigeration became available, the springhouse, in which the children, disobeying warnings from their elders, might dip their fingers into the pans of milk set in the water to cool and come up with a rich dollop of cream. For recreation out front they can play on a rope swing under a tree, whereas luring them from the back of the lot is a cluster of Astrachan apple trees whose fruit ripens early so that the children can climb the low branches and fill their hands and pockets with as many apples as they like and then lie on the summer grass to eat with juice-glistening faces.

"Best of all, though," writes Lela, "was the hollow. . . . This was really a shallow ravine that a stream had cut some hundreds of yards back of Grandma's house. Its sides sloped to the edges of the creek, which meandered along to a spot close to the lower fence line where it had obligingly hesitated and hollowed out a depression that made us a fine swimming pool." Right by this swimming pool is the center of all their outdoor play, the Indian Mound, of unknown origin, whose flat top makes a good place for a fort or observation point or even a stage on which the Anderson children can act the parts of the different story characters they had read about in their winter books. And so they sometimes act out fairy tales, including the Bluebeard story, while one of the girls plays Sister Ann sitting in a tower built of stray branches. On rainy days they transfer their play-acting to the attic of the farmhouse. In the attic, Lela writes in her biographical notes,

> were trunks and boxes filled with old clothing and pictures and all kinds of discarded trinkets and oddments. There were some old guns on a shelf, and there were strings of dried apples and usually some nuts left over from winter. But best of all there were all the magazines that had accumulated through the winter and that had been saved for us to read. I think that we enjoyed the Just So Stories [sic] best that first summer but there were other good ones.

She also writes in that account:

> We were the only grandchildren in the family and it seemed as if in Grandma's eyes we could do no wrong. Perhaps children now wouldn't enjoy such a season, for they all seem to want activities provided and fancy toys to amuse them. For us there was nothing like that but we didn't want it. For us there were few restrictions and little supervised play but there were all kinds of interesting places to explore and games that we made for ourselves.

Grandmother Shepard, assisted by her unmarried daughter Emma, cooks her simple meals in an old elevated cast-iron stove that burns wood grown on the property. She is not a tall woman, but very fat, with blue eyes and fair hair done up in little curls at the back of her neck. As is always the case in the summer, she wears her Mother Hubbard dress, much like today's shift. Meanwhile, old Mr. Shepard, when he is not staggering in with a load of wood from the pile in back, is more than likely seated outside the kitchen door with his chair tilted against the wall, where he can chew his beloved tobacco in complete freedom. Poor man, his good Presbyterian wife absolutely will not tolerate a spittoon or the chewing of the weed anywhere in "her" part of the domicile, which means that he sleeps in the converted woodshed attached to the back of the house. (He will chew his last plug this coming winter, pass away, and leave his widow and Emma alone to run the farm.)

People entering the kitchen from the yard wash their hands in a tin washbasin placed outside the door, scrubbing themselves with strong yellow soap that Mrs. Shepard has made herself by boiling lye and grease together in the great iron kettle in the yard. The lye she has extracted by letting rainwater leach through a barrel of wood ashes; the grease she has saved from her cooking. It is not the fancy, perfumed soap bought at Blair's country store, but it works.

Once inside the house, the visitor can quaff a dipperful of pure springwater from a wooden pail kept ready in the pantry. Supper is served at five-thirty on a drop-leaf table in the kitchen, while sunlight streams through the ruffled curtains on the windows, and the hosts—Mrs. Shepard, her husband, and Emma—have the satisfaction of knowing that practically everything there to eat, except for the coffee and salt, was produced on the farm: the baked corn bread from ears raised in the garden, the cottage cheese made on the back of the stove; ham or bacon from hogs raised out back and smoked on the premises, or spicy sausages filled in the old-fashioned way, or beef salted and dried according to custom immemorial. The preserved sauerkraut is home-made too; likewise the canned fruit and dried apples, and the pickled pigs' feet, and the mouth-watering cucumber dills.

After the dishes are washed, the women hang up their aprons and change from heavy work clothes to light, starched ones and then join the men in the low, wide parlor whose ceiling is covered with cheesecloth. While the clock ticks loudly, they perform by the light of a rose-colored oil lamp such house-hold tasks as making quilt blocks, sewing carpet rags together, patching clothes, and cutting out dresses, while the girls wind into huge balls, ready for the weaver, the bright strips of carpet rags. Mrs. Shepard, who learned to sew long before the sewing machine had been invented and when dresses were made of silk so stiff that they could stand alone, is a strict taskmistress at teaching the girls the art of the needle.

But all this is hardly considered work, for they meanwhile amuse them-selves with conversation for an hour or two until bedtime. The children lounge at their ease on the rag-carpeted floor and listen to local gossip, to stories of pioneer days, to arguments about politics, and to reports of church affairs, while outside the crickets chirp and a lone whippoorwill pours his mournful note adrift on the night air and makes the children pleased they are safe and cozy indoors. But at the first yawn all of them are hustled into muslin nightgowns, sent up the ladder into the attic, Max and Harold at one end and the girls at the other, separated by the chimney, and then tucked between cool, fresh sheets for the night's repose.

But just as soon as they hear the rattle of the milk pail in the morning and the crackling of kindling in the stove below, and see the orange pumpkin of the sun over the barn roof, they are up and ready for any adventure from King Arthur to Ali Baba and the Forty Thieves.

The Reverend Anderson, in charge of some church or other in the region, comes around once or twice during the summer to convey the family from Atlantic to nearby Geneva to visit his parent, stern Grandfather Anderson, a visit that Max could well forgo. Grandmother Shepard's is heavenly, no one can do any wrong here, but at the other place . . . well, that is another story.

For the side trip, father hitches old Molly to the buggy, mother rides with him in the front seat holding the baby, and the four children sit in back, where they clutch the duster over their knees to help keep their good clothes clean. Max might have on his starched sailor's collar and woolen jacket; and each sister, a butterfly bow in her hair, her ankle-length dress bound about the waist with a wide taffeta sash tied into a bow at the back.

The ride eastward has its points of interest for the children. They pass farms where Houdan chickens and graceful peacocks strut about. When they reach Porter's Corners Methodist Church, standing white and lone under the tall trees, they can tell they are at the halfway mark. Molly pricks her ears forward and steps faster, for she knows of the watering trough here made from a fire-hollowed log and fed all day with delicious springwater.

Once at the Anderson farm they see sheep pasturing under the oaks across the road from the main house. From these comes the white wool that Grandmother Anderson cards, colors, and spins—using an old upright wheel that she owns—and finally weaves into blankets. We approach the house from down a driveway lined with peach trees and get a view of a young apple orchard among whose protecting trees stand hen houses and beehives. Shading the springhouse is an old grapevine bearing green clusters of fruit that the children are sure to sample sometime before they leave. White-bearded Grandfather James Anderson, a bit lame from an old wound, walks out with his cane to greet everyone. With him is his still spry wife of many winters. But Max does not care much for either of them, unlike what Ethel and Lela feel. He would remember his Grandmother Polly Anderson as a "peppery, finger-slim old lady with the blackest eyes I ever saw in a human head, light on her feet as a girl, fluttering like a leaf about the kitchen. . . . I don't remember that she ever addressed a word to me, but I'm quite certain that I was in her way."[36]

Just as at the Shepard house, the children play on rainy days in the attic, where relics are stored from generations past. Here is a stereoscope with a box of pictures of exotic scenes to look at; a set of "tiddleywinks"; a kaleidoscope warranted to display two thousand lovely patterns of colored glass in the cylinder; boxes of shiny steel buttons and buckles; a clock; some umbrellas; trunks crammed with old-fashioned clothing just right for children to put on in masquerades; and—of special interest to Max—rusty old guns, powder horns, and bullet molds. Uncle Frank's shotgun is up here, too, but now unusable because it had blown up one day when he was out squirrel hunting and hurt him—but not seriously. With the guns and other hunting paraphernalia of the woodsman, they can now play Daniel Boone stalking Indians under the shadowy eaves, or perhaps a game they call "Pilgrims Going Home from Church,"* in which the players do not follow any set rules, some of the protective escort even defecting to the Indians and hiding behind the chimney ready to dash out in pursuit of the Pilgrims!

But they must be discreet with the guns, for Max can recall a certain dire incident that happened in the house some years back when he found in a closet a Civil War carbine, got a cartridge jammed in the breech, and then who should come in but Grandfather Anderson himself!—"a fierce, bent old man, with gray bristling eye-brows that rayed out over eyes shooting fire." Caught *in flagrante delicto!* "[T]he old gentleman found some words to say that seared my thinking for days," Max recalled from that occasion. "'You want to murder the family and commit suicide?' he inquired angrily. Then he went on muttering to himself. 'Who in Goshen left this thing full of ammunition? Been lying here ever since it came back from Lee's surrender, full of death and destruction! How am I going to get that bullet out of the works? You pile out of here, and if you touch a gun again on this property I'll whale you myself.'"

"I got out," Max recalled.

And it was probably during that same earlier summer that he crossed Grandfather again, according to what Max remembers. He and Lela were sailing duck feather boats on the little brook that coursed from the spring-house to the barn when Grandfather swooped down upon them like a vulture. 'What are you doing now?' he demanded. 'Sailing boats,' I answered. 'Aye! You're spoiling the drinking water for the horses!' he said bitterly. 'You don't care how much work you make for me! Now I've got to get a rake and clean every feather out of the culvert before it clogs! I've got enough to do, and here you come adding to it! You couldn't clean it out! Oh, no, but you can dirty it up!' And he got out his rake and cleaned the water carefully. We slunk away, Lela and I."

---

*Inspired, no doubt, by a well-known painting with that title by G. H. Houghton.

"Aunt Emma [Lincoln's sister] was another fierce one with a tongue that cracked around my bare legs," Max goes on. One photograph of this formidable creature shows plain, mannish features and dark, short-cropped hair. "Aunt Rellie was a little older, and not so fiery, but stern enough when I rode the old mare and was brushed off her back in the orchard. At Grandfather's house I was always in trouble."[37]

In the house there is a tall staircase that curly-haired Max loves to slide down. One day, one of the adults in the household threatens to cut off his pretty curls if he ever plays on the banisters again.

Sometimes the children amuse themselves by hiding in the tall grasses that bend over the brook and waiting there for Emma's ducks with their green-black heads to swim along (*they* are free to pollute the water all they want!); and just as one draws near, Max or one of the other children reaches out and seizes him while he squawks and flaps the air with his wings and splashes them good for presuming to get in *his* way.

Uncle Frank A. Anderson, also at the farm, is for Max probably the most interesting if not the most likable of the Reverend Anderson's brothers and sisters. If Rip Van Winkle were to be reborn, he might well choose to be another Uncle Frank. Being a valetudinarian, maybe secretly grateful for it, young Frank does not have to work as hard as the others at the farm; consequently, he gardens a bit but not so much as to risk getting himself labeled as ambitious, thank you; does as little hunting and fishing as possible, and then only for pleasure; takes long walks in the woods; reads much but studies for no profession or trade; writes a crude kind of poetry and gets it published in local journals; has the habit of separating each vegetable and meat on his dinner plate (he would rather they be served as separate courses); and knows the call of the night birds so well that he whistles to them from the porch for the delight of the children.

As a lifelong bachelor he treasures his independence too much ever to get married, though he is said to have had a "wife" without the bother of marrying her[38]—an arrangement that must have shocked his pious brother the minister, and if so Uncle Frank could not have cared less. He does not own any mountain, unlike Max's hero Van Dorn in *High Tor,* whom he otherwise resembles in divers ways, but year in and year out he is completely happy. Long afterward, when rich Max is sentimental about the Geneva farm and wants to assist his poor old uncle under some cover that will save his pride, he sends him $240 a month to buy back the place in Max's name and allows him to live on it free of rent and eke out a subsistence from the land.[39]

One thing likely to interest little Max at Geneva is his uncle's playing on the cottage organ, at which time he accompanies himself with a mellow tenor voice. Perhaps Max will play on it a little, and maybe sing too if coaxed, for he has a melodious voice that will one day get him into a male quartet; right now, it is a matter of learning by ear, but later on he will be able to read the notes and still later, as a man, compose the lyrics for several plays such as *Truckline Cafe*,[40] and the librettos for *Knickerbocker Holiday, Ulysses Africanus, Anne of the Thousand Days,* and *Lost in the Stars.* That is all for the future. Right now, his desire to learn the piano at home, for instance, will mean an uphill struggle against the backwoods notions of Reverend Anderson, who despite his own love of singing will one day imply that his son is a sissy or unmanly for ordering a book of piano lessons and then having the nerve to go over to the church with his profane scores and practice on the instrument there rather than on the one in the house (which might have been occupied by the other children, who also loved music).

And the parson will react the same way when Max begins to write poetry.[41] Never mind that Lincoln Anderson liked the poems of James Whitcomb Riley and some of the New Englanders. Evidently, Lincoln Anderson regarded music and poetry mainly as decorative things for use in his church services or for social occasions; the music always being played by a woman at the piano or organ, and the poetry a light variety composed by clever and educated men who were conveniently dead so that one didn't have to confront and be embarrassed by any of their sissified ways. It is pleasant to report, however, that this "singing and reading" family, as Lela describes it, had not only a piano but an organ by the time Max was old enough to play on them.[42]

Nor does the music in Max's life merely serve the needs of the future dramaturgist. It is always going to give him immense pleasure and consolation, being "the one part of his father's church that meant a good deal to him," his son Alan asserts unhesitatingly,[43] sounding depths of feeling and enlarging Max's sense of beauty in ways always denied him by formal religion itself. It is not hard to imagine the nine-year-old Max at Geneva thrilling to the playing of a transcription of Bach's "Arioso" or Handel's "Largo,"* the lofty strains speaking to him of some more than earthly yearning of the human spirit. According to what his son Terence affirms, even in his adult years this apostate from the Church would play old Church hymns for the sheer pleasure of hearing them again. To Hesper, his piano technique always resembled the organ. And when he played on the piano, it was with a special kind of emotional feeling all his own that emphasized the resonance and sonorousness of the chords, the sweetness of the chords themselves, yet without losing the melody. He would slow the melody more than most

---

*This is mentioned in *The Star-Wagon.*

people would in order to gain a rich, lingering effect. A favorite was "Greensleeves."[44]

Uncle Frank sees his one-day-to-become-famous nephew as a rather lazy youth, something of a dreamer. In later years he reports that Max would be riding along on his bicycle and then suddenly stop in the road or along the path, and sit there, as if he were thinking out some problem. And that Max, not physically aggressive, would be somewhere in the outer circle watching if a fight were in progress, unlike his younger brother Harold, who would likely be one of the combatants in the brawl.[45]

Not long after returning to New Brighton, the minister accepted a "call" to the Pine Street Baptist Church in the capital city of Harrisburg, Pennsylvania, an old-fashioned, gaslit, horse-and-buggy city, most of whose inhabitants were government employees and their families. A Major Elkins had promised him the position of chaplain of the state senate, a supplementary income, but the position went instead to another pastor, one who was a Harvard man and a graduate of the Philadelphia Theological Seminary.

There being no parsonage available to them this time, the Andersons moved into a three-story brick house in a block of six of them at 112 Cumberland Street, within shouting distance of the Susquehanna River. The other places where they had lived had yards big enough to support a garden and a playing area and had wide, unpaved streets; here, the backyard was tiny and bare, and the house fronted directly onto a brick sidewalk and a brick street.

Once or twice the minister rented a boat and took the children for a ride on the river, a deep stream and sometimes so swift that it was considered dangerous even for rowing. One day Max, always considered a lot of fun to be with, took Harold and the girls over to the point at Rockville to hunt for the big chestnuts grown there.

Much of the time they were in Harrisburg, however, they were ill: Ruth caught malaria and lost all her hair; some of the others had measles, earaches, and septic sore throat; and the father came down with a reaction to being vaccinated with unsafe smallpox vaccine. But the parson cheered them up by buying for them some used books consisting of "odds and ends of novels," including a set of Charles Dickens (always a favorite with Max, even in his adult years when he rarely read novels), a set of the main American poets, and histories of France and England. Max's favorites—at least by the time he reached high school—were the poets. These books represented to the deprived children a veritable treasure; they read them "almost to pieces," Lela said. In his "Love Letter to a University," Max notes: "Before I finished the eighth grade I had discovered and read most of the well-known novelists,

Dickens, Stevenson, Scott, Dumas, Cooper, and a vast sampling of others."

In those times the families of Protestant ministers found it most difficult or impossible to make close friendships outside the family circle because any partiality shown toward someone not in the bosom of the faith reacted unfavorably on the minister. This bigotry helps account for the fact that the Andersons lived so much to themselves and felt such an intense family loyalty. In a letter to Max in 1956, Ethel said that she had not realized just how extremely narrow-minded the people of the Reverend Anderson's congregations were until the family moved to Harrisburg.

And the minister, being a new man intent on proving himself wherever he moved, was not one to fight community prejudice; in fact, he had begun to absorb it. When he learned that Ethel's teacher, Miss Culbertson, was allowing her students to "skip" around the classroom during recess period when it was too cold to play outdoors, he made "an issue" of it and called it "dancing"—to him a wickedness on the order of attending playhouses. And Baptist provinciality and snobbery made things difficult for some who wanted to attend the best schools. For instance, Ethel, having won top honors in a citywide spelling contest, was allowed to select as her reward any local girls' school that she desired for the fall. She had heard that on State Street near the capital buildings there was a "fabulous" and exclusive one, and in the fall it proved to be everything she had hoped for. Marvelous! But now witness the wise members of the Pine Street Baptist Church: They moaned to the Reverend Anderson that it simply did not look well for his daughter to be making friends with outsiders on State Street, whereupon the preacher had to conclude that this fraternization would harm him in his work. And so he took his innocent, unsuspecting, knowledge-hungry little girl to task and forced her to withdraw![46]

Low-lying Harrisburg being malarial at that time and unhealthful for people susceptible to ear infections, the Anderson family must have felt deeply relieved when they rode off to Atlantic at the next summer vacation. This time everyone stayed later than usual on the farm because the Reverend Anderson, and Max too, needed to help with the haying. (In fact, every summer from the time he was able to work until well after he went to the university, Max did farm labor.) When wild geese began to honk their way South and maples to flare yellow from the hills, and when school bells were about to ring again in Harrisburg, the family began packing to go home. Someone had the idea that Max should stay on through the winter to help with the farm chores and attend school in Atlantic, particularly since he was happy there and had not yet recovered from the mastoid infection of the winter before. The drier climate of the region did seem to agree with him.

A more compelling argument might have been the one that Max discloses in his Columbia memoir, which was that "pickings were lean in Harrisburg." In a similar situation in the first chapter of *Morning Winter and Night*, Jamie's callous father tells the mother to leave Jamie on the grandmother's farm because they won't be charged for the "fodder"—as if the boy were some kind of livestock to stake out. And so the real Max was left behind at Atlantic. But the emotional consequences of this act on the sensitive boy were clearly traumatic. Gilda tells us that from this incident dates a certain dreadful, recurring dream of his lasting well into adulthood in which he always figured as a child being abandoned. The boxes and crates were packed into the wagon, his family—including his beloved mother—climbed aboard, and off they drove down the road waving to him. Poor little Max was left behind, heartbroken, terrified, not knowing if they were ever coming back.[47]

Grandmother Shepard cuddled and loved Max as usual. No doubt he read some in the few books she owned, which seemed to have included the Bible, Milton's *Poems,* and a volume of Burns. Somewhere he got *Kidnapped* and *A Study in Scarlet,*[48] works that Lela says she and the other children had read. But the one person who, of all his childhood acquaintances, probably had the greatest influence upon his imaginative development was kindly Aunt Emma of the deformed right hand. In a set of biographical notes sent to me, Lela writes:

> . . . during the winter days and evenings she showed him a side that he had not known. She was a wonderful story teller of both real and imagined incidents and she could take the most trivial happening and dress it up into a tale that would challenge her hearer's interest. She saw to it that Max got his lessons but she rewarded him by being interested in anything that he did or said. She told him stories about his ancestors—stories that he remembered so well that in his later life he asked her to write them down for him. . . .

The earliest prediction of his literary bent came in the form of some rhymed verses that he wrote under a tree on the farm;[49] one poem was about driving the cows home, another about a chipmunk that had bitten his finger. He was especially shy during this period of his early youth, and he kept his writing to himself so effectively that his family might never have learned of the poems had not Aunt Emma encouraged him to put them into his letters sent home.[50] The next year, when Lela drove out to the farm again, she found Max healthier and grown some; moreover, he was now trained in Aunt

Emma's method of telling stories, which method he delighted in practicing on the family once they got back to Harrisburg.

The next move was to the village of Jefferson, Ohio, where the young William Dean Howells had once worked. There they occupied the First Baptist Church's rather new parsonage on 88 West Walnut Street.[51] In Jefferson, Max began courting girls, and here he fell in love with light-haired, blue-eyed, and turned-up-nose little Hallie Loomis. Her father owned a 150-acre farm on which lay an apple orchard. After church he walked her home, and after school he carried her books. Hallie's ancestors had built the large, brick church where the Reverend Anderson was to preach for a year. Though the church was lighted by electricity, the Johnson pipe organ had to be pumped laboriously by hand, by someone strong and yet small enough for the little room or box provided for that purpose. Max, needing the extra money, consented to do the pumping, while Hallie sang in the choir, an experience he later rendered touchingly in *The Star-Wagon*.[52] Those who have read the latter will recall Hallie Arlington, the wild "other girl," the wealthy one that inventor Stephen Minch marries on trial after he takes his time journey back to the eastern Ohio of 1902—which is precisely when Max was living in Jefferson.

Few characters in Max Anderson's writings are known to be modeled after particular people in his life, but unquestionably the real Hallie Loomis inspired to some extent the girl in the play as well as the other one in the novel—at the very least, contributing their idealized or madonna qualities. Indeed, the fictionalized girls have such similar roles that we naturally suspect the existence of a prototype: In both works, the Hallie figure is visualized in retrospect or re-created from the past, is physically attractive, lives in a small, Midwestern community, goes swimming nude out in the country in the presence of the hero, is from a family that is better off financially than his, has a brief romantic relationship with him, and is finally rejected when he senses some flaw in her personal makeup. In Anderson's unpublished drama *Sea-Wife* there is still another Hallie, the unfaithful wife of Macquarrie, who has nothing in common with the other two Hallies except sexual indiscretion.

Anderson supposedly assured his daughter, Hesper, of the real-life basis of Hallie Haviland, and moreover told her many times and at length about the actual Hallie of his youth: His eyes would mist over with memory as he recalled the little angel he had seen in Jefferson ride by in her parents' phaeton or surrey and vanish in the dust while he, an awkward farm boy, stood gawking beside the road and feeling unworthy of her. But at night he would sneak from his bed and cross fields just to be able to gaze at her window.[53] Here we have the innocent origin for those composites he later imagined for his works. The real Hallie Loomis, who grew up and attended the University of Pittsburgh and became a professional librarian, told me that she was indeed aware that Anderson had paid her the tribute of using her name for an imagined girl in *The Star-Wagon*. On the other hand, she is most anxious to disavow any of the indecency of her namesakes, protesting with believable fervor that she was but an inexperienced child in Jefferson, that she had no sexual relationship with Max or with anyone else during that period, and that she didn't even know at that time what a loose girl was. She wants Anderson's love for her to stand as the unsullied thing it is, because it is no small honor in this mixed-up world to have been loved by a great author.[54]

Anderson's own testimony dispels any doubt that they had shared a strong and lasting attachment. He wrote to Hallie near the end of his life that he was "remembering the winter as we knew it in Jefferson—a winter when I think we were both fearfully in love with each other. At the ages of eleven or twelve or thereabouts![55] And the romance didn't terminate with the winter! Well, you were beautiful and I was a galumphing pre-adolescent boy. Quite a wonderful time to have been alive."[56]

Not among his more pleasant memories was the one connected with his trying to open a can of corned beef with the key, and cutting his hand so deeply across the palm that it spurted blood all over the floor, whereupon Ethel ran for the doctor while Lela hurried into the cellar to get a kind of first-aid right out of folk medicine, which was a fistful of cobwebs that she washed and then packed into the cut so that it would stop bleeding and have a fibrous bridge across which the new tissue might grow. With the doctor's help, or in spite of it, the wound healed well and left little scar.

One memory he probably treasured was his December 25 bobsled ride to Hallie's grandmother's house in Austinburg, a house once used as an underground slave station. There, Max and his hosts celebrated with an oyster supper the birthday of his girlfriend's brother, Bennet.[57]

The Reverend Anderson waxed unhappy with his salary before the year was out and felt sure he could fare better farther west. And in due time an offer arrived from Algona, Iowa. Once again came the elaborate and troublesome preparations needed for moving. It was not easy for the family to crate the furniture for railroad shipment and to pack clothes and food for a family swollen now to nine, two members of whom were infant twins, one of them nursing on a bottle for which existed no modern refrigeration and probably no fresh milk to buy along the route. Also, somebody had to get the railroad tickets and arrange for a month of housing at Algona until the furniture could arrive. Max was always kept busy at such times hammering crates together.

But in February 1903 they were off to Algona at last, and little Hallie is said to have cried her eyes out as she saw Max leave her sight forever. Long years afterward she wrote to him in behalf of the Cleveland Gilpin Players, a Negro group that wanted to produce his popular *Lost in the Stars,* and just for her sake he granted them a special reduced royalty.[58]

In Chicago the children glimpsed their first ships before plunging into the thinly populated prairie country for another one-year stand in another village of dirt roads on the recently won frontier as the parson continued his search for the will-o'-the-wisp of economic security. From now on they would see monotonous miles of open plains.

By today's standards life was harsh then and people lacked many of the luxuries now taken for granted. Algona, like the other settlements they were to know in the Midwest, had outdoor privies, and "When one took a bath it was in a wash-tub with water heated on the stove," novelist Louis L'Amour writes. L'Amour goes on to speak of an eminent New York physician of the period, a Dr. Sargent, who declared that he saw no value at all in bathing, that it was just a waste of time. He was not considered a crackpot, either. Houses were almost always frame and were lit by kerosene lamps; in the winter, often cruelly cold, they were heated by coal or wood stoves.

Businesses were dependent on the farmers, who in turn depended on a fickle Mother Nature to give them good crops of corn and therefore big herds of cattle and pigs. Visitors to the general stores enjoyed the wonderful odors of leather and tobacco and could buy there just about anything needed for the house and farm. Medical training was weak almost everywhere, few M.D.'s having more than two years of medical schooling, and many of them simply acquiring their skills by working with other doctors.[59] Salaries were generally low. When Ethel began teaching school later in Goodrich, North Dakota, she received fifty-five dollars a month. Horses and buggies still being standard transportation, the Reverend Anderson always bought himself a good team of animals whenever he moved into a new town, and sold it when he left. Big drays took the place of trucks everywhere and were drawn by huge draft horses specially bred for that purpose.

Reports from *outside* the family invariably depict it as hard off in these migratory years, although Lela and Kenneth play down the hardships, perhaps because they did not seem hardships to them at the time. The family was not down-and-out poor, not to the extent that the children ever went hungry or wore rags or that the mother ever took in washing or that the father applied for local charity. Nor were the Andersons ever looked down upon by the community.

The overworked and often tired parson's wife, weakened by repeated childbirths, was ever trying to economize by sewing dresses and blouses and shirts; however, she could not make trousers and coats but had to pay precious coin for them at the store. The youngsters wore hand-me-downs. And everyone would have been in actual distress had not well-wishers in the community donated some clothes. Add to these domestic straits a run-down church and a congregation unresponsive to the parson's enthusiasm. Small wonder, then, that he so quickly accepted a pulpit in the village of New Hampton: There they would stay for a record-breaking three and a half years, the longest Max was ever to live in a community during his youth.

New Hampton, Iowa, was rather sluggish but had a more thriving church, and the salary was a trifle bigger. As usual, Max took part-time and summer jobs, and once he began high school he became the printer's devil on the school paper, learned to set type with a stick, and discovered—as had so many youths before him who grew up to be famous writers—the thrill that comes from seeing one's own words set up in type. In the shop he printed a curious card for himself, "Cymbelline, Blackfriar's Theater. Admit one."[60] Already he was feeling the wondrous power of Shakespeare that would help mold *Elizabeth the Queen* and other plays.

In the small high school he took literature, rhetoric, geography, history, civics, botany, algebra, geometry (he never cared for mathematics), economics, and German.[61] German was required because of the German immigrant population. At last he began to catch up on some of the schooling he had missed because of illness. Here during his junior year he developed a "crush" on the popular new teacher in the school, Miss Bertha Alexander, who taught him English and Lela Latin. Miss Alexander's radiant personality met with rapid appreciation. She was a pretty woman of about twenty-two on her first teaching job, and she came from Burlington, Iowa; she lived with two other teachers in a local rooming house where the Anderson children and other fans of hers flocked for visits, at which time they sang while she played the piano. It seems that either here or in the high school she had a conference with Max and told him it was quite all right to be the way he was, to have his consuming love for poetry and music, and to want to create these things. Moreover, she recognized his writing talent. But just as it takes more than one wave to bring the tide in, this liberating angel was unable completely to free him from the feeling of stigma generated everywhere in the Middle West, that for a man to write poetry was unbecomingly effeminate and peculiar. We know that despite Miss Alexander's encouragement, he could see that hardly anyone else in the school wrote the stuff either. It remained for the university experience to prove to him that such writing was respectable after all.[62]

His eyes being weak, he was not able to hit the ball when he played baseball, did only fair at the broad jump, and no better at the high jump.[63] His weight was against him in leaping. But he did play some football until he injured his back, an accident that seemed trivial at the time but which gave him pain for the rest of his life. He seemed a spunky lad willing to try almost anything his companions did. He was by no means a sissy.

Certainly Max did not neglect the queen of the arts, music. With Tom Swale and a girl named Jo Shepard he played in a violin trio, earning his own money to pay for the instrument and lessons. He belonged to several school choruses, including the Glee Club, and sang in a pleasant low bass that his music teacher commended. He, Melvin Orms, Ralph Chambers (who would later marry Max's sister Ethel), and Charles Gerholdt formed a vocal quartet that had a lot of fun on the last Friday of each month when the high school held a program, and sometimes they sang at the local Baptist church. Melvin Orms, a year behind him in school, says that one event in particular remains in his memory about their musical association:

> My folks had a good Edison phonograph and a good supply of records. Occasionally the boys would come to the farm and we would listen to the records on Sunday afternoons. One Sunday we decided to record one of our songs as Dad had a recording attachment to the machine. We had gotten half-way thru the song "Carry Me Back to Old Virginny" when something tickled Max and he threw up his hands and let out a big "whoop" and burst out laughing. That finished the recording but the record was quite a prize [It was later sold by mistake with the machine].[64]

Judging from what Lela records in her unpublished "Life," this period of their residence on Chestnut Street in New Hampton seems to have been about the happiest and most fulfilling that the family had had up to that time:

> Dad was successful in his ministry; Mother wasn't having a baby, so she could take part in the church and community; Ruth and the twins were cute and a lot of fun; Harold was healthy and happy and well liked; we three older children, for the first time in our lives, had stayed long enough in one place so that we felt we belonged in the life of the town. We sang and read and had parties and hayrides and candy pulls. We even played Flinch until one of the "pillars of the church" decided

that it was a card game which might lead to gambling, so we were ordered to stop that form of diversion.[65]

Reading was so constant among them that it seemed to Max their only occupation. The mother and father bought books whenever they could, at sales usually, and what they did not buy, the children did.[66] Scholar Allan G. Halline, who suspected that Emerson's concept of the "beneficent tendency" of the universe influenced Max, wrote to the adult playwright and got the admission that he had certainly grown up on Emerson but could not be sure how much that had affected him—maybe a great deal.[67] Emerson's assertion that "Society everywhere is in conspiracy against the manhood of every one of its members" fits remarkably the mind that created such beleaguered but defiant individualists as Van Van Dorn in *High Tor* and Alan McClean in *Both Your Houses*.

Max was reading Henry David Thoreau at about this time, too, and he was to share with Thoreau not only a profound distrust of "big" government[68] but also a lofty if sometimes errant individualism that is Thoreauvian if not Emersonian.

In a drugstore in New Hampton he bought cheap copies of Shelley and the Globe edition of Shakespeare, and he ordered a paperbound copy of Keats.[69] The title of his play *The Eve of St. Mark* is taken from a Keats poem. As a matter of fact, Keats and Shakespeare were to become his favorites above all other poets. And when it came to dramas, Shakespeare was to him the Merlin of language, while all the other dramatists merely played around with magic.[70]

Somewhere along the way he developed a love for the poems of Matthew Arnold, who voiced a melancholy skepticism and classical restraint that seem peculiarly congenial to Max's own temperament; and he would one day gain from Arnold the inspiration to write his one-acter *Sea-Wife*, based on the poem "The Forsaken Merman." The only later poet to interest him greatly was Conrad Aiken.[71]

When he read poetry he felt, he says,

the way a porpoise must feel as he turns through the giant happiness of sea water. Then I tried writing it, and discovered that the imagining, the word-finding, and the setting down of a poem were more intense delights than the reading of even the greatest poems by other men. It wasn't often that the impulse came over me, but when it did, and a poem resulted, I had a taste of what, for lack of a better figure, men call "heaven."

But he adds that this recreation of his was purely private and personal, for the writing of poetry, especially by males, was not countenanced in the prairie states. "It was committed to paper, in secret, like a crime. . . ."[72]

Max dated many girls, including the lovely Jo Shepard, Helen Greenawald, Helen Breeding, and his choice of them all, Leona Kemman, who suffered from anemia. He was therefore having an enjoyable time in the village and was well on his way toward graduating from high school when his father, as expected, grew restless again and accepted a pulpit farther west, in Jamestown, North Dakota. But Max rebelled. He wanted to stay right where he was. And so it was arranged for him to live with the family of Helen Breeding; he would earn his room and board by working in their furniture store after school.

One night early that fall in Jamestown when Lela and Ethel were about to retire in the front upstairs bedroom, they heard familiar footsteps on the front boardwalk. "That's Max!" they exclaimed. It was he, all right. Some time later when they heard that his beloved Leona had died that summer, they knew why he had come home.[73] Somehow he recovered.

In the light of the stimulation Max received from later teachers in North Dakota, Lela is confident that his decision to move made a crucial difference in his professional writing career. Without that he might have married some girl like Helen Breeding and learned the furniture business and turned out to be another frustrated writer.

A detailed picture of Jamestown of that era comes from the pens of Edna LaMoore Waldo, who was one year behind Max in high school and had a study hall with him, and her much younger brother Louis L'Amour.[74] It mainly agrees with Lela's recollection. The town had a population of about fifty-six hundred when the future playwright arrived in 1907, was pioneer and provincial by almost any standard—some families still living in sod houses—but compared with other communities in the Plains states had some features that a newcomer not used to metropolitan life might have appreciated. Jamestown lies in a valley where the placid streams of the James and Pipestem intersect, both of them thickly lined with cottonwood and elm, chokeberry and box elder, in whose shades along the banks people could picnic. (Max had a lifelong fascination with water, whether as rain or river, bay or ocean; consequently, he must often have rambled along these streams.) In autumn people raked their leaves into the gutters and burned them, setting adrift on the cool air unforgettable smoky fragrances.

Though deep snows were common and subzero blizzards whipped howling in with every winter, springtime was always delightful, with the crocus or pasqueflower poking up through the snow. Bookstores were nonexistent, but the city hall held a fairly good though compact lending library, which the Anderson children haunted constantly. The household of the veterinarian, LaMoore, where Max and Lela visited, had a collection of not more than two hundred choice books that included the Stoddard Lectures on world travels; some novels by Scott, Kingsley, Stevenson, Henty, and Alger; volumes of poems by Whittier, Longfellow, and others; and a five-volume history of the world. Whether Max ever read from this collection is not known.

He felt no need to study the Bible itself; he said in the Columbia interview that he learned the contents well by merely listening to his father.[75] And even if Max were not the son of a clergyman, it would have been hard for him to escape the pervasive influence that the Bible, and the Church too, had on almost all the citizenry save for the wild Gypsies who rode into Jamestown from their farms. Nor could the negative example (as Max saw it) of his father's evangelistic salesmanship succeed in eradicating religion from his consciousness, as proved in after years when he declared himself an atheist but kept on writing eloquently about the spirit and, in *Journey to Jerusalem,* about Jesus Christ himself.

For spectator entertainment there were boxing bouts, Sunday afternoon band concerts, minstrel shows, circuses, and carnivals. The large Opera House was said to be the finest theater on the Northern Pacific railway line between Minneapolis or Chicago and the West Coast. All the important actors were "on the road" then and would continue to be until motion pictures arrived in force; all the actors traveling on the Northern Pacific came to Jamestown and stopped off to perform in order to defray expenses. But the ferment of theatrical activity that Louis L'Amour and his sister recall—as many as twenty-eight shows, most of them plays, in one season— seems to have taken place largely in the decade after Max left, though unquestionably some of it was going on in 1907-8, when the Andersons were in town.

The Reverend Anderson never attended any of these imagined hotbeds of wickedness, and of course he never wanted his growing children to go, but they went whenever they insisted. Probably the shortage of money was more effective than the father's disapproval in curtailing their attendance. No record survives as to what plays Max saw in Jamestown, if indeed he saw any at all, even though tickets were said to be modestly priced—according to the standards of the well-off LaMoores, who could well afford them. Edna Waldo writes that bored actors visited the high school sometimes, and it was the custom for the leading actor to make a speech.

Had not Max completed his English requirements back in New Hampton, he would almost certainly have sat in the English class of Miss Jennie L. Hall, a tall, lean, dark-haired, and energetic lady with a fine feeling for language. She unquestionably knew him and thought him something "special," according to what Lela recalls. And Miss Hall would have found it hard to overlook Max Anderson in a graduating class of only nineteen, he being older than the average senior and a six-footer in a day when six-footers were not as common as now, and being like herself an enthusiast for literature. Besides that, she was the school's strict principal, and he soon built up an amazing record for tardiness to classes.

Max excelled in "school music"[76] (for a long time in his youth it was a toss-up whether he would pursue a career in music[77]): He sang, and played the piano, and even composed. His grade average of 83.6 percent for the year would not have impressed the studious Miss Hall, but she *would* have approved of his membership in a literary society and his entry into a declamation contest among whose five contestants was one of her star students, Edna LaMoore.

Max, though public speaking irked him, was lured into the contest by the handsome prizes. From his voluminous readings in poetry he chose to give a recitation from "Morte d'Arthur," a piece characteristic of him in being strictly literary but which could no more appeal to his audience fresh out of the cornfields than a halter to a restive bull. He himself liked the selection, however, and worked hard on it. But when he lost out to a boy who made the crowd laugh, he was stricken to the heart. No wonder, says Lela, that Max long felt poets and poetry were so little appreciated in the towns of the Middle West. Ironically enough, out of all the contestants only he and Edna lost—the only two who ever went on to college and had any kind of career. It is pleasant to think that Miss Jennie Hall encouraged him to push on with his literary interests.

With high school graduation approaching, his father urged him to enter the clergy, but he refused. And then his father urged him and the other boys to take up farming for a living.[78] But Max had no desire to bury his soul under a haystack, although he seems to have had no interest in entering any of the usual professions either, probably because his severely limited experience and equally limited money cut off most career possibilities at the start.

After he got his diploma he worked as a fire-up man in the roundhouse of the Northern Pacific, a job so dirty and grimy that he was coal black from head to toe by quitting time. He used to claim that he met Lela on the street one day, as he trudged home from work, and she did not even recognize him. But the drudgery was colorful, Max recalls:

I was on the midnight to noon shift. . . . Those were the ordinary working hours in those days. I didn't have the haziest idea of what the job was when I got it, but I showed up the first night, was handed over to the chief fire-up man and told to watch him. He and his assistant had a list. They'd consult the list, fire a locomotive with a blow torch, get the pressure up, and then go on to the next one.

Well, after about a half-hour of this, the chief got mad at something and quit. So the assistant and I took over the list, and we fired up the locomotives and got up the steam. Then the assistant got mad, and he quit. And there I was by myself, frantically looking at the list, and trying to fire the locomotives and get up the steam. But I was falling way behind, and everyone was swearing at me. Meanwhile, No. 1 and No. 2, the crack fliers, were due to pull out, and I hadn't got to them yet. Well, I finally got them going, and I remember the engine of No. 2 crawling out under only 30 pounds of pressure, with the fireman cursing me all the way down the track.[79]

It is incongruous to imagine the future author of gracefully beautiful dramas like *Elizabeth the Queen* and *High Tor* as this bespectacled, sooty-faced Ariel who looks rather like the Calibans among whom he labors as he moves from engine to engine and lugs his blowtorch in his husky arms.

STUDENT AND TEACHER

Max narrowly made it to the university. The family had always assumed that he would go someday, but when the moment of truth arrived in 1908, no provision had been made to send him off to ivied halls. Unlike today, there were no federal loans for that purpose; a bank loan was out of the question, since the family had no sufficient collateral; and scholarships were as scarce as November strawberries for students like Max who did not rank at the very top of their class. Years of repeated illness and a built-up resistance to the academic system of dispensing knowledge had taken their toll on his grade point average. But a few doors down the street from him in Jamestown lived a friend named Garth Howland, who planned to enter the University of North Dakota in the fall, and Garth convinced him that if only he could get started at the university, enough part-time work would happen along to support him. "Don't worry about the money!" Garth said in effect.[1]

Almost 40 percent of the students then at the University of North Dakota were working their way through. But Max needed money to start on; a student needed $116 per year just to pay for board, room, and fees.[2] In this crisis his devoted older sister Ethel came to the rescue. It was she whom the Reverend Anderson had blocked from attending the school of her choice in Harrisburg; and later on she had dropped out of high school and got a teaching certificate. In a fine gesture that must have been decisive for her poor brother, she offered to send him at least $10 a month from her meager teaching salary at Goodrich, North Dakota. Ten dollars does not seem like much now, but in 1908 in New York City, for instance, one could buy a steak dinner with mushrooms for $.35. In old age, Ethel would write to her still immensely grateful brother that when she realized she would never be able to fulfill her own dream of going to college, she resolved that her brothers and sisters would not suffer the same defeat, not if *she* could help it.[3] In light of what she did for him that crucial first year—when the whole nation was wracked by a financial depression—one can understand why he in turn was so generous to her when he became a successful playwright.

At the time Max moved into Sayre Hall out on the fringe of the campus,[4] the University of North Dakota consisted of little more than a few brick buildings, most of them new, at the end of a trolley line running out from Grand Forks, which boasted a population of almost fifteen thousand. It was an encampment in the wilderness.

This was the region of the country that was marked on the old maps as the Great American Desert; all around lay the vast stretch of naked and wind-swept prairie. Except along the coulee which ran through the campus, all the trees were just slender saplings,[5] youthful but promising—like the pioneer sons and daughters who were arriving from farms and frontier hamlets all over the Dakotas. The whole student body numbered less than five hundred, about a fourth of them immigrants. All dormitories featured double beds. The regulations were most restrictive as compared with those on today's campuses: Residents were permitted to stay away from the dormitories only two nights during the semester, and girls had to get written permission from their parents to be in town after six o'clock except when chaperoned or going to church. Everyone had to sign in and out. Drinking and smoking were so abhorrent to the administration that if a male student were caught on or off campus committing either of these sins, he would be expelled from the dormitory; and, if a girl, expelled from the university. Max, who smoked, joined the others in going across the Great Northern tracks to light up, and some of the more daring made forays into the red-light district of town.

It is never easy to describe well a complex organization like a university, but this particular one was at once friendly and straitlaced, intellectual and informal, familylike and rambunctious. Sometimes President Merrifield could be seen visiting the men's dormitories for a friendly chat. Social and intellectual organizations on campus held their own with intercollegiate athletics. Classes were small. "School spirit" flourished, albeit at times with startling violence, and rowdyism grew common during President Merrifield's last year in office, which corresponded with Max's freshman year. The school historian writes that "organized hazing in its more vicious forms was on the verge of becoming a permanent campus problem ... accompanied as it was by class rivalries so heightened that mass fights were a constant threat, particularly in the early fall." He goes on to tell us that frequently

> erupting in the buildings, they could and did produce smashed furniture and broken windows. One brawl that developed when seniors attempted to break up a junior class sleighing party was serious enough to be noticed by the Minneapolis *Tribune*. When in 1908 posters were circulated forbidding freshmen to wear derbies or class pins or "to fuss with girls outside their own class," the resulting free-for-all swirling from the railroad station and gymnasium attracted a large crowd, disrupted classes, and was halted only by Merrifield's personal intervention.

The historian writes that on one occasion the students were so impudently aggressive that they tried to break up a faculty meeting by making a racket outside the meeting room door.[6]

It does not seem that Max was involved in any of these disturbances; he was always physically unaggressive and mild of manner until driven to desperation, at which he might explode with Jovian wrath—as he did once when his scrappy brother Harold had harassed him so much in play that he finally could not bear it any longer and, as Lawrence tells it, picked up the lad and hurled him right through a screen door. Harold was surprised but not injured.

Anyway, Max was altogether too occupied with his busy schedule to frolic even if he had wanted to. He must have missed out on some of the purely harmless recreation that makes the college experience so fondly remembered in after years and which would have leavened his increasingly serious personality. But sheer survival was at stake. He donned an apron and waited on tables at Van Gladen's dairy lunch and at the Commons. During his second year he found a sleep-robbing night job at the copy desk of the *Grand Forks Herald* where, as one of the two staff members serving under the editor-in-chief, he composed headlines and edited the news as it came in hot over the wires. When summer arrived, he drifted back to his familiar role of farm boy: in Jamestown, in Cando,[7] and at least once in Bottineau on the farm of his future father-in-law, James J. Haskett. At times he went back to the old grind of fire-up man in the roundhouse at Jamestown. Never in all his days was he to reap any pleasure from farming or any other kind of physical labor, but Lela credits to such outdoor work in his youth his recovery from early chronic illnesses, and the good health he needed for the demands of professional life.

At the end of Max's first school year, when he was barely able to support himself, Ethel quit her teaching post and moved with the family to Grand Forks, where they rented a house on University Avenue and took in a boarder. Thereupon Max left Budge Hall, to which he had moved from Sayre, and had an easier life at home, where he doubtless enjoyed better rations than the spartan diet of whole wheat bread and bananas he had become used to. But the Andersons still were hard pressed to make ends meet. At this time Ethel and Lela made a hopeless but gallant attempt to attend the university themselves. Lela had graduated from high school with honors and had won two scholarships to as many colleges, but she gave these up in favor of the Grand Forks venture. Though the girls completed the first year in good order, they soon realized that family finances would not permit them to continue (suitable part-time jobs for girls were hard to find).[8] Their dreams for college were shattered forever. They and most of the other children, lacking opportunities also, got caught in a bumper-to-bumper life in a slow lane that grew even worse during the Great Depression of the 1930s.

On campus and off, peg-top trousers were the rule with men's dress, and commonly turtleneck sweaters too, the latter being serviceable for slipping on in a hurry to get breakfast before the cafeteria door closed. The sweater kept one from having to wear that fashionable torture instrument left over from the Victorian era, namely the shirt with the high starched or celluloid collar. With the shirt went a bow tie, Max Anderson having a long, flowing type associated with poets of that period. He may have carried, like other youths, one of the thick Ingersoll dollar pocket watches, which he could haul out by means of a fob—wristwatches were not yet common. An early photograph shows him wearing pincer-type eyeglasses—perhaps in imitation of Professor Koch, his drama teacher—with a long black silk cord fixed to a buttonhole or lapel and then looped lordly over the ear. Coeds had their pincer eyeglasses anchored to the hair by means of a tiny chain and hairpin, and the hair itself commonly had pompadour rolls on the front, "buns" in back, and "rats," which elaborate configurations were easy for men to hide behind in class. Outside of class women might wear "Merry Widow" hats with a wingspan of two to three feet, which made navigation difficult when boarding streetcars. Their long dresses actually swept the earth, and if any fair creature uncovered even the least glimpse of stocking or flesh, *that* was sexy! One of Max's contemporaries at the University of North Dakota, C. L. Robertson, remembers:

One day when it was raining a college girl got off the streetcar at a crossing downtown, lifted her skirts in a grand sweep to keep them out of contact with the mud and almost caused the streetcar to be over-turned by the rush of men to see the display of limbs—legs were "limbs" in those days.[9]

Max, darkly handsome as a student, had a generous helping of what is popularly called "sex appeal." It hovered about him like a musk. "Girls fell for him. He could have almost anyone he wanted," his sister Lela declares with obvious pride;[10] and other sources duly support this claim. Little Margaret Ethel Haskett quickly became his favorite girl on campus. She was a Davis Hall bluestocking who had been dating the "campus catch," one Van Gladen, but she dropped Van when the new boy from Jamestown appeared. Margaret, helping to edit the school paper, soon got Max interested in that project.[11] But had she so desired, this winsome creature could almost as easily have gotten him interested in the migratory habits of the Canadian goose. Once they met, they were inseparable.

Margaret, who stood about five-two, was slim, small-breasted, with even features, a fair translucent skin, widespread blue eyes, dark brows, and straight-cut long black hair with a hint of gunmetal blue lurking in the shadows. With regard to everyday dress, she was most particular about selecting good shoes but otherwise spent little time on her personal appearance—probably because there was no need to, since Mother Nature had endowed her amply to start with. By all accounts she was witty, quick with clever retorts, vivacious, free-spirited, but conventional in outward behavior except for smoking in a day when women were not supposed to. Like Max, she was something of a dreamer.[12]

Some of her teachers thought her a better student than Max. She won first prize during her senior year in the university essay-writing contest.[13] She evidently had a strongly independent streak governed by fierce loyalties and idealistic convictions, as illustrated by her unwillingness to stay with her sorority, Phi Kappa Chi, when it supposedly denied a Negro admission or some membership right;[14] and also by her refusal of the Phi Beta Kappa key because Max was not offered one too.[15] She also had the agreeable gift of being able to talk *with* people—for example, children—rather than talking down to them. When her twelve-year-old niece Margaret H. Haskett visited her in New City long after her marriage, this lady who always seemed to be in a hurry on ordinary occasions took time to walk with the little girl down a country road and talk to her quietly about the countryside, making her feel as if she were on the grown-up's level, and after the visit was over sent her delightful gifts that she knew would please a young girl's heart.[16]

Just as happened with Max, the birth of Margaret Ethel Haskett was not officially recorded. Available family and school records agree in telling us that she was born on July 15, 1886, in the long since vanished village of Auburn, about eight miles from Carberry in the province of Manitoba, Canada. Family tradition has it that she was born prematurely and much underweight (so tiny a babe that, as the saying goes, she could curl up on a dime and leave nine cents' change) and had to be rushed down to the States for medical treatment soon after delivery. Tradition also says that she was a weakly infant who subsisted for a while on soda crackers—she was never a physically strong person, in contrast with her stubborn spirit—and always had to husband her energies.

Like Max, Margaret had a large number of brothers and sisters, eight finally, and all of these save for little sister Elizabeth were quite overawed by the tall and heavy autocratic father, who had farming in his blood. Both of Margaret's parents were Irish Catholic. Unlike the Reverend Anderson, James J. Haskett grew wealthy—after he wisely moved his operations to Bottineau, North Dakota, where he could count on having the few more frost-free days that were essential to his wheat growing—and in the full flush of his prosperity owned 1,030 acres of farm land at Bottineau and was worth perhaps $100,000.[17]

When Max was not squiring Margaret around and not writing free verse for the school paper, which he also edited; and not busy putting together (in his senior year) the school annual, *The Dacotah;* and not slaving at his successive part-time jobs; and not getting bruised from playing center and right guard on the varsity football team, a brief diversion for him[18]—that is, when he was free for his proper learning role at the university, he was so tired that, as he relates in the Columbia memoir, he slept by day in his classes. Not surprisingly, then, he made some D's in French, chemistry, philosophy, and history. But he made C's in half his subjects; B's in Church history, English, French, and sociology; and all his A's in English.[19] Being a rapid and voracious reader, Max completed some of this course work by examination, reducing to three the school years he needed for his bachelor's degree.[20] No doubt he would have earned higher grades if he had not been so continually weary and pressed for time. But grades seemed unimportant to him; his interests lay elsewhere.

Professor Gottfried Hult is said to have given him an incomplete in Greek one spring because "He'd gone on a reading spree in the library and couldn't be bothered about coming to classes."[21] All indications show that our student was so independent he much preferred working at his own pace and regarded university routine as an artificial set of rituals to be gotten through quickly so that he could continue educating himself. In fact, as his son Quentin discloses, Max at last developed a "profound suspicion" of academic institutions, especially as they proposed to train students for careers in the arts.[22] Several sources for this book told of Max's conviction that any student with enough talent ought to be able to carve out for himself some kind of meaningful career in the creative or performing arts without the bother of having to sit around in college halls. To Max, by midcareer, college was the haunt of the effete genteel and possibly the failed artist. But, unlike Jack London, he never discouraged his own children from going if they wanted to, and three of them went.

Frederick J. Brockhoff, one of his classmates in the courses on Shakespeare, recalls Max's "keen sense of humor," his "quiet reaction to a humorous passage [in one of the comedies]. He never reacted loudly—just with a sly, quiet smile."[23] The parson's son impressed students as being rather cynical about men who wielded great political power, an attitude that would be common in his best plays. Another classmate, C. L. Robertson, remembers that Max had a low, rich voice and was "friendly enough when one got to know him, but was not a great mixer [and never was]—he hardly had time to be"; also, that some of the envious students thought he bluffed a good deal and tried to impress his professors. But most likely this charge had its origin in the blurb found under his picture in the 1912 *Dacotah*. Max himself probably wrote the blurb and thereby founded the charge. The blurb runs: ". . . he is our greatest exponent of the intellectual bluff."

This same Robertson tells us that Margaret "stirred [her boyfriend] into action—he seemed inclined to be easy-going."[24] Appearances must have been deceiving, for Max was from the beginning far too active in studies, extracurricular school affairs, and part-time work to be called "easy-going."

Margaret was almost two and a half years older than her boyfriend and had arrived in Grand Forks years before he did, in order to attend the University of North Dakota Preparatory School;[25] consequently, she already knew about the university courses and professors and could give him many a handy tip. To his later friend Frank Ernest Hill, Max would confide that this girl was the first person he met to whom he could ever speak fully.[26]

Although he was to write two plays for production at the university, his foremost interest was lyrical poetry, and he was apparently much influenced by his readings in Keats, Tennyson, and perhaps George Sterling, who was then in vogue. None of the poems he wrote at this time can be considered as anything other than juvenilia, even though they surpass in quality much of what was getting published by some big-name poets. Several of his lyrics can be found in the pages of *The Dacotah* annuals,[27] for instance in the 1910 one edited by Margaret, where one encounters such titles as "So Long Ago," "There Comes a Time," and probably the best of all, "Again":

> *As Circe, on her lonely isle*
> *In the Tyrene Sea,*
> *Bending, within her castle dim,*
> *Over a crystal goblet's rim,*
> *On her lips a smile,*
> *Tempered the draughts of mystery—*
> *Tempered the fateful, luring wine*
> *With power to make men swine;*
> *So in these later, living days*
> *Over a chafing-dish there bent*
> *Full of dark intent,*
> *A maiden, face ablaze,*
> *And with the old unholy glee*
> *Made fudge to make a hog of me.*

Another lyric of his in *The Dacotah* and almost as good is "Whether the Dark Had Ushered in the Rain."[28] His mature poetry, except as found in the plays themselves, never rose far enough above this level and is never anthologized today.

Other writings of his in *The Dacotah* pages include a dramatic skit titled "Recently Discovered Fragment of the Epimetheus Shorn of Pharistes" and consisting of topical references to University of North Dakota life put into so-called classical dramatic form; also, a short story called "The Furrow."[29] He is said to have taken his poetry over to the house of Mrs. Florence B. Hult for criticism.[30] Florence wrote poetry herself.

Max took a total of eight courses under Florence's husband, the learned and lovable Professor Gottfried Hult, these being Greek language, literature, and philosophy, in the latter of which the student took considerable interest.[31] Long afterward, in his *Barefoot in Athens,* Max was to challenge the interpretation of Socrates' character that he had learned under Hult, but the more immediate value of this philosophical instruction was in filling in the spiritual gap made by his defection from Christianity. Like his more famous student, the teacher was the son of a Protestant minister and was raised and educated mainly in the Midwest. At the time of their first meeting, Hult already had a small following as a published poet in such journals as *Century Magazine,* where his verse resembled that done by the "Genteel" school of

Richard Henry Stoddard, Edmund Clarence Stedman, and Richard Watson Gilder, which is to say that Hult was a competent but minor writer of traditional verse during the twilight age that followed the demise of the Cambridge and Concord giants but coming before the Chicago Renaissance with its Carl Sandburg and Vachel Lindsay and Edgar Lee Masters. Hult's contemporary, Edwin Arlington Robinson, quite outdistanced him in quality of performance.

Hult's personal eccentricities, such as informal dress and office cooking, were better known locally than were his writings, but the latter were sometimes eccentric too. For instance, the professor considered it foolish to abandon in poetry time-honored Anglo-Saxon four-letter words in favor of Greek or Latin equivalents, and in one of his poems, written in about 1908, he employed the expression "the trees shit their leaves" instead of "shed" them, the usage causing some raised eyebrows, but people thought him to be merely queer rather than dirty.[32] In *What Price Glory*—the first stage success after leaving the university and Hult's immediate influence—Max used several of these forbidden Anglo-Saxon words.

It is curious that both these men who started out as poets—Hult in rhyme and Max in free verse—would in the early 1930s devote themselves earnestly to writing poetic dramas about famous historical figures. It is quite possible that Max's success on Broadway spurred the teacher on: In 1940, Hult published his *Inverted Torches,* containing the plays *The Messiah* and *Galileo.* Neither of these were ever produced. In a sense, Max's meteoric career in the commercial theater was a fulfillment of the teacher's dreams.

Our student took eight courses in English under Vernon P. Squires, his major professor, a reactionary among the faculty with respect to enforcing student discipline but who was later to help Max get a graduate assistantship at Stanford. Max took care not to lampoon *him* in the satirical senior class play he was to write. In his third and final year he took sociology from Professor John M. Gillette, a Midwestern leader in the Socialist party and in whose course Max gave a report on Thorstein Veblen's *The Leisure Class;* and Max credited to this particular course the "seeds of dissolution" that made him a socialist for a while after graduation[33] and probably had something to do with his pacifism as well. History he had in the classes of the nationally known Professor Orin G. Libby, whose radical views about Queen Elizabeth I and Queen Mary (of Scotland) must have made an impression on Max Anderson's thinking and influenced his conception of those monarchs in *Elizabeth the Queen* and *Mary of Scotland,* respectively. C. L. Robertson, seated in those classes with him, says that Libby shared with Max the view unpopular with many other historians of that day, which was that Elizabeth was far from being a virgin saint and that Mary was by no means a she-devil.[34]

Max was exceedingly fortunate in getting such professors as Hult, Squires, Gillette, and Libby, all of them "wonderful teachers," according to Lela, teachers who "seemed to see Max's possibilities and they helped him."[35] But the one who probably helped him the most was none of these; rather, it was the little dynamo called Frederick Henry Koch,[36] the handsome, dark-haired instructor of dramatic literature who was fresh out of Harvard and the Emerson College of Oratory in Boston, the teacher *extraordinaire* who would be known throughout American educational circles as the country's leading promoter of folk plays. If ever a teacher burned his candle at both ends for all things theatrical, it was Koch. If ever a teacher were like sunshine, warming his students, making them glow with his own abundant love for Shakespeare and the other masters of thespian magic, it was Koch. If ever a teacher could find the creative spark which he believed present in everyone, moreover could kindle that spark and tend it and make it blaze into sometimes original works of art, that too was Koch. In his dramatic readings in the classroom he squeaked and growled, whispered and shouted, cried and laughed, accompanying his delivery with masterful command of gesture; and on the dramatic stage he acted to great applause.[37]

When Koch first arrived on the Plains campus in 1905 he heard from the students that they had been producing nothing whatever in the way of authentic plays but only farces and minstrel shows, maybe because the faculty itself was prejudiced against drama. Still more disappointing, he found neither theater building nor formal stage on campus—not even office space reserved for him! But Koch laid plans to change all that. This young man had precisely what the university needed: vision along with the ability to get things done under inhospitable conditions. And before the year was out he staged R. B. Sheridan's *The Rivals,* casting in the lead role of Bob Acres a choice such as a PR man could hardly have improved on, the university's star football hero, John H. Conmy. Now who could dare say that plays are for namby-pambies and sissies? Or that plays, a supposedly tawdry, bohemian art lacking in respectability, would corrupt these sturdy sons and daughters of the soil?

After Koch produced the comedy in the Metropolitan Theatre in Grand Forks at June commencement, he proceeded to take it on tour through many little towns of the Dakotas, wherever the rail lines would allow, even though they had no guarantee in any of these places and only eighty dollars to start with. Upon arriving in a town, he had the actors draw lots to see which two would advertise the play by parading through the town in eighteenth-century costume and giving out handbills that announced the evening performance in the opera house. It was a highly successful tour in that everyone had a good time and no deficit resulted. In succeeding summers his eager and spirited troupers performed again in those same towns, now to crowded houses, with such works as Oliver Goldsmith's *She Stoops to Conquer* and Dickens' *Tom Pinch*.[38] Soon his amateur student players were known throughout the Northwest Territory.[39]

Koch, with his hail-fellow-well-met, breezy Western manner, belted Norfolk tweed jacket, flowing Windsor tie, and pince-nez glasses with the black ribbon about his neck—and in Mark Twain's words, "restless as a man who had swallowed a spring mattress"—contrasted sharply with the usual conservative professorial types. Nor did he feel at home with the regular academic routine. Unconventional with a capital U. There is every reason to believe that Maxwell Anderson warmed up to him quickly; they were known to be good friends from that time onward. Koch's classroom method was informal, familylike, relaxed, and the heart of it was the development of enthusiasm for literature (and from 1914 onward, when he began regular instruction in playwriting, the development of confidence in oneself). He was no niggard with grades, it's said, and he paid scant attention to formal criticism and historical scholarship. The scientific and scholarly professors pooh-poohed his methods, but he didn't care. "It is not the history of the flower nor its name that is meaningful," his biographers Selden and Sphangos quote him as saying. Rather, "In the deepest sense, it is the flower itself, the beautiful flower!"

He showed infinite patience with students and took a more than avuncular pride in what they accomplished as *his* Playmakers or *his* former students gone on to success somewhere (his assiduously compiled scrapbooks recorded their triumphs). In his dashing manner he was always the unashamed actor, the beautiful and inspiring egotist. Never, as some teachers are fond of doing, did he cut a student's written work to the bone and risk leaving the poor fellow discouraged and resentful; rather, he preferred to let the class offer constructive suggestions in a communal effort toward improvement. His famous former student Paul Green, from the University of North Carolina years, says:

> More than once I heard him say, "The longer I live the surer I am that what people need is not criticism but encouragement." And Proff [the pet name Green gave to him] did encourage people. He made them feel they could do things, beautiful and noble things.[40]

To the shy and gentle Max Anderson, used to a dogmatic father who had a

direct pipeline to God Almighty on all the great questions of life, this peda-
gogical approach must have been salutary indeed.

Koch took leave during Max's freshman year to return to Harvard for work
on his master's degree. At Harvard he came again under the spell of Professor
George Pierce Baker, who now taught a famous playwriting class. From
Baker he was inspired to form a "school" of regional dramatists modeled
somewhat after the then highly lauded Irish group of Padraic Colum and
Douglas Hyde, Lady Gregory and George Moore, J. M. Synge and William
Butler Yeats, which would interpret the rich variety of American folk expe-
riences in plays worthy of the country's vision, struggles, and achievement.[41]
And this gifted enthusiast finally carried out the plan, too, albeit on a smaller
scale, first at the University of North Dakota and later at the University of
North Carolina. No wonder his friend Archibald Henderson dubbed him
"Freddy Folkplay": "Wherever he dropped the seeds of art, talent and inspira-
tion have sprung up like magic and flourished luxuriantly."[42]

At the risk of getting ahead of our story, it should be remarked that Max
Anderson was completely sympathetic with his teacher's enterprise once it
started; and it appears that he kept in mind long afterward the desire to write
native drama, which Koch himself realized when he observed that Max's first
Broadway work, *White Desert* (1923), contained a strong folk element and
delineated the countryside Anderson knew best: North Dakota's vast and
lonely winter plain.[43] The folk element is also pronounced in his *Sea-Wife*
(1926) and *High Tor* (1937).

After getting his master's degree, Koch began an extended trip abroad
during which he met in Athens a pretty, eighteen-year-old girl, Loretta Hani-
gan. Ever the fervent romantic, three days later at the Acropolis he proposed
to her, and they were married the next year.[44]

Max, already excited about Shakespeare, took courses in that subject from
Koch when he got back from Europe, and probably found, as did so many
other students, something electric about his teaching.[45] An even closer association took place. In January of his sophomore year Max met with Margaret
Haskett, Garth Howland, and eight other people at the home of a physician
where Koch, presiding—whenever Koch was present, he always presided—
established the university's first dramatic club. This was the Sock and Buskin
Society, organized for the "study of the literature of the drama and the
promotion of the art of the theater . . . ," one of whose aims included getting a
university theater. At first the club was a center for dramatic presentations,
but later on for original playwriting.[46] Membership in it was highly select:
The candidate had to submit to one of the following three competitive trials:
(1) present a dramatic piece for reading; (2) present an article of twelve

hundred words or more on some aspect of modern drama or theater; (3) present an original play. Max gained his charter membership by reading before the society a paper called "The New Theatre," and he became one of Koch's two assistants. Every month the group gave some kind of dramatic performance before the student body, and in June it staged an outdoor production of *Twelfth Night*, the first of its kind on campus. Max tried out for the role of Captain in Act I, but he failed miserably and had to be replaced.[47] Such a failure in delivering just two lines of dialogue would discourage any ordinary young man from ever venturing farther into theater. But Max was no more ordinary than the little man who fired him. They were both stage-struck but in different ways.

Although Koch had an undeniable impact on his intellectual development once they met, no one can say that Koch inspired the first Anderson play of which we have record, a seniors' musical comedy with the Shakespearean title *Lost Labors Love,* written in Max's freshman year in collaboration with R. H. Montgomery.[48] But this future maker of playwrights clearly had much to do with Max's final college play, *The Masque of Pedagogues,* done when the author was a senior.[49] In it we note already the Elizabethan devices of verse dialogue and songs that later figure in Anderson's mature plays about Anne Boleyn, Queen Elizabeth, and Mary of Scotland.

The Masque of Pedagogues reflects Max's main literary interests at the time in that it contains five references to Shakespeare and two to Keats. Its plot is clearly a takeoff on Christopher Marlowe's *Doctor Faustus:* Lucifer visits certain scholars at the University of North Dakota and with bribes of preferred treatment in hell tries to learn from them some exquisite new kinds of torture to use down there. The professors, of course, are all gleefully expert in devising insufferably difficult assignments and examinations. Witness Professor Henry Le Daum (under whom Max took French) as he gives out one of his fiendish assignments to an imaginary class:

> For tomorrow, I want you to draw a map of Australia, and put in all the cities and towns which have any direct bearing on French history. Also, I want you to draw separate maps in color of all the countries of South America, including principal mountain ranges, towns, residences of famous men, holy shrines, and large coffee plantations. Include a diagram of the wind velocities in different latitudes, and don't forget Mercator's projections. There's a large banyan tree on the west coast of Chili that must not be forgotten. . . . Also, read Rousseau's Emile in the original and be ready to recite on any part of it. . . . read through the first two books of Hugo's Les Misérables. . . . If you have any time left,

read the history of Santa Cruz, on the reserve shelf, and write out the verb meaning "to die."[50]

Max's skill at satirizing the weaknesses of his teachers did not spare the charismatic Professor Koch, either.[51] The hit, reproduced below, captures neatly the man's love for emoting about Shakespeare, the enthusiasm verging upon the impressionistic and sentimental, the role of girl students making up an emotional claque for anything sad, the ignoring of published criticism, the easy testing:

Enter Prof. Koch and three coy maidens.

PROF. KOCH: (adjusting a flower in his buttonhole*) How pastoral it will be to hold class here on the greensward! Come, let us sit down here in a charmed circle and commune together upon the beauties of Nature and our immortal William,—our dearest Shakespeare. (They seat themselves on the grass.) Let us dispense with our texts today. I will not ask questions and you will not need the notes in the back of the book. Let us simply go over those passages which we have found the most wonderful and thrilling in all the work of the great bard. You will remember in Macbeth,

> "Duncan is in his grave;
> After life's fitful fever he sleeps well;
> Treason hath done his worst, nor steel nor poison,
> Malice Domestic, foreign levy, nothing
> Can touch him farther."

(As he repeats the above, the maidens take out their handkerchiefs and weep.) But now, let us have something sprightlier; something more like the hey-day of youth, in which we find ourselves. Here is the passage which my wife has often told me is the most beautiful thing in Shakespeare. I always take my wife's opinion as solid ground on which to build. She is so perfectly sane and unbiased in her decisions. Listen to this old, familiar passage again and see if I am not right in doing so.

> "Hark, Hark, the lark at Heaven's gate sings,
> And Phoebus 'gins to rise;
> His steeds to water at those springs
> On chaliced flowers that lies.
> With everything that pretty is

---

*Koch was an avid flower gardener.

My lady sweet, arise,
Arise, arise!"

1ST COY MAIDEN: Oh, Prof. Koch, I think that is just too lovely.
2ND COY MAIDEN: Oh, so do I.
3RD COY MAIDEN: And I.

PROF KOCH: Thanks so much. My artist's soul must have appreciation.
You shall all get A for today's work.[52]

Koch endeared himself as an inspiring and germinal personality long afterward, not only to Max Anderson but also to many former Dakota Playmakers
and Carolina Playmakers, as shown by the testimonials of those who attained
positions of influence or fame in radio, TV, theater, book writing, teaching,
and other fields. The following is a brief list of such grateful people: Paul
Green (*The Lost Colony, The House of Connelly*), Betty Smith (*A Tree
Grows in Brooklyn*), Josephina Niggli (*Mexican Village*), Foster Fitz-Simons
(*Bright Leaf*), Thomas Wolfe (*Look Homeward, Angel*), Daphne Athos (*The
Weather of the Heart*), Jonathan Daniels (*A Southerner Discovers the
South*), Howard Richardson (*Dark of the Moon*), Shepperd Strudwick
(actor), and George V. Denny, Jr. (founder and moderator of "Town Hall of
the Air").[53]

The Masque of Pedagogues is scarcely the work to illustrate the influence
of Koch at his best, but it is a revelation of some of Max's abiding literary
tastes.[54]

One cannot help feeling that if he had only been in one of Freddy Folk-
play's classes starting about 1914, when native plays were being turned out,
he might have begun his professional career in the theater long before he
did.[55] Koch never claimed to have "discovered" Max as a writer or to have
shaped his talent, but he never tired of telling people that the world-
renowned Maxwell Anderson was once upon a time one of his students.[56]

Shortly after Max and Margaret graduated in 1911, we find them in Bottineau, North Dakota, where sprawled the Hasketts' big farm. On August 1
there, in a ceremony conducted by Monsignor Joseph Andrews of St. Mark's
Parish, the renegade son of a Baptist preacher married the independent-
minded Catholic girl.[57] Like Romeo and Juliet's, it was a marriage pleasing to
neither family at the time[58] and destined for disaster. The witnesses for the
ceremony included H[arry] E. Haskett and Elizabeth Haskett, the bride's
younger brother and sister, both of whom may presumably have been among

those few who were sympathetic to the nuptials. The elder Hasketts were unhappy to bring even a nominal Protestant into the family. Moreover, the well-heeled James J. Haskett, for whom Anderson had sweated at least one summer as a field hand at twenty-five to thirty dollars a month, resented the union because he feared Max would not be a good provider.[59]

The Reverend Anderson had a horror of Catholics at this stage of his life, although in old age he married one after his first wife died. He never could accept Margaret's professing to be an agnostic; for this and perhaps other reasons they detested each other.[60] It is not surprising, then, that Max brought none of his own family along for his own wedding.[61] And he added two years when he listed his age on the marriage certificate as twenty-five, perhaps to make the twenty-five-year-old Margaret feel better. He never had much patience with legal forms.

Of the next two years, when Max taught high school in the village of Minnewaukan,[62] among the wheat lands of North Dakota, we know little. This particular school had only two teachers, and Max was the principal. The house that he and his bride moved into in Minnewaukan had four rooms lined up one behind the other, a company house in a row of several on the street. The Andersons must have had their share of suffering in this land of annual blizzards and subzero temperatures where winds up to sixty miles an hour fill the air with flying snow and reduce visibility almost to zero, where killing frosts come as late as May. They kept a big coal fire going in the living room up front; also in the kitchen range, until it "clinkered out" and some-one had to unclog it and start a new fire.[63] One who knew the Andersons at this time reported that they had no furniture in the whole place except a bed; they relied heavily on packing boxes and trunks.[64] But enough furniture had accumulated by the time Lela began making her visits that she found the house comfortably furnished.[65] Quentin, their first child, was born the year after they arrived.[66]

Their home became the center for local intelligentsia discussing such things as art and socialism, all of which apparently irritated their provincial neighbors, to whom the fine arts suggested immorality and to whom a teacher of radical politics was anathema. As usual, Anderson devoted much of his spare time to writing lyrical verse. Nearby was a lake that had given its name to the community of Minnewaukan; and though it had dried almost to a marsh by the time Anderson arrived, it exercised such a fascination for him that he wrote a poem about it called "Judith of Minnewaukan."[67]

At this point in history, when passions ran high because of the possibility that America might get embroiled in World War I, when in fact most of the

populace began to favor doing so, Max courageously joined his fellow social-
ists in taking an antiwar stand and, in his case, "talked pacifism" to his
students. This deliberate, open pacifism enraged the star-spangled school
board, which promptly terminated his contract.[68]

Luckily, Mr. and Mrs. Maxwell Anderson had saved enough money from his
small salary so that they could take off for graduate school in California.[69] His
friend Professor Squires had arranged a graduate assistantship for him at
Leland Stanford University, where Anderson could earn an M.A. that would
qualify him for a teaching slot at a college.[70] Perhaps he would be happier
teaching older, more mature students.

Stanford was still being led by Dr. David Starr Jordan, its first chancellor
and one of the noblest and most distinguished public figures of his day, who
had made it a leading American university. A prominent ichthyologist and
writer, chief director of the World Peace Foundation from 1910 to 1914,
and president of the World Peace Congress in 1915, Jordan was apparently
the first to make concerted studies of the genetic effects of war, as recorded
in his two books *The Human Harvest* and *War's Aftermath*. In these he
argued cogently that the most intelligent and physically endowed in a generation are likely to perish in battle and leave behind them the inferior breed
who will in turn sire the following generation. This is but one of the catastro-
phic drawbacks of war that he noted.[71]

In the fall of 1913, the Andersons moved into a low-rent house in a meadow
about a mile from the university, in a district called University Park. They took
turns riding off to classes on a bicycle; when one of them went to school,
the other stayed at home and tended the baby; when the scholar returned,
the baby-sitter took off. The arrangement worked well, and all indications
showed that they were happy as a couple. Margaret, however, was never
to complete requirements for her master's degree. This brilliant lady,
who had been considered by some at the University of North Dakota to
have more talent than Max, let her husband do all the writing when she
recognized his superior gifts; she devoted herself to running the household.[72] It was the familiar and age-old tale of the wife gladly and loyally
subordinating her identity as an intellectual being to her husband's, but
in her case as dangerous as it was commendable, for she was to find herself without a career of her own to pursue when the marriage was coming
apart.

Anderson took a part-time job as a janitor in a country school until the
assistantship in the English Department opened up after Christmas.[73] Various
published accounts, including some generated much later by the playwright
himself, imply that he was a regular member of the Stanford teaching staff,

whereas the official records do not show that. As a graduate assistant he gave some limited instruction, maybe of the "bonehead" sort on the freshman level.[74] His good friend Frank Hill, teaching there at the time, tells us that this big, robust fellow fresh out of the Midwestern snowfields was not happy at Stanford:

> I think he would have been happy if Stanford had been happier with him, but there was a quality in Max, in his writing and I imagine it was also in his speaking: he was immensely truthful, and I imagine would get up there before the class and say things that seemed rather extreme. At any rate, people in the department didn't quite like the way his classes were going, and Max was worried about it.[75]

Because the new teacher was an ingenuous man by nature and impatient of insincerity on the part of others, one can imagine him answering students ruthfully on his feelings about current European power politics, war, patriotism for the profit of special-interest groups, capitalist oppression, and the venality of public leaders. He could have shocked his nonhumanist subject majors, those from the families of H. L. Mencken's "booboisie," by telling them that creating poetry is far more important than engineering or banking or merchandising or lawyering, or certain occupations they might be in training to enter. As a grader of themes he was not the kind to flatter pretentious or incompetent writers. He to whom reading and writing skills had come early, had come easily, differed from his old teacher Professor Koch not in lacking enthusiasm—for Max was always enthusiastic in the classroom—but in not being hopeful when he saw so much dullness and mediocrity around him. Before many years were to pass, Anderson would decide that any meaningful improvement in the literary culture or writing ability of the student in the English class was a lonely enterprise carried out by the student himself independent of and without help from the teacher. "The boy who loves literature will read it in the library; the others suffer many purposeless and grilling hours."[76]

On the English faculty Dr. Henry David Gray was noted for his published studies of Elizabethan drama and Emerson, also for the fact that he wrote plays, his *Gallops* having actually had a New York production in 1906.[77] They were not very good plays, true, but one of them *did* get produced, and that was saying something to aspiring young writers from the provinces like Max, who were beginning to get theater in their blood. Gray was a superb lecturer with a flair for the dramatic; his only noticeable flaw as a personality seems to have been a habit of laughing in an effeminate manner, though he was no homosexual. Just as soon as Frank Hill joined the department, Gray delighted in telling him about a certain new student he had in his drama class, a man called Max Anderson, who had written a strikingly effective one-acter laid in the Dakota wilderness. It was about a highly religious couple, isolated with little food and nothing at all to stave off the awesome cold, who finally resort to burning that holy of holies, the Bible, so that they can get some heat. A "magnificent stroke," Gray called it![78]

This was one of three one-act plays that Anderson was to write for Dr. Gray's classes. Here is where he got his first and only formal instruction in how to build plays.

Long afterward Dr. Gray remembered his student as a relatively poor, wistful-looking young man who was not at all impressed with his importance as an artist. He recalled that Anderson set about his classwork quietly and bore "no look of an eager and soul-tortured young genius." He smiled little; more often, he wore a "quizzical expression" that suggested a smile not willing to break out. Gray thought of him as more of a poet than a potential playwright and found in some of his verse an "extraordinary insight" and "haunting quality."

> But I confess, to my chagrin, that I saw little promise of a Broadway success in Anderson when he took the course in Playwriting at Stanford. I can remember the work of a dozen or twenty students who have taken that course and written plays for it which gave me more hope than I received from anything that Maxwell Anderson submitted.
> —David Gray, "Anderson at Stanford,"
> *Prompter,* Vol. IV, No. 3 (Mar. 1938),
> p. 7 (Palo Alto Community Players, Palo
> Alto, Calif.)

Anderson in his own recollection was not kind either. His personality sketch "The Scholar Too Late," written in the elegantly dignified and rhythmical prose characteristic of his best essays, shows a satirical version of the teacher. "If you are familiar with the erudite and uninteresting in literature," Anderson opens up with obvious distaste, "you will know that Professor Maurice has no rival as an authority in Restoration drama. . . . His swift easy gestures and cultivated merriment over the things of literary yesterdays have the tragic meaning of a gay harlequin before a tall sable curtain." Maurice loathes lecturing and scholarly research in spite of his facility at these things and in spite of the popularity they bring him; what he wants most of all is to write great plays and poems, but these he can never do because his talent

never rises above cleverness and showmanship. And so he finds in the ener-
vating drudgery of his teaching an excuse for his failure as an artist. A sad and
bitter man beneath his glittering exterior[79]—surely an object lesson for
Anderson, showing what *he* might become if he made a career of college
teaching.

At the Round Table meetings held two afternoons a week at a spot the
members had selected along the Lagunita, Anderson was one of about ten
young, hopeful authors who met to read aloud and discuss their writings.
Gray recalls that the preacher's son was always attentive and interested but
did not throw himself into the discussions as the abler students usually did.
But Anderson showed himself very able at exposing pretentious language in
a fragment of verse drama that Gray read aloud to the group. Most of the
Round Table members were turning out poetry. A surprising number of the
group would end up with successful careers in journalism, publishing, and
education. Hill numbered among these young people; he was Max's own age.
When World War I broke out and America intervened in the conflict, this
six-footer who had never even driven an automobile left the Stanford faculty
to become an Army airplane pilot; and after the armistice he had a varied
career as poet, journalist, publisher, translator, book reviewer, magazine
editor, and biographer.

Also among the members was the gangling Robert Luthur Duffus with his
bobbing Adam's apple. Ill at ease except with Round Table companions, he
was at that time an editorial writer on the *San Francisco Evening Bulletin*
but had dreams of becoming a writer of fiction. And true enough, he was to
be the author of several novels but be better known for his long career as an
editorial writer on *The New York Times.*

One of the students in the group was dark-haired, quiet, bespectacled
Bruce Ormsby Bliven, a year younger than Anderson, and like him from a
Midwestern farm background. Bliven contributed articles to the campus
humor paper called the *Chaparral.* Someday he would be managing editor of
the *Globe,* and after that editor of the *New Republic.*

All of these young men would cross paths with Anderson during his years
in journalism. It seems that his friend and fellow student Margery Bailey, who
later became a professor on the Stanford faculty, was also a member of the
Round Table.[80]

No doubt these aspiring writers gave each other valuable intellectual
stimulation at the Round Table. But none of them managed to inspire Max
Anderson to abandon his plans for teaching and to turn, instead, to full-time
writing. He must have been unsure of his powers. Poetry was the main thing
at the Round Table, not drama, and poetry suited Max just fine. But he had

sense enough to know that he would have to live in a garret if he were to become a full-time poet.

At the end of the school year he took his master's degree in English after writing a thesis completely characteristic of him: "Immortality in the Plays and Sonnets of Shakespeare."[81]

Perhaps Max was unable to secure the position he wanted on a college faculty, or did not try, for we next find him teaching high school English again, this time in Polytechnic in nearby San Francisco. We know little about these years. The official school records for Polytechnic High School of that period have long been destroyed, none of Anderson's relatives seems to have left reminiscences of visits with him, Quentin was too young to remember much, and only one short, inconsequential letter from Anderson at the time has surfaced.[82] No new dramas written; some poems, however, placed here and there; the main literary event being the publication of six of his poems in *A Stanford Book of Verse.*[83] He gained some extra money by furnishing items for the *San Francisco Evening Bulletin* during the time that the famous reform journalist Fremont Older was still editor.[84]

At one time the Andersons lived in Palo Alto; at another, in a San Francisco apartment which Quentin, then only about five, remembers as having a Murphy bed that lowered from the wall when needed and as being within earshot of a neighboring park or zoo from which he could hear at night the cry of a peacock.[85]

In English classes "Maxie," as he was called in those days by his admiring female fans but never to his face, sat at his desk composing poetry while the students took examinations or wrote themes.[86] As one of his adoring pupils recalls, he was a "shy, handsome man with the build of a football hero, who taught Chaucer and Shakespeare like an author revealing his own works, blushing and perspiring as he read their poetry, magnetizing me into loving it as he did and revering the men who had written it."[87] When I asked her for more information, I received the following charming letter:

. . . all the girls were in love with him, including myself. . . . he was then writing poetry which he free-lanced to FPA's [Franklin P. Adams'] column in the [*New York*] *Herald Tribune* and to *The Nation* signing it M. A. I think, but cannot be sure, that he "got into trouble" with the stuffy old S. F. School Department for publishing "love poetry" and especially in that suspect *Nation*! . . . I know that in my senior year, he put on the old English morality play *Everyman*, because he gave me the part of Beauty in it, which part had exactly one line to recite. "I take my tap, in my lap, and am gone." Exit Beauty, carrying her little satin "tap," which stage-director Anderson would not permit me to call "cap" because that was *not* how the play was written! . . . I can say from personal experience that he was a truly inspiring teacher for those who had a love for the written word. That was all he needed to strike the spark. . . . This has been a long reach back into time. I hope that it gives you a glimmer of the young Maxwell . . . setting afire the hobble-skirted maidens of San Francisco by his incomparable recitations of, say, the sonnets of Shakespeare; pink-cheeked and perspiring, always looking a little too big for his clothes.[88]

This devoted pupil was Kathryn C. Hulme, who grew up to write, among many other things, the best-selling novel *The Nun's Story.*

On April 6, 1917, while Anderson was teaching his last semester of classes at Polytechnic, the United States declared war on Germany and quickly began drafting its millions of able-bodied young men.

When summer arrived and his teaching was over, Anderson, who was exempt from the draft because of nearsightedness, took a bachelor's vacation with his Stanford friend Robert Duffus, who was exempt because of a heart murmur, and with a Dutch-born architect named Herman Rosse. The three of them set out on a two-day bicycle trip across the Santa Cruz Mountains to Half Moon Bay, which lies just a few miles south of the Golden Gate. Those were the days before real-estate developers had transformed the California coastline into one long stretch of megalopolis and suburbia. The friends took their outing like true vagabonds; they brought a little food with them but no blankets. When they at last arrived at the beach and were going to bed down for the night they found the place cold and drafty, so they decided to find shelter a bit inland, on the lee side of a pasture next to a road. Much of the night they kept sliding down into the road. Quite early the next morning the trio pushed their bicycles back up the slope to the ocean until they sighted a roadhouse where they could get breakfast. The manager and waitress were suspicious and must have figured that these dirty and disheveled men were wandering bohemians or, still worse, draft dodgers fleeing from the sheriff.

In their discussions Herman had the audacity to take no sides in the war, doubtful that even an Allied victory was all right; Robert argued against the draft (aha!) but wanted the Allies to win; and Max, who had entertained them all by quoting from his remarkable memory some melancholy lines from Swinburne's "The Garden of Proserpine," remarked in his quiet way that a good poem was a long sight better than any war. These views, if overheard, may well have disgusted the manager, to whom men able to traverse mountain roads with such flimsy gear ought to be willing to die for their country. We can imagine his further surprise if he saw Anderson, waiting for the ham and eggs, get up and play on the piano music that he had composed for an operetta at the University of North Dakota, and when, for an encore, Duffus did Chopin's "Seventh Prelude."

Later that summer Anderson and Duffus, carrying almost no equipment, set out from the Mission of San Juan Batista, just west of San Jose, to walk to the coast. Anderson was again responding to the strange draw of water in his life. As the pair wended their route southward, the smell of the Pacific Ocean grew ever stronger. Along the way they happened upon a man past military age who looked them over questioningly:

"You boys going down to enlist?"

To avoid trouble one of our hikers said they were. The stranger nodded with approval:

"Wish I was young enough," he said with a sigh.

"The hell he does," Max growled.

Duffus writes in his memoir that they reached in their pleasant journey the Pajaro Valley where, in the unpoetically named town of Watsonville, they "stopped in a scrubby, enchanted restaurant, the booming of the sea was so near and the air so salty," and then walked northward along the shoreline of the Bay of Monterey. Once again, no prearrangements for getting regular meals or shelter at night. They traveled free of responsibilities and appointments and deadlines, like the breakers that rolled in about their feet, like the gulls that wheeled and cried overhead. The war itself seemed very far away. In the middle of the night they lay down to sleep in a stack of sweet-smelling alfalfa while overhead the constellations wheeled about the North Star. At dawn the pair of friends, unshaven and dirty, went down to the beach below Santa Cruz and began their northward trek to that city, from which they then took a train home.[89]

The fall saw Anderson at Whittier College, a Quaker school named after the poet, where Max was made head of the English Department. Maybe Anderson believed that a pacifist would find congenial company there. If he thought so, he was to be mightily deceived!

At the time Anderson began work at Whittier College the fate of the Allied armies in Europe hung in doubt. On the home front the war mobilization with its compulsory military service affected every niche of American life, and the outwardly peaceful Quaker school was no exception. Whittier College at that time had a dozen teachers to handle about eighty students, most of the latter being women.[90] It was a quiet school, the last big excitement having been the Friday night when some students locked a cow in the chapel, whereupon Bossy left her scented offerings in many a pew and finally got wedged so firmly between the seats that people had to lift her out with a crane. The best speaker the chapel ever had, said the students.[91]

The institution was rigidly controlled by a board of conservative and mostly Quaker trustees who, in common with American Friends elsewhere, were not all united in their opposition to the draft and, moreover, were very much subject to the pressures of war delirium from the surrounding community.[92] The school was tolerant of heathens as such; for example, before Anderson came, it hired an Episcopalian, Dr. Herbert F. Allen, to teach English; and when Allen left, it hired the onetime-Baptist-turned-agnostic Anderson; but in other ways it gave short shrift to boat rockers. Whittier College not being well financed, the trustees had the unenviable problem of trying to remain liberal enough to please their non-Quaker donors and at the same time be faithful enough to the ideals of their moneyed supporters among the Friends.

Heralding Anderson's arrival were the routine thumbnail sketches of him in the *Whittier College Bulletin* and in the *Quaker Campus* newspaper saying that he was the newly appointed Professor of English.[93] Once classes began, the students seemed pleased with what they were learning under the "Bolshevik" (at that time meaning a radical, not a Communist).[94] Raymond C. Hunnicutt, who took playwriting under Professor Anderson, reported that he still had some of the plays that he wrote for the courses; and Thomas Kimber was reportedly enthusiastic about his own courses with the professor.[95] The only negative note from the classroom level comes from Carl E. S. Strem, a student there in 1918, who once heard Max Anderson read aloud to a group a play which he had apparently written; Strem considered the performance a bore.[96] But there is at least one such listener in every crowd.

In December their second child, Alan Haskett, was born. Now with this new responsibility weighing upon him, the rebellious father got in trouble again with officialdom.

Several explanations have come down to us for Anderson's sudden departure from Whittier after only one year of service. The explanation he gives on page nine of the Columbia memoir is that he was "let out" because he could not bear to sit on the chapel platform during prayers. "They didn't like that, so I left." But in a much earlier interview, with newspaperwoman Helen Deutsch, he supposedly told her that, one day, after reading to a class a military poem called "Prayer Before Battle"—assigned to the class for study—he closed his textbook, gazed out over his spectacles, and made a shocking comment. He quietly said that matters would be most unfortunate if the enemy—the Axis powers—happened to be praying in just such a

Christian way for *their* success on the battlefield and for the destruction of *their* enemy, because heaven would likely get confused and not know which side to champion. (Perhaps he was recalling a similar incident from one of the novels by Voltaire.) Anderson found himself fired within a week.[97]

This incident must have been the last in a series of offenses against official decorum at Whittier. One such earlier incident, and the most curious of all, has recently come to light in Charles W. Cooper's official history of the college, where we find some details about the affair of Arthur F. Camp, a senior student who resisted the draft.[98] Camp, whose application as a conscientious objector had been denied, was drafted anyway, but he refused to report at the induction center. After being jailed as a deserter, Camp decided to accept induction rather than rot away in prison for the remainder of the war, and he ended up serving his country as a loyal member of the U.S. Army. The alleged basis of his claim as a conscientious objector was that the American policy in Europe would not resolve any of the important problems there because President Woodrow Wilson was but an ivory-tower scholar incapable of judging European trends and thought; and still more, that Europe would be embroiled in fighting again within thirty years—maybe within twenty years. Hence, American involvement would be pointless and stupid. During his detention by the authorities, Camp had sent to the editor of the *Quaker Campus* newspaper an open letter in which he defended his refusal to serve; however, the student committee that published the newspaper refused to print the letter. Now Max Anderson, to whom it must have seemed a classic case of civil disobedience reminiscent of Henry David Thoreau, flew to the rescue. He wrote a letter of his own that was printed on November 1:

> To the Editor of the Quaker Campus:
> It has come to my ears that a former honored member of Whittier College has been drafted, has refused to serve, and is now enduring a Los Angeles jail because he has conscientious scruples which make it impossible for him to enter the army. . . .
> I have talked with Arthur Camp very little, but in doing so have formed a high opinion of his ability and his motives. It takes a brave and high-spirited man to take the stand which he has taken. He deserves to be heard on the subject which seems important enough to him so that he is willing to sacrifice reputation, friends, and future to uphold his views. And where can he be heard more naturally, where should he be more welcome, than in the columns of the paper of his college? If there is criticism of the government in this college it should be represented

in the paper. It is a weak and shaky government that cannot stand criticism, and it is a weak and shaky intellect that never has any criticism to offer. If our very colleges are to stifle thought, where is the thinking to be done? . . . There is always something to run from if you are coward enough to run. Whatever may be thought of the opinions of Camp, he has proved himself no coward.

MAXWELL ANDERSON[99]

Of course, Anderson's letter brought *him* under school and community pressure now. The school dean tried to mediate, but the teacher refused to accommodate himself to the atmosphere of intolerance—just as some of his mature plays (*Gods of the Lightning, Winterset, Wingless Victory,* and *Lost in the Stars*) oppose intolerance. In the following spring, the *Quaker Campus* announced his resignation—a euphemistic label for what really happened—and regretted his departure, predicting great things for him as a poet.[100] Had the local panjandrums chanced to read his recent poem "Sic Semper" in the avant-garde journal *New Republic,* where he wrote, "We have had enough of kings/And of fools that stutter and creep," they might have broken a blood vessel in their rush to get rid of him. The poem enthusiastically endorses the Russian Revolution.[101]

It is sadly ironic that, because Arthur Camp was away from Whittier at the time of the furor over the letter, he did not learn until quite recently what the mild-mannered professor of English had done in his behalf—and also suffered in his behalf.

Whittier College left a bad taste with Anderson all the way through the 1930s, insofar as we can judge from hints in his plays. In *Valley Forge,* the starving soldier Alcock in Washington's army is scornful that Quakers would prefer to sell their hogs to the British forces rather than deliver them up to the cause of freedom (Act I, Scene 1); in *Knickerbocker Holiday,* Councilman Tienhoven considers it more festive to hang a Quaker than a Baptist because the former takes a longer time to die (Act I). But by the time of World War II Anderson must have gotten over the chagrin, for he permitted the college to stage one of his dramas.[102]

After Whittier he was fed up with chalk dust, partly because he was too much of an individualist and a rebel to become the submissive teacher demanded by most school administrators, partly because his own high standards had caused him to lose faith in his or anyone else's ability to teach students to write and to love literature (an ironically mistaken conclusion, if we are to believe his students' testimonials),[103] and partly because he wanted more money.[104] His moonlighting experiences on the *Grand Forks Herald* and the *San Francisco Bulletin* had taught him that there was an easier living to be made in journalism. But what he may not have known was that he was too original, too much of an artist to content himself for long with routine newspaper work, a business that neither asks for nor rewards even the greatest of literary talent. What must have been going through the mind of this unbending individualist at this time was the desire to make as good a living as he could while waiting for the right literary opportunity to arrive. Meanwhile, he could discover and perfect what he wanted to do with his pen.

CASTING ABOUT FOR A CAREER

Compost

As I searched my mind for words that might epitomize these daily papers—yellow, crawling, foul with filth—surely it was fortune put in my way the advertisement of an honest man in a needed trade: Manure delivered by car or wagon load; we pay for garbage.[1]

Through his Stanford friend Duffus, who was working on the *San Francisco Evening Bulletin,* Anderson procured a job there[2] and moved his family to Palo Alto and later on to San Francisco. He returned to journalism just after that most famous, most feared, and most loved editor on the West Coast, Fremont Older, had sold out his interest in the *Bulletin* and taken over the *San Francisco Evening Call-Post,* in whose pages he had begun to serialize his amazing crusades against crime, including municipal corruption. The separate installments excited Anderson so much that he urged Older to put them into a book—which was eventually done.[3]

The ex-professor soon displeased the new management of the *Bulletin* by submitting an editorial in which he claimed it was financially impossible (which it was) for Germany to reimburse the Allies for all their costs in the war. The management thought he was excessively outspoken and rejected the piece, and soon they sent him a note stating they appreciated his literary talent but that he ought to start looking around for another post.[4]

Luckily, his newspaper experience in Grand Forks enabled him to get a job right away on the copy desk of the rival *San Francisco Chronicle*.[5] Not long after that, an epidemic of influenza swept out of the U.S. Army's Camp Fremont and struck the city hard. The Anderson house was so located that Anderson had to go through one of the camp's gates each time he went to and from the paper, always burdened with the responsibility of having to remember the latest password, which changed all the time. He is said to have never left his house without fear of getting shot by the sentries or being tossed into the stockade. When he was subsequently laid up for a long time in bed, it was not owing to the army's bullets but from its influenza; and when he returned to his desk on the *Chronicle* he discovered that he had been fired. With a wife and two small children to support, Anderson was in dire straits.[6]

During all his time in the Bay Area we have no evidence that he showed any pronounced interest in the professional theater, either by writing for it or by going to productions. "My contact with the theater was mainly through the play I'd read." As said earlier, in Grand Forks he had seen Alla Nazimova perform in *A Doll's House*. In San Francisco he watched Forbes Robinson act in *The Passing of the Third Floor Back*: also, the golden-voiced Sarah Bernhardt in a scene from *Cyrano de Bergerac*. And he saw little else than these works—"pretty sketchy things," he admits.[7]

His substantial playwriting talent lay bottled up. And turn wheresoever he did in teaching and journalism, his frustration at not finding the right outlet for his creative energy was cutting into the soul like an ingrowing nail, making him increasingly bitter. "He was a complete pessimist," his good friend Hill recalls. "He absolutely thought the world was going to hell and there was nothing that could be done about it." Before very long, Anderson's colleagues would say that his motto was, "It doesn't matter."[8]

One day when the proverbial wolf was howling at the door, he received a letter from Alvin Johnson, a former Stanford man now on the *New Republic*, where Anderson had once placed an article and some poems, including "Sic Semper." It was "Sic Semper" that had impressed Johnson deeply, not because the poem favored the new Russian Communist state but because it was, in Johnson's words, a "poem of exultation over the fall of the age-old oppressive dynasties of Russia, Germany, and Austria." It "breathed the spirit of the Peasant Revolts and the storming of the Bastille."

The upshot: He wanted Anderson on the *New Republic*.[9]

The parson's son considered this one of the luckiest moments of his life. And to think that Johnson made the offer mainly on the strength of one poem!

After borrowing fifteen hundred dollars from two retired spinster schoolteachers who dwelled next door to him, he headed with his family to O. Henry's Baghdad on the Hudson,[10] arriving in New York in December 1918. The kindness shown to him by those spinsters may have been repaid in more than cash—by the gentle affection with which he handled many an inglorious citizen in his plays. They also serve who only lend and wait.

Unfortunately for his employment on the *New Republic,* Anderson had no real interest in the very thing that Alvin Johnson had wanted him for, which was politics, national or international. Max did not know much about these subjects, claiming with Will Rogers that all he knew was what he read in the papers. But Johnson warned him at the outset, "If you persist in being interested in books and literary matters, you can ride yourself right up a tree and get nowhere. . . ."[11]

In its brief history the *New Republic* had been (and still is) a small but influential magazine of liberal pretensions noted for excellent book and drama reviews and for political articles tinged at one period with Marxist sympathies. When Anderson arrived, the staff included Johnson, formerly a professor of economics at Stanford and now in his spare time a novelist and short-story writer; Irish critic and historian Francis Hackett (who would one day spring an unsuccessful lawsuit on Anderson in connection with *Anne of the Thousand Days*); former Harvard philosophy teacher Walter Lippmann; book reviewer Philip Littell, whose play *Septimus* had run in New York in 1909[12]; and the founding editor-in-chief himself, fifty-year-old Herbert David Croly, a saturnine, formidable, tactless, even intimidating man who from the very first did not hit it off with Johnson's new recruit.[13] Every day the jolly Croly would lunch with his editors; and because Croly was known to have a high-handed, anti-egalitarian attitude toward the common man, he probably argued often from this point of view with our rough-edged, uncompromising democrat. Croly was known for lapsing into long silences and watching his opponent sit and sweat. Within six months he picked an argument in which he was in error—and fired Anderson.[14]

One more journalism job down the drain.

Just as school ties with Stanford had helped him get on the *New Republic,* they did so again with the *Globe and Commercial Advertiser.* Bruce Bliven, now managing editor there, invited him and Robert Duffus to join the staff. Then Anderson arranged for Hill to get on too. Under the management of

Scottish-born Henry John Wright, a tall, courteous gentleman with the face of a statesman and a twinkle in his eye and a reverence for the King's English, the *Globe* was a widely read and exceptionally liberal Republican organ of the sort that Anderson might have enjoyed working on. And he did like it there.[15] At first.

Wright had *carte blanche* from the owner to run the paper just as he liked. The owner, a goggle-eyed paperhanger named Searles, had acquired the *Globe* through his marriage to the widow of a California millionaire. According to the anecdote that Wright told Hill, some of the jealous relatives of the new Mrs. Searles sued to break the will of her late husband, and for their purpose hired noted attorney Joseph Choate. When the case came to court, Choate put Searles on the stand and by means of subtle questioning made him confess that he had practically nothing in common with his rich wife except for an interest in racehorses. Choate aimed his index finger at Searles and shouted, "Did you marry this woman, sir, for lust or for lucre?" Whereupon the defendant, eyes protruding more than ever, replied in all honesty: "For both, sir, for both." Wright had never seen Choate so completely flabbergasted. Of course, Searles kept his fortune.

As a rule, Anderson did not write editorials easily, but he sometimes wrote brilliant ones. And sometimes duds. The duds bothered the elderly Wright, and he would call in Hill to share his worries about their burly colleague, asking in effect, "Why can't he omit the duds and just write the other ones?" As a matter of fact, Anderson was getting a reputation in the city for outstanding journalism. But the pea under the mattress bothered poor Wright. He remembered only too well another brilliant writer he used to have on the staff, the impossible maverick and caustic wit Frank M. Colby, contributor of fine reviews and excellent essays, some of the latter ending up in *The New Yorker*. He, too, was given to strangely unpredictable writing. To have another Colby on the *Globe* would be just too much! Wright recalled that once, when the *Globe* was all ready to go to press, he at the last minute discovered that they lacked Colby's scheduled editorial, which was to commemorate the recently deceased Hamilton Wright Mabie. The latter was a deservedly forgotten Victorian essayist best known for his high moral tone and his penchant for platitudes. At last the tardy one came forward and announced, "Oh, here's this little paragraph that you asked me to write." The wickedly terse Colby, who cared little for the Victorian essayist, had phrased his paragraph approximately as follows: "Hamilton Wright Mabie was a lecturer and popular writer who.took ladies to the edge of literature and left them there."[16]

The editors under Wright were all young men who would rise early and study the latest issues of *The New York Times,* the *Herald,* the *Tribune,* and the *World*—the big morning papers—to get ideas for editorials. Then they went into a two-hour conference with Wright at a quarter to nine, at which time he would either propose the big topic of the day or ask some of his men if they had seen anything that morning that looked promising to write on. Each editor had three or four ideas to lay out for discussion, and old Mr. Wright enjoyed this play of minds with younger men. He was gentlemanly enough not to force them into adopting topics on which the group could not agree. Anderson generally had a greater fund of information to draw upon than did Hill, who probably for that reason chose to do his writing in a lighter vein. Anderson, Hill, and Duffus were all staunch liberals, and as such were against monopolies and for organized labor; and the first ten amendments to the U.S. Constitution were in their eyes the Ten Commandments of good government.[17]

But by late 1920 we find Anderson unhappy as a well-paid journalist and at the same time more active than ever with his beloved poetry. He planned with a group of friends to publish *The Measure: A Journal of Poetry,* which was to accomplish in New York what Harriet Monroe's well-known *Poetry: A Magazine of Verse* had long been accomplishing in Chicago to introduce new poetic talents to the world. He and his editorial group for the magazine disagreed with some of Monroe's literary judgments and planned to exclude works by Amy Lowell and Louis Untermeyer while including those by, for example, Conrad Aiken.[18] It seems that Anderson first suggested the idea for the new journal to Hill and to a young woman named Louise Townsend Nicholl, then on the staff of the *New York Evening Post,* or she suggested it to them. In addition to these the nine[19] original poet-founders were Padraic Colum, Agnes Kendrick Gray, Carolyn Hall, David Morton, George O'Neil, and Genevieve Taggard. Contrary to what Hill recalls, the Irish playwright and poet Colum played a substantial role in *The Measure,* during the first two years alone contributing almost as many poems, reviews, and editorials as did Hill, although not as many as did Anderson. From this group of nine regular editors they elected an acting editor and an assistant to handle the monthly publications for each successive quarter. Anderson was elected acting editor for the first quarter, Colum for the second, Nicholl for the third, and Hill for the fourth. Eventually they brought into the organization such new member-poets as Kenneth Slade Alling, Hervey Allen (best known today as the author of the novel *Anthony Adverse*), Pitts Sanborn, Joseph Auslander, Winifred Welles, and Robert Hillyer, with his golden hair and blue eyes, sensitive features and exquisite manners—what Hill considered the ideal-*looking* poet.

For the first time, apparently, Anderson was in an intellectually stimulating group of creative artists, some of whom, though minor, had either made a reputation already, as in the case of Colum, or were soon going to. Oftentimes Margaret Anderson joined the other wives in coming to the meetings.

Board members had equal power in running the journal and agreed not to publish anything they could not all approve. The first number appeared in March 1921 as a little pamphlet of twenty-six pages selling for a quarter and containing short works by some on the board as well as by Conrad Aiken, Wallace Stevens, Alfred Kreymborg, and Robert Frost. In the editorial, with the self-deprecating title "Thunder in the Index," Anderson said nothing revolutionary. There was not even the note of jubilation or expectant hope that one associates with the opening of great enterprises. Rather he had the tone of a man who was about to attend the funeral of his best friend and who goes about it bravely:

> This is not, at any rate, an age favorable to great poetry. . . . There are not, let us confess, any great poets writing at this time in English. . . . The inference is that he [Conrad Aiken, perhaps his favorite of all living poets] can't find a theme in our Sahara of unbelief and commercial sharp-practice. Contemporary prophecy, what there is of it, is spoken in asides, in hints and falterings. In no previous age have fundamentals been questioned as they are questioned now. The very value of art, of life, grows dubious.
>
> THE MEASURE, then, is a hope against hope, a venture in the face of despair, a fiddling while Rome burns. . . . We are no more certain of the value of fiddling than you are, but we know no other activity so satisfactory. It may be discovered that poetry and art are out of place in the new tradesman's civilization about to be erected on the ashes. . . . But there are enough poetry lovers left alive to keep us going a while with sympathy and manuscripts.

He goes on to say in a bleak assessment of what mankind has produced thus far that "we have maintained all literature at great expense for a number of centuries in order to produce five or six invaluable books, ten or twelve invaluable poems," and that *The Measure* will be lucky if it can publish even one masterpiece during its whole career. The spirit of the age is such that he doubts that a poetic revival is imminent.[20]

We know that this is a characteristic attitude for Anderson during his early and middle years, a *Verzweifelungsmüt,* a part of his tragic temper, colored ineluctably by what must have been his own frustrations. Here he was entering middle age with a family to support and spending his spare time trying to advance the careers of younger poets like Hillyer—already earmarked for success. But Anderson pursued poetry's beautiful shape even in the valley of despair. Among the huge collection of Andersonia lodged in the archives of the University of Texas there is an undated, unpublished sonnet of his that relates in touching manner his struggles and hopes, his joys in creating the living lines, and yet, too, his lament at not having scaled the alpine heights:

I Have Outlived All Poets Who Died Young

I have outlived all poets who died young.
Too many years of comfort, nor have made
One song that I could strike up unafraid
In Paradise, after the lads had sung.
Still I build line on line, still not the less
Search the sharp strings for music of my own,
At the blank midday with my moonstone,
Begin, darkly begin again, confess
The words unworthy, throw the paper down.
Then I have sworn one would be better dead
Having done great things, than at middle age
A middling craftsman with a name unknown—
And when I spoke I lied. The song is bread;
A day for singing is the only wage.

During the first year with the magazine Max Anderson and Frank Hill bore the burden of paying contributors thirty or forty dollars every now and then, which disbursement seemed fair at the time since these two earned the highest salaries from their regular *Globe* work, but because each had a wife and some children to support, the money drain proved too much even for the sake of the muse, and Anderson soon proposed that they kill off *The Measure.* The other members, however, howled in protest and insisted on keeping the journal alive, whereupon in October of the second year the editor printed an announcement that Anderson and Hill had left the board with regret "because of too great stress of other work . . .," which in Anderson's case was probably an accurate excuse, because it just so happened that he was writing at this time the play *Benvenuto.*

After rounding up some patrons the remaining members continued *The Measure* for several more years,[21] a pioneer among many "little magazines" of poetry that were to flourish in the twentieth century, providing an outlet for the works of numerous talented artists besides those named earlier, the list including Louise Bogan, Hart Crane, Rolfe Humphries, Walter de la Mare, John Dos Passos (better known as a novelist), Carl Sandburg, Rabindranath Tagore (Nobel Prize winner), and Elinor Wylie. It is one of the supreme ironies of Anderson's life that he, who yearned beyond all else to make a career of poetry but whose reach exceeded his grasp in this medium, originated one of the most outstanding poetry magazines ever to appear in America.

His fascination with poetry was intense and lasting.

One day an engineer named Lieberman, who worked at the Curtiss aircraft company, stopped by the *Globe* and in the course of a conversation with Hill, a free-lancer on the side, said that he ought to write some aviation articles for which he (Lieberman) would supply technical information. Anderson was nearby, at that time grown into a tall, impressive-looking man with dark hair and an unusually large head; with "the look of a person who is going to amount to something," Hill recalled later; so impressive that when the pair of them met new people, the latter would ignore Hill and fix their attention on his friend. After listening to Lieberman's suggestion about the new assignment, Hill excused himself by saying that he was fully busy those days writing poetry, whereupon the philistine dropped a "quasi-derogatory remark." It was at this point that Anderson wheeled on him in one of those rare moments of anger:

"Now, Lieberman, you know damned well that poetry is more important than engineering."

Hill tells us that Lieberman was so "overawed" that he "just shut up."[22]

Anderson is usually described as a shy, withdrawn figure who avoided not only crowds and celebrity-hunters but also most invitations to make speeches. He usually preferred his company in the form of tiny groups in a domestic setting: He, his wife, and one or two other couples of old acquaintance would be ample. A characteristic pose is that of him leaning forward with his hands in his lap while he listens intently to the speaker. He almost never "held forth" at the dinner table or elsewhere—unlike his dominating father. It is curious that about the time he was on the New York newspapers, perhaps starting as early as 1922, he belonged to a discussion group called "The Dinner Club" that had been formed by two *Globe* lawyers named Carl Stern and Walter Pollack. Duffus and Hill belonged, as well as noted historian and English professor and literary editor Carl Van Doren; William L. Chenery, the soon-to-become editor of *Collier's;* and the highly influential economist and semanticist Stuart Chase. The club met about five times annually in various spots in the city, the first time in a restaurant; members had cocktails followed by a good dinner. One or more members were selected to plan each meeting, choose a subject, and have one of their number lead off the discussion. Unfortunately, Hill, who is our sole source of information about this club at the time, does not give us any details of what went on or what Anderson's role was at these undoubtedly stimulating dinners.[23]

While Anderson was helping to launch *The Measure* upon its short but brilliant career, he heard that the *Globe* would soon be sold. Many a head might roll under a new ownership. One day at work he got a mysterious, anonymous telephone call from a man who said that he had a matter of some interest to discuss and asked whether Anderson might have lunch with him. Anderson did. The mysterious caller turned out to be a lawyer working for the *New York World,* and he was acting as an emissary from the executive editor, Herbert Bayard Swope. The lawyer revealed that spies on the *World* had been reading all the *Globe* editorials lately and learned that one Maxwell Anderson had been responsible for writing most of the ones they particularly liked. And since the *World* was looking for new blood for its editorial staff, and since they offered a substantial rise in salary over what he was now getting, why not go over to talk with Frank Cobb, head of the editorial staff?

This Anderson did right away. Soon he was the prize catch on the staff of the city's leading Democratic paper, ensconced among mostly older men who had already made their reputations; men like Cobb, one of the most prominent and respected newspapermen of his era and adviser to President Woodrow Wilson; like Walter Lippmann (soon to come over from the *New Republic*); like Don Carlos Seitz, poet and biographer; like Swope, winner of the first Pulitzer Prize, earned as a war correspondent during World War I; and like Deems Taylor, music critic for the paper and also the composer of an orchestral suite and several operas. And then there was the crippled book reviewer Laurence Stallings, whose meeting with Anderson was to change the course of their lives. It would have been hard to find a more distinguished group of men on any other newspaper in America.

Cobb, with a commanding voice that spat out words like a machine gun does bullets, called in our newcomer one day and told him that he hoped he would take over the editorship! Instead of being joyful, Anderson replied frankly that he had no aspirations as a newsman, that he was merely interested in making a living; and worse still for the ears of a veteran like Cobb, he cared not a tinker's damn about politics, the very meat and potatoes of any ambitious writer on a metropolitan paper. Nor did Anderson change his mind. At last, as he explains in his memoir, he was restricted to writing "all the decorative editorials, about the flowers, the human interest things."[24]

As practically everyone knows who has studied Anderson's life, he is indissolubly linked with the little community of New City, nestled forty miles north of the metropolis. The sight of the region evokes a long-vanished America of autumnal landscapes and river vistas, sailboats and paddlewheelers, recorded nostalgically for us by Cropsey, Coleman, Bierstadt, Durand, and others of the Hudson River School. New City lies alongside those magnificent escarpments called palisades, the jewels of the Hudson River Valley, in Rockland County, New York. The county is aptly named, because in this picturesque land of rushing streams, oaks and elms, beeches and tulip trees, and flower gardens enough to please Flora herself, there are everywhere rocks and more rocks of all sizes and shapes strewn across the landscape as if by a mighty hand, but except in the highest elevations softened by a civilizing green carpet of lawns and hedges, vineyards and orchards; by many attractive old houses; and by a maze of shaded and sometimes stone-walled country lanes. Here in this once rural hinterland, starting in 1922, Anderson was to live for most of his creative years, longer than the combined total that Mark Twain dwelled in Hannibal, than Melville sailed the Atlantic and Pacific, than O'Neill vagabonded on the high seas and in the waterfront slums of coastal cities. The influence of the region on his life and art cannot be lightly dismissed.

The region around New City is steeped in history, legend, and the supernatural. Known to every schoolboy is the Dutch occupation of New Netherland, which included a vast territory on both sides of the Hudson in what are now the states of New York and New Jersey. On the west bank of the river, where New City lies, is the prominent landmark known as High Tor, a basaltic mountain towering 832 feet above the port of Haverstraw, in whose suburbs Major John André had his unfortunate rendezvous with Benedict Arnold at Treason House. The Tor is less than three miles as the raven flies from Anderson's old farmhouse at 170 South Mountain Road where, from his attic study, he could see the peak. This projection is on the river end of the crescent known as South Mountain, which arches like a boomerang toward Mount Ivy and shelters under its curve the village of New City as well as the twisting and precipitous lane called South Mountain Road. From the crest of High Tor, Indians in 1609 spied Henry Hudson's *Half Moon* as it glided on its maiden voyage up that stream in search of the Northwest Passage. In 1777, during the American Revolution, a beacon on the mountain warned Washington's soldiers that British gunboats were tacking up the river. Night travelers on Storm King Highway sometimes report seeing the ghost of General "Mad" Anthony Wayne riding his favorite horse.

In the old days when blizzards and winter ice storms whipped down on the countryside from the Hudson Highlands, the families huddled about their hearths and told queer tales of ghosts and other strange sights. One such account dealt with the dwarfs who were said to live in the gloomy forests of Donderberg Mountain. These creatures were fat as butterballs but peppery of disposition; and the most irritable of them all was their chieftain, called the Heer. One of his peculiarities was that he demanded a salute from mortals who rounded that curve of the river over which his mountain stood guard. Whenever a sloop captain dared to sail by the Donderberg without lowering his mainsail as a token of deference, the Heer screamed to him through his trumpet and raised such a violent squall as to capsize the boat. One day a captain, unafraid of the Heer or simply a scoffer at superstition, had the audacity to refuse the salute, whereupon such a terrific squall struck the boat that all aboard feared they were lost. Fortunately, a pastor on board had the presence of mind to sing as loudly as he could the song of St. Nicholas—who was a patron of sailors—which song chanced to please the Heer and he calmed the elements. But the Heer is said to have paid a final warning by snatching the nightcap off the parson's wife and whisking it off to hang from a church steeple in Esopus.

Another legend is that when storm clouds and lightning come to vex the otherwise tranquil waters of the Tappan Zee, that lakelike bulge of the river between Tarrytown and Nyack, one can see the frightening *Storm Ship* with its wild crew clinging to the ratlines and howling with the wind. Residents in those parts considered this to be the specter of the *Half Moon* foreboding evil or ill fortune.

One of the most curious county tales is supposed to be the Legend of Hugo, named after a Rosicrucian who in the eighteenth century came over with a band of ironworkers from the Harz Mountains of Germany. As an alchemist and dabbler in the occult, he had heard the American Indian legend that for the protection of mankind the evil spirits of lust and greed had been imprisoned in the bowels of the Tor. He had also heard the legend that the youngest of the Magi, fresh from seeing the infant Christ, wanted to test his religiosity by going to High Tor and exorcising those same evil spirits. Why he didn't just leave well enough alone and keep them imprisoned there is a mystery no one has explained. This misguided Magus, therefore, journeyed across the world until he at last reached the mystic mountain, where he built an altar on the summit and tried to drive out the evil spirits. But the Magus failed and died of a broken heart. Hugo, though recalling all of this, was not to be deterred: Where Christianity had failed, perhaps plain old-fashioned mysticism might succeed. He built a forge on the peak and set about trying to convert the spirits. The latter answered him, bribing him with limitless wealth and power if only he would drop all that tent revival nonsense about conversion and set them free; in fact, it was simple, for all he had to do was read aloud some strange characters inscribed on the back of a huge salamander that lived under the forge. He declined. The salamander, angry at not getting his back read, rose out of the fire one night and scared Hugo's wife to death, gave her little boy a fatal burn, and drove the mystic himself raving mad into the woods.

Only his daughter, Mary, remained. One day a beautiful young man visited her hut asking for shelter. Mary soon found occasion to relate her family's misfortunes to this mysterious stranger, who in turn prayed with her and promised to help. He even went a bit further and seduced her. Then one night, after they realized they were in love with each other, he did what beautiful young strangers commonly do in such fairy tales—he disclosed his secret identity. No earthly being in disguise was he, but the Angel of Fire sent down from heaven to assist mankind, a kind of New World Prometheus; but something had gone wrong on earth, the spirits of lust and greed had corrupted him, changed him into a heat-resistant salamander, and inscribed on his back the secret letters which, if spoken aloud, would release the demons from the mountain.

When Hugo had refused to read them aloud, the demons took revenge by proxy in ordering the salamander/Angel of Fire to kill the mother and the boy, drive Hugo crazy, and assume the form of a man so that he could debauch the girl. Just as the spirit-seducer was confessing this to the girl, crazy Hugo happened to be wandering near and overheard the words and recovered his senses, whereupon he let out a shriek sufficient to waken the evil spirits from any orgiastic dreams they might have been having, seized the young guest, and threw him into the flames. But fairy tales usually have happy endings for beautiful young men who give their hearts to forest maidens: because his love for Mary had been genuine, he was changed back into an angel and sent drifting skyward until lost from sight.[25]

It seems that Anderson first saw the picturesque countryside around New City during a walking visit that he made in the spring of 1921 just after he began work on the *World*.[26] New City at that time was just a village with no more than six stores, an inn, a courthouse, a garage, and a couple of churches. He had heard indirectly from Mrs. Mary Mowbray Clark, proprietess of the fashionable Sunwise Turn bookstore in New York City—a gathering place for young artist-writers—that some property to his liking might be had along South Mountain Road,[27] which lay three miles north of the village. The road constituted a little artist colony, very thinly populated at the time, that had a strong appeal to those like Anderson who hated the city and valued the fresh air and independence offered by rustic living. Some people found the rents in Greenwich Village too high: One lady painter moved to the road because she didn't want to go on paying a ten-dollar rent every month. Nobody on South Mountain Road had a lawn. It was mostly brush country, much of it having been farmed; clumps of trees bordered the west branch of the Hackensack River that curled alongside the road and grew thicker on Mrs. Mary Clark's property, where they formed a little forest of splendid oaks, beeches, and elms. Mrs. Clark would leave her old Dutch house each morning and walk over the mountain to the town of Mount Ivy and then commute to her bookstore, returning the same way each evening.[28]

During Anderson's walk along the road that day, which must have been delightful with the dogwoods in bloom all over South Mountain, he asked directions from a local artist whom he spied digging in her garden, one Amy Murray, a poet-singer-harpist in her fifties who hailed from Scotland. Once when she was young and beautiful, she had strummed her clairschach in most of the big cities of America, but now she spent her days writing verse, tending her spectacular flower garden, and keeping house for young Rollo Peters, a Shakespearean actor. A neighbor recalls that Amy "lived on corn-flakes, and that was about it," she was so poor.[29] Anderson probably invited her to send samples of her poetry to *The Measure;* and the fact that six of her poems soon appeared in that journal, in which he had a controlling interest, suggests that this greathearted man might have wanted his poor neighbor to have something extra with her cornflakes. He was always playing Maecenas to some deserving but hard-luck artist once his income began to allow it, particularly among the residents of South Mountain Road. In after years, he even wrote a preface to her book of poems called *November Hereabout,*[30] and in so doing probably helped her get it accepted for publication.

Later that day he found and agreed to buy the special place he was looking for, which consisted of an old frame farmhouse with an ancient stone wall in front and a waterfall out back, all set on three acres of mostly cleared land. The asking price was three thousand dollars. Soon after that he went over to Nyack and requested Mr. Walmsley, the cashier at the First National Bank there, to lend him the down payment he needed. Anderson, never one to bother himself with the details of finance—business matters usually bored him—took an amusingly naïve approach to getting the loan from Mr. Walmsley. The latter asked, how much was the down payment? Five hundred. And how much did he want to borrow? Five hundred. But what, then, was he putting into the house himself? Why, the wife and children, of course! Anderson got his money and moved into 170 South Mountain Road.[31]

At the time of this writing it is a large, thoroughly renovated place with many modern conveniences. There is a raised patio in back, a swimming pond made by damming the stream, a stone bathhouse beside the pond, and a tennis court, together with shrubs and flowering trees. But on that long-ago April day Anderson saw just a simple, homely, boxlike structure with a honeysuckled front porch that was just a stone's throw away from and in clear view of the dirt road. There was a much better house for sale across the road, but he'd decided not to take it. No waterfall. His house was built so that heat from burning logs in the fireplace would rise to the second floor and warm it too if one opened the door to the stairwell. But no indoor toilet, no electricity, no telephone, no garage to house his secondhand Packard, no running water, not even a well. Even so, there was water aplenty: it was swirling at the bottom of the precipitous gorge and waiting to be carried up in buckets by hand.

Stone walls divided the old farm into seven parts; hence, Anderson dubbed his place Seven Fields. The site had both isolation and rustic beauty. Hardly anyone ever drove down that plain dirt thoroughfare except, at long intervals, some local farmer on his way to or from the market. On the way inland from the Hudson the visitor encountered a large ledge of rock that was difficult to drive over to reach the Anderson place just beyond on the left, and the ledge intimidated many, causing them to turn back; this impasse was one of the reasons he liked the location.[32]

But marvel of marvels, the waterfall! And in his own backyard! From the window of the attic, which he planned to use as a study, he looked down on a spectacular cataract that coursed through a redstone ravine containing caves with artifacts once used by Indians.[33] He could take a bracing morning bath by standing under the cataract of crystal water, the latter uncontaminated as yet by suburban pollution. In addition, the steady, murmuring music of the fall, sounding like spring rain showering the leafy canopy of the forest—a phenomenon pleasantly audible to the visitor there today—penetrated Anderson's window in the attic and furnished a soothing, dreamy background for him while he worked.

Except for winters spent in the comfort of the city until such time as he could renovate the old house, he would live here on this farm, "camping out" as he called it, the windows not even getting curtains for several years.[34] He rose at six in the morning, built the fires from wood grown on the property, hauled up from the ravine the buckets of water Margaret needed during the day, fed the cows and pigs and chickens, and did a little gardening in his spare time. He bicycled to the railroad station at Haverstraw, to take the train to Weehawken, New Jersey, then the ferry across the river to Manhattan, then the subway downtown to the *World* offices.[35] In his spartan taste for country living he reminds us of his hero Van Dorn in *High Tor.*

Later, when *What Price Glory* brought in plenty of money, he entered into a deal with two friends to buy a large tract of adjoining land and divide it among them. This gave Anderson a total of thirty acres.[36] At that time the old house was remodeled by a painter-sculptor from the neighborhood, Carroll French, who with his actress wife, Dett, used to tour villages in the East with a horse-drawn wagon doing puppet shows. They became close friends of the Andersons. French seemed unable to lay a chestnut board or beam anywhere in the farmhouse without introducing some delicate carving of local flora or fauna, or sometimes storybook characters, for instance on the handsome Dutch door at the front entrance and on cupboards both upstairs and downstairs. Wherever his chisel touched, some bit of beauty sprang to light. Anderson thoroughly enjoyed the house after French got through with the remodeling. It is sad to reflect that when the sculptor grew too old and weak to carve anymore, and lonely because his wife was in a home for the aged and did not even recognize him when he visited her, he grew despondent and finally drowned himself in the swimming pond back of this house that he had filled with enchantment.[37]

Another artist in the neighborhood was Kansas-born Henry Varnum Poor, who had studied at Stanford and also in France; he had started out as a painter and finally became one of the finest ceramicists of his day. In the woods he had a stone house that he had built with his own hands. He and Anderson were the same age and were both strong, portly, bearlike but gentle men. These two gave their neighbor Marion Hargrove the feeling of being in an elevator with a pregnant woman who is surely going to bump into something.[38] Henry's picture of High Tor, *Grey Dawn,* hangs in the Metropolitan Museum of Art. He painted a dozen panels for the U.S. Department of Justice Building, and a large mural called *Conservation of Wild Life* for the U.S. Department of Interior Building. Like the dramatist, this blond man was most attractive to women. Flame-haired Millia Davenport, and Ruth Reeves, and just about all the other good-looking, unmarried women on the road were in love with handsome Henry and contrived ways to snare him, but the woman who got him at last was no beauty at all; rather, she was the dark and garrulous, striking and fiery little Bessie Breuer, a magazine writer who would soon switch to fiction.[39] Among her novels was *Memory of Love,* a startlingly beautiful account of passion and heartbreaking renunciation in the life of a philandering cad—a far better work, by the way, than her glacially static *Take Care of My Roses,*[40] which in treating of Anderson's marriage inadvertently reveals her sour-grapes attitude toward him for achieving wealth and fame. To Bessie, true art and commercial success very seldom went together.

She was notably fond of dancing whenever she attended parties on the road; the bouncy little woman was so indefatigable that she wore out her partners and generally ended up dancing by herself. Rumor has it that she finally trapped Henry Poor by playing the Florence Nightingale act on him when he was ill with the flu. She went over to his house and nursed him and never bothered to leave after that.[41]

Henry seems to have been more versatile than Bessie, even venturing into the fields of architecture and writing. During World War II, he went on a government-sponsored artist's project to Alaska; and when he returned home bursting with ideas for a book about his adventures, he announced that it would bear the title *An Artist Sees Alaska*. In announcing his plan he seemed to be encroaching on Bessie's territory. Bessie believed that any artist of real merit always suffered the torments of hell in giving birth to the work of art. Imagine, then, the disgust with which she watched Henry clear the kitchen table, slap down a pad of paper, and blithely start writing with a confounded fountain pen! And he didn't suffer at all! His book proved to be readable anyway.[42]

In addition to the Poors there dwelled at least four other couples in that neighborhood during the 1920s who were enjoying a more or less extended honeymoon together before getting married—which some of them finally did. This group of irregulars included a professor's rebel daughter, Millia Davenport, designer of theatrical costumes; Margery Content, who did nothing creative herself but lived with painter Michael Carr; designer of fabrics Ruth Reeves, whose live-in was a man younger than herself; and also Martha Ryther. These were the people who set the tone for the social life there and led some outraged residents of nearby Haverstraw to label South Mountain Road as a "free-love colony."

It was common during warm weather along the road to see nude adults of both sexes sunbathing or splashing around in the creek bottom. The privacy of the stream that flowed along the valley floor must have led Anderson and his young wife to enjoy many such innocent outings together. Alan Anderson inherited from his parents three strikingly clear, undated photographs taken of his mother by some admiring amateur photographer; they reveal Margaret gloriously *au naturel* in a woodland setting. One of the pictures shows her shapely backside, she standing erect with long hair cascading like a dark midnight waterfall about her thighs; the other two show her from the side and front, a fragile and yet lovely young woman running gracefully like a classic nymph through the woods. The camera angle suggests a tall photographer like her husband. There is a tribute to her in his poem "She Said, Though You Should Weave," which he published in the *New Republic* in July 1922, where we read of her small body standing straight and slim under the mossed cataract.

The road community was in no sense profligate and debauched. But such was the general permissiveness in that neighborhood that Anderson's younger brother Kenneth, at one time a resident there, was glad when he transferred himself and his wife into the relatively conventional precincts of Washington, D.C., where he found a job with the Brookings Institute and an environment that he felt was better suited to bringing up children.[43]

In those idyllic times before the neighborhood grew moneyed and "respectable" and began to attract more and more childless couples, there were numerous children around for the Anderson boys to play with. Among these must be counted the Hills. Also, those belonging to architect Herman Rosse, mentioned earlier—the man who did the decorations in the Peace Palace at the Hague. Mrs. Zeus Rosse, who at six feet stood two inches taller than her husband, must have had the example of the Greek god in mind when she insisted against her husband's protest that she, too, have twelve children. "But Zeus," he lamented, ". . . I am an artist, I cannot afford to keep twelve children." But they had ten by the time he went back to Holland.[44]

Anderson was a devoted father to his boys Quentin, Alan, and Terence, in that order of birth. When they were tiny he often read stories to them at bedtime, just as most fathers would, and when they grew older played outdoor games with them on the lawn, and, of course, he took them to the theater.[45] But it is no exaggeration to say that they enjoyed an enormous freedom, indulged at every turn once the father came into big money, and grew up as unmanaged and carefree as the wild honeysuckle on the fences along South Mountain Road.

But for specific failings, let us consult Alan:

> I think that there's a kind of single-mindedness about [becoming or being a writer] that can endanger your other relationships—it needn't necessarily, depending on the kind of person you are—but it really means that so much of your energy and attention is focused on your effort that you are bound to lose track of other things around you. And I think he over-simplified his role as a father. He would look around and hope that we were happy and do something to try to make us feel happy. And I think he loved us! But he didn't spend a lot of time being a parent, thinking about the role of a father. . . .
>
> I think that one of the ways that Dad failed as a father, as a parent,

was that he ... worked very hard at being a writer, he had to—it was hard for him to get a chance [in his youth] to read as much as he wanted to—his father made him turn the light out—he had to work hard for a living. ... And he really did it just by sheer guts. ... But what he didn't do is to tell *us* that you had to go through all that to be a writer [Alan himself had tried briefly to be one after he came out of the army at the end of World War II, but he met with no success] ... that you had to work damned hard if you wanted to be a writer, or do anything that involved that kind of concentrated dedication.

Alan adds that his father would sometimes ask, "Do you need money?" in the hope that this would make it clear that he cared.[46] If his later practice is indicative of how he was as a young father, we may trust the report of his third wife, Gilda, that Anderson had constructive sessions with various of his children, at which times he was not trying to foist money on them as if to buy their love.[47] Like Alan, Maxwell's youngest brother, Lawrence, stresses the warmth of the man's personality; he goes even further by saying how uncanny the man was at discovering the needs, emotional and otherwise, of family members and then without being asked doing something always appropriate to satisfy those needs.[48]

Not only did Anderson not believe in using corporal punishment on children, he almost never raised his voice in anger at his own; the only exception that Terence recalls was the time when he and Alan were banging merrily away with a sledgehammer at a supporting post inside the farmhouse, making the old building shudder with their blows, whereupon the father yelled out to them the single word "HEY!" It was the loudest and most vehement tongue-lashing they ever suffered from him.[49]

Once little Quentin fell down with a paring knife and severed the big artery that led to one of his legs. The first doctors to examine him were certain that he would have to have the limb amputated. The thought of this drastic operation left Anderson horrified. He pleaded so desperately with them to save his son's leg that they agreed to take a chance on a new experimental operation favored by a certain young doctor who had recently come back from the war. Under the latter's direction, the team channeled the arterial blood into smaller arteries where they could nourish the tissues, the operation was a success, and Quentin kept his leg, thanks largely to his father's refusal to give up.[50]

Hill, who soon bought a farm across the street from Anderson, found the artistic and social milieu in New City extremely interesting and congenial, although Mrs. Hill (daughter of a college professor) did not feel at all comfortable around her free-thinking neighbors and ached to move away (which they eventually did). All these artists, Hill assures us, were of the "slashing, free type" except he and Anderson, of course, who were by no means bohemians—and were refreshing to observe because they marked a departure from the stuffy conventions of Victorianism in bourgeois American society. "Nobody born after 1920," Hill assures us, "can possibly realize the stifling effect of the conventions as they existed, say, up to 1910."[51]

A succession of American writers that included Theodore Dreiser, Sherwood Anderson, Sinclair Lewis, and Eugene O'Neill had been (and still were) forces of liberation by introducing into their art hitherto forbidden subject matter, exposing the humdrum and repressive nature of village and small-town life, championing the role of the artist in an increasingly commercialized society, and in general exposing as artificial if not downright dishonest the genteel vision of American life as found in most current magazines, books, and stage productions. The businessman rather than the artist was the hero, and the public saw nothing excessively materialistic, or simplistic either, about the rags-to-riches philosophy inherent in Horatio Alger's books. The American artist was so undervalued at home that when President Coolidge was confronted by a French delegation asking whether the United States wanted to take part in an international art exhibition scheduled for Paris, he replied, "No," because he didn't believe there were any painters in America.[52]

Against this kind of stuffy provinciality compounded with ignorance the artists who lived along South Mountain Road were carrying out their own forms of revolt, although these people were for the most part serious, hardworking, and productive. In New York City and in other metropolitan areas of the country one could see the "Roaring Twenties" going full blast. But this saturnalia was not typical of the road people. They were not debauched, but like the partygoers in F. Scott Fitzgerald's stories, they too rebelled against Prohibition, not by relying on speakeasies and bootleggers for their liquor but by brewing it at home from fruits grown in the region. It all started when Anderson discovered large quantities of wild grapes growing along the creek and had his Negro maid, Lou, make some wine from them. Word of his success spread through the valley so quickly that Hill, for instance, was soon turning out six different varieties of wine made from domesticated grapes, elderberries, cherries, etc.[53] No doubt these two fellow poets shared many a convivial evening together as they discussed over brimming glasses the state of the arts. Anderson, however, was not a heavy drinker; he never drank anything to excess, unless it was coffee.

In addition to those previously named, the neighborhood became at various times the residence of many creative, performing, and directing artists, of which not a few achieved national recognition. Eunice Tietjens, poet and playwright, was briefly a neighbor to Anderson; he consoled her when her play *Arabesque* failed on the Broadway stage.[54] Harold Hickerson, who was to collaborate with Anderson on *Gods of the Lightning,* rented the Hill house across the road. Hugo Robus did sculptures. Painters in the neighborhood included Morris Kantor, the man who finally married Martha Ryther, another painter. Among the several actors living there the most famous was Burgess Meredith, who grew prominent from taking roles in Anderson's plays; he bought Treason House and lived there with his actress-wife Paulette Goddard; later, after these two were divorced, he married Kaja and had Henry Poor build him a house along the road. Broadway directors who made the district their home included Alan H. Anderson and John Houseman. Along the road also dwelled cartoonist Bill Mauldin (famous for his humorously realistic drawings of front-line soldiers during World War II) and Milton Caniff (creator of the "Steve Canyon" and "Terry and the Pirates" comic strips). Writer Marion Hargrove moved there after World War II and became closely attached to the Anderson family. A bit later came musical composer Alan Jay Lerner, then husband of screen actress Nancy Olsen;[55] he bought Burgess' second house and resided there until he separated from Olsen. Poor's daughter, Anne, still lives in her father's house and has made a profession of painting and teaching.

Of all the artists through the years, Anderson's best friend after Hill left was the internationally famous musical composer Kurt Weill. He met Weill at a party at the home of press agent Helen Deutsch. And a most fortunate meeting it was. The two talked about what the German-born composer had done in Europe. Anderson grew very interested and finally asked, "Why don't you come out and visit me in New City?" So Helen Deutsch drove Weill and his actress-singer wife, Lotte Lenya, out to South Mountain Road one day,[56] and it didn't take them long to fall in love with the neighborhood. The opportunity for the author of *Die Dreigroschenoper* (a modernized version of John Gay's *The Beggar's Opera*) to work closely with a by then well-established playwright, who himself was fascinated by good music and had had some songwriting experience, was something that he could hardly turn down. The Weills bought Rollo Peters' ancient residence, Brook House, which stood alongside the creek next to the road. And that's how their long and happy and fruitful association began. The wood path between their houses wore smooth from the many visits they made back and forth.[57]

Several of the Anderson relatives interviewed for this book spoke of Weill's delightful personality. One reason he was so beloved was that he was sensitive to the feelings of coworkers. Anderson tells the following amusing anecdote about his little friend:

> Once when Kurt was in Boston with the try-out of a musical he came downstairs to have breakfast with the producers, the lyric writer, and the man who wrote the book for the show. He found them all sitting about the table over black coffee discussing the problems of the play and the sleepless night they had spent. Each one described the sleeping pills or prescription which he had tried and which had failed and then turned to Kurt and asked wearily how he slept. "Oh, fine," Kurt said, because he had slept well, and always did. Then he realized that they all hated him for that answer, and he added gloomily, "But I had bad dreams."[58]

Anderson's nearest neighbor at the time he moved to New City was young playwright John Howard Lawson, who rented the farmhouse across the way. Lawson was a radical with a flyweight talent who pursued experimental forms of dramaturgy, including Expressionism, and had just written as his first play a strange creation he called *Roger Bloomer*. The Theatre Guild had thought enough of it to accept it for production and advance him the usual five-hundred-dollar royalty, a sum that awed Max Anderson when he first heard about it. Just recently he had had to borrow that amount from the bank as the down payment on his farm. Lawson was seven years younger than himself. And he'd hit pay dirt on the first try. He could not help comparing that man's success with his own failure thus far to make a living off poetry.[59]

It wasn't that Lawson had gotten a play accepted, it was that he had gotten that five hundred dollars so easily. "I wanted to make money," Anderson confessed. It was as simple as that.

One evening, when the new playwright was away, his proud wife invited Anderson and two or three other neighbors over to hear her do a reading of *Roger Bloomer*. Anderson listened carefully to this supposedly marvelous play that could earn so much. And at the close of the reading he thought, "Well, if that's a play, I can certainly write a better one than that!"[60]

Having gotten fired up over the prospect of making a bundle of money with his pen, the next step was for him to find a proper subject. Margaret had been reading a recent, three-volume biography of that gifted rogue Benvenuto Cellini, whose life is chock-full of sensational adventures, and he decided that this might be the very source he needed. However, he was so hot to begin composing that he couldn't bear to wade through the whole biography; so he formed a plot outline from the first half of Volume I and sat down by the waterfall to do what turned out to be his first full-length play, *Benvenuto*. Once completed it consisted of a prologue and nine scenes showing the adventures of Cellini at the court of Francis I in Paris during 1540. The conflict in the story is between the King's mistress, Madame d'Etampes, and Cellini; the latter has gained influence with the King at the expense of d'Etampes' favorite artist and is in a position to harm her because he is privy to her unfaithfulness. The hero at the close loses his girlfriend to suicide and narrowly escapes death himself.[61]

Among the weaknesses of this melodramatic effusion must be counted not only the presence of an unworthy adversary (d'Etampes is just a royal whore) but also an unsatisfying ending. Realizing that he had created a dud, Anderson put *Benvenuto* aside. One of the things he learned from this experience was not to write about artists—his prejudice on this subject was to remain with him throughout his career.[62] Perhaps he also learned, if he didn't know it already, that he had a romantic's love for remote times, for colorful people of history, for the pomp and circumstance of the royal court, for love intrigues in the palaces of nobles, for famous lost causes, and for heroic gestures even at the edge of the grave.

He detested the label romantic,[63] but what else is one to call him after reading the letter he sent to critic Heywood Broun the very next year?

A great play cannot deal with ordinary people speaking commonplaces. It cannot deal with ordinary life. It has to concern itself with definitely unusual individuals in unusual situations, lifted by extraordinary emotions to extraordinary actions. And if it is to have the depth and reach of tragedy, it must pass before a setting that has in it something mysterious and titanic. It must rise above the usages of law, custom and religion into an elemental, spacious and timeless world, which we have all glimpsed but will never inhabit.

—[October (19?), 1923]
Letters, pp. 19-20

We will see this program carried out in his important verse plays of the 1930s.

Even after the failure of *Benvenuto* the vision of those five hundred dollars still gleamed undiminished before his eyes. Broadway was surely his oyster, and he would find a way to pry it open yet.

The record he left of his early attempts to reach the stage is interesting but incomplete.[64] At about this time he must have recalled the advice that Professor Koch was giving to his drama classes—teacher and student had kept in touch—which was to choose a subject from those blue remembered hills of home, those quaint and lively experiences of common people in a known regional setting. He was willing to try a new angle, and he had nothing to lose but his time. It just so happened that his wife told him a story about the early troubles that her parents had had on a North Dakota claim, and out of this he conceived the plot for his tragedy *White Desert*. The setting was North Dakota, the time the year of his birth, and the characters people of pioneer stock such as he had known. And since he had been longing for years to make a living from poetry, he decided to arrange the dialogue to look and read like poetry, a daring and momentous decision.

In opting for poetic drama he was doubtless conditioned by his extensive readings in the Elizabethans and almost certainly by the comforting knowledge that at least a few modern dramas such as Edmund Rostand's *Cyrano de Bergerac* had been eminently successful despite their versification. Besides that, *White Desert* was going to be a tragedy, and he knew with Aristotle that all the great tragedies use poetry because of the necessary heightening of emotion it provides. To him, prose represented the language for information, poetry the language for emotion. He realized that such figures as Synge and O'Casey, whom he admired, had succeeded in forcing poetry to convey emotion by establishing unfamiliar rhythms of speech, and he thought the usual prose of the theater was inarticulate.[65] In this as well as in all his later verse dramas he used an unrhymed iambic pentameter, or blank verse, a pattern that is fairly unobtrusive to read.

Why did he bother to do the play in blank verse when he must have known that a verse play *period* is what usually closes on Saturday night? This he explained many years later in a letter to a Stanford student in which he said that he chose iambic pentameter because experience has shown that it combines the greatest loftiness and intensity with the least artificiality. And if it is not stilted on the page it sounds natural when spoken by an actor. By contrast, free verse resembles inflated and complicated prose when it is uttered on the stage.[66] As for possibly failing on Saturday night, he knew he always had his *World* job to fall back upon, unpleasant as it was.

The book editor on the *World*, Laurence Stallings, took an interest in the play and showed it to the music critic on the paper, Deems Taylor, who in turn happened to be friendly with a Broadway producer named Brock Pemberton. The gallant Pemberton decided to take it. And that's how Anderson got his five hundred dollars at last. The money fever was raging now.[67]

Pemberton, or someone else in the company, grew nervous about the poetry and had the piece typed up like prose so that the actors wouldn't get self-conscious as they read the lines aloud.[68] On October 18, 1923, the work by the new author went on the boards at the Princess Theatre in New York City, with Frank Shannon and Beth Merrill in the lead roles.

The following synopsis is provided because *White Desert* has never been published and is therefore not available to the general reader, and because the drama illustrates Anderson's all-too-human attitude toward wifely infidelity, which will crop up later in another connection. A young farmer, Michael Kane, who suffers from a rigidly repressed sexuality, cannot understand how his beautiful wife, Mary, can be pure and at the same time enjoy sex with him. He recalls uneasily that she had once given herself to him when they were engaged. His twisted attitude soon leads to unwarranted suspicion—and tragedy. In the middle of winter the Kanes entertain their nearest neighbors, Sverre and Annie Peterson, who have come to welcome the newlyweds to their otherwise cheerless North Dakota homestead. Sverre is a romantic, bantering man, pleased with the arrival of the beautiful Mary—who is younger and better looking than his own spouse; in fact, he is so pleased that Michael is eaten by jealousy. Mary, meanwhile, is so happy at having company that, when the few chairs are occupied, she thinks nothing of sitting on the bed with Sverre as they chat, an innocent familiarity that strikes Michael as an erotic no-no. And once the Petersons leave, he accuses her of moral looseness. That night the puritan cannot sleep for worry. When he interrogates her the next day on the subject of sex, she staggers him by freely admitting she has pleasure with him in bed. Disgusted with this, he hurls scarlet names at her. It was her purity, he said, that attracted him to her in the first place. At first Mary thinks that this is all a cruel joke, but when his abuse continues she defiantly threatens to get even with him. Angry, Michael leaves for town on a two-day trip to get supplies.

Now enters a blizzard to shut folk indoors. Sverre chances to get lost on the way home, and Mary, seizing the opportunity to seduce him, entices him to spend the night with her in the house. All goes as she had planned. When Michael returns he feels guilty about his intolerance and suspicion; he says that he should have recognized that she was merely human, as he was. And she, in turn, confesses her copulation of the night before. Staggering surprise! But he recognizes that he had driven her into that sin, and the two of them effect a reconciliation. Just then Sverre reappears, the too-tangible reminder of what she did, and Michael knows that he cannot readily forgive her in spite of himself. And knowing that her act is irrevocable, their marriage shattered, Mary begins to walk off across the snowy fields with her fellow sinner.

A jealous rage boils inside Michael at this juncture; he races indoors, grabs a rifle, and shoots her dead.[69] The important point in understanding the author's own attitude then and later toward the unfaithful wife is not that Michael killed her in a rage but that he could not fully forgive her despite his self-enlightenment on the human condition.

This demand for woman's fidelity is embedded also in Anderson's dramatic theory that a theater audience watching a play will resent woman's "inclination toward the Cressid"—that is, her unfaithfulness to the lover. His theory does not require man's sexual restraint or fidelity, but other virtues instead.[70] He is fairly consistent in his writings when he treats this theme.

White Desert ran for only twelve performances. Anderson didn't think it was a very good play, and the critics were only too willing to agree with him. But they admitted that he was a writer of promise, which opinion gave him the fortitude to continue playwriting[71] although he was to abandon for some years his aim to place a poetic tragedy on the commercial stage.

Feeling definitely committed to the theater now, he started straightaway on another work, which he planned with the actor who had taken the role of Sverre, George Abbott. Abbott needed to travel to Boone, North Carolina, to soak up a Southern accent for another stage role he had been offered, and he invited Anderson to go along so that the two of them could work together a few hours each day on *A Holy Terror,* as the joint venture was finally titled. This was to be a story about the famous Hatfield-McCoy feud. Anderson didn't like what they came up with in the way of a script, but the producer, John Golden, bought out his interest for a thousand dollars, and everybody was happy—for a while. With his partner's name removed, Abbott then collaborated with Winchell Smith to finish *A Holy Terror,* now transformed into melodrama, which work quickly failed after it reached the stage in the fall of 1925.[72] But long before then Anderson had written something far better, this time with a friend of his on the staff of the *World.*

GLORY

I magine, if you will, that it is Friday evening on the fifth of September 1924, and we are visitors to New York City. We are standing just outside the Plymouth Theatre on Forty-fifth Street. Since it is only eight o'clock, we have a little time on our hands before the play begins. We are a half block west of that storied avenue—actually, the longest in the world—of huge billboards and flashing slogans, brilliant colors and gaudy designs, garish glitter and dreams known everywhere as Broadway. On rooftops in the district are spectacular ads for Lucky Strike, White Rock, Squibb's Dental Cream, Corticelli's Silk Thread; on one roofline a Wrigley's Gum sign stretches one whole block between Forty-third and Forty-fourth streets.[1] Now with Prohibition there are speakeasies in the neighborhood. Occasionally walking past us are war veterans, some identified by a pinned-up empty sleeve or trouser leg, mute reminder of an agony at Flanders or the Marne or Château-Thierry. Here at the Plymouth people in evening dress line up before the ticket window to see a new play whose name is blazoned across the marquee as *What Price Glory*—minus the question mark that later generations will give it—written by two new playwrights, Maxwell Anderson and Laurence Stallings. Few theatergoers know much about either of them. Stallings' gall-bitter war novel *Plumes* was published this very year but has not yet caught on with the public. The authors, it is said, are professional journalists on the

World and don't have a single artistic or commercial success to their credit.

Come to think of it, why risk an evening again with Mr. Anderson, whose *White Desert* fared so poorly at the Princess Theatre? There is still time to walk over to the Republic to see the heartwarming sentimental comedy *Abie's Irish Rose,* a commercial success now in its third year. There there is the Arthur Hammerstein musical *Rose-Marie,* which recently opened at the Imperial. George Kelly, uncle of the famous movie actress and Princess of Monaco, Grace Kelly, has a new satire on the boards titled *The Show-Off,* about braggart philistinism and success worship—ironically curious fare on Broadway, where every night some writer for the stage caters to these very tastes. And popular actor Walter Huston is starring in a hit called *The Easy Mark* on Thirty-ninth Street. If we wanted more serious drama, we might consider that strange and troubling Eugene O'Neill, who has his *All God's Chillun Got Wings* running at the Greenwich Village Theatre. But tonight we happen to prefer a little laughter thrown in with the soul-searching, and there are mighty few laughs in any of those torridly sensational O'Neill plays.

Many show patrons tonight will attend the dazzling Ziegfeld *Follies*— Florenz Ziegfeld is noted for impeccable taste in all his productions—or perhaps Earl Carroll's *Vanities* or George White's *Scandals,* these last two patterned after the successful Ziegfeld format. All feature the pulchritudinous girls, the erotic display of flesh, the scenic spectacle, the rollicking vaudeville.

For sheer novelty, many will be going to the new medium known as the movies: In one of these flickering celluloid wonders, Sabatini's *Captain Blood* has sailed into town with a crew of swaggering pirates, but the boisterous cries and hearty oaths are muted in this silent-film version.

As we stand looking at the theater ads in our copy of *The New York Times,* we see many plays advertised. It is a healthy and vigorous period for the thespian arts, even though the vast majority of the American plays are sheer claptrap, uninspired by a single line of lasting merit. But where there is an active theater, there is hope of seeing a good play at least now and then.

We decide to take a chance on *What Price Glory* here at the Plymouth and proceed to buy our tickets. The building itself is rather new but already has a distinguished history. Here, for example, audiences saw the first New York production of Ibsen's *The Wild Duck* in English. Figuring in that Ibsen première had been the famous Russian actress Alla Nazimova, who went on to act memorably in *Hedda Gabler* and *A Doll's House.* (Then she took the latter work on tour to Grand Forks, North Dakota, where in the opera house sat one of tonight's dramatists, Maxwell Anderson, seeing one of the very first plays in his life.[2]) Here in the Plymouth the celebrated John Barrymore had acted in a dramatization of Tolstoy's *Redemption;* and, the next year, he had teamed up with his brother Lionel in *The Jest.*³ Of course, there had been artistic as well as commercial failures at the Plymouth in its brief history— there might be another one tonight—but these are to be expected in a business where well over half of all Broadway plays never earn a profit. But, since it costs little nowadays to stage a play, many producers are willing to gamble in the hope of striking it rich with an occasional smash hit. And so we wonder whether tonight's producer of *What Price Glory,* Arthur Hopkins, will get any return on his investment, which is rumored to be in the neighborhood of ten thousand dollars.⁴

Once inside the Plymouth we climb up to the second balcony, where we find the whole area empty except for two large middle-aged men seated near each other. From reports we recognize them as the authors, but why their wives are not with them on this important occasion is a mystery. Perhaps they wanted to spare the women the shock of seeing what would likely be a failure. (Margaret Anderson surely suffered enough when *White Desert* failed.)

We recognize Laurence Tucker Stallings as the slightly taller man, the one with the unruly reddish-brown hair, blue eyes, Cupid's-bow mouth, and especially the heavy artificial right leg that always gives him discomfort. Not many years ago this Georgian was attending Wake Forest College and getting suspended for indulging in his favorite pastime, gambling—considered a serious offense in those days at a Baptist school. Fortunately at Wake Forest zoology interested him, too, this subject taught by the president himself, Dr. William Louis Poteat, whose nubile daughter Helen proved to be the youth's chief zoological interest. After his graduation he married Helen and began work on the *Atlanta Journal.* Then in 1917 he happened to drop into the Marine Corps recruiting office in Atlanta, where he helped the leading sergeant arrange enticing newspaper articles; before the day was over, the articles proved so heady an enticement to Stallings that he himself enlisted. Later he won a lieutenant's commission and went off to Europe in the 4th Brigade of the 2nd Division, ready to help fight the war that President Wilson promised would end all wars.

Stallings had been reared in the Southern romantic tradition of viewing war as chock-full of chivalric heroism and glory, a notion soon blasted out of him in the savage fight for Belleau Wood, where German machine-gun bullets riddled his right knee just a few days after he had been promoted to captain. He spent the next eight months laid up in hospitals in France, then two years in hospitals in the United States, all the time in agonizing pain, until surgeons finally cut off his injured leg just above the knee.

Once out of the hospital for good, he attended graduate school at George-town University, and a bit later he worked on the *Washington Times*. Then on to New York. And all the while his shattered leg helped make him more and more bitter about Wilson's war, and all wars, for that matter. His autobi-ographical novel *Plumes* mirrors that state of mind: At the story's end the boy Dickie asks his war-crippled father, "What is a general?" and gets the sardonic reply, "A man ... who makes little boys sleep in graves."[5]

Now he's a literary editor—a book reviewer—on the *World*. He impresses those around him as being an exceptionally entertaining albeit nonstop talker with a superb memory—able, like his friend Anderson, to quote Shake-speare by the yard—and gifted with an excellent and often bawdy sense of humor.[6] Many years later Anderson will say of him, "He was a very good idea man, with an extraordinary vocabulary, and a wide range of interests, a lot of knowledge," but unfortunately not able to write a play[7]—by himself, that is.

While we wait for the curtain to rise, let us imagine further that we accost the man wearing the glasses and try to find out how *What Price Glory* all began. Anderson, though a physically powerful and thick-set fellow measur-ing five feet, eleven inches tall and weighing about two hundred pounds, is obviously a shy bird. With his massive head, wavy brown hair, thoughtful dark brown eyes looking mildly at us through spectacles, and bow tie with suit, he looks for all the world like a handsome professor from one of our colleges. He speaks slowly in a low, sonorous voice, but only after he has thought about what he wants to say and is ready to say it, in marked contrast with Stallings' effusive personality. We soon learn that Anderson doesn't like to gossip or indulge in idle chatter, that he even becomes anything from displeased to quite angry when he feels that the people talking to him are superficial, pompous, or bogus.[8]

From him we learn that there is a lunchroom just below the floor where the *World* has its editorial offices and that the two friends had been in the habit of lunching there together. Stallings used to tell him of the colorful adventures he had had as a marine officer in the 2nd Division. He was primed up on the subject not merely because of his antiwar feelings, a sentiment fully shared by Anderson, but also because he was working with Herman Mankiewicz on a musical comedy about Haiti under the leatherneck occupa-tion. In one of his lunchtime anecdotes he raved about a marine who had come in from battle screaming about the horrible things that were happen-ing to everybody, and calling out, "What price glory, now?"[9] Somewhere in these anecdotes figured a Philip Townsend Case, captain of the 5th Marine Regiment, in which Stallings had served as lieutenant. "Stallings used to say," a friend of his remarked, "that Case was the most extraordinary commanding officer he had ever seen—if Case had been in charge of the Army he would have fought right on to Berlin."

The facts about Case subsequently were included in the portrayal of the play's Captain Flagg, but the latter's swaggering features derived from another captain Stallings knew. (In later years, when Case had heard more than he wanted to about this sensational play, he took a powerful dislike to being identified, even in fun, with the roaring and whoring Captain Flagg.)[10] All these anecdotes fascinated Anderson, all the more since he had never seen combat. He knew there was the stuff for a good play in all this, and he urged his colleague to tell more and more.

One night he and Stallings used *World* tickets to take them to the opening of what turned out to be a wretched play. As they were leaving the theater, the ex-marine observed to his friend:

"That was awful. I could write a better one myself."

"Why don't you?" said Max. "Or why not collaborate with me?"[11] But Stallings thought little of the idea, no doubt because writing it would steal time from his musical comedy. He told his friend, however, "Go ahead and see what you can do with it."[12]

Because Anderson's duties as editorial writer left him with plenty of free time, he started to work on the play right away, choosing as his studio a table in the public library on Forty-second Street because the small apartment he was then living in with his wife and three children was simply not conducive to composing drama. And so, using abundant notes taken down from his talks with the ex-marine, he went down to the library for six straight nights after dinner and wrote "in a high fever of enthusiasm" a longhand draft. This writing in longhand—never typing—was to be his custom with all his dramas. (After the play had been produced, Anderson saw a cartoon in *The New Yorker* showing a couple walking notebook in hand into the public library and looking for the spot on which *What Price Glory* was composed.[13]) He picked the title himself, deriving it from Stallings' remark about the distraught marine. As for the rest of the play, Anderson is supposed to have told one of his friends that he patterned it somewhat after *Henry IV,* Part I,[14] the main resemblances being the use of an actual war background, the satirical thrusts at heroism, the roistering and swearing and wenching that occur away from the battlefront, and the alternations of scenes of comedy with those of dire combat.

After about a week Anderson showed his draft to his colleague, who fortunately had begun to lose interest in the musical comedy, and confessed that the wine-cellar part (Act II of the finished drama[15]) was incomplete but that he, Anderson, could not finish it unaided because he lacked military experience. Then he told Stallings what was supposed to happen and gave him a written version to start on: This much we know to be true about Anderson's contribution, in marked contrast with what he said many years later when he generously credited the war hero with *all* of Act II. This particular act is indeed so stylistically different from the others that some readers might be tempted to believe that Stallings wrote it entirely, whereas in truth he only reworked what Anderson had already set down.[16] At any rate, given something tangible to revise, the ex-marine went into action on the play immediately and completed the wine-cellar part in one afternoon, making the leatherneck speech vivid and colorful and racy, as befits actual frontline troops. The work was done so rapidly that the time from Stallings' lunchtime yarns to curtain rise at the Plymouth was less than six months.

Getting the vision down on paper was one thing; getting it accepted for the stage was quite another. Buried in the desk drawers of aspiring writers all over the country are no doubt thousands of plays that, for one reason or another, never get accepted. How did *What Price Glory* manage to avoid this graveyard of shattered hopes?

On the evening of the day that the typist had finished making the typescript copy and turned it in, Stallings went over to the Hotel Brevoort, where he met a potbellied, big-jowled man with owlish eyes behind circular spectacles. This was Alexander Woollcott, the influential drama critic on *The New York Evening Sun,* the fancifully styled writer of books about theater, and the *bon vivant* of delights gustatory. Woollcott with his gift for exciting narrative and frankly exhibitionist eccentricities would soon become on radio, a few years hence, the idol of millions with his "Town Crier" program. But even now he had a sizable following. "Wit's End" was the name Dorothy Parker gave to his New York City apartment,[17] where, dressed in nothing more than pajama bottoms and dressing gown, the full moon of his belly exposed, he would waddle to the door to receive guests "like a fat duchess holding out her dirty rings to be kissed."[18]

Woollcott could be petty and impatient, high-handed and cruel, not only with newcomers but even with friends: He earned and deserved the lasting hatred of many. When actress Margalo Gillmore tried to introduce to him in the Algonquin Hotel a young actor who professed to admire his writings, the response was chilling: "Oh," sneered Woollcott, not bothering to look up from the menu, "can he read?" Whenever His Mightiness deigned to greet someone, it was usually with "Hello, repulsive!"[19] He told one young woman she was so stupid that her brains were popcorn soaked in urine. Such sadistic behavior was amusing, he thought. Nevertheless, this *poseur* with the affected airs of a spoiled eunuch (he *was* sexually underdeveloped) was worshipped or dreaded, liked or shunned, by just about every person of note on Broadway and its environs.[20]

Woollcott was a conspicuous member of the well-known Round Table of writers, newsmen, actors, and artists who assembled informally for lunch every day in the dining room of the Algonquin. For the most part they were young people in their twenties just beginning their careers. Members of this sophisticated group included poet and short story writer and obliging lie-around Dorothy Parker, looking softly feminine and helpless with her big doe eyes and her hand placed on her listener's forearm but formidable with that tongue of hers. When asked by her fellow wit Franklin P. Adams to use the word *horticulture* in a lively sentence, she replied: "You can lead a horticulture but you can't make her think."[21] It was the same petite, dark-haired Miss Parker who is said to have invented the advertising epigram, "Brevity is the soul of lingerie."[22] The *bons mots* attributed to her are legion.

Other women in the group were Edna Ferber (dramatist and novelist), Gertrude Atherton (novelist and biographer), Jane Grant (*Times* reporter and wife of Harold Ross, who would soon found *The New Yorker*), Ruth Hale (Heywood Broun's wife—these bluestockings insisted on keeping their maiden names), and Peggy Wood and Tallulah Bankhead (both of them actresses). Another sophisticate there was the lecherous Grand Mogul of Gagdom, George S. Kaufman, already launched upon his long series of successfully collaborated plays that would one day include *The Man Who Came to Dinner,* where we can see Woollcott burned nicely to a crisp in the figure of insufferable Sheridan Whiteside.*

Future playwright Robert E. Sherwood was among them too; in fact, it is said that he used to duck into the Algonquin partly to get away from the midgets who performed in the now-vanished Hippodrome across the way on Forty-fourth Street. Just before he became a movie reviewer on the old humor magazine *Life,* he had a job with *Vanity Fair,* whose offices were near the Hippodrome, and this remarkably tall fellow of 6 feet, 6½ inches sometimes asked his fellow editors Robert Benchley and Dorothy Parker to walk along with him to protect him from the midgets at the amusement palace. Maybe he thought 5-foot Dorothy Parker would be a good match for them.

---

*Woollcott, whose egocentricity was exceeded only by his desire to seize the main chance, considered the portrait a tribute and played the role of Whiteside in a touring company soon after the play came out in 1939.

Otherwise, the midgets would be sure to sneak up behind him and hoot and jeer and make a grab for his knees and yell up to him for a weather report. He was helpless to deal with them.[23]

Nor should we exclude from the long list of Round Table wits such figures as Robert Benchley (whimsical essayist and soon-to-become screen actor), Heywood Broun (drama critic), Joseph Hergesheimer (novelist), Marc Connelly (dramatist), Brock Pemberton (theatrical producer), and Harpo Marx (actor). The list changed considerably over the years.[24]

To some degree this was a self-admiration coterie, aptly symbolized by the mirrored wall that threw back upon them their own reflections at the long table that was their original location before the hotel manager, Frank Case, moved his prize menagerie off to the round table in the Rose Room, where they lunched on ham and eggs, hamburgers, apple pie, and coffee while they made jokes about each other and, just as likely, those not present.[25] Sometimes they could be pretty severe with each other's writings too.

It was into this circle that the crowd-shy and city-hating Max Anderson came once because he particularly admired wit. His daughter Hesper, our sole authority for this visit, does not tell us when it happened, but it must have been sometime before 1928, since this is the terminal date that Frank Case gives for the existence of the original Round Table. According to what Anderson told her, he felt that these quipsters thought him tame. He who was so skillful with puns and so delightfully funny in his comedies had a kind of humor unsuited for oral fireworks. It was best enjoyed in a small circle of intimates or on the written page. He was so shy of and distracted by strange company, especially those who require us to perform on demand, that he would be likely to formulate the witty comeback some time later, when it was too late.[26]

Anderson did not deal in made-up jokes, certainly not in gags saved up day after day for the right moment to insert them into the verbal exchange, which was standard procedure there. Nor did he go in for needling and back-stabbing his acquaintances—once again, considered jolly fun at the Algonquin. However, although this merciless crew sometimes murdered an innocent reputation in order to get the clever retort in, they did a public service when they flailed the socially pretentious, the hypocrites, and the bores.[27]

This was just the hothouse atmosphere that Alexander Woollcott flourished in. As dramatic reviewer on the *Sun* he dwelled among that tiny group of elites who could make or break a new play in the city. While Stallings was sipping coffee or bootleg whiskey there with him in the Hotel Brevoort just after *What Price Glory* had come back from the typist, he told the paunchy journalist about the play and how he thought it contained roles for J. M. Kerrigan and Lionel Barrymore. A novice's pipe dream! the experienced Woollcott must have thought. Stallings went on to wonder aloud how to get the work to the attention of Barrymore or, maybe better still, Arthur Hopkins, his manager. (Producers were known as managers in those days.) Another pipe dream!

At that very moment Hopkins himself walked into the room!

Stallings opened the dialogue by declaring that he had a play he wanted Hopkins to read. The manager, a habitually taciturn man, simply told him to send the script over to him.

Hopkins, of all managers in the business, was notoriously inefficient in reading new plays submitted for approval. Typescripts, each clamoring for attention, each promising to be tomorrow's hit, flew into his office like wind-driven snow and piled higher and higher and lay there indefinitely. Rumor had it that cabdrivers on West Forty-fifth Street knew that if they found typescripts left in their cabs by forgetful passengers, they were to send them over to Hopkins' office at the Plymouth. He collected waifs and strays.

Therefore, Hopkins' invitation offered no more cheer than a flickering candle in a blizzard. Nor did he say anything at all for a while. Ages passed. Whereupon Stallings seems to have taken it upon himself to break through the wall of silence—if one were ever to get the little man to talk again.

No, he wouldn't send it over! Stallings grumped, for the manager wouldn't read it.

At this juncture the wily Woollcott, who knew about Hopkins' method of handling new plays that he wasn't especially eager to read (and war plays were not in vogue then), gave a pleasant leer. Hopkins must have spotted the leer. And he was probably taken aback by the brave recalcitrance of this newcomer. Whichever of these did the trick is uncertain, but he broke down in that hour and made the concession that the impasse so clearly demanded: The manager said he'd read the typescript that very night and send him an answer on Monday.

When Stallings hobbled into the *World* offices on Monday morning, he heard that Hopkins had telephoned for him but supposed that the man merely wanted to learn the address for returning the rejected typescript. He therefore played it safe and waited for a repeat call. And sure enough, a few minutes later the telephone rang again: He and his colleague Anderson were to go over to the manager's office to sign the contracts and pick up the advance.[28] Oh, happy Monday!

On the other hand, Hopkins had his reservations. In his autobiography he tells us that he considered the play to be such a bitter and intransigent indictment of war that it might never prove popular.[29] But it seems that quality interested him more than popularity. He was a strange figure for the world of show business in that he didn't feel any need to seek slavishly the approbation of others in order to justify his career. He writes in his autobiography: "No creative work can express the person who is afraid to stand alone."[30] For such a man, *What Price Glory* seemed made to order.

Anderson and Stallings were fortunate to acquire this courageous director-manager, who was known for taking a chance with a newcomer (for example, O'Neill and his *Anna Christie*) and for avoiding the superficial style of production elsewhere in vogue. Over the years the gentle, uncomplaining, courteous, astrology-trusting but lovable man had been doing much to raise the level of theater. According to Anderson, Hopkins made no "obvious effort" in directing the play, and yet things somehow got done: "You never heard him speak to an actor. You never saw him make any suggestions or heard him make any suggestions. Things just happened, but they happened smoothly and perfectly."[31] Not only his directing experience but also his years as a booking agent in an amusement park syndicate and later in a vaudeville circuit had taught him how to handle temperamental actors.

As is usual with New York plays, Hopkins took this one out of town for a tryout, in this instance to Stamford, Connecticut. At one of the dress rehearsals the prototype of Flagg arrived, none other than the fearless Philip Townsend Case, and he gave Hopkins and the others an opportunity to learn how far his casting of Louis Wolheim was from the original. The contrast must have surprised just about everyone. Actor Wolheim, a former college professor,[32] had a flat-nosed, pugnacious, craggy face that looked as if it had been battered too often in varsity boxing matches. And what did the man he was to play look like, the belligerent Case, he whose reputation as a fire-eating bulldog had preceded him? The warrior who could leap into the jaws of death and come out with a gold filling? Case turned out to be a rather small, dapper man with pink cheeks and a noticeable lisp! Of such mortal stuff are the real heroes of this world made.

"Stallings," he told them, recounting their service together in France, "was brave but excitable. When we first smelled gas Stallings started to shout, 'Gas! Gas!' I said, 'Shut up you son-of-a-bitch.' He got one whiff of gas, and thought the war was over."[33]

Hopkins invited Case to attend their New York opening when they got there and reserved a box for him.

On the evening of their first performance in Stamford, one of Maxwell Anderson's former students from Polytechnic High School in San Francisco, Kathryn C. Hulme, just happened to be present and watched how her

"Maxie" comported himself on that special occasion. She spied a ponderous figure of despair pacing back and forth in the dark area behind the theater seats, perspiring and wringing his big farm-boy hands and looking woebegone.[34] He was preparing for the worst.

But all went well in Stamford. Still, there was no telling how the New York audiences, much less the critics, would like the play.

It is now eight-thirty and curtain time in New York for the première performance. The curtain rises. In a few minutes Louis Wolheim appears. And the handsome William Boyd in the role of the other main character, Sergeant Quirt. He is not to be confused with that other William Boyd, famous by midcentury as the cowboy star Hopalong Cassidy.

What Price Glory, set in France during the last phase of World War I, after the Americans have entered the conflict, presents two battle-hardened troopers who have seen a lot of each other during their many years of service in the U.S. Marine Corps. Captain Flagg has been wrangling with his first sergeant, Quirt, over the favors of a provincial wench named Charmaine. After her father, Cognac Pete, protests to Flagg that the sergeant has seduced his *petite enfant innocente* (*she* being seduced?—what a laugh!), Flagg seizes this juicy opportunity to get even with the other marine: He bellows to Quirt that he must marry the girl and turn over his soldier pay. But orders from higher up save the sergeant at the last minute; they must be off to action at the front. The first and third acts are all comedy, but Act II, whose setting is the wine cellar of a French house, introduces a bloody naturalism that is new in the history of drama about war. The realistic speech and liberal use of profanity are also new. Dirty marines, tired from fighting, discuss the havoc of war as casualties are carried in; a hardened pharmacist's mate gets ready to carry out surgical operations under their very noses; the brutality and pointlessness of combat are everywhere evident in this hole of misery; an hysterical lieutenant, afflicted with shell shock, breaks down at the sight of another man's injuries. Act III finds Quirt wounded but ready to let a game of cards decide which of the two marines will win the floozy—this prize symbolic of the territorial gains of so much modern warfare—but orders arrive sending both of them off to the fighting again. As true soldiers they obey.

The debunking of war in *What Price Glory* is all the more effective through having as heroes professional marines rather than draftees; the theatergoer is thus led to believe he is on the "inside," privy to terrible secrets, and that if the professionals themselves find so much wrong with military operations and so little to inspire one with valor that they spend most of their time quarreling over a slut, then things are desperate and shocking indeed! Flagg and Quirt are the conventional warrior-heroes of literature when they loyally obey the call to battle, but in their hearts they seem to bear a slogan popular among the pacifists of the Vietnam War era: "Make love, not war."

The play runs smoothly, so smoothly that, as the curtain drops down on the final act there is—could one believe it!—yes, thunderous applause! We sense something else going on down there too, but none of us up here can see it; a bit later we hear that patrons in the orchestra were so jubilant that many actually stood up on their seats and cheered![35]

The pandemonium even catches Captain Case off guard. He had arrived at the Plymouth thirty minutes late with a fellow marine officer, both of them intoxicated, and they were shown to their box, where they quickly fell asleep.[36] But the racket wakes up Case, and he is surprised to find himself a bit of a celebrity.

No question that *What Price Glory* is a winner. While the huzzahs are still sounding in our ears, Stallings leans over and puts an arm around his coauthor and tells him that this is the first time he has realized what the play is all about. Had Stallings been out drinking with Case, perhaps?

Certainly Max Anderson knows what the play is all about. And he knows something else, too, that he had helped write what he thought was merely a potboiler, for he wanted only to make money.[37] And now the two of them are going to make gobs of it. And even more important, now a whole new career is opening up for Anderson. Life will never be the same again for him after tonight.

Woollcott's review in *The Sun* the next day was extremely favorable: "No war play written in the English language since the German guns boomed under the walls of Liege, ten years ago, has been so true, so alive, so salty and richly satisfying." This was the bellwether of a series of notices that helped launch *What Price Glory* upon a long and triumphant stage career. Walter Winchell once observed of the erratic and sometimes sentimental Woollcott that he *always* applauded the season's first production because he didn't want to "stone the first cast,"[38] but we should not take the *bon mot* too seriously in this instance, for other reviewers on the same day were also enthusiastic, as witness Heywood Broun in the *World*. George Jean Nathan wrote that it was "the finest thing of its kind I have seen . . . infinitely superior to every other play born of the late war. . . ."[39]

Such was the contagious spirit of the play that Robert E. Sherwood, himself wounded during the war and still suffering from an excruciating facial tic, and many years later one of Max Anderson's close friends and a colleague in

The Playwrights Producing Company, attended a sparkling performance and decided then and there that it would be simply wonderful to be a playwright.[40] His own antiwar play, *The Road to Rome,* appeared not long afterward.

The profanity in *What Price Glory* had all by itself such an impact that it gave rise to an amusing anecdote: An elderly, dignified-looking woman, who had been silent during the first act, dropped something accidentally during intermission; she turned to her escort and said, "I seem to have dropped my Goddam program."[41]

The very next day following the première, when the reviews showed the play a success beyond all doubt, Anderson made the greatest decision of his life, to leave his desk on the *World,* never to return, never to do journalism again. One of the elderly editorial writers there, L. R. E. Paulin, who had been in the city for at least two decades and knew how very heavily the odds were stacked against a repeat performance on Broadway, told him to put his royalty money away and forget it, because he'd probably never have another hit in his lifetime; he should play it safe and stay in journalism.

But Anderson didn't listen to him. Anderson's was the fulfillment of almost every newspaperman's dream: to bid the paper goodbye and write books for a living. In middle age, at a time when almost all aspiring literary artists have either abandoned writing as a career or metamorphosed into teachers or editors or newspapermen, he was *leaving* journalism for an exciting, creative career. He was his own man now. No more need to worry about his radical libertarianism upsetting whatever employer he might have, causing hard feelings, and getting himself fired for the nth time. He was so happy and pleased with himself that he didn't quite know what to do, and yet the occasion clearly called for some kind of celebration. Being a man of modest tastes and averse to self-advertisement in its lavish forms, he did something rather characteristic of him by buying himself a cane and strolling down Fifth Avenue, twirling it in the faces of no doubt curious passersby.[42]

Stallings, for his part, bought himself a new Chevrolet, and in a scene reminiscent of Diamond Jim Brady, drove the machine too fast along East River Drive without properly breaking in the engine until—poor celebrity!— the engine seized in that shiny, spanking new car. Maybe that is why we hear about him buying also around this time a luxurious Hispano-Suiza sports car.[43] Soon he would go out to Hollywood and help transform his novel *Plumes* into the film *The Big Parade,* another smashing money winner.

What Price Glory, with its "toot goddam sweet" and other profanities, stirred up a hornet's nest among the puritans and other guardians of public decency. Secretary of the Navy Curtis D. Wilbur branded the play as nothing less than a shame, "full of gutter language," and assured folks that the clean-living and clean-speaking lads in today's navy no longer spoke anything like Flagg's smutty vernacular.[44] Wilbur was getting all his impressions on this matter from a subordinate who, like himself, had taken care not to contaminate his mind by going to a production: This was the commander of the Brooklyn Navy Yard, Rear Admiral Charles P. Plunkett.[45] Plunkett had complained to his boss that the entertainment in question had violated a federal law that prohibited a nonserviceman from wearing a United States uniform on the stage in such a way that it brought discredit to the services. The steaming admiral also tried to rouse United States District Attorney Colonel William Hayward, but Hayward, with experience leading New York's Negro troops during the war, found nothing disturbing about the language and declined to prosecute.[46] Not to be ouflanked, Plunkett fired letters of protest to the city district attorney and to Mayor John F. Hylan, who responded by ordering some of his officials to confer with Plunkett and with Major General Robert Lee Bullard, the ranking army officer in New York, to try to remove the offensive content in the play.[47]

Hylan was also in a dither about the nudity in Earl Carroll's *Vanities*. He was perhaps all the more zealous to get action against Carroll and Hopkins now that the city had lost in the Court of Appeals its right to close up an offending naughty-naughty called *The Demi-Virgin*.

Suddenly the chief nemesis of *What Price Glory*, Admiral Plunkett, got torpedoed out of action. The cessation of hostility from that quarter may very well have come from the publication of a satiric letter in Heywood Broun's column in the *World*. There we read that during his service in France in the AEF, Plunkett daily sent letters reeking with horrible profanity to his rival-in-arms General Chamberlaine; he fumed about not being permitted to break out of Houssamont and transport his huge, sixteen-inch naval guns up to the front on their railroad cars. Finally, he disobeyed the general's orders and broke out, but when he reached the front he discovered to his astonishment that the guns faced in the wrong direction and that there was no turntable in Flanders capable of rotating the long cars they were on. At learning of his fool predicament, the admiral "took a spraddle-legged stance about ten feet to the right of the rear truck and Oh! Oh! Oh!"—spat blue flames![48]

With the admiral knocked out of action, that left General Bullard to battle for the honor of the armed forces. The general, however, refused to cooperate in censoring. But the city district attorney and the police had been set in motion by now, and soon two policemen sent around to the Plymouth to investigate found in the dialogue many words that they said offended them. Meanwhile, details of this *cause célèbre* as reported in the city papers—

sometimes on the front page—provided a kind of advertising impossible to buy. One night, manned police wagons were parked in nearby streets, ready to make a raid if the district attorney so decided. The climax of this whole affair came when Police Inspector West and three other officials arrived at the Plymouth, asked to see Hopkins, and demanded a copy of the script. Hopkins put them off by replying that he had already given his spare one to the federal authorities. Undaunted by this, the officials decided to stay and watch the show, taking the precaution to post a stenographer on the stage to take down any instances of blue dialogue. This was too much heat for Hopkins. He assembled his cast and told them to delete the profane words, about twenty in all, but to continue to act in a profane style.[49] The evening performance went on as scheduled except that thirty-five minions of the law stood outside in readiness to storm in when called upon, but when the curtain rustled down they were all dismissed. Someone asked Inspector West if he liked the show, and he replied that he enjoyed it immensely. After the patrol wagons returned to the garage, the forbidden dialogue crept back into play performances just as before.[50]

The Churchman, an Episcopalian weekly, assailed Mayor Hylan for appointing military men to censor the work in the first place. Why not have clergymen censor objectionable plays that deal with parsons—for example, *Rain?* And capitalists censor stage capitalists? Absurd![51] A Unitarian preacher, Charles Potter, came to the defense of the original text and said that he, for one, regretted the excision (however temporary) of those coarse words. To Potter, *What Price Glory* gave an excellent picture of the brutal life led by professional soldiers.[52]

This unconventional, earthy language, shocking though it was at the time, does give one a fair notion of what barracks speech is like—after being scrubbed and fumigated. It also led to a more intense realism in the American theater. Motion pictures followed suit by giving a realistic rather than a sentimental treatment of war. Hopkins, who was certainly in a position to know, records that this work opened the floodgates to a stream of needless profanity in playhouses during the following seasons because producers were misled into believing that profanity was the key to their play's success.[53]

Thanks partly to this windfall of free publicity, Arthur Hopkins drew in $10,000 a week profit on his investment.[54] The royalties to the playwrights followed some formula about which there is a good deal of uncertainty; their contract was drawn up some years before The Dramatists Guild brought out its "Minimum Basic Agreement between Authors and Managers" and put royalties on a uniform scale for everyone. Back in 1914 this same manager had given beginning playwright Elmer Rice 5 percent of the weekly gross and an advance of $500 upon accepting *On Trial,* but by 1926, two years after signing the contract for *What Price Glory,* Anderson wrote for a journal that authors were receiving 5 percent on the first $5,000 weekly gross, 7½ percent on the next $2,000, and 10 percent on everything over $7,000.[55] Arrangements continued to be very fluid, however, until the "Minimum Basic Agreement" went into effect and managers began to honor it everywhere; until then the beginning author negotiated at a disadvantage, to put it mildly, except with a few men like Arthur Hopkins.

With his sudden earnings, Anderson repaid the last of the $1,500 he had borrowed in San Francisco so that he could travel East, bought two farms in western New York for relatives of his, began remodeling his farmhouse on South Mountain Road, and moved from his tiny apartment on 70 Perry Street to more comfortable quarters at 171 West 12th Street. The change of apartment was a big event to his little son Quentin, who remembers three things about the change: His mother quickly ordered in a whole assortment of liquors; she bought some delicious sweetmeats; and he, Quentin, was greatly impressed when introduced at last to the one and only Captain Case, whom he had seen represented in the theater.[56]

Anderson's brother Lawrence recounts one notably heartwarming thing Max did for his mother when he came into sudden affluence. At the time of the incident she was visiting with the Maxwell Andersons in the old farmhouse in New City. This is the story in Lawrence's own words:

> . . . the whole family had never had any money of consequence. . . .
> He was in the upstairs hall of the old house and he met with mother about it there. "Mother, wouldn't you like to go to New York on a shopping trip? You've never done anything like that. Really get something nice." And she said she'd never thought about doing anything of that kind. "Well, I've written out a check for you and I want you to go and get some nice things for yourself." And he handed her a check and it was for $1,000. She had never seen $1,000 in her life before.[57]

That would have been equivalent to at least $8,000 in today's money.

How much Anderson was earning every week can be glimpsed in the following anecdote which Professor Koch, his drama teacher from the University of North Dakota, liked to tell about his former student:

> Chatting and drinking beer together in New York after Anderson's great war play *What Price Glory* had become a smashing success on Broadway, Anderson interjected, "Proff [sic], don't you remember

that I had my beginnings with you at Grand Forks? I was an actor for you once?"

"You were not," exclaimed Koch skeptically.

"Well," Anderson said, "have you forgotten, too, that I was a charter member of your Dakota Playmakers?" Koch replied, "No, I remember that, and all that you were good for was to read papers; you were never an actor."

"Yes, I was," retorted Anderson. "Don't you remember the production of *Twelfth Night* by the Sock and Buskin? You cast me for the smallest part in the whole show. I was the Captain who appeared in Act I, scene 1 only. I had two lines to say, but as an actor I was so rotten that after the second rehearsal you fired me."

Koch felt himself put "on the spot" for one moment and dexterously changed the subject. "Now I remember," he said, "but hold on Max, what are your royalties now on *What Price Glory?*"

"Oh, my share of the royalties is about a thousand dollars a week," preened Anderson. "But we're just getting started; we're planning to have a second company open in Chicago soon, and we are also going to have five road companies; then we will sell the motion picture rights for it."

"A thousand dollars a week—" replied Koch, "that's not bad for a starter, is it? But at least, Max, give me credit for having fired a rotten actor to save a good playwright!"[58]

What Price Glory piled up 299 performances during its first New York run. Buoyed up by the tumultuous applause, actor Louis Wolheim clearly thought he could make a career of playing Flagg, much as O'Neill's father had done with the Count of Monte Cristo. During that season young Paul Green was just beginning his dramatic career after having courses under Koch at the University of North Carolina; Green went backstage and paid Wolheim a call while the latter was wiping off makeup and exclaimed in a voice rich with the music of Southern hills, "Oh boy, what a play!" Yeah, the greatest play since Shakespeare!" the other crowed and added, "It's going to run forever!"[59] Certainly it did have an extraordinary run for nonmusical realistic fare. There were road companies and occasional revivals, and of course the highly profitable movie versions: By early 1931 Anderson's royalties from the *first* such version totaled $28,333.33, and two more were yet to come![60] It is too bad, however, that he didn't put much of his earnings into savings and investments so that he could prepare for the lean years. But he knew and cared little about how big money breeds itself.[61] Among the very few investments he made in his long career, aside from buying U.S. savings bonds, an acreage in Maine, and some property near High Tor, we note the purchase of thirty shares of stock in Rotary Motors Co., a Delaware firm; but he soon lost track of the firm, and by 1934 he was writing to see whether it still existed.[62]

What Price Glory, though not as good as several of Anderson's plays in the 1930s, was always to remain for him something special—far more so than even *White Desert,* which belongs in his favorite genre of poetic tragedy. Even in his last years, when reviews were rarely to his liking, when he refused even to read reviews, he could always reflect that once upon a lovely time patrons actually did stand up on their seats and cheer at one of his plays. And manager Arthur Hopkins always felt that, of all his numerous productions, this one was in some respects the best of them all.[63]

THE ARRIVAL OF THE
FEMME FATALE

During the period immediately after he finished writing *What Price Glory*, when Anderson was discovering through trial and error the types of material he was best suited to, he wrote a drama of "strange and peculiar beauty," as Barrett Clark called it,[1] which has neither been published nor professionally staged. This is *Sea-Wife*, completed sometime in 1924. It is a good example of his already strong predilection toward romance where fantasy brushes its velvet wings against the calico lives of ordinary people and where the dialogue lifts the imagination aloft on cadences of noble rhetoric and lyric poetry. The admitted source is Matthew Arnold's poem "The Forsaken Merman," where a sea king yearns for his mortal wife, who had deserted him to return to the companionship of her race. But Anderson shifts the focus to the wife and places the action in a tiny community on an island off the coast of Maine. In this one-act play, Margaret has just come back to her fisherman husband, Dan, after a mysterious three-year absence during which she has lived with a sea king and borne him children, and now she faces the disbelief of her husband and the hostility of bigoted villagers. She has the uncanny misfortune to inhabit what are to her two very real worlds, the supernatural and the natural—much as do the marooned Dutchmen in *High Tor*—and cannot fully adjust to either.[2] Incidentally, the play's witch, Biddy Stewart, may have been inspired by the alleged witch Biddy Weed, who lived on the edge of the Enchanted Meadow lying between Valley Cottage and Central Nyack.[3]

In 1925, Anderson and Stallings collaborated again, on a swashbuckling romance called *First Flight*, about the young lover Andrew Jackson; and also on *The Buccaneer*, about the pirate Captain Henry Morgan. But neither play was strong enough to run for more than twenty performances, and today they have little if any interest for the serious student of the theater. Anderson, unaided, would shortly do far better. As for his coauthor, Stallings would never come up with another stage winner again, though he kept busy. After the twin failures just noted, he spent much time in Hollywood turning out operas, motion-picture scenarios, and dramatizations of other people's novels.

Despite these two failures, Anderson decided that he would adapt a novel for his next stage play (at the risk of getting ahead of our story it can be said that he would be more successful with adaptations than collaborations). Accordingly, that same fall of 1925 brought moderate commercial success at the Greenwich Village Theatre[4] with his *Outside Looking In*, taken from Jim Tully's sociological study of hobos called *Beggars of Life*. He shared royalties with the novelist. Future film actors James Cagney and Charles A. Bickford took the roles of Little Red and Oklahoma Red, respectively. But as art, *Outside Looking In* doesn't compare favorably with Anderson's best work and is rarely reprinted, even though it is superior to much of what does get anthologized.

Meanwhile, his marriage was breaking up. It is difficult to ascertain just when the domestic troubles first began, but there are hints of them in his intensely personal essay "An Age of Hired Men," which came out in *The Freeman* late in 1920. Here Anderson evokes Francis Bacon's statement that a married man, by virtue of having a wife and children, has given hostages to fortune: "Without a shadow of doubt marriage and children, as we know them at present, constitute the most effective brakes on progress toward generally recognized ideals, the most immoveable barriers in the way of individual and industrial justice." No happy spouse could have written that. Nowhere in the essay is there a cheerful note on behalf of the conjugal state. In 1926, after Margaret had been through the strain of bearing the last of her children, she underwent a serious operation to realign the tissues of her reproductive tract; it is possible that her medical condition before and even long after the operation interfered with her sex life[5] and helped drive the husband to seek a new bed partner.

Perhaps his habit of isolating himself often and for prolonged periods while writing—away "in a world of his own," as his brother Kenneth said of him[6]—finally began to bother Margaret. Max learned that he could use his latest project as an excuse to bow out of dull parties or other social engagements that his more outgoing wife had planned for him. After all those long years of sweat and privation, she may have argued that they were now entitled to enjoy their reward, to travel more, and to entertain in the style that becomes the family of a celebrated man.

But he grew bored with parties unless they consisted of a few intimate friends, and he didn't like to travel much because his work regularly took him on the road for weeks at a time during tryouts. It was no fun living out of suitcases in one strange hotel after another. His brother Kenneth tells us that Margaret wanted to enlarge their social life, but Max resisted; and his brother Lawrence puts the matter more emphatically in saying, "[Max] was unhappy about her interest in making the social climb, which didn't appeal to him at all."[7]

As their relationship grew worse, Margaret, who was still very attractive, began to accept attentions from three unidentified young men, which situation would have provided Max with an additional reason for going his own way. She tried desperately to create for herself some kind of independent and meaningful life, an enterprise that presumably was difficult for her after loyally subordinating her interests to his for almost two decades. She even began to attend a school in New York.[8] It is not clear whether they were actually separated, but when they took vacations in Europe they went separately. From various postal cards sent back to the children we learn that in the middle of 1926 Margaret was visiting in Paris and in Ireland, where she found a cousin of hers; in July of that year Anderson was in Plymouth, England.[9] Their vacations apart from each other apparently cleared the air for a while, for we soon find them living together again, perhaps in the New York apartment.

From an undated letter to Kenneth that Margaret wrote not long after her return to America, we get a good idea of her feelings at the time. Kenneth, who had once lived with them while attending school, had written to see whether he might be allowed to return and live with them again, but she refuses him flatly: "For you do interrupt us. Our real selves are not present where you are. Many brothers and sisters put up with this false relationship all their lives. . . . Very likely if you were anywhere near our age and interests we'd put up with it too." She writes that except for her brother Jim, with whom she professes to have nothing in common, she has seen none of the Hasketts since the second year of her marriage. Max, she informs this would-be visitor, wants to be left alone, and to that end has made gifts of money to various needy relatives in order to "get them off his mind and not continually on it." But Max has gone so far in being generous that she must take steps, as usual, to protect him against the consequences: an increasing familial dependency. (It is almost as if she had in mind that old French proverb which runs, "No good deed will go unpunished!") She tells Kenneth:

> My feeling about Max is the only thing I care about in life and I could put up with anything he wanted. I came back from Europe believing I could face a future—with him—containing any number of relatives. But just as surely will I refuse to put up with anything that he doesn't want—and that interferes with his work and life.[10]

But her resolve finally was not enough.

It is curious and probably not without significance to his marital crisis that he wrote the comedic play *Saturday's Children* in 1926 and had it staged in January of the following year, Humphrey Bogart and Ruth Gordon in the lead roles, a play whose theme is that marriage destroys romance. Surely this theme was attractive to him for more than dramatic or commercial reasons. He admits that Ibsen's *Love's Comedy* may have been the source,[11] but his known marital difficulties during this time must have made the theme singularly appealing to him. The characters Bobby and Rims are young people trapped into marriage by a designing relative and are now seeing their love destroyed by economic worries. Bobby tells her husband, Rims, after they begin to experience the treadmill of housekeeping that she almost wishes she were married to someone else so that she could have the excitement of meeting Rims as a lover at secret rendezvous. The *raissoneur* in the play, Mr. Halevy, reinforces the fantasy by telling her that she would have been better off having an affair because marriage, far from being romantic, actually consists of a succession of dishpans and quarrels and bills. Before long their problems drive them asunder and we find Bobby living alone in an apartment building where her chastity is guarded by a strict landlady. In the final scene we see Rims climbing through her window for a romantic reunion, enacting the role of the clandestine lover now that conventional marriage has failed to provide happiness. In the excitement of their coupling, however, we are supposed to forget that the problems of dishpans and so forth have not gone away—and won't.[12]

Saturday's Children swiftly became Anderson's third popular success, running for 310 performances (almost three times as many as *Outside Looking In*) and then later revived.[13] By now, producers and directors were seeking him out. And also actresses. Kenneth tells us that these temptations of the flesh were such that Margaret began jumping like hot corn in a popper.[14]

Difficulties at home made him all the more susceptible to these sirens; undoubtedly he had intimacies. But he was never known for being promiscuous.[15]

Margaret's sky came plummeting down when Mab Maynard arrived. The latter appeared, appropriately enough, in the year that brought Anderson's drama about marital problems, *Saturday's Children,*[16] and when he was the talk of the town and earning big money again. He is said to have first met her in an elevator, at which time he asked if she wanted to act.[17] The heroine of his play *Gypsy,* scheduled to open that fall at the Klaw Theatre, bears some ominous resemblances to and is curiously prophetic about this newcomer in his life, Mab Maynard. In that play Ellen is a neurotic and dishonest creature who suffers from bad heredity and equally bad upbringing, who marries against her better judgment, who proves unfaithful, and who then kills herself with gas.[18] It is not known whether Anderson had met Mab before writing the play and, if so, whether the circumstances of her life had colored his depiction of Ellen.

This new woman in his life was like one of those lovely, expensive dolls that Lela used to admire in department-store windows when she was a girl.[19] She had a slim figure, violet eyes, dark brown hair, and a band of palest freckles that tiptoed across her upper cheeks when she stayed in the sun too long. She was only five feet tall and weighed a hundred pounds at most. Truly a doll woman.

Mab was her stage name as well as the one she used in private life once she reached New York, but she was born Gertrude Higger on September 27, 1904, in Montreal, Canada, the elder daughter of Benjamin Higger and his wife, Anna.[20] Both parents were Russian Jews, Mr. Higger having emigrated from Rogovo, Lithuania (at that time part of Russia), to the United States, where he shortly became a naturalized citizen; his future wife, Anna Lerner, had emigrated from a small village in Russia to Canada when she was but four years old. Mr. Higger married Anna in Montreal, where her family had settled, and then moved to Baltimore and became a foreman in a cigar factory and taught that trade to his wife. All during this time the family dwelled in poor neighborhoods and had very few luxuries; and because both parents worked away from home, the children were left unsupervised constantly and had to learn from an early age to take care of themselves. Being the firstborn and beautiful and also willing to speak up for herself, Gertrude was her mother's pet and had the advantage of getting whatever new clothes were to be had, but she also spoke up for Libbe, her quiet and meek sister. Gertrude was fun-loving, made many friends as she grew older, liked crowds, and everyone seemed to like her.[21] She also picked up an inordinate love of gambling with cards, a habit that remained with her for the rest of her life.

In 1909, shortly before the father died, he and his wife returned to Montreal with the two children. There Mrs. Higger became a widow, fell into disgrace with her relatives,[22] and found that she had to leave town quickly. Following a cold goodbye to her mother—not in her home but by appointment in the street—and no farewell at all at the train station, for no one had come to see them off, the little family fled south to Cleveland. The Lerner kinsmen, however, wanted to force the daughters back to Montreal because Gertrude had been born there, and to this end they sent a representative scurrying after Mrs. Higger. Eventually the squabble reached court, and the children were taken out of school and placed in a shelter home pending the outcome of the hearing. At last the youngsters were called before the judge and asked whether they wanted to go back to Canada in the event that the decision went against the mother. The court finally decided that neither of the children could be deported, since Mr. Higger was shown to be a U.S. citizen when they were born.

But the shame of the court hearing was followed by still more shame: For various reasons the mother deposited her little girls in the Jewish Orphan Home, a B'nai B'rith organization on Woodland Avenue. In the orphanage Gertrude wrote short stories, acted in plays, and took part in sports, giving no evidence of that depressed and neurotic condition that afflicted the last years of her life. A bright girl, she preferred intellectual companions when she could find them and grew bored with silly parlor games that didn't tax the mind.

Then Mrs. Higger found herself a new husband, Albert Klein; and now as Mrs. Klein she took them out of the orphanage when Gertrude was sixteen and had the audacity to insist that the elder daughter go to work and help support her (just as Libbe must do when she reached sixteen), even though it meant dropping out of high school.[23] (In later years the mother would visit Gertrude in New City and demand that her daughter entertain her; if refused, she would grow emotionally ill. She wanted celebrities to fuss over her so that she might later brag about their acquaintance.) This unnatural dependence, emotional and economic, irked both daughters and no doubt helped drive Gertrude away from home. Immediately upon release from the orphanage, Gertrude found work as a stenographer for a Cleveland attorney and took night courses to finish high school. She also began to save money. In the fall of 1923 she enrolled at Ohio State University, but the stay was brief: She failed all courses she attempted during the quarter, evidently because of heavy absenteeism;[24] she must have had a change of career plans following her marriage in December to the tall, shambling, aquiline-featured singer Charles V. Maynard, a student there. The Kleins, as expected, bitterly opposed her marrying a gentile.

We next learn about her going to New York City—whether in the company of her husband is uncertain—and attending the American Academy of Dramatic Art,[25] doing some modeling, and performing in a vaudeville act where she was billed as "The Beautiful Mab Maynard," astonishing audiences by controlling her breath and muscles in such a way that a group of men could not lift her.[26] Along with finding a career she found her new name of "Mab" and dropped forever the middle initial "H" and whatever that stood for,[27] along with the uneuphonious surname of "Higger"; moreover, she never again alluded to the family religion, partly for reason of social ambition and partly because Judaism was associated inseparably with the impoverished and unhappy past that she wanted to forget.

Soon after she met Anderson she went to work as his secretary, typing up his plays and handling his correspondence. Doubtless Mab hoped to get a part in one of the plays; indeed, she would figure in several of them during the 1930s, even though by all accounts she was a mediocre actress.[28] But no one questioned that she was a marvel at typing and also at figuring out Anderson's not always legible handwriting; moreover, she had an efficient, critical, systematic mind that would prove useful with clerical chores.[29]

Though basically an unspontaneous, humorless person—never good at making up puns or enjoying those that Anderson invented in profusion—she at least had the virtue, we are told, of never being in the least catty about people behind their backs. Nor was she flamboyant, like some actresses—a trait that would have driven him up a wall—but his country-in-laws, the Chambers, who did not commonly see stage folk, considered her a little artificial.[30]

Mab was one of those determined, energetic, ambitious young women who, though lacking marked talent of their own or advanced education, are nevertheless drawn to men of talent who make lots of money that these women can spend to create their own special world of luxury and fashion. Taking into account the uncertainties and deprivations of her youth, we can appreciate why Mab so determinedly put her faith in materialism. She went so far as to look down on people who didn't have much money, and she measured artistic success mainly if not exclusively by what it earned.[31]

The lure of dollars was important in drawing Anderson into playwriting, but after he was assured of a more or less dependable income from his craft he began to take the ascetic view that ownership of money robbed the artist of something vital inside: consequently, he gave away to his family whatever he earned.[32] As a result, this generosity often obliged him to earn still more money. But if he was serious in believing that money harmed him as an artist, he was almost certainly rationalizing his extravagant generosity and poor business sense. Someone should have reminded him that his idol, Shakespeare, did quite all right for himself though encumbered with rich holdings in Stratford-on-Avon.

Money may not have been the crucial reason that Mab was drawn to him, but it certainly was a potent one. However, she no doubt honestly admired him as a person and as an artist. Soon a romance flowered between the thirty-nine-year-old man and twenty-three-year-old woman. Gossip has it that he sometimes took her as well as Margaret out to the farmhouse together, and while Margaret looked on he would playfully pull Mab onto his lap. In the beginning the gesture meant nothing romantic, perhaps—or was he deliberately trying to make his wife jealous, or more likely still, to pay her back for her flirtations with the young men mentioned earlier? We may never know. But the proximity of an attractive secretary who was eager to serve— nay, adoringly attentive whenever he broached any of his domestic or theatrical problems, and who was in her own way as ambitious as he was—spelled temptation. It was natural that his gratitude would become admiration; his sympathy for her troubled past a passionate attachment. Later on, apparently as an act of selfishness or cruelty toward his wife, he took Mab out to the farm alone on weekends and in doing so raised the eyebrows of his New City neighbors, a closely knit group most of whom liked Margaret and took her side in the emerging scandal. It is uncertain whether he informed Margaret of what was going on before the affair became public, but she somehow learned the truth and was furious![33]

Margaret's supporters included his housekeeper, tongue-wagging Martha Stamper. Martha was a strikingly handsome, big-bosomed woman who had been hired at eighteen to nurse Quentin after a leg accident. Later on, Margaret, who never found much poetry in household maintenance, gladly took the impressionable Martha under her wing and taught her all the exciting secrets of cooking one steamy meal after another and scrubbing sinksful of greasy pans. Her service with the Andersons included not only mothering all the boys until they grew up but Hesper, too, when she came along. Immensely grateful, even half in love with the playwright himself, she considered Margaret something of a saint and spent the next twenty years making certain that no one, above all Mab Maynard, ever forgot it. As a sly and adept liar Martha became the sometimes lovable enemy in the camp, reading open letters that lay around, monitoring telephone calls, and spreading often vicious gossip from one end of the road to the other.[34]

Information on the Andersons' marital problems is scarce, for the couple was not in the habit of complaining to other people, and the children were too young to be aware of most of what was going on, but indications are that Max considered his wife faultless in the breakup and that even her flirtations with the three young men were harmlessly chaste.[35] Margaret at middle age and after bearing three children may well have lost all sexual attraction for him. And she may well have had personality faults that he couldn't live with, but the fact is that we don't hear about them. Anderson was slipping like quicksilver through her fingers, and there was nothing she could do about it except suffer. It came as a shock to Kenneth when Margaret, who seemed to be in good physical health, told him in her fortieth year that she was sure she didn't have much longer to live.[36]

However reprehensible Anderson's treatment of his wife, we would understand him better if we had some glimpses of that radical spirit that was definitely his during this time and that found expression in his attitude toward certain human institutions and customs. It was only natural that this spirit would overflow into his marital and love relations. Many years later he wrote about a widespread mood he had shared during the 1920s:

> We saw clearly in those high-minded times that the race was not going to live by the Old or the New Testament. It was going to live in the light of scientific day, making its choices freely among the fruits of the new trees of knowledge. . . . God was to be replaced by a sort of higher expedience, arrived at by laboratory methods. *There was no sin except that which made for inefficiency. Honor was a holdover from the past, retained mainly for business reasons. The need for sexual restraint was abolished by the discovery of contraceptives. . . . Love should be free. . . .* [italics mine].[37]

All his life he was a champion of liberty and justice, particularly as these applied to the individual citizen in conflict with overly zealous minions of the law. Alan and Terence told me an anecdote about the time their father exploded with anger at a guard in Grand Central Station. He and Mab had been waiting for a long time and, wanting to rest, found no seats handy. Anderson noticed a ledge nearby and sat down on it. Spotting him, a policeman barked, "You can't sit there!" Anderson looked over at the guard and said simply, "I'm tired. Don't bother me." And there he continued to rest, all two hundred pounds of him. Then the policeman came over and gave him an order, "Get up!" Still Anderson wouldn't move. Like his hero Brom in *Knick-*

erbocker Holiday, he had the peculiar resistance of the American to being ordered around. Mab could tell that he was becoming angry because, at such times, he grew very quiet and concise of statement; in this case he said, "Go away." At that, the bluecoat made the mistake of grabbing his lapels. Suddenly Anderson gave his tormenter a very firm push that sent him reeling backward on his uniformed behind. It required two policemen to force the angry Anderson up the stairway to the office of the station police, where he was asked if it was true that he had shoved that holy of holies, the guard. "Yes," Anderson replied, "and I'll do it again, too!"

Quite soon the official realized that he had in his office no crank or ordinary New Yorker but the celebrated author of *What Price Glory;* furthermore, that the dramatist was well within his rights to resist the physical harassment. Thereupon the official apologized and asked him to sign a statement the effect of which would clear the police of any wrongdoing—now that the tables were turned!—but Anderson refused: "I won't sign anything." Try as the police could, they did not budge him from his fierce resolve, and finally they had to let him walk out of there a free man without signing the release.

This anger of the beleaguered citizen is something that in 1928 he infused into his fiery but minor work *Gods of the Lightning*—based on an internationally famous legal trial of that decade[38]—and which would turn up again in *Both Your Houses, Winterset,* and *High Tor.*

Some time after he had started courting Mab, the dramatist took his little sons Terence and Alan to her apartment in Greenwich Village.[39] There would have been no point in taking along the eldest son, Quentin, because he already knew about and openly disliked this Wicked Witch of the Canadian North who was causing his mother grief.[40] Even Terence resented her.[41]

Mab was still married to the singer Maynard, but he was conveniently away at the time. The most probable reason for the visit was that the intrigue was well advanced by now, they had discussed getting divorces from their respective mates, and she wanted to see how the children got along with her as a replacement mother. Not being a maternal soul, she had reason to be nervous about marrying into a ready-made family. When the trio arrived at the apartment they found Mab dressed in finery for the occasion, she wearing what could have been a lover's gift from Anderson, a white fox fur cape. Even this early she freely indulged her lifelong taste for luxury. Mab was simply not one of those women who are content to drink Kool-Aid from a jelly glass.

She showed her guests about the place, let the children admire the two

French swords hanging above the fireplace, served them refreshments, and gave each boy a cut-glass paperweight from a pair that they had been eying. The boys took the precious gifts home with them. Long afterward, when she happened to visit at their house, she spotted the blue paperweight that she had given Alan and pounced on it crying, "THAT'S MINE!" and took it back, having forgotten that she had ever given it away. He had cherished the gift originally and was astonished that she could not remember her own attempt at generosity and friendship.

Not until many years later would the boys be able to recognize her smoldering sensuality and her reputed skill for bending men to her desire.[42] These qualities must have been very real to the Reverend Anderson, for she quickly made him an admiring follower when the two met at Lela's farm in western New York.[43] Her daughter, Hesper, says that Mab prided herself on being able to capture any man she wanted, and in this connection recalls a story told her about Paula and Lee Strasberg, one of the founders of the Group Theatre. It runs this way: Paula was much in love with Lee but he was in love with someone else. So Mab instructed the unhappy Paula in this wise: "Look, you listen to me, and I'll tell you every move to make. . . . You want Lee Strasberg? I'll tell you everything to do." Exactly what the man-baiting advice was is not recalled, but Paula used it and brought her man to the altar.[44]

In the spring of 1929 Mab went to Hollywood with her husband not long after Anderson had arrived there with his wife and children for his first stint at writing motion-picture scripts.[45] We can't be sure whether the playwright had invited her or whether Margaret was aware that her rival was in town. A photograph from this visit shows a playful Anderson in a bathing suit, cigarette in mouth, laughing as he tries to pull the fully clothed Mab along with him for what looks like a swim at the beach.[46] When he was not playing around with Mrs. Maynard he spent much of his time adapting Erich Maria Remarque's novel *All Quiet on the Western Front* for director Lewis Milestone. It was an early talking film. Anderson rented a house on the water and did his work there, not bothering to go to the studio much; nor did he watch any of the filming or go to see the completed film, which thanks to his contribution won an Academy Award.

We learn from Mab's Hotel Dorset notes (a chronology filed among the Anderson memorabilia at the University of Texas) that she broke up with her husband, Charles, in the spring of 1930 and flew to New York. Very likely the affair with Max had something to do with this breakup. According to what Gilda Anderson told me, it was in the throes of splitting with Charles that Mab made an abortive attempt at killing herself.

In that same year Anderson went to work at another studio, MGM, and wrote scripts for *Trader Horn* and *The Phantom of the Opera*, but in these two instances receiving no credit,[47] a neglect that seems not to have disheartened him where Hollywood was concerned: He cared only for the money.

Very likely to give himself some relief from the tedium of laying out a scenario that he knew some hack would doctor later on, he began writing a legitimate stage drama, *Elizabeth the Queen*, in which Mab was to have a minor role. (He usually worked on a play every time he did a stint in Hollywood.) This became his first artistically successful use of dramatic poetry intended for the professional stage. In reading it we are taken into England's most splendid age for an exciting story of the conflict between royal love and the hunger for power, laid against a background rich in atmosphere and color.

Sir Walter Raleigh, jealous of his rival the Earl of Essex, who is the Queen's lover, plots against him with the aid of the secretary of state, Sir Robert Cecil. The plotters believe that the young man is a rebel at heart and they want to lure him into accepting a military command where he will be tempted into rebellion and thus bring himself to ruin. At council they succeed in baiting him into taking command of a hopeless military expedition against Ireland. Before Essex leaves, Elizabeth, now saddened by his reckless desire to prove himself in leadership, gives him her father's ring with the explanation that she would be willing to forgive him anything at all if he should ever deliver it back to her. Essex then goes abroad. Before long, Raleigh and Cecil try to win to their side the crafty Francis Bacon, who knows but does not reveal that they have been intercepting and tampering with the mail sent by Essex and Elizabeth. Her pride hurt by her lover's failure to answer her letters, Elizabeth angrily orders him back to England. The young earl, stung to the quick by being so ordered, decides to capture London and seize the crown. Once his troops have taken the palace, he confronts the Queen, becomes reconciled with her, and together they discover the treachery that had caused their differences. It now looks as if all will go well. But the ambitious Essex decides that he cannot be satisfied unless he rules jointly with her. This the Queen cannot tolerate! By promising compliance, she inveigles him to disband his guard; and once this happens, she has him arrested for treason. Thanks to him she has learned the bitter lesson that whoever would rule a kingdom must not be hindered by considerations of mercy, friendship, and love.

During the hour just before execution, the Queen waits for her erstwhile lover to send the ring as a sign that he wants forgiveness, for the woman in her has now relented and in her anguish is willing to grant him almost anything. When the ring doesn't arrive, she orders that he be brought in. She offers him his life, but he refuses. He explains that he has learned a terrible lesson about himself, which is that he would try again for the throne if given a chance, but realizes that she would make a better ruler; he himself would only embroil the kingdom in expensive and needless wars. As he starts to go, she breaks down and cries after him to take the throne. She cannot bear living without him! But the noble Essex pretends not to hear and walks onward toward his execution, for he knows that it is better to die young and untarnished than to live long and rule unwisely. Elizabeth, frantic with grief, is left Queen of "emptiness and death."

Anderson admitted that Lytton Strachey's brilliant best seller *Elizabeth and Essex* had inspired his endeavor, but he insisted that he used neither the colorful rendering of history in Strachey nor the versions that he found in other sources.[48] But it is undeniable that Strachey's critical, ironical, iconoclastic attitude toward public leaders and institutions found in Anderson a kindred spirit. Anderson's subsequent popularity as an historical playwright—a label, however, that would have made him scoff — paralleled the vogue for historical books that was rampant in the 1930s following the achievements of Strachey and such American novelists as Hervey Allen (*Anthony Adverse*). And though Anderson began writing such plays quite early, as witness *Benvenuto,* not until the vogue began did his own career in that genre get launched.

In such plays he presented history as a cruel spectacle of opportunists infected with an ineluctable desire to rule over others; who are by the nature of their office subject to enormous temptations, overwhelming them if they stay in office long; who sacrifice their youthful ideals, if any, to keep the blind machinery of government running; who include among their benighted numbers not only emperors and kings and queens but also American congressmen; and who end up trampling under their heels the sensitive and the idealistic. Anderson would have agreed with Lord Acton's famous dictum, "Power tends to corrupt; absolute power corrupts absolutely."[49] And similarly he would have agreed with Thomas Jefferson and Henry David Thoreau, both of whom held that the less government the better because a swollen government, however benignly it begins, harbors the cancer of totalitarianism.

The several ways in which *Elizabeth the Queen* deviates unashamedly from recorded history, together with Anderson's known seriousness as an artist, suggest that he might have been using some theory worth our attention. Indeed, in some of his later English history plays[50] a kind of theory emerges. For example, in *Mary of Scotland* he has his cruel Queen Elizabeth snarl that she, and not the so-called historians, will dictate what the surviving record will be about her innocent prisoner Mary, therefore that Mary will but waste her time if she expects to be vindicated at last.[51] Being given the grim news that the ruler determines the final record, we must conclude that art—such as Anderson provides us—can be just as valid as any written history, and perhaps more so. In one of his less beastly moods Henry VIII in *Anne of the Thousand Days* declares that the artistic interpreter of events is superior to the mere chronicler; it is true that the interpreter never records exactly what happened, but because of his imaginative probing behind the scenes and into the minds of the characters, what he does write comes closer to the truth than does the so-called historical record of what happened or was spoken.[52] Moreover, we are led to believe via Anderson's unpublished *Richard and Anne* that art can be far more real and fascinating than formal history, even if the artist unintentionally employs lies that were passed on to him. The last-named play consists of a contemporary staging of Shakespeare's *Richard III* wherein ghosts of the original characters drift in and try to set straight the record that evil Henry VII had falsified in order to defame his predecessor, Richard III, who, we learn, was not actually a monster, despite what Shakespeare had told us. Shakespeare, we are informed, had inherited the lies and then, by means of a glorious imagination, made from them a version that seems satisfyingly real.[53] So, if Shakespeare took liberties, what is to stop Max Anderson?

But the English actress who was to star in *Elizabeth the Queen* objected to these very liberties. This was Lynn Fontanne, wife of actor Alfred Lunt, who was cast as Essex. The Lunts comprised a distinguished man-and-wife team, and the Theatre Guild had taken an option on the play as a vehicle for this pair and had hired Philip Moeller to do the directing. Luckily for all concerned, Lunt insisted that he and his wife overlook the so-called inaccuracies because the script was otherwise so virile and well constructed; and, besides, Anderson had promised he would rewrite some scenes and create some new ones before rehearsals started.

For the benefit of those not familiar with the inner workings of Broadway production, everyone expects the writer of any new play to do considerable revision during rehearsals and out-of-town (New York being "town") tryouts. Unlike in Hollywood, no one can tamper with the script without the writer's permission, but he is obligated to stand by and write on demand. As it turned out in *Elizabeth the Queen,* however, the real changes Miss Fontanne had in mind had much less to do with historical accuracy than with getting more scenes written to show tender love as well as conflict between the royal lovers, the point being to emphasize the Lunts' favorite kind of story, the witty war between the sexes.

It is not recorded how far Anderson went along with these demands. He was known for being obstinate about compromising what he called the "dream" or "conviction" that was central in whatever he wrote, but he was willing to bend a little in minor matters.[54]

As rehearsals drew near, Anderson did not supply the new dialogue promised—not that he refused—nor did he lift a pen after rehearsals started; the fact is, he happened to be in one of those creative dry spells common at times to all who follow the Muses. This situation naturally left Moeller and Fontanne irritated. Another irritant was Anderson's decision to put Mab into the cast as one of the Queen's ladies-in-waiting; he had earlier arranged a walk-on part for her, but presumably she lifted her melting violet eyes to him and asked for something better—and of course got it.[55] The other two ladies-in-waiting were Phoebe Brand, who would one day marry the actor slated for Francis Bacon, Morris Carnovsky; and also Edla Frankau, daughter of set designer Aline Bernstein (Thomas Wolfe's mistress). Mab and Edla had been so hot to get into just any Broadway show that they accepted as salary a mere pittance; they did not need the money, unlike poor Phoebe.

In the aftermath of the stock market crash in the fall of '29, the Great Depression meant a hand-to-mouth existence for the millions thrown out of work, the few jobs available had many takers, and salaries sank painfully low. But Edla could look to the rich Bernsteins for money. And Mab to Anderson. Ever since Mab had separated from her husband for good in the spring of 1930,[56] Anderson apparently had become her primary means of support even though they did not live together. Phoebe, with a diminished wardrobe and little to live on, took it upon herself to make her two pampered companions realize that their willingness to work for practically nothing had the effect of lowering the salary figure offered to her. But once she had made this clarification, the three of them became friends and often met with Anderson and Carnovsky after the show to play word games and gamble a bit at poker—they noticed that Mab had a passion for this.[57]

The first rehearsal brought big trouble. There on the stage stood Lynn Fontanne, in real life just as vain and used to having her way as was the Queen she was enacting; but possessed of unquestioned technical skill, personality that commanded attention from an audience, years of experience behind her on the London and New York stages, competence at handling sophisticated roles, and a generous measure of matronly good looks.[58] She was an apt choice to re-create the imperious Tudor Queen. Up to her walked a tiny woman who was obviously inexperienced, seemingly but a girl, and pretty enough to arouse a twinge of envy in the fortyish Lynn Fontanne. The lady-in-waiting respectfully approached the Queen, curtsied, and prepared to utter her first line, "Your Majesty."

The harsh voice grated on Miss Fontanne's cultivated ear like a fingernail drawn sharply across a blackboard. Somebody—probably the prima donna herself—then had a tête-à-tête with director Moeller, and he in turn got up the courage to face Anderson to say that he considered it insulting to the famous Lunts to allow such a complete amateur, devoid of acting experience and unable to speak English decently, to occupy the same stage with them! How Anderson took this is not recorded. Nevertheless, he did insist that Mab stay on. And as if to underscore his point he stalked through the stage doorway, and it was three days before the production staff saw his bristling moustache again.

Miss Fontanne noted as the play went along that he was conducting an open affair with her lady-in-waiting, with the "young girl" Mab Anthony (Mab's current stage handle), an affair so indiscreet that Mrs. Anderson could easily have known all about it and probably did. Accordingly, Miss Fontanne began to look at him with a decidedly jaundiced eye.[59] It was not his infidelity as such that bothered her but his going about it with what she considered a lack of subtlety and sophistication. Evidently she might have approved even of his bedding down with all her ladies-in-waiting—and Penelope Gray thrown in for good measure—just as long as he had been properly discreet. But discreet was not Anderson's way.

In the meantime, the Guild was growing more and more anxious as the New York opening approached, and Anderson still had not come up with any of the needed revisions.

When Elizabeth the Queen made its out-of-town debut, in Philadelphia, the reviews were disastrous. The new writing was needed urgently, but every morning that he was asked for it Anderson replied that he just didn't feel like writing. Finally the Guild producers, Lawrence Langner and Theresa Helburn, decided to close the show so they could cut their losses. But when the Lunts offered to buy it from the Guild and do it themselves, the Guild changed its mind and decided to give Anderson another try: They put off the New York opening and arranged a long tour during which they hoped to make all the required changes, and the first stop would be Baltimore.

The weather in Baltimore brought such a heavy rainstorm that it drenched staff and actors as they went back and forth to Ford Theatre. Anderson holed up in his room at the Belvedere Hotel while the torrents of rain poured down. On the Tuesday morning following the Baltimore opening, Langner met him in his hotel foyer and asked what had by now become a bitter litany, whether he had anything ready that day. To Langner's surprise

Anderson handed him sheet after sheet of what turned out to be a completely revised play, including the new parts.

"When did all this writing occur?" Langner asked.

"Well, Lawrence," replied Max with an enigmatic smile, "I really only
write well when it rains."[60]

Thus he discovered one of Anderson's strangest secrets. If it had been only
a matter of accepting Langner's word, we might have reason to doubt such a
singular explanation. Lynn Fontanne, exaggerating a bit, added that he could
write *only* when it rained;[61] and Theresa Helburn even tells us that whenever
the Guild was producing one of Anderson's plays—they did *Mary of Scotland, Both Your Houses, Valley Forge,* and *The Masque of Kings*—she and
her group used to pray for rain so that Anderson would stay home and get his
writing done for them.[62] Moreover, Alan informs us that his father "liked
nothing better than to be at his desk when he could hear rain falling on the
roof. He drove everyone else mad because he insisted that his favorite
weather was RAIN! And he meant it."[63] Of course, Anderson worked in other
kinds of weather, but water in its varied forms—as lakes, rivers, waterfalls,
oceans, fog, and liquid or frozen rain—seemed to fertilize his imagination as
nothing else could. Water occurs within his plays too: *Mary of Scotland,
Winterset,* and *High Tor* all contain sleet or rain; furthermore, not only do
these same dramas use at least one setting that adjoins a large mass of water,
but so do *Sea-Wife, The Wingless Victory, Key Largo, The Miracle of the
Danube, The Eve of St. Mark,* and *Storm Operation.*

Getting back to the tour of *Elizabeth the Queen,* it rained in Pittsburgh, it
rained in Cincinnati, and it rained in St. Louis; and all the while Anderson
worked furiously at strengthening the script; and as improvements occurred,
reviewers grew kinder. At last, on November 3, 1930, the play opened in
New York at the Guild Theatre.

If Anderson behaved on opening night in the typical manner described to
me by Alan and Lela, he sat or stood around in the back of the theater, maybe
pacing back and forth like a caged bear, trying to keep out of sight so that no
one up front would be tempted to call "author!" at the end of the performance and have him come up for a bow. He was just plain shy. He wouldn't
mingle with the crowd in the lobby during intermission, where he might be
recognized and slapped on the back and asked to autograph a program.
There would be no use trying to make an appointment with him to go out
later for a night on the town, for he would have his heart set on fleeing the
bright lights of the city just as soon as the show ended and retreating to
Rockland County until the next theater business compelled him to return.

It was unfortunate that Lee Simonson had created such dull and drab sets for *Elizabeth the Queen,* for they fell short of conveying the splendor, the extravagance, the magnificence that one expects of Elizabethan style, but the powerful story coupled with the superb acting of the Lunts made up for this deficiency. Sets and costumes together had cost only $13,525.[64] But the Guild had a hit. There were seventeen curtain calls. Stark Young in his review in the *New Republic* had some reservations, but when it came to assessing the portrayal of Elizabeth he was ecstatic.[65] Alexander Woollcott and Wolcott Gibbs and John Hutchins also wrote about it favorably. Though most people came to see Miss Fontanne's makeup for this role of roles—she in a crimson wig, high forehead, shaved eyebrows, built-up aquiline nose, and folds of flesh made to simulate the aged monarch as represented in seventeenth-century prints—the script easily surpassed anything that Anderson had done thus far.

This was the first and perhaps the best of the Tudor dramas, one that is frequently reprinted in anthologies. Unfortunately, some later commentators have devoted too much attention to his so-called "imitativeness" of style— the use of a witty fool, court repartee, puns, a very loose blank verse mixed with prose. Unfair though it is, some went on to imply that other plays of his are similarly indebted to the Bard, as if to write any form of blank-verse history play was ipso facto Shakespearean. No one would question, however, that *Elizabeth the Queen* marked a brilliant opening for his golden decade of the 1930s, when no longer would Broadway speak so much of what O'Neill was doing, for O'Neill was in limbo, but wonder at this remarkable new talent that was daring to bring back poetry to the theater.

When the old Greek gods made a present to some mortal, it was to be feared that they might take away something crucial at the same time; and so it was in the late winter of 1930-31, in this season of artistic and commercial triumph, that Anderson suffered a blow that left him desolate. He was at the time living, at least during winters, in the West 112th Street house that he had bought about four years earlier, after moving from the apartment on 12th Street. One day he and Margaret got into such a fight with each other that they were shouting on the stairs, while 12-year-old Alan lay sick with the flu on the third floor and heard them. Though Alan didn't understand what the noise was all about, it made him unhappy to know that the grown-ups were quarreling. Gee! That's *angry!* was his thought at this first—and last— flare-up he was ever to overhear between his parents.[66] Most likely Mab's name came up, but so could have the names of several other attractive young women, such as actress Laurette Taylor, whom the playwright was not long afterward known to be dating.[67] Maybe he had irritated Margaret by declaring for the nth time that he would have no part of some invitation that she had accepted for them. More likely, he had irritated her by saying that he was going to leave for Nova Scotia to get materials for a new play he had in mind. Leave again! . . . so soon after the long road tour with *Elizabeth the Queen!* Was this new trip merely an excuse to be with Mrs. Maynard? We don't know, but he did go to Nova Scotia.[68]

After he left for the trip northward the terrible fate that Margaret had prophesied for herself came to pass. With one of her women friends she was driving her car along Riverside Drive when, suddenly, she collapsed over the steering wheel and lost control of the car. It was headed for a crash. Accounts differ a little over what happened next, but it seems that a motorist whose name was Eddie saw the car about to veer off the road, and he had the presence of mind to drive his own car in front of the other one to stop it.[69] Stop it he did, and when Anderson learned about this act of heroism, he showed his gratitude by giving Eddie a job as his chauffeur.[70]

The unconscious Margaret was taken immediately to a hospital. The next day, *The New York Times* carried a notice of her death by stroke.[71] Hesper tells a sentimental story, handed on to her by her mother, Mab, that while Margaret was dying she extracted a promise from a now repentant Anderson that he would for her sake never marry Mab.[72] One is reminded of what King George II of England is said to have promised his dying wife after she had begged him to remarry once she was gone: *"Non—j'aurai—des maîtresses"* (No—I shall have—mistresses), to which the Queen responded: *"Ah, mon Dieu! Cela n'empêche pas"* (Oh, my God! That doesn't make any difference).[73] No doubt Hesper's story, if true, would explain her father's subsequent conduct, but what actually did happen? There is certainly nothing in the surviving papers to back up this romantic tale; the oral account from Lawrence places Anderson completely out of town when the death occurred; and both Lela and Kenneth tell us that no deathbed scene could possibly have taken place for the simple reason that Margaret was pronounced dead upon arrival at the hospital. The end came almost instantaneously.[74]

The dreadful news reached Anderson quickly and he hurried back to New York. Somehow the children had not been told of the catastrophe; it remained for him to tell them. Alan recalls that his father climbed the stairs to his room where he was still sick with the flu and told him in a voice choked with grief the simple statement, "She's gone." As quickly as he understood, Alan burst into tears, and then the father, seeing his son cry, cried also. It must have been shortly afterward, when the family gathered together in the house to take stock of their loss, that Terence, nine at the time, walked over to his father and looked up at him and said in a pitiful voice, "We are not ever going to have any fun, are we—anymore?"[75]

One thing that Anderson was almost feverish to learn from the autopsy was whether he himself—through his infidelity, or more directly through the emotional upheaval in which he had left her—had been the cause of her death. He just *had* to learn! Maybe she had taken poison or too much liquor or an overdose of drugs. His future daughter-in-law Meg (Margaret Elizabeth Pickett) was gathered with a lot of other people in his upstairs study on 112th Street when he finally got the telephone call about the autopsy, and after he was through on the telephone he went over to Meg and said to her with enormous relief in his voice that Margaret had died of a strictly natural cause.[76]

Yet he could not be certain that his actions had not contributed in some degree to her strange and sudden demise; therefore, a measure of guilt lingered to torture him for the remainder of his days. Darkness surrounds some questions in his life, but most informants concur on this matter of long-felt guilt. "I should never have done it to her," he told his last wife, Gilda, many years later.

In his old age he was to write a poem about his long-lost Margaret, a poem filled with tender sorrow:

The children were hard to care for
Through the long days
Did you know then
That I would weep now?
. . . .
You were angry once
You wept in the night
Once you said
If it does not end soon
It will all end
Between you and me.[77]

A sculptor friend prepared a death mask of Margaret, and the body was cremated. The ashes were put into an urn inside a little walnut box that Anderson was to keep for several years in his attic study in the old farmhouse, and after that in a closet in the New House next door, and finally in his cabin in the woods.[78]

One of the saddest of all chores was to pack up his wife's clothes to send them off to her mother, who was herself physically incapacitated from three strokes. He enclosed besides many beautiful imported dresses some pairs of fashionable and expensive shoes, some of them brand new, but designed for such an exquisitely tiny foot that no one among the Hasketts could be found to wear them.[79] So grieved did Anderson become that in a letter to his brother-in-law James E. Haskett he wrote that he doubted he would ever compose another play.[80] Indeed, the creative slump lasted well into the fall of 1931, when he began *Night over Taos* after reading Harvey Fergusson's series of six articles on the Rio Grande Valley published in *American Mercury*.[81] Even by the tenth anniversary of her death he was still sorrowful, as he wrote again to James: ". . . I guess there'll never be anybody quite like Margaret, the longer I live the more I miss her."[82]

The feeling of remorse his children talk about was real enough but, human nature being the sometimes inconsistent thing it is, Anderson continued to see Mab. By now he must have begun to feel that any self-imposed renunciation of their love—had he ever entertained the idea of renunciation, which is most doubtful—might sound noble to a Victorian ear but would in his case be unrealistic and unnatural because he was deeply attached to her by now and felt that he needed her all the more in his grief and loneliness. Kenneth tells us that his famous brother, despite the somber appearance in published photographs and an Olympian reserve in handling newsmen, was deeply human: "Max always needed someone to love—and who loved him *without reservation*" (italics mine).[83] During this same troubled period Anderson dated at least two other actresses, but Mab remained the center of his interest.[84]

The summer of 1931 saw him and Mab together at Brookfield Center, the Group Theatre's workshop about five miles from Danbury, Connecticut. The Group Theatre, which had evolved from the Theatre Guild largely under the inspiration and leadership of Harold Clurman, reflected the unrest of the times (the Depression had thrown many theater people out of work) and a desire for higher artistic ideals such as one could find in a repertory company. During its ten-year history, actors in the Group Theatre would include Elia Kazan, Clifford Odets (better known as a playwright), Franchot Tone, J. Edward Bromberg, Morris Carnovsky, and Stella Adler. In addition to Clurman, the directors would include Cheryl Crawford and Lee Strasberg.

Phoebe Brand and Morris Carnovsky first persuaded Anderson to visit this organization; and then when Mab somehow got a bit part in their forthcoming production of Paul Green's *The House of Connelly*,[85] he rented a house nearby so he could spend part of the summer with them attending rehearsals and conducting friendly arguments with Clurman about current drama. No doubt it was largely at Mab's suggestion or as a means of pleasing her that he threw parties for them at his house. She herself always had that innocent delight in parties that a duck shows when set loose in a mill pond. But Anderson was happy just in being able to make other people happy; he also enjoyed the buoyancy and youth of these earnest people who were doing something hitherto quite rare in the story of the American theater, which was to start an ensemble group devoted to using definite principles in its training. In addition, he was attracted to Brookfield Center because the actors and directors of the Group Theatre produced their own plays, a practice unheard of since the businessman had invaded the theater and taken over that function.

During this summer Clurman asked him to help finance their operations; he got in response at least $1,700.[86] Very early next year the two worked out an arrangement for producing *Night over Taos*—and, of course, Mab would have a role in it as Conchita. Anderson pared his script down to the bone to please the production staff, but this latest experiment of his in versification failed almost as miserably on the stage as did the first one, *White Desert*.[87] The failure was partly due to a bad production. Still, he does not seem to have suffered emotionally from this setback. His usual practice was to lay the failed work aside quickly and not attempt another production of it, for he felt that the really worthwhile plays had to have an immediate success on the stage in order to gain assurance of survival: He wrote that in the history of the theater no playwright ever left behind a quantity of unappreciated material that gradually acquired recognition; poets and novelists have done so, but not playwrights.[88] It was the first time or never.

THE GOLDEN YEARS

A good example of Anderson's theme of the corruption of power is his satirical play *Both Your Houses,* one of his many outstanding contributions to the theater during the 1930s. This play was intended to be a blast at the Hoover administration, according to what he wrote to his lawyer Samuel J. Silverman (see *Letters,* p. 239), but the producer, Jed Harris, kept the play for so long that when it finally reached the boards of the Royale Theatre on March 6, 1933, President Franklin Roosevelt was already in office and the topicality was almost lost.

Freshman Congressman Alan McClean, whose surname aptly suggests his sterling character, becomes angry at learning about an omnibus House appropriation bill that is freighted with graft and "pork barrel." He sets about trying to kill the legislation in committee. His colleagues, however, are so routinely dishonest that they are surprised he would raise any objections. The rather likable old rascal Sol Fitzmaurice, who is the most completely realized figure in the play, has tagged onto the bill a provision that will anchor the Atlantic Fleet off his private resort area! McClean decides to outwit the charlatans at their own game: He loads onto the bill such flagrantly extravagant riders that, he hopes, it will surely fail when it reaches a vote in Congress. But the legislators are so lost to conscience and reason that it passes anyway. As the play ends, McClean leaves office determined to broadcast the truth about political crookedness in the government. We are left with the conclusion that any meaningful reform is almost hopeless; the temptation to power and money is too firmly entrenched in the very nature of government.

Theater attendance sagged so much that the show was in danger of closing rather soon. But to the rescue came the Pulitzer Prize committee and recognized with its accolade for the 1932-33 season that *Both Your Houses,* depite its gloomy assessment of Congress, represented a valuable piece of dramatic literature. Whereupon the play went on to ring up 120 performances, but clearly not enough to bring the author any big money.

On the other hand, movie script writing paid well indeed. For Anderson it was a swift albeit painful way to subsidize his efforts at legitimate drama. And so, in the spring of 1933 he and Mab were in Santa Barbara, California; this time he would write scenarios for *Death Takes a Holiday* and *We Live Again* (based on Tolstoy's novel *Resurrection*).[1] But Mab must have returned East for an acting job almost immediately. During the evenings, after boring sessions of scenario writing were done, he worked on his new play *Mary of Scotland.* He may well have designed the role of Mary for Helen Hayes, who makes that claim; it was she who first enacted the role; but as the shortest actress on the American stage she felt oddly chosen to portray one of the tallest queens in history—that is, until Anderson reassured her by saying that she would not be playing history's Queen at all but *his* Queen.[2] He must have considered that Miss Hayes' small size would make her seem all the more like a victim, more sympathetic in the eyes of the audience, in that gripping last scene in prison where she at last confronts the evil, and of course taller, Elizabeth (Helen Mencken).

Mary of Scotland is of special interest because it was here that Anderson for the first time made full use of the theory of tragedy that he was to set forth in published essays years later.[3] In this connection the critic Allan Halline reasons plausibly that Anderson was like most playwrights in creating the work first and then theorizing later about what he had done.[4] Perhaps the reader will agree that this is a good time in which to study this theory in some detail, especially since most of the plays from 1933 onward make some attempt to apply it. In examining the successful plays dating from antiquity onward, Anderson formulated from them a list of rules for serious drama, including tragedy, which the artist has to follow if he is to obtain more than accidental success on the stage. These are the rules:

1. The play concerns the mind or heart of a person, not mainly external events.

2. The story is about a conflict between the forces of good and evil inside a single human being. The audience from age to age will define what good and evil mean.

3. The protagonist, who represents the good forces, must win; if he represents evil, he must yield to the good forces and acknowledge defeat.

4. The play's protagonist cannot be perfect, else he cannot improve; and he must emerge at the close of the play as more admirable than at the start.

5. The protagonist must be exceptional; or, if he is a man in the street, he must epitomize qualities of excellence that the audience can admire.

6. Excellence on the stage must always be moral excellence. The hero's struggle to improve his material circumstances does not make interesting drama unless his character goes through a trial and comes out better than before.

7. A healthy moral atmosphere is essential. The audience will not permit evil to triumph on the stage.

8. The theater audience likes these human qualities on the stage: man's positive character and strength of conviction, woman's fidelity and passionate faith. The audience especially dislikes these qualities: man's cowardice and refusal to fight for a belief; woman's infidelity.

Partly as the result of such discoveries, Max Anderson concluded that the theater's purpose is to locate, and hold up for our view, those qualities in the human race that are admirable; moreover—and here is the most astonishing idea of all—that "the theater is a religious institution devoted entirely to the exaltation of the spirit of man. . . . It is a church without a creed, but there is no doubt in my mind that our theater, instead of being, as the evangelical ministers used to believe, the gateway to hell, is as much a worship as the theater of the Greeks, and has exactly the same meaning in our lives." As evidence, he stated, "The plays that please most and run longest in these dusty alleys are representative of human loyalty, courage, love that purges the soul, grief that ennobles." In short, the theater is the cathedral of the spirit, "the central artistic symbol of the struggle of good and evil within men."[5]

His friend Hill summarized the foregoing when he opined that "Max actually developed a philosophy out of what he thought the public wanted, and then within that he brought in his pessimistic philosophy to condemn the things he didn't like, so that you had a combination." He goes on to add:

"I remember that we were going home one time on the train. This was rather early in his career. He said, 'Frank, people like quarrels. They like a fight on the stage.' He was thinking aloud of what audiences liked. By and by he rationalized this and got it down to the point where he accepted, more or less, a philosophy which was accepted by the public, and then gave it a little edge from his own bitterness, and that was what he came up with in the end. Which always seemed to me to be a very interesting phenomenon. I always thought that if Max had happened to have a bit more of a positive philosophy of his own, he could have worked out something that would have given more size to what he had to say; that he had the resources for saying anything. It was terrific. There was simply no limit, almost, you might say, to what he could have done. He did quite well, of course. Still, his philosophy was, more or less, his limitation."[6]

We should note as well that this traditionalist among the playwrights reread Aristotle's *Poetics* and came up with some more intriguing conclusions, albeit of a nonreligious and nonphilosophical nature. He discovered that the recognition scene described there—though commonly an artificial device; for example, the penetration of a hidden identity or disguise—was a technique that the old Greeks had used most convincingly in some of their greatest plays. He found, furthermore, that the device occurs in a subtler form in the plays of Shakespeare and the moderns. By such pragmatic means Anderson arrived *at his own* version of the recognition scene. As he understood it, the protagonist in a modern drama almost invariably discovers, usually near the end of Act II in a three-act play or near the end of Act III in a five-act play, something in himself or in his environment about which he had been ignorant or had imperfectly understood. In the play the hero will make such a discovery and it will in consequence deeply affect his thought and emotions and radically alter his conduct.[7] Incidentally, Anderson is the only American playwright to date, other than Arthur Miller,[8] who has furnished us with a systematic theory of tragedy. Anderson had applied some of this theory in *Elizabeth the Queen* but never fully developed it until *Mary of Scotland* came along; and while it is true that his greatest works usually employ it, their success is mainly due to the complexity of characterizations and to the imaginative poetry that is sometimes lyric and sometimes meditative.

Sometime during the summer of 1933 Mab got a divorce from Maynard. While her lover was winding up his work in California, she spent her days at Green Mansions, the Group Theatre's workshop in Warrensburg, New York, rehearsing for a role in Sidney Kingsley's *Men in White*. They had cast her as a sick girl covered with bandages and a white sheet on a hospital bed, attended by a nurse (Phoebe Brand).[9] None could fault Mab on her voice *this* time, because she did not have a single line to speak.

That fall, Anderson's *Mary of Scotland* proved to be a critical and popular success at the Alvin Theatre, where it was to run for 248 performances. During that season Kingsley's *Men in White* was established as a hit, too. The Mab who appeared nightly on the stage as a sick girl had a real medical problem: She was pregnant.[10] At this time she was living on Riverside Drive. Mrs. Julie Sloane (widow of publisher William Sloane), who became Mab's neighbor years later in New City, told me that she, Mrs. Sloane, used to go to an apartment building on Riverside Drive to visit a friend; one day she looked out of the friend's window and saw an expensive, shiny yellow car parked outside. When she asked about it she was told that it belonged to the famous Maxwell Anderson, who came to visit a tenant in the building, a drama student named Mab.

The extant letters he had written to Mab and to Lela during the months when he was on the West Coast do not speak of an impending engagement or wedding; the words "husband" and "wife" are not used even fancifully. The letter he wrote to her in late July, just days or a week or two away from his return East and from a wedding he was to claim, shows that the love relationship is fairly settled, unstirred by any new and momentous change in his life such as a marriage would represent. In the letter one would expect him to mention at least briefly the plans for a wedding, but he does not. Of course, his letters are not characteristically emotional anyway, except when he is keelhauling a critic who has been audacious enough to attack one of his plays. The tone here is that of the long-time lover or husband who feels secure in his relationship and therefore has no need to prove anything to the woman who is already his.[11]

His younger brother Lawrence, twenty at the time, was a guest in the 112th Street brownstone during August when Mab and Max took off down the coast together; and when they returned, Mab flushed with happiness like a new bride, Max told him that they had been married and taken their honeymoon on an island in Chesapeake Bay. Lawrence got the idea that the marriage was performed by a justice of the peace in Delaware or Maryland (most of the islands in Chesapeake Bay are in Maryland).[12] And there is hardly any question that Max actually did stay on such an island at the time represented. The first that Lela heard of the union was at a family gathering in the fall during which Max arrived and announced that he was a husband and told them the name of his wife.[13] None of his relatives, not even his own children, had been forewarned of or witnessed the ceremony.[14]

In the course of years family rumors circulated that no legal wedding had occurred. Quentin and Terence were both sure—but could not prove—that their lovely new stepmother, who presumed to replace their Margaret, lived among them under questionable circumstances.[15]

One theory of a few female members of the family is that Anderson could not bring himself to marry Mab because in his subconscious mind he considered her a whore for having slept with him; therefore, he would defile Margaret's memory if he went through with a ceremony. The theory is analogous to the one about the deathbed promise to Margaret and is scarcely more plausible.[16]

Kenneth strongly suspected that his brother had not gone through a legal wedding ceremony. Kenneth concluded that since Max was familiar with the medieval Scottish conjugal rite known as "hand fast," which dispensed with legal and churchly forms and consisted of simply an exchange of vows with a mutual declaration that the couple are man and wife, he might have chosen to go that route. Bizarre as it sounds, this is the most likely explanation of what happened on that island in Chesapeake Bay or wherever it was that they made their momentous decision, because there certainly is no evidence that they applied for or received a marriage license. Even their daughter, Hesper, feels certain that the parents never wed in the legal sense of that word.[17] Such a union was not unusual in New York artistic circles then.

Long years after the supposed event, Max's third wife, Gilda, asked him why there had been no wedding. "The gist of his answer," the last Mrs. Maxwell Anderson recalls, "was that everyone thought them married and a wedding would have announced to the world that they were not . . . perhaps Hesper had come along by then" (ellipsis Gilda's).[18]

Nevertheless, one is entitled to try to find some cogent reason why the couple had not made their union legal *before* people had gotten used to considering them joined in holy wedlock, and the answer surely lies in his rebellious spirit *at that particular time,* in his attitude toward certain human institutions. When he had married Margaret, he was not as advanced in that rebellion; and by the time he married his third wife, he must have had reason to regret those years of unblessed conjugality and felt it necessary to prove to the new woman that he genuinely loved her, wanted to spend the rest of his life with her, and was not just having a post-Mab affair.[19]

Returning to his arrangement with Mab, it seems likely that he timed the announcement of his "marriage" as a cover for her pregnancy. One other pressing reason for acting fast was that he had arranged to move the Reverend and Mrs. Lincoln Anderson into the Hope House down the road from him in New City in order to get medical attention for his mother. The latter had been in poor health as the result of several strokes, her troubles having begun some years earlier at a party where a guest unwittingly mixed into the salad some poisonous herbs intended for a poultice; Mrs. Anderson ate some and grew deathly ill, and her health was never good after that incident.[20]

But it is important to note that, however unconventional, whether there was an old-fashioned Scottish rite or not, it was to him a most serious match, subject to all the loyalties and responsibilities known to couples who are legally married. He had in mind no short-term affair or anything savoring of an affair. No "open marriage," either, such as Elmer Rice had.[21] The fact that Mab wore a wedding ring[22] indicates that she took her new status of Mrs. Maxwell Anderson equally seriously.

Soon after the couple left their winter quarters in the 112th Street brownstone came the building of a new house for them next door to and somewhat to the rear of the old farmhouse. The latter was still not suitable for year-round living, and the plan called for Anderson to give up the city brownstone and move out into the country permanently. He bribed his eldest son, Quentin, with the offer of the old farmhouse, which could be renovated, on condition that Quentin marry his girlfriend, Meg, and settle there with her and take care of his younger brothers, Alan and Terence.

Quentin agreed.[23] Already it was quite evident that Mab was not going to be much of a mother to her stepchildren; perhaps she considered it a lost cause, there being no love one way or another; but Anderson loved them all and obviously found it convenient to keep the children close by in order to check on them from time to time. Mab got along well, however, with her husband's brother Lawrence, then living in the Hope House down the road: Lawrence was close to her in age and idolized his playwright brother as a father figure. Doubtless she was all the more grateful to Lawrence now that Terence and Quentin would not accept her.[24]

Anderson's original idea was to have his friend Henry Varnum Poor construct for them a simple English cottage with rushes on the floor, and this was what actually went up—at first, but minus the rushes.[25] Hardly had they moved in when this dream of modest, rustic retirement evanesced; Mab's advanced pregnancy was the reason, and besides, her life-style found the cottage too crowded. She wanted ample room for entertaining. And so they called in Poor again with his crew of friends and neighbors, some of them skilled artisans, and no doubt all of them grateful to get work in those Depression years, and the result was a large house that consisted of at least ten rooms and four baths plus an adjoining garage apartment. In its heyday when freshly painted, the furniture and tapestries bright and clean, and the grounds meticulously landscaped, the place must have been far more attractive than it is today in its slightly run-down condition, with paint peeling off the ceiling. Anderson was delighted with it. But undeniably there is a certain gallimaufry about the architecture because the new house had developed in two distinct phases that never completely harmonized: First had come the small, two story cottage previously mentioned. Then an anteroom was attached to join up with the three-story addition that quite dwarfed the original. For the outside walls Poor had imported cinder block from Ohio, waterproofed it, and painted it a ghostly white.[26] On the outside the house is unimpressive, but on the inside it reveals merit in the form of careful, meticulous, and sometimes inspired design, as where the workmen had put bookshelves and radiators into recesses within the walls and installed large windows and glass patio doors that make the occupant feel a part of the wooded landscape.

Soon after the enlarged house was finished, a writer from the magazine *House Beautiful* wrote an article about how functional and "modern" and "honest" and "straightforward" the design was—rather lukewarm praise— and how the New House got along well enough without trim and molding, how the huge fireplace with its tall copper hood threw heat out into the room, how the tightly wound spiral staircase saved space. The writer reported that Guilbert Rose had designed and woven the fabrics used in the draperies, that Maurice Heaton had molded much of the glass, that Carroll French had made the furniture, and that three other neighbors had done all the paintings.[27] Poor's decorative handmade tiles adorned windowsills and the two fireplaces. Huge beechwood logs hauled in from the neighboring woods and scraped clean now buttressed the downstairs ceilings. Floors throughout were made of solid oak pegged down; on the upper stories they were covered with cork. In its size and originality and workmanship the house reflected something of the tenant Anderson, whereas in the evolution from simple cottage to baronial residence it reflected the change that Mab with her society ambitions and luxurious demands was bringing into his life. In a letter to me, Lawrence Anderson recalled only fond memories of the house:

> It was a home with lots of room for family and friends, pleasant dinners by the fire, occasional parties with a few close friends, and much writing, writing, writing. . . . It was a lovely place away from the world, deep in the woods, surrounded by carefully tended gardens.

And the brother added with a touch of fancy: "From the windows could be seen the bright flash of the beacon on top of High Tor, and in storms the little, lost Dutchmen could be heard playing at their game of bowls" (from his September 15, 1978, letter).

In August, after the cottage stage of the house was finished, Mab gave birth to a blonde-haired, blue-eyed girl. Anderson named her Hesper, after the Evening Star, because he thought this first daughter of his would also be his last child.[28] His pride changed to sorrow a week later when his mother, Premma, died following a long illness in which he had spent a small fortune trying to find a cure for her.

With cancer eating away at his vitals, and with only eighteen months to live, Lincoln Anderson took a new wife and moved to Lakeland, Florida. He left behind in Max Anderson's care Max's youngest brother, Lawrence.

By the flagstones at the entrance of the old farmhouse today the visitor can spy some tiny blue flowers that are descendants of those that Margaret had kneeled among and tended with loving fingers many seasons ago. Elsewhere in the yard are three yellow rose bushes that Mrs. Alan Anderson, resident there now, had rescued from the thousands that once tossed their gorgeous heads in Mab's formal gardens next door.[29] The roses are bright, scented remembrances of still another vanished household, still another tale of love, dreams come true, domestic quarrels, sexual passion gone astray, sorrow, and early death.

Like his other wives, Mab took delight in gardening, but thanks partly to the means at her disposal and partly to a deep hunger for beautiful things, she outdid the other two in the planning, the expense, the varieties, and the sheer lavishness of floral display. It was as if she had to compete with the finest that her society friends had to offer. Perhaps owing to her upbringing with her neurotic mother, and her years in the orphanage—unloved and unloving—she could devote to flowers that reserve of tender affection she found it hard to bestow on people.[30] And almost any gardener knows that plants are marvelously manageable and responsive and rewarding in ways that people, including stubborn playwrights and temperamental daughters, never are.

Soon after the cottage or its enlargement was complete, Mab ordered in bulldozers to push back the woods, always her enemy in green, and strip away the upper layer of rocky soil for a set of glorious gardens that would do credit to her new elevation as Mrs. Maxwell Anderson. There were to be separate formal gardens for roses, for other perennials, and for annuals. She would have a rock garden carefully spaced by stone pathways and borders, a brook to purl through it, and over the brook a little bridge shaded by a Japanese cherry tree. Anderson was no gardener, but he always enjoyed flowers, enjoyed pleasing her even more, and gave her *carte blanche* to spend what she liked. To her, then, it was damn the cost! Better by far than having him simply throw that money away on his drove of relations or dole it out in loans forgotten and irrecoverable. Consequently, in that era of vast unemployment and bread lines and depressed wages, she must have had a clear conscience when she ordered in thousands of dollars' worth of rich topsoil to lay over the bedrock.[31]

For the object of her special attention, the rose garden, she had workmen set out beds of many different hybrid teas chosen for their massed color effect and ravishing scents and approved tulip form; she even had a greenhouse built to extend the floral season, with the result that she had flowers to fill all the household vases to overflowing the year round. It was common on early spring days to see this tiny woman, clenching a gold cigarette holder between her teeth while smoke wreathed upward among her curls, working energetically up to her elbows in the dark, moist earth as she placed bone meal for the roots of some prize-winning floribunda just arrived. Of course, she had to have a full-time gardener to prune and to set out the new stock and to apply the doses of manure water; also to help her—for she rarely stood idly by watching—tear out the pestilential weeds and drown the gnawing Japanese beetles in jars of kerosene. But for the weekly spraying so essential to producing showplace blooms Mab called in one of the nation's leading experts on rose culture, Sylvia Westcott. Nothing but the best for Mab's roses.

"The rock garden is beautiful," Max's secretary wrote to Mab when she was away once some years later, "[the] primroses and poetica and the new ferns and mint down by the water are lovely. The tulips are just coming into full bloom. . . ."[32] Elsewhere stood shrubs of daphne. At various times one could find beds of poppies bearing all the tints of the rainbow, peonies colorful enough to rival the splendor of Joseph's coat, tall spikes of gladioli, shy violets hiding their purple among the low green foliage, showy irises with sword-shaped leaves, blue delphiniums, narcissus bearing among the petals their tiny cups; along with fragrant hyacinths, stocks, and scabious, asters and snapdragons, nasturtiums and zinnias, petunias and begonias, anemones and phlox. Here and there sweet peas clambered up a trellis.

But after one of her many arguments with her husband, or after some other frustrating domestic experience, it was sad to hear the little gardener remark sometimes, she who had spells of melancholy verging on suicide, this Persephone among her asphodels: "Life isn't worth living."[33]

Year after year the planting continued, one generation of flora giving way to another as taste or whim changed. During World War II a vegetable garden—then known as a "victory garden"—lay to the right of the front driveway. At one time there were grapes and strawberries, maybe as a concession to her husband, who made periodic gestures toward self-sufficiency that even led him to use a horse and buggy for shopping at the village store.[34] He was probably responsible for their ordering in enough young fruit tree stock to give them a small orchard—at least two varieties each of apples, pears, peaches, plums, cherries, quince, plus a mulberry. For help in taking care of all these trees they called upon Bartlett's, a professional firm.

There were happy days when the Group Theatre people came out into the country for weekends of partying and swimming. Mab relished these times, whereas her husband, a retiring soul, looked on with quiet, philosophical amusement. Sometimes one could find him with the others in the pool just above the waterfall where the stream had been dammed for that purpose; he preferred to enjoy himself by hanging by his hands under the diving board or along the dam, where he could thrill to the cold of the mountain stream and perchance feel a trout brush against him. These stage folk visiting him were for the most part city innocents, used to a world of concrete sidewalks and subway trains and high-speed elevators. At times he must have thought them a parcel of fools. Certainly his daughter-in-law Meg did. The down-to-earth Meg was present at some of these gatherings and was amazed at how naïve the thespians were about country things: One actress, for instance, wandered out into the garden, where she discovered a spear of asparagus jutting out of the ground, picked it, and ran back screeching to her wide-eyed companions, "Look what came up out of the ground! Can you believe that this came up out of the ground? Wowee!"[35]

No doubt these visitors thought Anderson quaint for turning up so often in work boots and one of the many pairs of shiny, loose-fitting pants that he ordered by the dozen from Sears, Roebuck catalogues.[36] Even with all his periodic wealth and nearness to the city, Anderson still had the fascination of the isolated Midwestern farm boy for the mail-order catalogue, the magic book that brings in wonders from the outside world.

But the serpent called acrimony early invaded the connubial garden. Some of the conflicts observed in the marriage with Margaret occurred again, since Mab also yearned for a more active social role and more travel than Max was willing to participate in. A big age difference made the relationship more ticklish this time. Repetition can put an end to the wife's honeymoon tolerance of little quirks and peccadilloes; what had once seemed to her a lovable eccentricity can become in a little while a nagging oddity. Simone de Beauvoir writes in her book *The Second Sex* that when a woman marries a poet, one of the first things she notices is that he fails to flush the toilet. The man whose independence of thought had upset the trustees of Whittier College and the editors of several newspapers was not likely to be easy to live with. In their quarrels Mab often threatened to leave him, and did leave him once during the 1930s, when Martha packed little Hesper into the backseat of the family car in the middle of the night and, with Mab, rode off to Florida to stay awhile with Mrs. Klein—a refuge guaranteed to be temporary.[37]

It is hard to believe, however, that, given the kind of success worshipper Mab was, she could ever seriously consider leaving Max for good; no, not give up all that attention and exposure she enjoyed every time she strolled into posh New York restaurants and received on sight the best table. The name of Mrs. Maxwell Anderson was a badge of pride for one who had been a penniless tatterdemalion in a Cleveland orphan home.

A peace-loving soul, Anderson usually avoided confrontations and quarrels around the household; his typical response was silence and withdrawal. Though he was happy with and devoted to Mab for many years—more devoted to her than she was to him, the evidence seems to indicate—they did have quarrels about the way to raise Hesper, the princess of the cinder block castle, at which times he might retreat from his wife's tongue by going out to his study in the woods or taking a walk until tempers cooled.

When Hesper was a tender seven, Mab was already having so much trouble riding herd on her that she wanted to send her off to a boarding school, but Anderson flatly refused.[38] Very early the child became intimately attached to her devoted father, a situation made more complicated by her distaste for her mother (the touch of her hand was too much for Hesper to bear). Just as Anderson had rebelled against his father the preacher, Hesper rebelled twice as vehemently against her mother and played her off against her spouse to boot.

Today, Hesper finds it difficult to be objective about her mother. But she finds it just as difficult to be objective about that loving and yet aloof, sympathetic, and yet ultimately unfathomable father who once dwelled familiarly among them.

If we can believe what Hesper writes about her girlhood in the sketch called "Someone Else," she had a fertile and sometimes morbid imagination that played on family secrets. When she asked her brothers or Martha what Margaret had died of, the answer was always, "She died of a broken heart." Somehow Hesper convinced herself that her parents had killed Margaret, whose body then disappeared and whose ashes were moved around several times before going out to the cabin; they were now rumored to lie in a cedar chest on the third floor along with her yellowed letters. This, to a tiny child whose bedroom adjoined the stairs to the third floor, was terrifying. She could never summon the courage to climb to the third floor to see for herself. Shadows seen flickering on the stairs became Margaret's ghost seeking vengeance against her, the seed of the intruding new woman, and Hesper went to sleep with the blankets clutched over her head. With such an imagination at work, it's no wonder that she grew up to be a script writer for Hollywood melodramas!

Mab used to throw elaborate birthday parties for the poor little rich girl, but instead of inviting to them a flock of laughing and joyful children—albeit few of any kind dwelled on the road when Hesper was growing up—Mab invited adults, many of them from the city, who would come bearing gifts and then sit around self-consciously sipping champagne and munching birthday cake and caviar.[39] The Anderson boys might come over from next door. The only other child guest was Hesper's friend Sandra, the daughter of Mary Mowbray Clark. And as Hesper looked around for adults to emulate when she grew up, she noted that practically the only ones her parents seemingly approved of had artistic talent, which restriction signified personal failure for her if she couldn't manage to enter such a career; and it was the same problem that her older brothers had already begun to confront.

Her parents' abandonment of religion had its effect on Hesper, too. When Mab's sister, Libbe, visited the household in New City, Mab begged her not to bring up the subject of religion in the presence of the children,[40] and thus the whole rich heritage of Judaism was lost to the girl: She was left to find her own spiritual salvation among the stones and thorns of adult life. But Mab might very well have been keeping the Jewishness a secret so as to protect Hesper from the bigots that lived beyond South Mountain Road. The family friend Lotte Lenya told this biographer that Mab was frightened by the beating that Peter Poor (son of Henry Varnum Poor) suffered at school when the children learned that he was half-Jewish.

Hesper, when tiny, looked pert and pretty and altogether darling as she toddled around in her sunbonnet while her mother played Charmaine in a Suffern theater production of *What Price Glory* in the 1930s. And was she spoiled! Waited on and coddled right and left; she could do no wrong. One night the nurse, baby-sitting with her, frantically telephoned the parents that their little towhead was cheerfully cutting up the expensive lace tablecloth with a pair of scissors, and the nurse wanted to know what to do about it. "Just go ahead and let her," came the reply.

Mab is said to have had a fetish about personal beauty and demanded that her daughter stay attractive and not change, as she unfortunately did, into a plain-faced and chubby teenager, at which time Mab made her the butt of some cruel remarks.[41] After the girl reached her teens, Mab sent her to the exclusive Hewitt day school for girls, where the students wore uniforms and no makeup and received excellent academic training. It happened to be the school that the movie actresses Barbara Hutton and Julie Harris, and likewise fashionable socialite Margaret Perry, had attended. Hesper believes that her mother chose the school largely for social reasons—with such a cachet about her, the daughter might meet and marry a Rockefeller or a Ford!—but whatever the reason, Hesper could not tolerate the place for more than a few weeks and finally refused to attend classes anymore. Mab was crushed.

Some reports tell us that Max was a better parent than Mab, but such reports come from biased sources and evidently do not take into account his excessive indulgence of the children and his overweening desire to run away from domestic conflicts. Right or wrong, such a personality is going to be popular among the children and probably the neighbors as well. He had something of Rip Van Winkle's easygoing charm. By contrast, Mab was much more ambitious for the child's sake, more aggressive, more demanding of discipline. And since she was the one who had to confront Hesper and her tantrums on a daily basis, whereas Max was safely away in the woods writing, Mab's failures were naturally more conspicuous. All evidence indicates that Hesper Anderson was most difficult to raise. Mab didn't know how to cope with the distrust and hatred and, finally, rebellion that her methods generated. Considering the fact that Hesper—as she freely admits—played one parent against the other to such an extent that Mab hardly had a chance of victory, one tends to feel sorry for Mab. But one looks almost in vain for anecdotes that put her in a favorable light today, in spite of what must have been her undeniable qualities as hostess, as reader of Max's crabbed manuscripts, as patient wife for a husband who didn't like to go out much, and as energetic civic leader in causes too numerous to mention here.

Mab, however, seems to have had a strain of clumsiness in her social relations. In one story we are told that she was giving a party at the New House the month when Hesper reached puberty. Hesper drew her mother aside during the festivities and whispered, with mingled embarrassment and happiness, that she had just minutes before started her first period. Mab was, of course, happy for her. But after the youngster had retreated upstairs, she overheard her mother telling the assembled company the wonderful news that her daughter was now a woman! It was hours before the new woman dared to face people again.[42]

Once in a crowded department store elevator Mab asked her daughter, in a voice loud enough for all to hear, "What size bra do you wear, dear?"[43] The girl's embarrassment can be imagined.

Finally there is a story that suggests what Mab Maynard was doing with the "beautiful people" when her husband wasn't around. As said earlier, she had a weakness for poker. Anderson, however, played only one type of poker, a game called red dog, in which all cards are wild; neither Mab nor her friends would go for that. The night before this incident, Mab had been at the house of the composer Alan Jay Lerner nearby, where a poker game had been under way. Hesper, supposing it would be a lark to tease her mother, remarked laughingly to guests out on the terrace that she had heard Mab's car pull up into the driveway at the unholy hour of seven that morning. Suddenly Mab's face twisted with fury; she raced across the terrace and slapped the little informer on the face with all the power of her elfin body. She screamed that Hesper, warned several times over not to invade her privacy, must never, never, *never* tell what hour she got home! This startling flare-up, which Anderson witnessed, seems not to have made him suspicious of his wife's indiscretions with other men. And Hesper, a naïve twelve at the time, has always rejected any possibility that her mother was being unfaithful, for affairs just didn't happen among the knights and ladies of the cinder block castle. But in her "Someone Else" she records that, after Mab died, she told her older brother Quentin about the slapping incident, whereupon he was appalled at her naïveté and hinted that her mother had had "constant affairs." Hesper did not believe him.[44]

For one reason or another—envy could be among them—Mab made some enemies in the ranks of the Anderson relatives; and since the unpleasant reports about her derive almost exclusively from the enemies, we must be wary lest we receive a one-sided picture of the woman. But she does seem to have been a lovely little snob, a snob who was insensitive toward the feelings of those she considered her social inferiors. There is nothing atypical in Meg's anecdote about how her mother-in-law greeted her one Thanksgiving: "I didn't get dressed up today, because I knew you would be in rags anyway."[45] (The remark was not intended to be funny.) Mab's snobbery was such that hardly any of her husband's old friends came calling anymore, including one of his dearest, the poet Hill, who resided just across the road. Hill's was a sad case. Knowing that he had neither wealth nor national following, she found ways to put him into his ever so modest place. Hill wrote about the matter, ". . . I came to feel that I was not quite important enough, or at least not in the sphere where Max's work lay. I don't think Max felt that way at all. I always had the feeling that Max and I were on terms of perfect intimacy, and that at any time we could go back and be just the same as we were."[46] Max apparently was unaware of what his wife was doing to his friendships.

"I had known a lot of wealthy people but they didn't put on the dog like *that!*" recalls Nancy Anderson about life in the New House. The servants there included, in addition to a gardener, a hired man, a butler-chauffeur, a cleaning woman, a nurse for the baby, and a cook. When Anderson came back in the afternoon from his writing, Martha would bring in a beautifully arranged tray that often contained caviar, Japanese green tea, crystallized honey to sweeten it with, and English muffins or specially prepared toast triangles. Mab was quick to catch on to what was fashionable cuisine. Sometimes she would spend most of the day preparing a special meat dish.[47]

The fashionable world that Mab burned to compete in included such socialites as Margaret Perry, Paulette Goddard, and Elsa Maxwell, and Mab spared nothing to stay in the race. All of these were her friends; they visited back and forth. The homely Elsa was noted for her lavish balls, such as the Pet Hates Ball, which each partygoer attended in the disguise of his or her *bête noire,* and the assets she required of her guests seem to have been those that Mab required of hers: not too many brains, except in parties of six to eight, and obedience to the wishes of the hostess. As for the woman, she should be beautiful (never mind how the hostess looks!), dress beautifully, and be vivacious and animated. As for the man, he should be good-looking (most important!), his tailor should be of the finest, he mustn't be so much married that he's unwilling to charm or flatter the ladies, he should not only dance well but also be willing to do so, and he should have manners, to wit: He should reply to all invitations he receives, carry the champagne home under his belt rather than under his arm, and politely refrain from throwing bottles out of windows.[48]

On many a weekend, limousines rolled over the stone bridge and up the long, curved driveway, lined with birches and dogwoods, to the entrance of the New House, where they discharged such social luminaries as actors Rex Harrison and his wife, Lilli Palmer; maybe Valentina, the chic couturier who designed Mab's stunning dresses; possibly the fleshy figure of Elsa Maxwell. Such glamorous ones Mab admired and took upon herself to invite for an afternoon or a weekend, either without consulting her husband or with his grudging consent; and unless the guests included, say, Rex and Lilli, whom Anderson liked, he might very well escape beforehand to his retreat in the woods "to work" or, as Mab suspected with good reason, to lie around and read *Kidnapped* for the fifth time rather than have to deal with tiresome visitors.

On these weekends the house was aglow with flowers. Mab, adorned with heavy gold charm bracelets on her arms, flashed her partygoing smiles. It was fun time for her. Like her mother, she luxuriated in the presence of celebrities. But where was the distinguished husband for whose sake these guests had arrived? "Oh, he's out in the cabin, wouldn't you know, working on 'the latest,' " Mab might exclaim with a forced laugh. And she would be left alone to entertain them until he came back, which he might not do at all until he heard the last limousine purr off to the city. This scenario of the disappearing husband and the hurt wife would be repeated over and over for almost twenty years.

The swank social life that stimulated her, that made her face light up like a department store window at Christmastide, had no interest for him. He disliked the usual run of parties frequented by Elsa Maxwell's crowd. He hated to dress up for formal occasions—getting him into a business suit was accomplishment enough—at which time he favored wearing one of his tan or brown tweed suits, a camel brown coat, and a dark brown fedora hat. His overweening preference for the Anderson plaid created problems some-times. He had Thoreau's distrust of wearing fashionable clothes just to please another's eye.

No doubt Max went too far in avoiding frivolity, for in his makeup there was a strain of puritanism coming unbidden from his father's church, a bit of the work ethic that distrusted any concentrated, prolonged displays of fun because these resulted in attitudes, he felt, that wasted whatever was noblest in the human spirit. Maybe, as his son Alan suggests, being frivolous made him feel unconsciously guilty. Alan recalls that when someone told the father a piece of gossip, he would not give his informant even the gratification of an "Oh, really?" which most people would, but simply stared at him in silence.[49]

It would help us to know Anderson and the highly individualistic slant of his art if we were to make a visit to his famous cabin in the woods.[50] A privileged visit it would be, too, because only a scant number in his lifetime had ever seen the place, and no contemporary photographs survive. If it is springtime, we will have to wade there through freshets; if winter, dig our way through snowdrifts. Let's play safe and choose summer instead. Broken twigs and matted leaves strew the pathway. Around the cabin are sweetgums and ashes that provide shade and help blot out that intrusive world Anderson is trying to escape. Not far from the doorway gurgles a little spring—as expected, water is somewhere nearby. We are surprised to find the cabin so small, smaller even than Thoreau's at Walden Pond, and more simple still. Carroll French had designed and built it for Max as a prefabricated unit, then taken it to the woods in sections and assembled it there on a concrete slab that measures ten feet by twelve. The outer walls are made of random wooden siding (not logs); the roof of wooden shingles is covered with green moss. Green shades drawn down in all three windows enhance the sylvan effect. The wooden door of this hermitage is fitted with giant hinges and contains on the upper surface some of French's quaint carvings, but when we try to open it we find the door fastened shut by means of a cleverly concealed long iron rod thrust horizontally from the corner of the hut, where the bushes hide the device.

We enter at last. In the little room our noses detect the odor of mildew; even the books smell of mildew. Bookshelves surround the room and contain ancient Greek plays, one or more titles by Aristotle (including *Poetics*), works by and about Shakespeare, some volumes of the standard poets (including Keats and Arnold), essays, biographies, histories, and scientific treatises (Anderson reads a lot of science).[51] But there are few novels; the few there are include some old favorites by Stevenson and Dickens; also, Twain's *Huckleberry Finn;* and, depending upon what year we make our visit, Steinbeck's *Tortilla Flat* (Anderson enjoyed it immensely) and Paton's *Cry, the Beloved Country.*[52] There are even some books about Iceland and the Shetland Islands. Scatter rugs lie about the floor. We see a cardboard box containing canned fish such as kippered herring. In one corner of the room stands a large pine table used as a desk, and on it a row of books; and in front of the desk is a Windsor chair. A chaise longue, in which he also writes, rests catercornered across the room. When he feels like taking a nap or just resting his back from the old football injury, he can walk over to an iron cot beside which lies a pile of more books. Accounts differ on how much time he spends lying on the cot, but it could not be much because of his tremendous output of plays and letters.[53] The final piece of furniture in the small room is an airtight "dumpy, black-iron [wood burning] stove; bought from a second-hand man for fifteen dollars . . . looking like Napoleon after Waterloo, sulking in a corner."[54] Lighting comes from kerosene lamps on tables and hanging from wall hooks. No typewriter is visible in the cabin.

Judging from the books present and from what we have heard, the dramatists that he had read admiringly, and continued to read, in his mature years include Molière, Goethe, Ferenc Molnár (*Liliom*), Ibsen, Sidney Howard (*They Knew What They Wanted*), Marc Connelly (*Green Pastures*), Robert E. Sherwood (*Abe Lincoln in Illinois*), George Bernard Shaw (whom he praises in his essay "St. Bernard" as the best of all modern playwrights), Sean O'Casey (*Plough and the Stars*), J. M. Synge, and Eugene O'Neill—though Anderson could not bear to sit through a showing of *The Iceman Cometh.*[55] But he believed that none of the moderns could hold a candle up to the great dramatists of the past because, except for O'Casey, none were poets.[56]

After we step out of the cabin and glance again at the roof we discover the reason for the odor of mildew inside. On the roof ridge are fastened two water sprinklers connected by pipes with an electric pump down below, which in turn sucks water from the spring close by. And near the door is a valve which Anderson can turn on—say, in the sultry August heat—and the cabin will be bathed with the delicious sound and coolness of rain drip-dropping in the woods! Then he can pull down the shades, relax in the Windsor chair, and set to work.

Anderson rarely made notes for a play he intended to write. The typical procedure required that, after finding his subject and characters, he soon did the recognition scene. Next he sketched briefly the divisions of the play and wrote the script in a kind of pleasant torture. The script he set down in a big ledger containing one hundred fifty to three hundred pages. The complete script, running not more than a hundred pages, represented three distinct phases of development, each one so clearly demarcated in the ledger that today one can easily follow the sequence of what he did even though the handwriting is often far from clear; that is, he prepared in the notebook the original plus two stages of revision.[57]

By choosing ledgers rather than loose sheets of paper for his writing, he forced himself to be careful so that no pages would have to be torn out and spoil the neat appearance. The general impression given by these ledgers is that of a writer who thinks each play through so carefully in advance that when it comes time to commit himself to paper he incurs no hindrance in the flow of language.[58]

After putting the script through the three phases of development mentioned earlier, he carried the ledger to his wife for typing (during the last few years of her life, Mab turned over that task to Lawrence's wife, Lillian).[59] Max subsequently assigned Mab a small percentage of the royalty for her secretarial work—which practice would also apply to the third wife—partly in order to benefit from a provision in the federal income-tax law by which a writer can claim a deduction for secretarial help.[60] In this way Mab assisted him much as authors' wives have done down through the centuries when they served as copyists or proofreaders or became audiences for the "latest" item from the writing desk, as witness what happened in the families of Nathaniel Hawthorne, Samuel Clemens, and Ernest Hemingway. Unlike Mrs. Clemens, Mab seems not to have imposed any clear-cut instance of censorship.

At the end of the working day he would often bring in a new scene and read it aloud to the family. Mab was a sympathetic and intelligent listener.[61] The boys, living next door, often came over for visits; no doubt he could discern on their faces how well he had succeeded in comic passages—more so than in the case of Mab, who had no sense of humor. The fact that the surviving scripts never show an alien hand at work makes us believe Alan when he declares that his stepmother's aid was predominantly secretarial, that his father did *all* the drafting and formal editing.[62] Once the play was typed it went back to the cabin, where Anderson made a further revision.

But once the creative fire had cooled, the act of revising bored him; there was no task that he hated more.[63] He told Elmer Rice, "I hear of these playwrights who go over and over scripts, reworking, and emerging with final brilliant versions, but in my case either the first draft looks good or it will never be any good."[64] And those plays he revised most extensively are with only a few exceptions his poorest ones. It is as if he had to conceive of a well-ordered narrative at the same time as he did the theme if he were going to turn out a good play.[65]

One reason for his impatience with revision has to do with all those years of journalistic grind in which everything was composed for a deadline that allowed little opportunity for redrafting, even if he had wanted it; he grew accustomed to pouring his heart into that first sustained effusion, and all else was anticlimax. Besides, many journalists turned creative writers are said to get bored and lazy after years of relying on the rewrite desk. Another reason for impatience lay in the need to write more and more plays and screenplays to keep up his enlarged scale of living, to fend off the creditors, and to support his flock of dependents. He once wrote to the wife of Professor Gottfried Hult, "I have a feeling that my own plays have suffered a great deal from being written to a demand [that they make money for theater managers] but that's the only way plays can be written profitably and I have tried to make an intelligent compromise between my soul and my living."[66]

Once he had finished with what was to him the onerous task of revising the first typescript version, a typist made an original and several copies from it; this new script was the one that went into rehearsal and, according to him, was the one usually published. The form of the work after it had gone through the meat grinder of rehearsals rarely suited his fancy.[67]

Anderson's good fortune with some of his most unconventional plays must have helped convince him that quality could be achieved on Broadway. Dorothy Thompson wrote to him for help in launching a repertory theater, but he gave her a "no" on the grounds that the conditions of the Great White Way had not hampered his own career and that the theater she proposed *would not make money* and would therefore founder.[68] (He disliked theater subsidized by government and public funds.) The letter to Thompson illustrates the crux of his motivations and the origin of some of his shortcomings as a playwright: his geniune desire to ensure the integrity of his art but at the same time demanding that that art pay well. Not for him the glory of resting on posthumous laurels at the price of losing immediate returns. And so, with the exception of *Sea-Wife,* he rarely gambled on a play for experimental or off-Broadway theaters.

Sometimes Anderson had particular actors in mind even before he wrote the plays; sometimes he decided upon the actors afterward and then tried to recruit them. We have already seen that he fashioned *Mary of Scotland* for Helen Hayes.[69] Because Anderson was concerned that his work gain immediate acceptance on the stage so that it would not, as he feared would otherwise happen, fall into permanent obscurity, he went out of his way to get the stars who would presumably guarantee success. Almost without question Anderson tried to model his career after that of Molière, for he wrote in "A Confession" that when Molière failed with one kind of play, he then turned out a different kind to please audiences; that Molière *consistently strove for quality as well as commercial success;* and that the Frenchman, too, realized that a play absolutely must gain immediate applause if it were to survive the ages.[70]

But even with all this attention to the commercial value of his art, he had a recurring need for money that drove him early and late to writing scenarios. Many of his own more popular plays found their way to the screen; indeed, income from selling film rights was to remain for the rest of his life a major source of income.[71] He didn't mind letting Hollywood turn his original plays into screen entertainment as long as he didn't have a hand in it. But the fact is, he hated writing screenplays—just as other famous American authors have hated it—and worked there only for the quick money. Hesper remembers that he sank into despondency each time he boarded the train for his trip westward into the Land of Celluloid; and when he worked on pictures his jowls were more noticeable, dropping lower and lower the more he stayed there; and when he talked on the telephone with some motion-picture magnate like Walter Wanger, his shoulders sagged. In dealing with some of these people his temper, usually kept under tight control, would sometimes erupt like Mount Saint Helens.[72]

Anderson's friend Paul Green, who ended up occasionally as a writer in movieland, recalls an incident illustrating their attitudes toward work out there:

> I remember one day at my house in Santa Monica. We were lying out on the grass in the sun and just talking about the movies. And Max's feelings about what they [the producers] were doing to the medium . . . were about the same as mine. . . . In describing some of the producers . . . he would sort of smile and say . . . "Ah, the sons-of-bitches!"[73]

At the risk of getting ahead of our narrative, it could be said that Anderson finally developed this scorn into an essay that damned the whole business of the cinema. In " 'Cut Is the Branch That Might Have Grown Full Straight '" he complains that the screenwriter is doomed to anonymity not merely because the product is ephemeral but also because his independence and individuality always get lost in the corporate mix where the producer is free to order changes in anything that the author writes, no matter how inspired and admirable. No work of genius can survive this treatment. Moreover, he tells us that, in comparison with the stage, films have as much chance for survival as-a celluloid cat would if he chased an asbestos rat through the flames of hell.[74]

The 1930s abounded in Anderson plays; almost all his great ones were written then. The output was such that most can be mentioned here only in passing. He had expected *Valley Forge* (1934) to be his best work yet, and he did careful research on the period from December 1777 through June 1778, at which time General George Washington and his Continental Army were suffering terrible hardships at Valley Forge and when only the most extraordinary efforts could keep these forces from disbanding. When a Mrs. Keehn on the staff of the Library of Congress offered to do research for him, he declined her assistance and explained that he always did such work himself so that the facts would stick in his mind better.[75]

It was characteristic of his thoroughness that he paid special attention to Washington's letters; not only did he borrow the nine volumes of *The Writings of George Washington from the Original Manuscript Sources, 1745-1799* that John C. Fitzpatrick had already edited and published, but he also asked Fitzpatrick to lend him page and galley proofs of the next three unpublished ones, thereby covering the crisis period depicted in *Valley Forge*.[76] Thus when Anderson places women in Washington's camp but excludes Martha Washington during the month of January, he does so with full support of the historical record. Nor did he invent Mrs. Mary Philipse Morris, who was a love in the general's youth; it appears, however, that Anderson fictionalizes when he brings the two together for an abortive love dalliance and has Mary unwittingly convey to the general the lie that the longed-for American-French Alliance will not occur.[77]

But *Valley Forge* failed for a number of reasons, one of which is related to dramatic structure—the drama did not steadily build in excitement to the close of the acts.[78]

Anderson wrote one of his masterpieces, *Winterset* (1935), in the cabin in the woods.[79] Almost every single study of Anderson's art agrees that with this play he demonstrated his most daring and at the same time most felicitous use of poetic dialogue. To future ages it will equal the best of O'Neill. Except in *White Desert* and *Sea-Wife,* Anderson had thus far restricted such dialogue to historical themes with tragic endings because, as one who had pored over the acknowledged classics of the stage, he had found no instance of a successful poetic drama using a contemporary setting.[80] Not even Shakespeare had dared to break the unwritten rule that the remote past is necessary to supply the emotional distance in which the poetic becomes acceptable to an audience. It is obviously far easier to imagine the Moorish general Othello talking in iambic pentameters to his lady-love than to imagine General Dwight Eisenhower doing the same to his.

Winterset may well owe its existence to a challenge made by a drama critic to Anderson in the winter of 1933-34 while *Mary of Scotland* was still enjoying its success on the stage. Walter Prichard Eaton, a teacher in the Yale drama department, wrote a laudatory assessment of Anderson's stage career up to and including his triumph with *Mary of Scotland;* it seems to have been one of those rare reviews that the playwright savored, mainly because it eschewed personality and concentrated on technique. "In an age when we have assumed that realism was king," Eaton wrote, "and we almost gleefully declared the poetic drama to be as dead as the Dodo, Maxwell Anderson has given us poetic plays and made us go to them in droves, and like them." In his most provocative statement, nevertheless, he said that Anderson had done so well with the poetic treatment of the Elizabethan age that "Can he [now] push on and create a poetic drama of modern life? If that isn't the artistic problem which lurks largest at the back of Anderson's mind, the present writer is a poor guesser." He cited the famous Indiana playwright William Vaughn Moody, author of verse dramas, as one who had been trying to create a modern play couched in verse but who had died before succeeding; maybe Anderson could "pick up the torch" and carry it forward.[81]

Anderson wrote to him that he didn't believe great dramatic verse could be written using a contemporary theme, but he clearly wanted the other man to prove him wrong. And Eaton obligingly persisted in trying to do that, cautioning that the absence of this genre didn't prove that it could not be developed. When asked for instances, Eaton went on to cite a number of them, such as Clemence Dane's recent Broadway entry *Come of Age,* which, unhappy to say, had closed after a short run.[82] Hardly an encouraging instance. But Eaton had planted the seed.

Anderson's meeting with lawyer Robert Montgomery, a fellow student from the University of North Dakota, gave Anderson the opener he needed. Montgomery told him that he shouldn't think so ill of the judge who had condemned poor Nicola Sacco and Bartolomeo Vanzetti, defendants in the notorious Sacco-Vanzetti trial of the 1920s, because the old fellow was almost mad now, going around asking person after person, "What was wrong about that? They were guilty. They were obviously guilty. I had to do this and this and this—legally I was in a box. I had to do it." This was how Judge Gaunt of *Winterset* came to be born; all the rest followed from that.[83] Therefore, in spite of Anderson's deep admiration for Shakespeare's art and in spite of critics' persistence in putting him in debt to Shakespeare, the mad judge did not originate in King Lear but in an actual person whom Anderson had written about years earlier in *Gods of the Lightning* and now saw in a new perspective.

The passage of years since *Gods of the Lightning* gave him the aesthetic distance he needed in handling the Sacco-Vanzetti case again so that, for this and other reasons, *Winterset* is much better as pure literature. In choosing for the first and only time to use the medium of verse to craft a contemporary tragedy, he said that he still found it difficult to find an "idiom" acceptable to audiences; he reasoned that poetry in a modern, upper-class milieu would require stylization that might well militate against the realism he felt was essential; nevertheless, he wanted to avoid the romantic devices of the "long ago" as much as the "far away" and still retain an air of strangeness. In order to achieve these various objectives he compromised.[84]

Winterset, which took slightly over two months to write,[85] has as its *mise en scène* a slum neighborhood in New York that sprawls at the base of a gigantic bridgehead of steel and masonry whose span arcs out diagonally over the heads of the audience in a manner symbolic of the contiguity of poverty and wealth, of defenseless little people below and inhuman power expressed in the technology of the bridge overhead, and yet of mankind's aspiring hopes everywhere. The characters utter a language cleansed of modern clichés, in spite of the tenement locale, and comprise an unusual crowd gathering together for disparate reasons during a December thunderstorm. The story that coalesces concerns a social order that discriminates against a disadvantaged class and benefits one class at the expense of another. Mio Romagna, an impassioned young wanderer, goes to a waterfront slum in hope of gaining evidence that will clear his father, who was unjustly executed by the state.

Initially, the title of this powerful work was *The Bridge,* but the final title owes its origin to the hero's speech in Act III in which he refers to the winter solstice:

Now all you silent powers
that make the sleet and dark, and never yet

have spoken, give us a sign, let the throw be ours
this once, on this longest night, when the winter sets
his foot on the threshold leading up to spring
and enters with remembered cold. . . .[86]

The first production of *Winterset* at the Martin Beck Theatre in the fall of 1935 was so astonishing and compelling that several reviewers returned for another performance; some read the text before writing their second notices; and some of these thoughtful second notices caused the play to be a smashing success at the box office and helped win for its author the first Drama Critics Circle Award ever presented.[87]

About two years later, Professor Frederick Koch wrote to Anderson from the University of North Carolina and said that for a long time he had intended to tell him how much he admired him for the excellent things he was doing in the theater. One passage from *Winterset* he especially admired and was in the habit of quoting from memory at classroom meetings and addresses, was Esdras' marvelous final speech over the fallen lovers:

. . . this is the glory of earth-born men and women,
not to cringe, never to yield, but standing,
take defeat implacable and defiant,
die unsubmitting. I wish that I'd died so,
long ago; before you're old you'll wish
that you had died as they have. On this star,
in this hard star-adventure, knowing not
what the fires mean to right and left, nor whether
a meaning was intended or presumed,
man can stand up, and look out blind, and say:
in all these turning lights I find no clue,
only a masterless night, and in my blood
no certain answer, yet is my mind my own,
yet is my heart a cry toward something dim
in distance, which is higher than I am
and makes me emperor of the endless dark
even in seeking![88]

Koch was so enthusiastic that he ranked the passage with the best of Sophocles and Shakespeare.[89] There is certainly nothing in all of O'Neill, that most unquotable of American dramatists despite his prestige, that can come anywhere close to it in originality and heroic grandeur.

The Wingless Victory (1936), which was Anderson's only play to emerge the next year, is a poetic tragedy based on the Medea myth and set in Salem, Massachusetts, in the year 1800. But so fertile was he that long before it reached the stage he had completed in the cabin in the woods the first draft of a far better work that was to win him his second Drama Critics Circle Award.[90]

No more convincing example of his brilliant versatility can be cited than the poetic comic-fantasy called *High Tor,* easily the best of its kind yet done by an American, arriving as a flash of gleaming silver in a midnight stream of tragedies. The germinal idea for this new composition apparently came to Anderson on a spring afternoon about mid-March in 1936. Having climbed with one of his sons to the summit of High Tor, he looked out over the famous river that had seen so many changes in its long history and remembered "the Dutch fleet which had sailed up the river and . . . the Indians who had once dwelt on the mountain. By association the legend of Rip Van Winkle came to mind." At least, this is the account as it comes down to us via some reporter or publicity agent. The unnamed source continues: "The phrase that came into his mind and began it all formed itself into something like this: 'A study of the evanescence of civilizations' . . ."[91] After thinking about the idea for two and a half months—true to his habit of elaborate planning in advance—Anderson set down the first lines in his ledger; a month later, the task was done.

His son Terence tells us that the labor of giving birth to *High Tor* was not only a painless experience for his father but also a very cheerful one for the entire family because Anderson would come back from his cabin near the end of the day, sit down on the left side of his big fireplace, and entertain them by reading aloud the part he had just completed. Everyone laughed at the antics of Biggs and Skimmerhorn in the bucket of the steam shovel.[92]

Indeed, it is a delightfully funny and at the same time a serious play. Just as with *Winterset,* the time setting is now. The story is about a crusty young individualist of Dutch descent, Van Van Dorn, who spends much of his time fending off beauty-blind trap rock men and their crooked representatives who want to swindle him out of his beloved mountain on the Hudson so they can tear it down for its road-building gravel. Adding to the excitement is a crew of Dutch phantoms marooned there centuries ago by the ship *Onrust;* they take out their resentment against the strangeness of the modern world they are forced to inhabit by hurling their bowling balls into the airplane beacon and smashing it.[93] A trio of amusing if conventionalized bank robbers take their stolen money to the mountain, where it tempts sticky-fingered Biggs and Skimmerhorn, a realtor and probate judge, respectively, into hilariously risible contretemps. As if all this were not variety enough, there is also a philosophical old Indian looking for a place to be buried. But all three major groups of characters—Van Dorn, phantoms, Indian—disparate though they appear to be—make for a thematically unified dramatic structure in that each one represents a cultural phase of history, each interesting in itself, which is about to be annihilated. One perceptive study of this work finds in it ". . . the nostalgia of the poet for fair things past and dead, and the anger of the citizen who sees greed personified in the unimaginative hogs who would despoil beauty for financial gain."[94]

There is one passage near the end of Act II in which Anderson evokes the memory of his long dead wife, about whom all his sons and even his widow are sure that he suffered guilt feelings through the years. At this time Margaret's funeral urn had been moved out of the big house (where it had been terrifying Hesper) and put it into the cabin, in which place he wrote *High Tor*. So tiny was the room that it would have been almost impossible for him not to see the urn as he worked, and one can easily imagine him being reminded of the early years of happiness he had shared with the radiant Margaret. Thus this drama, as so many others, was done in the shadow of mortality; the dead wife being with him still, as if her spirit were looking over his shoulder as he penned his lines. In the passage alluded to, the lovely Dutch phantom Lise is seen standing near Judith, her rival for Van Dorn, who lies sleeping nearby, and Lise sorrows for her lost life and probably a sweetheart, too, back among the cobblestone streets of a town in Holland ever so many years ago. Her brief affair with Van Dorn had not succeeded in assuaging her old grief. Judith asks her why she is crying, and Lise replies:

> Am I crying?
> Well, they're not for him, or you, these tears;
> Something so far away, so long ago,
> so hopeless, so fallen, so lost, so deep in dust
> the names wash from the urns, summons my tears,
> not love or longing. Only when you have him,
> love him a little better for your sake,
> for your sake only, knowing how bitterly
> I cried, for times past and things done.[95]

In addition to the mountain climb the author had made, several other factors had a part in the inception of this comic fantasy. Something of Uncle Frank Anderson went into the makeup of Van Van Dorn, but the resemblance to Henry David Thoreau is much more striking.[96] And just as Thoreau was a conservationist, so was Anderson. As a public-spirited citizen Anderson had joined neighbors to combat the New York State Trap Rock Company, whose steam shovels were aready disemboweling the earth to the south and east and threatened to rip down soon that part of South Mountain overshadowed by the Tor.[97]

And that naturally brings us to the eccentric and jealous local owner of High Tor, Elmer Van Orden. Alan tells us that his father had known Van Orden and had climbed his mountain many times before the play was ever written; moreover, Max had "patterned the character [Van Van Dorn] in the play after a young Elmer Van Orden, imagining what Elmer might have been like in his early years. . . ." Kenneth largely substantiates these claims, for he himself had been up the Tor with the playwright around 1922 and recalls that soon after that, Anderson had hired the Dutchman to build the chimney for the old farmhouse at the time French was renovating the interior. "Van Orden *is* Van Van Dorn," he insists.[98] Various newspaper accounts after *High Tor* reached Broadway identified Van Orden with the fictional hero.

But what was the real Elmer like? He was every bit as odd and crusty and idiosyncratic as his counterpart. Until his death on February 19, 1942, at the age of seventy-nine, he had lived as a bachelor recluse in an eighteenth-century, one-and-a-half-story farmhouse on the slope of the mountain with snakes and huckleberry bushes for neighbors. Way back before the Revolutionary War, King George III had given a land grant to one of Elmer's Dutch ancestors, and ever since that date succeeding generations of Van Ordens had owned the mountain estate. Elmer himself had lived there as a boy and loved his way of life. His was a shabby gentility, but he was content—except when trap rock men come nosing around or a sightseer climbed his mountain. With the aid of his small hired man and companion, August G. Weltie ("the boy," he called him affectionately), whom he had rescued as a teenager over a half century before from St. John's Orphan Home, in Brooklyn, and who claimed to be a friend of Maxwell Anderson's, he worked his self-sustaining farm without the aid of electricity and other modern conveniences, chopped his own wood for fires, fetched water from a frost-free spring near the house, and adamantly refused year after year to sell his property to anyone who would not preserve his beloved peak.

Surely he had heard what the quarriers had already done to nearby Mount Taurus. He knew what unconscionable power some of the big firms had for destroying natural beauty under the aegis of public service and progress. No doubt he had sympathized with a problem that Anderson had had soon after he moved into the neighborhood, which was that the Rockland Light and Power Company was planning to construct a high-tension line right over the waterfall. Anderson and his neighbor Ed Jones used to go out at night and pull up stakes to delay the development. Fortunately, Jones or some other neighbor is said to have checkmated the Company by—implausible as it sounds—erecting a house along the intended route.[99] (Some of the anger in this episode of the waterfall likely boiled over into the treatment of the businessmen in *High Tor.*)

Burgess Meredith, the friend whom Anderson had made famous through the role of Mio in *Winterset,* played the lead in *High Tor* also. He was now launched upon what was to be a long and highly successful stage and film career that would last into his old age. When Meredith was still rehearsing for his second Anderson play, he and a photographer climbed up the wooded slope to the top of the Tor for some publicity photographs and there ran into the formidable Van Orden for the first time. The latter was in no mood for pleasantries. "What the hell are you doing here?" the jealous owner shouted at them. After the visitors identified themselves and mentioned the stage play, the old codger snapped that, yes, he had heard something about it. Finally he showed enough interest to announce, "I'd like to see that goddam show."[100]

Meredith remembered that wish. Not long after the play opened at the Martin Beck Theatre to a long run greeted with critical applause, both Meredith and Anderson invited him to a matinee performance. The old man put on his Sunday-best black suit, fixed into his old-fashioned tie a diamond stickpin, seized his black cane, and rode into the big city, where he watched the imaginative re-creation of his life take place on the stage while he sat comfortably and chewed tobacco. After the show, he walked backstage, met the cast, and gave Anderson a good-natured argument about how the play ended. Van Dorn should not have sold the mountain! Never! Nor did Van Orden ever change his mind on that point.

From that time onward he gained a kind of fame along the Hudson and people began to appreciate, apparently for the first time, his efforts as a conservationist. Whenever theatrical folk wanted something "different" to do, it became the fashion with them to go up the river to see Elmer at High Tor.[101] Viennese artist Franz Felix made several portraits of him, and his New City neighbors honored him with a big party.

Life sometimes imitates art. Just as the play *High Tor* has the lovely Lise, a ghostly Dutch woman, having a brief and poignant love relationship with the hero, so there was a real ghost in Van Orden's life. As noted in an earlier chapter, the region of Rockland County abounds in tales of the supernatural. Mrs. Hume Dixon, a resident on South Mountain Road, supposedly witnessed the ghost of a woman in her ancient farmhouse, as she told one interviewer:

I have seen her many times. . . . But always in one place—at the head of the stairs, standing in an attitude of welcome, and invariably smiling. She seemed to be a young woman, dressed in some sort of linsey-woolsey material; the dress simply cut and gathered at the waist, with a full skirt. Her hair is a nondescript light brown, falling lightly around her shoulders—a sort of "early American" hair-do. . . . Her best feature is her mouth; large, and always curved in a warm, generous smile.

She has never bothered me in the least. I have grown quite accustomed to her, in fact, and in a lonely country house, her presence is almost welcome. Many times, when I have been working late in my study, on the second floor, I was aware that she was just outside the door, standing, as usual, at the head of the stairs. Who she was, or what was her history, though, I have never been able to find out.

In her capacity as civil defense worker during World War II, Mrs. Dixon once called on Elmer Van Orden to learn what his old house could offer as a shelter in case evacuees had to come in from New York City. Van Orden sat sick in his armchair, not far from death. During the course of her interview she happened to mention her place on South Mountain Road; and he who knew all the old houses and their families in the district nodded that he remembered it. Then she described her lovely ghost, whereupon his eyes brightened, he straightened up, and he announced with difficulty that he knew the spectral visitor well. In fact, he was once engaged to her! Something in the way he replied kept her from questioning him further. Later, at the general store, Mrs. Dixon met Weltie, who confirmed what his employer had said and added that the figure in linsey-woolsey was the only woman Van Orden had ever loved. It all happened very long ago; he couldn't recall her name. When the owner of High Tor died, Mrs. Dixon's friendly ghost never reappeared.[102]

Anderson, when he first heard the story, thought it fascinating, but it seems to have been completely unknown to him at the time he composed his famous drama.

A fund-raising Committee to Save High Tor got under way which included Anderson, producer Guthrie McClintic, the cast of *High Tor,* and numerous other celebrities. Schoolchildren donated their nickels and dimes. By means of many such contributions, the Hudson River Conservation Society and the Rockland County Conservation Association, of which Anderson was honorary chairman, at last bought up the whole Van Orden estate from his heirs for twelve thousand dollars and then gave the acreage around the summit to Palisades Interstate Park, where it is now safe forever from the likes of Biggs and Skimmerhorn.

In early February 1937, less than a month after his comic fantasy began entertaining crowds on the Great White Way, *The Masque of Kings* opened there at the Shubert Theatre. In this poetic tragedy Anderson supplies the answer for the mystery of January 30, 1889, when the heir to the Austro-Hungarian throne was found with his young mistress shot to death in a hunting lodge at Mayerling, Austria. It is characteristic of Anderson's idealistic heroes during this decade that Crown Prince Rudolph goes down to defeat in a good cause, defiant to the end, and unstained in character (except for keeping a mistress), rather than drag out his years growing cunning and hardened in a world inimical to justice and truth and good faith. The first published edition of *The Masque of Kings* had to be withdrawn from the market and a new one substituted because a Countess Larisch, whom he had supposed dead and had used as a smutty gossip in the play, proved to be very much alive and sued him for libel. The names Count and Countess Larisch were then switched to Baron and Baronin Neustadt, whereupon the suit was dropped.[103]

Still the plays poured forth, but they were most uneven in quality. Typical of the one-acters he turned out in this decade was *The Feast of Ortolans,* set in the time of the French Revolution. The National Broadcasting Company aired it in September,[104] a mere bagatelle.

That same September brought to the stage *The Star-Wagon,* which he had written as a potboiler,[105] but it proved to be one of his more charming works, which once again illustrates that authors are rarely good judges of what they write. *The Star-Wagon* is a science fantasy about a poor, unassuming scientist, Stephen Minch, who with his quaint assistant Hanus Wicks invents an amazing machine that carries them back to a town in eastern Ohio—as it turns out, to the very year during which Anderson was a boy in Jefferson—so that Stephen can find out whether he would have been happier if he had married the rich and sexy "other girl" instead of his tried-and-true Martha. This comedy contains, indeed, several of the well-tested ingredients that make for popular Broadway fare. Thanks to H. G. Wells' familiar novel *The Time Machine* and its successors, the theater audience was sure to have some appetite for the fantasy of time travel. Meredith again had the lead role in the first stage production; Lillian Gish was Martha; Kent Smith and Edmond O'Brien and Mildred Natwick took minor parts; and Anderson's son Alan played Ripple.

There is a certain heartwarming genuineness about *The Star-Wagon* that leads one to want to believe that Anderson poured in more than the usual quota of his private feelings and experience; moreover, that he must have enjoyed what he was putting on paper. It is no surprise, therefore, when he has the likable Hanus prefer rainy weather over sunny. An equally obvious parallel—at least in the eyes of those who knew Anderson well—consists of Stephen's role as inventor, because one of Anderson's hobbies was science, and he read a great deal about the subject and tried his hand at inventions. Lawrence claims that he and Max invented many things together, at least on paper, such as a rotary engine similar to the Wankel design and also a chain saw, long before these things appeared on the market. Lawrence goes on to say that much of the philosophical discussion in *The Star-Wagon* about reaching a life goal by taking the right-hand road or the left, and about what constitutes good fortune or bad fortune, all relates to conversations they had had together:

> Many times after all the rest of the household was asleep, Max would tap on my door and we would meet in the kitchen for coffee and conversation. Max's curiosity led us into discussions which covered almost every activity of mankind. Some of our thoughts eventually found their way into ... [*The Star-Wagon*], and my own philosophy was nurtured into a sturdy vine which still supports me in good times and bad.[106]

Some sections of the play are obvious appeals to sentiment, to the quaint charms of old-fashioned living, and to the clichés about true love and marriage, and yet in the context of the story these appeals are forgivable because they seem embedded in a richly remembered and ever so personal experience. Act II, Scene 2, done with a delicate nostalgia, would have a special charm for almost anyone. There in the choir loft in a small church we see Hanus pump the organ just as Anderson used to do in his father's church. In the choir is Hallie Arlington, based on Anderson's childhood friend Hallie Loomis. But where we see best the youthful Max—the Max tenderly yearning for and at the same time responsive to music—is when Stephen plays "Jerusalem the Golden" on the organ and both he and the singer, Martha, are profoundly moved by the rapturous notes set adrift in the church. The passage conveys well the evanescent joy that even ordinary music might bring to a sensitive but not especially articulate listener. Martha then tells him that they have to go now but he wants to linger because, he says, the music affects him; at this, she suddenly takes his hand in a communion of shared feeling. A few lines later Martha gives voice to that cultural claustrophobia written about by so many artists from the Middle West around the turn of the century. She says there is no one around capable of teaching them serious music, that they'd have to move where people love that art. What a world of youthful longing and frustration Anderson distilled into Martha's lament![107]

Alan informs us that his father based Stephen and Hanus "on a couple of old friends here in Rockland County [Lloyd Orser and Carroll French, a carpenter-mason and a sculptor, respectively], and on his own affection for honest, muddling, good people as opposed to efficient, successful and somewhat ruthless and cold people."[108]

Thanks largely to how *The Star-Wagon* was drawing in customers, the year 1937 was prosperous for Anderson. His secretary, Alfred Sturt, heard about a thousand acres of land for sale near Hudson, Maine, that his boss could get at eight dollars an acre; they would furnish a quiet, isolated retreat where Anderson could be alone when he needed to. Apparently it was a good long-term investment too. One argument appealing to Max was that Quentin could have a game reserve on which to hunt and fish whenever he liked. Of course Max bought the place, which proved to be the beginning of a sadly ludicrous financial scheme that would cost him thousands. Maybe everything would have been all right had he been content to make no improvements and let the place remain what it was, a wild but fenced-in deer refuge, but somehow he got the notion to ask his sister Dorothy Elizabeth (Beth) and her ne'er-do-well husband, Stanley Oliver, who were looking for something to do, to move in and raise minks commercially for him. He would be the absentee owner of the Anderson Fur Farm and supply them all the capital needed. It seemed like a scheme designed mainly to help his poor sister. None of them had ever raised the smelly little minks before, but the Olivers were willing to learn; the deal was made, and they moved in.

Breeding sheds went up and a stock of North Shore Labrador minks brought in. To save on cost, the Olivers fed horsemeat to the bushy-tailed guests, but soon the latter were running up a big feed bill by devouring the equivalent of a horse a day. Not long after operations began, the mink fur market took a plunge which, combined with perhaps other factors unknown to us, meant no profits for Maxwell Anderson; worse still, he got frequent appeals for more money to subsidize the operations. The money drain was such that after three years a desperate Mab tried to sell the ranch, but there were no takers. Beth wrote to New City that Stanley was sick and that she could hardly manage all the work alone; another time she wrote that he had recovered enough to abandon her and hop into bed with another woman, leaving Beth badly off for clothes and blaming herself for the separation.

Later on, divorced by now, she told the absentee owner of the crowning insult, namely that Stanley had secretly sold timber from the ranch and even a good deal of the fence—not all, however, because much of it had already sunk into the marshes like Anderson's investment—and pocketed all the money for himself. The minks were all gone by now. Finally, Anderson sold all the wooden buildings for a dollar and later on got rid of the land. The only profit to the Anderson household from all those years of investment and labor: one mink coat for Mab.[109]

Though Maxwell Anderson was widely known as a solitary and privacy-craving figure, he was also a founder and a longtime member of what is certainly one of the most enduring playwright-businessman organizations to appear since the seventeenth century. This was The Playwrights Producing Company, Inc.,[110] whose board of directors consisted almost entirely of playwrights who were producers of their own works.

The significance of this group is best understood by those who are acquainted with the grossly restrictive and overwhelmingly commercial conditions under which playwrights had labored in the generations before the founding of the company. The Theatrical Syndicate, formed in 1896 by a half-dozen unscrupulous businessmen, created a monopoly of theater in America via the control, including ownership in many instances, of its physical properties. The American theater of that period was not, as is the case today, synonymous with the New York stage; it was the "road," a network of thousands of playhouses in every city of any size and stretching from coast to coast. By means of "booking" arrangements the syndicate exercised its power over the scattered playhouses, guaranteeing to send on schedule attractive fare at set prices, but requiring in turn that the playhouses sign up only with them. This policy ruthlessly eliminated competition from independent acting troupes. And because the aim of the syndicate was to fill the house at each performance—that is, to make the most money possible—it chose to send on tour almost exclusively the tried-and-true popular shows, notably melodrama, while the experimental and less popular but often artistically superior plays went begging. Under such repressive conditions, new playwrights of significance had scarcely any chance to develop. Had Anderson tried to write for the theater during those days, he would surely have become frustrated and gone back to journalism. Nor were conditions for original playwrights any better when the rival monopoly of the Shubert brothers, Sam and Lee and J.J., began to compete with the syndicate and eventually replace it. During World War I, the "road" began to weaken and with it the monopolistic domination that had discouraged for so long on these shores the introduction of all but a tiny handful of daringly original dramas.

During the early days managers (as producers were called then) wielded for the most part outrageous control over dramatic writings, all aspects of production, and even subsidiary rights; this was true for conditions all the way up through the first quarter of this century. To say that the early American playwright (British, too, for that matter) was treated like a pariah is no exaggeration. Unlike today, when the dramatist is a prince receiving a liberal percentage of the box-office receipts, following a set scale for everyone in that craft, the unestablished playwright in the early days received a small salary, or flat payment for the script, or royalties amounting to 1 to 2 percent of the gross box-office receipts. The manager grabbed at least 50 percent of stock, amateur, and motion-picture rights![11] In 1905, when the thousand-foot reeler *Raffles* appeared, the first ever based on a play, the only person to share in the profits was the film maker, for the law at that time recognized no such property as "motion-picture rights." And just as theater managers were frequently arrogant in their treatment of the author and his script, film makers were even more so, stealing the plots and titles of plays without authorial content or recompense. When Elmer Rice was under contract to write scripts for Metro-Goldwyn-Mayer and wanted to sell one he had done in addition to the work required of him, his immediate superior agreed but only on condition that Rice invest half the sale money in a questionable oil company that the other man was organizing. The playwright agreed. The oil stock never earned a penny.[112] The theater manager sometimes required the dramatist to give him an option on motion-picture rights in return for a modest sum, and if the play proved to be a hit he would earn thousands from the sale of those rights. If the author dared to refuse selling him the option, the manager would hold up the stage production indefinitely.

Another irritant to an author was that the manager picked the cast and director without consulting him at all and made changes in the script as he saw fit. Elmer Rice said that he had once worked for a particularly stingy and ignorant vulgarian named Bill Brady, who seems to have been typical of his breed. Brady once put together a shoestring show using such "worn-out old sets and worn-out old actors . . . that one Wednesday it achieved a record: nobody, I mean *nobody,* bought a ticket for the matinee; at three o'clock they dismissed the cast. I've never, before or since, heard of a New York performance which drew not a single customer." Brady asked him on one occasion whether he had seen a certain Brady show that had failed by the end of the week; Rice replied "yes" and told him that it was wretched, but the frank response didn't bother Brady at all. All he wanted to know was whether Rice now could write something that would make use of the four leftover sets that were still in good condition. "He was obviously disappointed and bewildered when I refused," Rice said.[113]

Going to the other extreme, we have the benevolent autocrat of good taste in the manager Arthur Hopkins. In staging *What Price Glory* he had picked the cast, chosen the sets, appointed himself director, and gone so far as to delete some offending words in the dialogue without, it seems, consulting Anderson or Stallings, but Hopkins was fair-minded and liberal when it came to paying out royalties. Up until approximately the heyday of O'Neill, new and at the same time artistically important plays had a very hard time getting staged in America because, as implied earlier, the kind of fare most in demand—at least by the syndicates, who did all the distribution—was pure escapist entertainment; and since the manager's interest was simply to make money, it was strictly a businessman's theater, not an artist's.

But thanks to the rise of the Provincetown Players in 1916 and to the formation of the Theatre Guild in 1919, and to other causes that need not be mentioned here, more and more managers became willing to take a chance on work of artistic merit even though it carried more than the usual financial risk. In the battle of art versus commercialism, art was at last getting in a few sound punches.

Once authors saw that stagehands, musicians, and actors were beginning to unionize, they decided to protect themselves by founding The Dramatists Guild. The Guild members eventually formulated a revolutionary document called a "Minimum Basic Agreement between Authors and Managers" which they required managers to sign before consenting to have their works produced by them; and among various other provisions, the document required that the negotiating manager not tamper with the script without the author's consent, not sell the film rights, and not pick the director and cast without first getting the author's approval. All these provisions are now taken for granted in theatrical circles, but upon first seeing them the managers became almost apoplectic with anger and put up tremendous resistance. By 1926, however, the insistent playwrights finally forced most of the influential managers to sign the document, the main holdouts being the Shubert brothers, Anne Nichols (who still presided over her long-running *Abie's Irish Rose*), and one other, who continued to fulminate against the new provisions. It just so happens that three of the future members of the Playwrights Company—Elmer Rice, Robert E. Sherwood, and Sidney Howard—served their terms as president of The Dramatists Guild and as such defended the Minimum Basic Agreement against constant opposition from managers.[114]

Producer-director Theresa Helburn blasted the new contract, for in her eyes it made the manager into a "money-raising office boy." Furthermore, she complained, "A man may be a brilliant playwright but that does not mean he is also an expert or effectual producer. . . . There is no field, I suppose, in which writers make more frequent or more serious mistakes. . . . sometimes I wish authors would be content to be read and not heard."[115] This same Miss Helburn happened to be one of those on the board of directors of the Theatre Guild, whose stated policy was to *exclude* the playwright from all phases of production.

At least three playwright organizations had existed in the United States in the decade before the founding of the Playwrights Company. In the season of 1934-35 Arthur Hopkins had brought together briefly in an advisory and writing cabinet Maxwell Anderson, Sidney Howard, Robert E. Sherwood, Philip Barry, and Laurence Stallings, but it broke up when Barry decided that he didn't care to write in a cheek-by-jowl association, and Stallings displayed an apparent indifference to playwriting by heading off to Africa to work on newsreels.

Another similar organization was the Dramatists' Theatre, Inc., headed by a consortium of now obscure writers that included Edward Childs Carpenter and James Forbes. Nothing came of it either.

Still another group, this one definitely "leftist" politically, was the New Playwrights, whose most important member was Anderson's neighbor John Howard Lawson. It, too, vanished like a snowcone in August.[116]

Elmer Rice in his autobiography tells us about the revolt that he and four of his confreres carried out against the Theatre Guild and how they ended up founding the Playwrights Company:

In mid-November 1937 I attended a meeting of the council of the Dramatists' Guild. It was a dull day and a dull meeting. When it was over, I entered the elevator with Robert Sherwood and Maxwell Anderson. We agreed that a drink was in order. We went to a gloomy bar [Whaler Bar at the Midston Hotel] and, over our drinks, voiced our dissatisfaction with the theatre. My own views had been too well publicized to require much exposition, but Sherwood and Anderson spoke vehemently of their disenchantment with Broadway producers, particularly the Guild Theatre, which had presented many of their plays. They were harassed by disagreements about casting, revisions, and the disposition of subsidiary rights. If only their plays could be done as they wanted them to be done, without interference! We began exploring the feasibility of a group of playwrights organizing for the production of their own plays. . . . when Anderson and Sherwood asked if I would join them I immediately assented, for the proposed setup eliminated most of the conditions of the Broadway theatre which I had found unsatisfactory. We asked Sidney Howard if he wanted to come along with us; as we had anticipated, he was enthusiastic.[117]

The quartet of Anderson, Rice, Howard, and Sherwood decided that they needed a fifth member. Someone thought up the name of Philip Barry, but they turned him down because he had already proved himself too much of a loner; they instead picked S. N. Behrman. When they approached him, Behrman accepted but with reservations, for like Barry he felt uncomfortable writing in close association. (All of the five save for Behrman had already won the Pulitzer Prize at least once.) All of the members were friends; all were in middle age, Anderson being the eldest; all were well-established playwrights who had had works presented by the prestigious Theatre Guild; all were university men (three from Harvard); all were pacifists up through most of the 1930s; and three of the five had been journalists. What is of special significance is that they generally shared liberal, humanitarian views and injected into their writings some kind of serious conviction about social or political, military or religious issues of their day. No wonder they got along well—most of the time.

Wharton, the Playwrights Company's legal counsel, thought that the "merriest member of the group" was moon-faced Samuel Nathaniel Behrman—called "Sam" by his friends—who was a "perpetual fountain of wit, comment, and anecdote." Behrman treasured his colleagues mainly for their pleasant society and like Anderson cared not a whit for business discussions. Actually, Behrman didn't even want to produce his own plays,[118] but it took him many years to act on that conviction and resign. He was born into a Jewish middle-class family in the small town of Worcester, Massachusetts, on June 9, 1893, and early developed a love for English literature (his books *People in a Diary* and *Portrait of Max* show him to be an Anglophile). In his *The Worcester Account,* later dramatized as *The Cold Wind and the Warm,* he told about his boyhood. While he was still in high school he contrived a one-act play, which he then sold to a vaudeville company. But that wasn't all; he next mounted the stage to act in it. After attending Clark University he went on to Harvard, where he studied drama in the English '47 workshop taught by Professor George P. Baker, the same workshop attended over the years by Philip Barry, Sidney Howard (his classmate there), Frederick Koch, John Dos Passos, Eugene O'Neill, Edward Sheldon, and Thomas Wolfe. At Columbia University, where Behrman completed his work for the M.A., he came under the influence of John Erskine and also Brander Matthews, the first teacher to hold the position of professor of dramatic literature in any American university. After graduation, Behrman continued to write plays, and to support himself he turned out newspaper and magazine articles and worked as a theater press agent.

Like Max Anderson, Behrman began his dramatic career by doing collaborations with various people; none of these collaborations successful. *The Second Man,* finished while he was still at Columbia, was finally staged after he had spent eleven years trying to interest producers in it. In 1927 it became a success. This piece supports the values of upper-class society where one can choose to be wealthy and avoid involvement in the tough and unpleasant issues of the day, a stance that Behrman was to keep all his life—maybe to avoid losing that detachment he felt was necessary in the art of high comedy—and which marks him off so distinctly from Rice, Anderson, and the later Sherwood. *The Second Man* is in some ways representative of all his best work: characters from the social register who have a sophisticated, graceful, worldly air—notably a perceptive woman; a fairly light plot; and urbane and mildly amusing dialogue.

Behrman wrote slowly and put out a comedy about every two years, with the result that critics have admired his jewellike craftsmanship and incisively sketched characters; indeed, his main rival in America for drawing-room comedy is Philip Barry, whose vogue is in a tailspin. Behrman has been called with justice the American Congreve.[119] Among Behrman's best works are to be counted *Serena Blandish,* based on Enid Bagnold's novel; *Meteor; Brief Moment; Biography* (most likely his masterpiece); *Rain from Heaven; End of Summer* (his own favorite); *Amphitryon 38,* an adaptation from Giraudoux; *No Time for Comedy,* a personally revealing play in which Behrman "attempts to work out his own attitude toward the violent political events of the late Thirties"[120]); *Wine of Choice;* and *Jacobowsky and the Colonel,* still another of his many adaptations, this one from Franz Werfel. Like the other members of the Playwrights Company he did a stint in Hollywood now and then.

Though he was also a biographer and novelist, he will be remembered as a playwright, and his limitation there is that much of what he wrought follows a formula.[121]

In the year that the playwrights first met together to form their company, 1937, Behrman married Eliza Heifetz, sister of noted violinist Jascha Heifetz.[122]

Sidney Coe Howard was another member who married into a famous musical family: His second wife was the daughter of composer and conductor Walter Damrosch. Howard, with the short-cropped hair and lean, taut features and who looked like a marine officer in mufti, was a natural leader; about him lay what Wharton called a "curious quality of dominance." Such was his air of authority that when he was writing screenplays for David Selznick, a magnate notoriously late for appointments, Selznick took care never to be late to one with Howard. In his business letters to Wharton we can see a mind keen to discover weaknesses in the contract that was being drawn up for the fledgling organization.[123] Howard was a decisive man who spoke with a crisp clarity of speech.

He was born in Oakland, California, on June 26, 1891, the son of a steamship executive who had an intense interest in culture, and of a mother who was a trained musician. Howard attended the University of California and then went on to Harvard. On the Western Front during World War I, he served in the ambulance corps and later in the air branch as a commissioned pilot. After the war was over, he worked on *The New Republic,* the old *Life,* and *Hearst's International Magazine;* on the latter he was a radical reporter writing articles about industrial spying.

Like Anderson, Howard began his dramatic career by tackling a romantic subject in poetry, called *Swords,* in blank verse and treating with the Guelphs and Ghibellines. It failed on the stage. But in 1924 came *They Knew What They Wanted,* which brought him the Pulitzer Prize and substantial popularity; this was followed by the often-acted *Silver Cord,* a Freudian assault on momism that antedated Philip Wylie's *Generation of Vipers.* Other successful plays were *Yellow Jack* (with Paul de Kruif, about how the U.S. Army conquered yellow fever), *Alien Corn, The Ghost of Yankee Doodle,* and *The Late Christopher Bean* (adapted from René Fauchois).

Howard's twenty-four plays, many of them adaptations, reveal him as a person with considerable technical skill and no little courage, as where he reverses the Paolo-Francesca theme in *They Knew What They Wanted* to give an honest and practical even if sentimental and un*macho* solution to the problem of what the Napa Valley vintner does when he discovers that his mail-order wife has been seduced by his handsome young hired man. Although Howard was not strong in originality or given to experimentation, as were Anderson and Rice, he could write gripping story lines and lay bare the essential motives of his characters, many of whom furnished strong story roles for the leading actors and actresses of his day.

Howard assisted in several productions but before he could finish his first play for the Playwrights Company he became the victim of a freak farm accident. As he stood before his tractor and cranked it, not realizing that it was in gear, it leaped forward and crushed him to death. His passing was a shock to his colleagues. Behrman wept openly. As testimony to the high regard in which they held him, the company set up the Sidney Howard Memorial Award, which provided fifteen hundred dollars to the most promising new playwright of the year.[124]

The life of Elmer Rice, born Elmer Leopold Reizenstein in New York on September 28, 1892, is a success story on which even Horatio Alger could not have made improvements. As Rice tells us in his autobiography, *Minority Report,* he was the son of a poor and ignorant cigar maker of German-Jewish extraction. The father's epilepsy made him unable to work steadily; the family otherwise subsisted on the board money from an uncle and a grandfather until Rice himself went to work. As an only child (his younger brother died when Elmer was three), he grew up lonely in a culturally barren household that contained not a book until Elmer brought one home. He learned to read before starting school; the discovery of a public library in the neighborhood came into his life like an earthquake, and he read everything that suited his fancy—adventure stories, novels, plays; but his parents thought his preoccupation with reading was abnormal. The father picked on and criticized him constantly.

Elmer's grandfather took the little boy to the first plays he ever saw: These were dramatizations of Hans Christian Andersen's fairy tales done at the German Theater on Irving Place. His teeth grew unsightly because the family was too poor or negligent to get him proper dental care, and he became nearsighted long before anyone bought him glasses. This thin, homely, pugnacious-looking, red-haired genius grew up in a New York of street gangs, flickering five-cent cinemas, gaslights, elevated railways, horsecars, dung-laden thoroughfares, hurdy-gurdies, and itinerant vendors. At the end of his second year in the High School of Commerce, where he organized a literary society, his parents told him that they could no longer afford his education, whereupon he became a claims investigator and later a file clerk in his cousin's law office. Here is where most lads of promise would have dropped out of sight forever. But not the plucky little Elmer Rice. During evenings he attended New York Law School in which, bored with studies that were too easy for him, he often spent his time reading plays; and when he took the final examination two years later he supplied his answers in the form of blank verse, limericks, jokes, and quotations from Omar Khayyám, Shakespeare, and the Bible; but somehow he passed—and with honors. Though he also passed his bar examination, he decided to abandon law for a career in playwriting. He had found in the legal profession mainly a penchant for trickery, obfuscation, and moral blindness, all of which had no small part in shaping some of the plays he would write.

At the age of twenty-two Rice presented copies of *On Trial* to two producers; one of them, Arthur Hopkins, accepted it immediately, suggested an elaborate rewrite, and staged it before enthusiastic crowds. Rice made a hundred thousand dollars from it; and being a thrifty man, unlike Anderson, Rice probably put some away for hard times. In the murder mystery *On Trial* he used a rather new technique for the stage, the art of flashback, to show scenes that the trial witnesses describe. But it was a long time before he came up with his first major work and at the same time the first Expressionistic play in American drama, *The Adding Machine* (1923), a bizarre and unforgettable revelation of the modern robot man. *Street Scene,* with its realistic depiction of slum conditions, won him the Pulitzer Prize. Drawing upon the legal trickery he had witnessed so often in the court room while he was going to law school, he etched in acid his *Counselor-at-Law.* Actress Betty Field became his second wife; she starred in two of his plays, including his last important one, *Dream Girl,* whose heroine is the female equivalent of James Thurber's fictional Walter Mitty. Rice wrote many different types of plays—often at top speed, unfortunately[125]—including fantasies, comedies, melodramas, and Expressionistic fables. He was also active as theater director, novelist, and essayist.

More so than with the other Playwrights Company members, Rice was active in arbitration, anticensorship, and legal rights. He was president of the American Authors League, he founded The Dramatists Guild, and he served as board member of the American Civil Liberties Union. Equally important, he helped create the Federal Theater Project, famous in the 1930s for bringing inexpensive quality theater to millions of Americans who would never otherwise be able to afford a ticket, and he was in charge of the New York regional branch of it until the government forbade him to stage one of the widely applauded Living Newspaper skits called *Ethiopia* (an attack on the warmongering Mussolini regime). At this government censorship, Rice angrily resigned and not long afterward announced his retirement from the theater, took a slow trip around the world, and wrote a novel called *Imperial City.* He thought he might make a living from fiction. The Playwrights Company drew him out of retirement.

Wharton does not credit this dumpy little man with any of the charisma that Howard and Sherwood were said to possess, but Wharton praises Rice in the warmest terms for his loyalty to friends, his sympathy, his desire to help, and his unflagging energy in combating whatever he considered to be evil—and censorship was at the top of the list.[126]

In marked contrast with Rice is the gigantic Robert Emmet Sherwood, the man who turned out to be the acknowledged leader of the Playwrights Company after Howard's untimely death. Sherwood was a descendant of

Irish hero Robert Emmet, a grandson of novelist and article writer Mary E. W. Sherwood, and son of a highly successful investment broker and theater enthusiast. Sherwood's mother was a talented painter and illustrator who had won medals in Paris, Buffalo, St. Louis, and Chicago. It seemed natural that little Robert, born into the Sherwood household in New Rochelle, New York, on April 4, 1896, and weighing at birth fifteen pounds, would be big at something someday.

But at school it wasn't studies. At Milton Academy he was constantly in trouble and made mediocre grades, seemingly because of his preoccupation with extracurricular activities such as writing poems and stories for the literary magazine, creating and acting in plays—and setting fire to the building where his grades were filed (he then helped put out the blaze).

When he went to Harvard he failed freshman English—his best subject—and went on probation at the end of the year, once again a case of rebellion against academic discipline, but not laziness, for he was up to his ears writing items for the *Lampoon* and composing a play for the Hasty Pudding Club. It was the same kind of miserable academic record that F. Scott Fitzgerald was piling up at Princeton at about the same time. In Sherwood's sophomore year his grades were again atrocious, but he did manage to coauthor a play called *Barnum Was Right,* which toured several big cities a few years later. Before he reached his senior year, World War I began and he felt that he had to get involved; after the U.S. Army turned him down because of his height, he enlisted in the Canadian Black Watch regiment. He was sent to France where, in the fighting at Vimy Ridge, he was gassed and, upon going back into action at the front, was shot in the legs, brought back unconscious on a stretcher to Amiens, and spent several months in various hospitals. The horrors of battle, including his own legacy of a weakened heart and an excruciatingly painful *tic douloureux* (facial neuritis) that he would always suffer from, turned him, like so many other writers during the 1920s, into a hater of all war.

For a while he worked on *Vanity Fair,* the old *Life,* and *Scribner's.* Various reasons account for his turning to drama as a career: One was the pleasure he had taken in circuses he had witnessed as a child[127]; another, his having attended Anderson's *What Price Glory;* and still another, the stimulation he had received from visits to the Algonquin Round Table, whose habitués George Kaufman, Marc Connelly, and Edna Ferber were already writing plays. Sherwood with his glacially slow speech was nevertheless an accomplished wit at the Round Table. There he met the actress who was to be his first wife, Mary Brandon.

Hannibal having been a hero of his ever since school days, Sherwood read

Theodor Mommsen and other authorities about the great Carthaginian's campaigns in Italy in an effort to learn why Hannibal didn't destroy Rome when he had the chance, but not finding the answer in books he made a guess, and out of this came the hit *The Road to Rome*.

Sherwood's next commercial success was *Reunion in Vienna*. His *Acropolis*, which failed in London, is one of several instances in which his works parallel in subject matter those of Max Anderson: Each wrote a drama about ancient Athens, about the American Revolution, about the foolishness of war (Sherwood did several of these), about Americans fighting the Japanese in the Pacific during World War II, about a future American President, about a handsome married woman who goes into the camp of a famous general in the opposing army and tries to seduce him, about murder in a highway cafe out West, and about gangsters pursued by police. The two men were good friends, shared similar ideological views, wrote rather often for the popular market, framed works for some of the same actors and actresses who in turn were not above suggesting topics to the playwrights, and read and discussed each other's scripts as members of the Playwrights Company—all of these help explain the parallels.

Much of what Sherwood wrote is now considered trivial, and some of his more serious work is dated, but hardly anyone can question the genuine merit in *The Petrified Forest* and *Idiot's Delight*. The last important play he was ever to do was *Abe Lincoln in Illinois;* after that, the service of his country during wartime occupied much of his energy. The biography *Roosevelt and Hopkins* won him his last Pulitzer Prize.[128]

John F. Wharton, sandy of hair and pale of face, became for the group a combination business adviser, legal counsel, mediator, and—after his official role was ended—historian for the enterprise. Their getting him was a stroke of fortune. Even Rice, so suspicious of laywers, admired this man. By the time of his death in 1977, the quiet-voiced, kindly Wharton would be the author of three books and almost a hundred articles on economic and social problems; an officer in two musical organizations; a leader in ecology; a civil-defense worker (during World War II); and a winner of several awards (the magazine *Variety* dubbed him as "the man who had done the most for the theatre").[129]

The members of the Playwrights Company had each counted on investing ten thousand dollars in it, for at least a hundred thousand dollars was needed to get started; that left about fifty thousand dollars to come from outside backers. And among the most obvious of possible backers at that time was John Hay Whitney, wealthy dabbler in things theatrical, who happened to be a client of Wharton's. Through Howard's friendship with the lawyer the

Playwrights Company managed to talk to Whitney but were not able to make a satisfactory deal.[130] This was the beginning of their relationship with Wharton, who would remain with the company until it dissolved. They placed him immediately on an equal footing with themselves on all board decisions, which meant that, like them, he read every script, offered criticism, and passed on whether a given play reached the stage. No one can read his *Life among the Playwrights* without realizing that here is a shrewd but honest and likable figure, hopelessly stagestruck, enjoying immensely his singular relationship with the creative minds around him, and receiving the implicit trust of his sometimes temperamental colleagues.

He was born in a typical middle-class family in East Orange, New Jersey, where citizens looked askance at show people, and his mother told him that it was "unnatural" to have a nighttime career; consequently, though he became a theater buff at the age of eleven[131] and daydreamed about the excitement of playhouses, his mother turned him toward a career in law. After going to Columbia Law School he ended up in the prestigious firm of Cohen, Cole, Weiss, & Wharton, where many of his clients were important figures from film and stage.

On the day of the Playwrights Company's first meeting he took the nonartist's commonsense point of view and gave the talented men around him a friendly talk about the perils of emotional outbreaks; and knowing, also, that another danger lay in allowing friendship and admiration for each other to cloud their critical judgment, he warned them about this too.[132] Apparently no one took offense.

Other officials in the company who attended all meetings but were not on the board consisted of young Victor Samrock, the general manager, who had worked for the producing concern of Haight and Potter; and William Fields, the press representative, with experience serving the Ringling Brothers and Barnum & Bailey Circus.[133]

Basic capitalization for the company came from the sale of preferred stock; each playwright member, having invested $10,000, received 100 shares of preferred stock at $100 per share; and an additional 500 shares were sold to outside backers, most of whom Sherwood found at weekend parties on Long Island. The backers constituted a distinguished list, for they included three publishers, actor Raymond Massey, New York's future governor Averell Harriman, Mrs. Robert E. Sherwood, and the president of Columbia Broadcasting System.[134] In addition, there were 1,000 shares of Class A stock to be sold at $1.00 a share, and 1,500 of Class B stock to be sold at the same rate, both types bringing in $2,500. In the distribution of net profits each playwright would receive slightly over 11 percent, and Wharton 10 percent.[135]

On April 12, 1938, the five playwrights and John Warton signed a Basic Agreement for the Incorporation of the Playwrights Company, which ran, in part:

> The playwrights desire to organize a corporation by which plays hereafter written by the playwrights may be produced and exploited in the manner herein set forth; such corporation also to have the power to produce plays written by other dramatists.[136]

On July 1 they were legally incorporated by the state of Delaware. They set up temporary offices at 230 Park Avenue; later they moved to permanent offices on the thirty-eighth floor of the International Building at Rockefeller Center.[137]

The name they chose for their firm, Playwrights Company, stuck out like a lightning rod to attract bolts from Broadway's prophets of doom. Pundits accordingly gave them one season before going out of business, but all these pundits proved to be wrong. Over the course of its history, the company would add two additional artist members, Robert W. Anderson and Kurt Weill; and, when finances grew lean, the spectacularly successful real-estate operator Robert L. Stevens joined them in a reorganization that increasingly produced the plays of nonmembers. The company managed to survive for twenty-two years, at the end of which time new conditions in the theater joined to human mortality brought it to an end.[138]

Among the conditions they imposed upon themselves at the outset was that the company would get first option on any play that a member might write; if the group did not like the play, the writer was then free to peddle it elsewhere—and this sometimes happened. They also set a twenty-five-thousand-dollar production limit for any one show, a figure that seemed reasonable in those pre-inflation days but which had to be increased very soon when Anderson wrote a musical play. And most important of all for these artist-friends, each author had the final word on all details of production as long as he kept within the budget.[139]

As for what they expected to get out of this association, Max Anderson summed it up well years later. As he saw it, a playwright has always been a "bird of passage" in taking his scripts wherever he could find the best market; he had no business office he could call home, and what production arrangements he made did not last longer than the run of the play itself. And since the best plays written thus far had been done in the seventeenth century by people who were connected with stable production organizations consisting of dramatists and actors who owned stock in them and had a voice in their management, who is to say that something likewise good wouldn't come of the Playwrights Company? By a "pooling of brains and experience" he and his fellows had a better chance of expressing their individuality as artists than would be the case in agencies where profit is the sole or major consideration. (Since they didn't expect to get rich, they could at least afford to have their say.) They wanted to work with dramatists whose products they respected; the advice of such people would be valuable because it stemmed from considerable experience at the writing desk. In short, the Playwrights Company would provide a secure haven for their erstwhile "migratory careers." He thought that the biggest benefit for the members was that each could write just as he wanted and could produce his play as he pleased; no doubt he had in mind the elimination of many of those needless rewrites that he, for one, had had to make during Guild rehearsals.[140] And creative writing being the lonely enterprise it is, Anderson must have treasured the new arrangement all the more for the fellowship and intellectual stimuli it provided.

Most of the Playwrights Company members seem to have felt uncommon stimuli that first year, for by July 1, when they were formally a part of The Playwrights Producing Company, Inc., Anderson had shown a new facet of his talent by preparing his first musical play—as opposed to musical per se—which was *Knickerbocker Holiday*. Sherwood had written what was perhaps his magnum opus in *Abe Lincoln in Illinois*. Behrman had penned the most serious and subjective of all his comedies in the work significantly titled *No Time for Comedy*. And Rice was trying to finish *American Landscape*. All of these contributions would open on Broadway during the coming season; three of them would become hits—a most auspicious beginning for the Playwrights Company, which was supposed to fail within a year!

Burdened with his numerous financial obligations, Anderson decided to write a musical play because such a work, if successful on the stage, would bring in far more money than a straight play. Although *Winterset* and *High Tor* had been critically successful, neither one ran long enough—or was popular enough—to make a lot of money for him. He would "go commercial" this time.[141] It was embarrassing for him to be tardy in paying his ten thousand dollars to the Playwrights Company; after all, he had been one of those who had urged all the other playwrights to invest![142]

In early April 1938, when the Kurt Weills were guests at the Andersons', Max is said to have asked his friend, "Kurt, do you think we can make a musical comedy out of Washington Irving's *Knickerbocker History of New York*?" This is easily the most high-spirited and zany, charming and hilarious of all of Irving's creations, a veritable effusion of youthful fun in the guise of scholarship, perhaps the greatest of all burlesques on history. Weill agreed with him that they could do something with that quaint book. Since his own musical projects in New York were not flourishing, he was prepared to agree with almost any new project that his friend had in mind. The two of them then worked out the basic plot before Weill had to go to Hollywood later in the month, and Anderson's last words to him before parting were reportedly, "If the idea works out, I'll have the book ready upon your return."[143] They had already planned for the story's main events to occur during the troublesome reign of peg-legged Governor Peter Stuyvesant; also, for a love story about a young burgher who rebels against the dictatorial governor and a crooked town counselor. But during his associate's absence, Anderson developed the play along lines that must have finally discomfited Weill, satirist though he had been in Europe, for he happened to admire President Franklin D. Roosevelt: Just as Irving in his mock history had taken satirical shots at Thomas Jefferson in the person of Governor Wilhelmus Kieft, so Anderson decided to hit Roosevelt (and his New Deal administration) in the person of Stuyvesant.

The playwright took it upon himself to prepare the entire text as well as the librettos, doing the latter in the order in which he came to them.[144] One of his models for form seems to have been *The Mikado*.[145] It was the first time he had ever worked with Weill, or else Anderson might have known that Weill had rather definite ideas about where he wanted to insert the music and what kind of music it would be, and Weill wished that Anderson had planned all that more closely with him beforehand. But no hard feelings arose,[146] and he cheerfully went along with the political satire also.

Max Anderson had started out liking the aggressive Roosevelt,[147] whose emergency relief programs had begun to rescue the nation from the ravages of the Depression and give hope to millions, but as the years went by Anderson came to distrust the man for the increasing centralization of power that developed in the executive branch of government and threatened individual liberties. The personality of a single dominant figure, unprecedented in the boldness of his reforms, was being felt in the legislative and judicial branches of government as well. To Anderson, Roosevelt must have seemed on the verge of becoming a kind of despot. Nor was he alone in his fears about F.D.R. and the enlargement of the federal bureaucracy. The President already was fair game for attacks right and left, as witness Moss Hart and George S. Kaufman's successful musical farce *I'd Rather Be Right*, which in the preceding season had starred George M. Cohan (as F.D.R.) in a spoof of the New Deal.

At some point when the music was almost finished, the playwright-composer team invited out to New City young director Joshua Logan, at that time one of the notables of Broadway because of his triumphant Rogers and Hart musical *I Married an Angel*. Logan had long been an admirer of theirs: *What Price Glory* had been the big theatrical event of his life at fifteen; *The Threepenny Opera* had taken Berlin by storm when he was there, Lotte Lenya singing the role of Jenny. Incidentally, this director from the Deep South was going to be profoundly influenced by something that Anderson explained to him one day, namely the theory of the recognition scene, so much so that Logan employed it advantageously in every film and play he produced from that time onward. At his first meeting with the authors of *Knickerbocker Holiday* in New City, Logan listened to Weill play the piano and sing the new melodies. "My head was rattling a bit with what I'd heard," the director recalled. "It wasn't Dick Rogers, and Max wasn't Larry Hart, but everything about Kurt Weill was talent and enthusiasm. And Max's lyrics were poetic and funny. I knew I wanted to do the show and told them so. There was a small celebration consisting of clasped hands and squeezed shoulders. I was amazed by how much my approval meant to them."[148] After all, it *was* Anderson's first musical play since university days, and he was perhaps unsure of his technique; and Weill was eager to establish in America a reputation at least equal to what he had enjoyed in Germany.

A big problem arose. Brom Broeck had been written for actor Burgess Meredith, who at first wanted the part but then created trouble by backing out; there ensued a frantic and futile search to replace him with another young star who could project a likable rebel and could also sing. So there began a shift of emphasis in personalities that nearly ruined the play. Logan suggested that the Stuyvesant part be strengthened so that they could use it to attract a big star for the role now that Broeck's part could not draw a star; and that is what finally happened, the erstwhile villain moving into the spotlight, becoming halfway likable, too. Logan right away had perceived the attack on F.D.R. and secretly frowned on it, and maybe it was partly for this reason that he brought pressure on Anderson to humanize the portrait of the irascible Dutch governor. Someone suggested that the governor's role be filled by the fifty-four-year-old Walter Huston, at that time a celebrity for having had the lead in the stage and film versions of Sinclair Lewis's *Dodsworth*,[149] and Logan accordingly flew to Lake Arrowhead in California to read him the script of *Knickerbocker Holiday*.

Huston was a kind, lovable, even adorable man, but certainly a most unlikely choice to project any kind of Hitlerian dominance on the stage or anywhere else.[150] Even his photographs exude a happy, big-brother charm.

Nevertheless, Logan read the script to the actor and ended by singing the final lyric. Huston and his attractive wife, Nan, were enthusiastic.

"He's an old scoundrel," Huston concluded.

Logan began to feel a knot in his stomach. Was *this* actor going to back out too?

"Oh, I like the nasty part, except that the character's pretty skimpy."

"It can be longer," the director explained. Had Anderson authorized him to make this concession? We can't be sure.

"Not longer, just better. It's too one-note, too coolheaded. Couldn't this old bastard make love to that pretty young girl a bit? Not win her, just give her a squeeze or tickle her under the chin, and she could even consider him for a fraction of a second when she hears his song?"

"Song?"

"Sure—something nice I could sing to her. I like the other songs, 'The Scars' particularly, but I mean something, you know, a moment for the old son-of-a-bitch to be charming."

"No problem, Walter, you'll have the song you want. I guarantee it."[151] Hence the search for "September Song."

Even making allowances for a possible aberration of memory on Logan's part after a lapse of almost four decades, the foregoing exchange is a good example of what Anderson meant in his essay "Compromise and Keeping the Faith" about the necessity for the playwright to compromise on little points as long as he keeps the essential integrity of the play intact. Of course, we can't be sure just how far the director was authorized to go in his bargaining, but Anderson did finally agree, and the little adjustments did take place. The shifting of emphasis in *Knickerbocker Holiday* was, however, reaching a critical point.

The young director returned to New York with the good news—they had a star at last—and Weill immediately wired Huston the question: "What is the range of your voice?" Back came the answer: "I have no range. Appearing tonight on Bing Crosby program. Will sing a song for you."[152] Weill and Anderson got together and tuned in; what the actor crooned was one of his old vaudeville numbers. The voice was low and husky, full of gravel, yet the man clearly knew how to put over a song.

After the broadcast was over the musician turned to his friend and proposed, "Let's write a sentimental romantic song for him." Soon they set to their tasks—apparently the next day—and Max wrote the words in an hour and turned them over to his colleague who, by that evening, had the music prepared. That was how "September Song" was born. Weill's widow claims that the pair actually wrote three different versions, one of which was chosen for the play.[153]

Logan and Weill then sang "September Song" over the telephone to Huston. Afterward came a pause during which they listened intently for the vaudevillian's reaction. "Yes, yes, yes, yes, yes—play me the tune again," he urged. They did.

Huston amazed them by singing the whole piece back to them.[154] A good omen—the song had stuck with him. Maybe it would stick with the public too.

Members of the production cast were certain that the love duet "It Never Was You" would prove popular, but they were all surprised when "September Song," as crooned by the irresistible Huston, became the favorite. Crowds demanded it as an encore. The song so enchanted audiences elsewhere, too, that Huston even sang it at curtain calls in another show long after *Knickerbocker Holiday* had passed into theatrical history. It is still heard and enjoyed today by countless people, most of whom have no inkling of its origin. Of Max's many accomplishments this one hauntingly lovely song about a man's autumnal love for a girl would earn him, surprisingly enough, the most money of all through sales of records, sheet music, and other rights,[155] and it still gives tidy royalties to his estate and Weill's.[156]

In this rollicking costume story full of fat little Dutchmen with knee breeches and long pipes, the nominal hero is Brom, a Dutch variant of Van Dorn, who creates trouble for himself by accusing Mynheer Tienhoven of selling brandy and firearms to the Indians. The state council, not able to stand the exposure of one of its members, condemns Brom to be hung as part of some holiday festivities; the peg-legged Stuyvesant happens along, fortunately, and frees him, but changes his mind when he literally smells defiance in this new breed of American. Brom's view of government is characteristically Andersonian, for he thinks all governments are corrupt but that democracy has an enormous advantage over other forms of rule because it is so incompetent and awkward in its corruption. The play ends with Brom persuading the council to reassert its old democratic authority as the lesser of evils and thus keep the government small and funny.[157]

One can look in vain in the preface to *Knickerbocker Holiday* for any direct mention of Roosevelt, but the political target is sufficiently clear. Anderson tells us that under the cloak of emergency relief the "efficient" New Deal administration is sneaking in the welfare state, that all this creeping socialism will necessarily increase government control to the point of tyranny. Therefore, better by far to have a relatively inefficient democracy that at least enables people to remain free than to have the cold-blooded but "efficient" juggernaut of totalitarianism that is presently grinding over the peoples of Europe and Asia. Thus the preface reinforces the message in the play text.

Elmer Rice labels the play an attack on Roosevelt and what Anderson considered unwarranted methods of social reform, and says that he (Rice) and other members of the Playwrights Company, all of them Roosevelt supporters, had used cajolery to get Anderson to take out some of the "more pointed references to the New Deal."[158]

During a tryout in Washington, D.C., four days before the supposedly "big opening" at the Barrymore Theatre in New York, an unexpected distinguished guest took a box seat at the performance. This was President Roosevelt himself, no less. As the great man reached his box, Kurt Weill led the orchestra in playing "The Star-Spangled Banner," whereupon the President stood up, reminding Logan of a "caped statue of victory." Cheers rang through the house until Roosevelt sat down again. The play represented something special for him because this was only the second time he had attended the theater since reaching the White House. His friendship with Huston had drawn him, we know that; maybe something else did too. An anonymous reporter who covered this event noted that none of the many allusions to the events of the times were lost on the chief executive; Logan went even further and recorded in his memoirs that the whole audience looked compulsively at the President each time to learn if he was laughing— and he "howled at each joke. . . . To a blind man, it must have seemed like an empty auditorium except for one crazy, laughing fool."[159]

Stuyvesant's line "Democracy is government by amateurs" made the President's head go back in laughter, the reporter noted in the article. In that part where Stuyvesant planned to declare war on Connecticut so he could whip into shape his soft and timid army, and a fearful council member rose to ask whether they might not send Connecticut a letter instead and hand over Boston as a sop, both the President and the rest of the audience found a sally that Anderson probably had not intended at all, but they laughed heartily anyway. It just so happened that on the previous September 26 Roosevelt had sent a vain telegram of request to Hitler and Beneš that they settle the German-Czech controversy by negotiation rather than war. Other laughs came from the distinguished guest—and again we rely on the more sober reporter rather than Logan, with his penchant for exaggeration—when the councilman named Roosevelt, a fat and timorous little Dutchman, answered his name early at a roll call.[160]

President Roosevelt invited some of the cast to a party in the White House. Anderson refused to attend; probably he couldn't stomach the idea of shaking hands with a man he had satirized. When the others arrived in the Oval Office, Roosevelt was already there, seated, and they began to call out their requests for drinks. He told them in a loud voice that he had enjoyed the play very much—except for the "letter" joke, for he had sent a *telegram* to Hitler. When someone brought up the possibility that war with Germany was unavoidable, Roosevelt agreed.

"Unavoidable. Doesn't everyone know it? It's only a question of when. Maybe six months, maybe a year. If I hadn't sent that telegram, we'd be at war now." This last sentence contained the very kind of boast that would have made Anderson smile to hear it.

And the chief executive stared at Logan and pointed to him.

"*You* can do something too."

"Me? What?"

"Put some warnings into that play of yours. Make people know we are in danger. Stick a pin in them. We are going to be attacked, and the longer it takes us to know it, the greater the enemy's advantage."[161]

The play was already changed so much from its original that it couldn't bear further tampering, even in the cause of national defense. Anderson was to serve his country well, but in other ways.

Thanks to the extensive news coverage of the Roosevelt visit in newspapers, in magazines, and on the radio, the play attracted a lot of additional customers when it reached New York. *Time* magazine carried a cover picture of Huston in his costume. The reviews, however, were mixed: Joseph Wood Krutch praised the new show; Richard Watts, Jr., and others singled out Huston for encomiums; George Jean Nathan said that Anderson didn't know much about creating musical comedy. The critics generally ignored "September Song"—but it became a hit within a week or two. *Knicker-bocker Holiday* had a run of 168 performances in New York and also a nine-week tour, which gave Anderson a comfortable income for a while.[162]

Now that we have reached this high-water mark of popular if not artistic success, when Max Anderson had plenty of money again, it is appropriate to say a few things about his heartwarming generosity to family, friends, and strangers, starting with the stage success of *What Price Glory* and continuing for the rest of his life. Lela writes of her illustrious brother that

he never forgot his family and in one way or another he helped all of his brothers and sisters to an easier life than we had ever known. I shall never forget my own surprise and delight when he sent me a check for a hundred dollars at Christmas time in 1924. I had never seen so much money at one time before. A great deal of the pleasure that he derived from his success was that he could do things for the people he loved. For me and my family his help made a tremendous difference and quite changed the direction of our lives.[163]

He advanced the down payment on a farm that Lela and her husband wanted in Hinsdale, New York. Years later, he loaned them $1,950 at interest, and still later he sent checks to cover the educational expenses of their sons Keith and Avery.[164]

In his correspondence we learn that he paid the whole cost for the Hinsdale, New York, farm that he gave to his father and mother at the time the minister retired.[165] He also helped his sister Ethel and her husband, Ralph Chambers, to keep their farm going.[166]

Sometimes Kenneth aided him in such disbursements through his role as business manager of Anderson House Publishing Company, in which the playwright shared a joint partnership; out of the royalties from Maxwell Anderson plays a sizable chunk went into a special fund, and many a time the dramatist wrote or telephoned him to mail such-and-such an amount to relative "A" or "B," who needed it urgently, and Kenneth obliged him. For instance, in a letter dated December 15, 1933, Kenneth wrote to his famous brother that he had just sent a check to their needy sister Ruth. Another letter mentions a loan to Kenneth himself.[167] And so on. Anderson received very little money from Anderson House profits because of having skimmed off so much in advance for these numerous charities.[168]

There are the moneys, spoken of earlier, that went off to Uncle Frank Anderson, to Aunt Emma Harper, and to Margaret's mother, Mrs. Haskett. A loan of $500 went to Margaret's salesman brother James E. Haskett; $1,200 more loaned to James; and payments of $5.00 a week during the Depression to help support the out-of-work husband of James' sister, Elizabeth S. Hamilton—and when Mr. Hamilton found a job, the $5.00 was shifted to Anderson's sister Ruth.[169] The biggest regular monthly dole was apparently the $300 a month he sent year after year to Mab's extravagantly wasteful mother in Florida.[170] Due to the incompleteness of the record, one can assume that these samples—I found many more!—represent only a small fraction of Anderson's largess to the family. Much of the time he initiated the loan or gift, as if self-conscious about having all to himself so much of a good thing while knowing its potential for bringing even more happiness to someone down on his or her luck.

Apparently even the slightest request for a legitimate loan or gift was enough to make him get out the checkbook. An aspiring young writer told him that he was all primed to write a novel, and would do it too, but could one believe it? He owned no typewriter. No need to tell what Anderson bought him. This sort of generosity happened many times, according to Anderson's neighbor, Mrs. Julie Sloane.[171] He gave some land for a house to the brilliant piano teacher Julian Poor (Bessie's brother), the man who in Vienna had forever spoiled his chances for a concert career by freezing his fingers at practice in an unheated garret.[172] And then there was the Russian basso profundo Alexandre Mirsky, who with his hysterical wife, Helen, went through the motions of playing hired parents for the Anderson boys in the farmhouse while Anderson was away; though they were nonentities on the job, Anderson continued to smile on them and even paid for Alexandre's voice lessons. Anderson even got him a small role in *Valley Forge*.[173]

Anderson was generous in reading scripts mailed to him by aspiring young writers. Some of the plays submitted were in verse, for in the 1930s he was the world's leading exponent of dramatic verse and seemed in avant-garde circles to herald a revival of that genre. "What I long for more than anything else," he wrote to his friend Margery Bailey, once a classmate of his at Stanford and now a professor there, "is to see and welcome into the theater some youngster or youngsters who have an instinctive grasp of the problems it took me decades to approach solving, and who can write plays that will put the modern drama on a par, at least in attempt, with the best there's been." He went so far as to cooperate with her in setting up a national competition for verse plays and offering a cash prize of one hundred dollars and a production for the best script.[174] The contest went off as planned; out of ninety-eight scripts submitted, Florette Henri's *Surrey* was the winner, and Bailey forwarded it to Anderson so that he could consider it for a production on Broadway. Upon reading *Surrey* he thought that the girl had genuine dramatic talent but weakened her verse sometimes by decorating with borrowed ornaments.[175]

WORLD WAR II
AND THE
PROBLEM OF FAITH

B y early 1938 it was clear to many that vast thunderheads presaging
World War II were rising in Europe and Asia. It was only natural that
such events would affect the life and art of Maxwell Anderson, that
ardent champion of individual liberty. He was to involve himself in World
War II far more than in the first one, as reflected in the subject matter of his
plays, in personal visits to military camps and a war zone, and in various types
of refugee and civil-defense work.

On May 28 he aired on radio his one-acter about the Spanish Civil War
called *The Bastion Saint-Gervais;*[1] no one could miss its anti-fascist ring. Like
many Americans, he was beginning to sense the threat of numerous dictator-
ships newly risen around the world and the imminent possibility that America might be sucked into a global war. Directly and indirectly some of his
plays and other writings began to show a shift in his attitude toward democracy: At first he contented himself with attacking fascism (as we have
seen already in *Knickerbocker Holiday*), and then he began actively defending democracy as mankind's shining hope.

More evidence of change in his thinking occurred on the night of November 20, 1938, when the Playwrights Company gave benefit performances of
both *Knickerbocker Holiday* and *Abe Lincoln in Illinois,* and Anderson stood
up during an intermission in his play to ask the audience for contributions to

a relief fund for German refugees who were pouring into America. He must have been strongly worked up over his topic because public speeches were rare with him. His colleague Sherwood, during an intermission of *Abe Lincoln in Illinois* at the Plymouth Theatre, made a similar speech.[2] It would be several years before Anderson started keeping a diary, but Sherwood had already started one; in it he had recorded not many weeks earlier that he, for one, had to start battling for an end to America's isolation, that the hopes of humanity depended on America assuming its rightful role of leadership and all the attendant responsibilities.[3] And before very long he would act on his convictions by going to work for President Roosevelt as chief of the overseas branch of the Office of War Administration, even act as his adviser, and write many of his best speeches. He and Anderson differed widely in their attitude toward F.D.R., but they were of one mind about the threat of war, the need to rally Americans in defense of their country, and the plight of the refugees and the Western Allies.

During his theater speech, Anderson mentioned that everybody involved in the production of *Knickerbocker Holiday,* from stagehands to dramatist, was waiving that night's earnings so that all of the box-office receipts could go to the relief fund. He begged his audience to contribute also. The conclusion of his talk shows that somewhere between the completion of the play and the delivery of the speech—a matter of only a few months—the rapidly worsening international crisis had caused him to soften his opposition to increased federal control now that a war for survival loomed ahead:

> And now please forgive me if I add a personal word about the possibility of war between the democracies and the dictatorships. . . . It is in the American tradition to give generously in a time of calamity, and we must do that—but let us not be misled by our sympathy for the persecuted and oppressed into believing that we can make the world over by force of arms. Participation in a modern war means dictatorship, even for us, and the abrogation of our liberties. Dictatorships are hard to get rid of, liberties are hard to win back.
>
> But it may be that modern civilization has come to its great crisis. It may be that, much as we dislike war, much as we may fear the effect of the war upon our own liberties, we may be unable to avoid a conflict with the dictatorships of Europe and Asia. Just as this nation once discovered that it could not endure half slave and half free, the earth as a whole may soon discover that it cannot exist half free and democratic, half Nazie [sic] and enslaved.[4]

Other members of the Playwrights Company had also begun making their separate artistic responses to the challenge of war. Sherwood's *Abe Lincoln in Illinois* had an obvious patriotic appeal; the Lincoln story lured Eleanor Roosevelt to attend and write him a letter of congratulations.[5] Rice's *American Landscape* failed on the stage in December but it, too, affirmed the American way of life and its traditions.

In the spring of 1939 Anderson published *The Essence of Tragedy and Other Footnotes and Papers,* the title essay of which constitutes his most significant statement on dramatic theory. He also began work on his tragedy *Key Largo,* basing the name and the plot on an unidentified incident he said had happened the previous winter when he drove through Key Largo, Florida.[6] The story in it is reminiscent of Joseph Conrad's *Lord Jim* in that a young man, in a moment of trial, makes a fateful decision, grows ashamed of himself for it, and in a final deed of heroism wins back his lost honor. This play penetrates far more than did *What Price Glory* into the whys and wherefores of war. And although *Key Largo* adheres to Anderson's dramatic theory in every respect—the hero developing from weakness to self-realization—it was not destined to have a corresponding success with the American theater public when it finally reached the stage a few months later.[7]

But the play's main interest lies in its dramatic working out of Anderson's cosmic philosophy, which had arrived two years earlier in his beautiful and inspiring and heavily Existentialist essay called "Whatever Hope We Have." Before turning to instances of this philosophy in the play itself, it would be best to summarize the essay: Anderson tells us that there are only a few, often unreliable rules to guide us in matters of ordinary living; and as for the big questions, the universe is completely silent in giving us help. Man's essence is not what he happens to be at any given moment but what he imagines and wants to become. This is analogous to Keats' idea that we make our own souls. Moreover, Anderson believes that man lives an ephemeral life voyaging among the constellations where there is no certainty about the meaning of life or destiny save for an occasional insight offered by science or religious instruction, art, or the idealism of the young. He learns that great souls before him—Plato, Christ, Shakespeare, Bach, Beethoven—have set down, usually in symbolic form, their records of noble victory or suffering or defeat, and these records have the dual function of prophecy as well as motivation for man to pursue a far-off goal for the race. The net result is a racial dream that mankind can ultimately improve itself in wisdom and goodness.

"Whatever Hope We Have" informs us that Anderson acquired these views from what he had learned about the supreme achievements in music, poetry, and the graphic and fine arts; in the Sermon on the Mount; and in the last chapter of Ecclesiastes.[8] His idealism owes something (as pointed out earlier) to Emerson's essays; to one or more of the formal Existentialists; to the beautifully melancholy skepticism of Matthew Arnold, a favorite poet of his; to his readings in science; to his father's Christian humanism, despite fundamental differences in theology; and to his own idealistic and rebellious personality, which refused to acknowledge in history's long twilight of the gods any dimming of the human spirit. But various facets of his life show that he was far from content in having rejected all formal religion: Once the Christian feast was removed, there remained only poor man's porridge.

In the play *Key Largo* the hero is King McCloud, a young turncoat from the Spanish Civil War who is now trying to find in a Florida fishing resort some reintegration for his shattered spirit. The wise man who advises him is blind d'Alcala, father of McCloud's sweetheart, and he delivers such eloquently poetic lines as to make us believe that here is a chapter from Anderson's own spiritual testament. D'Alcala urges the turncoat to keep up a faith in this admittedly godless universe, but McCloud is now skeptical of all faiths whatsoever.

When the hero questions whether the universe is empty of any significance and supernaturalism, his question hearkens back to Epicurus' vision of the gods as serenely indifferent to man's needs and interests. More especially, his question has a melancholy, modern sound with its emptiness and negation and estrangement; it subsumes a complex of factors peculiar to modern civilization such as Frankensteinian technology enslaving its master, political institutions deaf to human needs, disruption of traditional religious order and certainty caused partly by the new sciences with their gospel of materialism and skepticism, partly by the insights afforded us by thinkers like Charles Darwin, Sören Kierkegaard, Freidrich Nietzsche, Karl Marx, Sigmund Freud, and Albert Einstein.

The playwright's persona in *Key Largo,* however, who is d'Alcala, answers all this with his cosmic philosophy. He says that again and again man rises from the muck of the evolutionary processes; looks around him; realizes to his profound distress that he is all alone on a godforsaken planet spinning through the interstellar void; and then sinks back in fear of this starkly brutal truth. Time and again man makes a religion out of his hope, follows it to the uttermost limits, and then the feeling of aloneness in the universe strikes him down like a disease. But in spite of this recurring disappointment man has a great and noble destiny, we are told, for he will someday be able to "face even the stars without despair,/and think without going mad" *(Key Largo,* page 114, Act II). Through his mouthpiece d'Alcala, Anderson gives us not only a cogent explanation of that peculiar sickness of our times, which is the mind's subtle attack on itself, but also a poignant hope that man must and will persevere as an idealist in a universe bereft of God and be guided along the way by some noble purpose that, however vague it may be now, is nevertheless sure.

By the summer of 1939 Anderson was in Hollywood again, grinding away at screenplays and refusing to fill out an application form for Social Security, which he considered an invasion of his rights.[9] He pointed out in a letter to theater critic Brooks Atkinson about this time that not even artists would be able to function well if federal power ever extended into the lives of individual citizens. "It's my opinion that the evils of capitalism are the evils of the jungle, the evils of collectivism those of the ant-hill. And since we must choose between them I prefer the jungle. After all, we evolved from the jungle. Nothing will ever evolve from the ant-hill."[10]

While in California he revised *Both Your Houses* for the Midsummer Drama Festival at the Pasadena Playhouse, which was to honor him by putting on a total of eight of his plays during the period from June 26 to August 19. He was the only playwright represented. It was a tribute to his high standing in the American theater. He changed the dialogue near the end of the story to make Congressman McClean now defend the American government as being the best in the world, the best ever planned by men, and to say that if any harm arises it is from the men who run it. The resulting script is a far cry from the 1933 published version in which McClean excoriates Congress for its rottenness; more to the point, it ends on a timely note of patriotism to fit Anderson's change of heart and the rapidly worsening international crisis. But the alteration of text is artistically superficial because he had left intact all the cynicism and hopelessness that permeate earlier sections of the work.[11] One other way in which Anderson tried to rally Americans to the cause of freedom was in adapting parts of *Valley Forge* for radio broadcast on September 13.[12]

By 1940 the United States was deeply divided in its attitude toward intervention in the European war. The *Chicago Tribune,* the America First organization, the Communist Party of Earl Browder, the Socialist Party of Norman Thomas, and Charles A. Lindbergh proclaimed that the war in Europe was not our war. The most powerful opposition to all these isolationists was the Committee to Defend America by Aiding the Allies, whose national chairman was the highly respected editor of the *Emporia Gazette* of Emporia, Kansas, a man named William Allen White. Robert E. Sherwood happened to be an active member of White's committee. On the day after the massive evacuation of Allied troops from Dunkirk was completed, the Playwrights Company met at Anderson's house to assist Sherwood in preparing a full-page news-paper ad headed with the caption "Stop Hitler Now!" It took a great sense of urgency to weld these men with their individualistic code and war-hating disposition into a common national cause. Even Behrman, the most unin-volved of the Playwrights Company in the great social and political causes of his time, labored all of one night helping Sherwood get the final copy ready. This ad, financed by contributions from the Playwrights Company members, Dorothy Backer, F. D. Cheney, George S. Kaufman, Henry R. Luce, Dwight D. Wiman, and many others, was published on June 10 and 11, 1940, not only in *The New York Times* but also in newspapers in Chicago, Dallas, Des Moines, Los Angeles—altogether over a thousand papers. The ad boldly called for people to write immediately to the President, senators, and congressmen and tell them that to defend America they must send food, guns, munitions, and planes to the Allies before it was too late. At his next press conference Roosevelt pronounced the "Stop Hitler Now!" ad an important piece of work;[13] he felt that he could now go ahead with his plan to send Lend-Lease aid to Britain. And none too soon. The Nazi hordes were rapidly swallowing up Europe. On the very day the ad first appeared, Mussolini attacked an already besieged France through the Riviera. If big France fell, what hope was there for little Britain just across the Channel?

On the evening of October 10 Maxwell Anderson presented in New York what was for him, an avowed atheist, one of his most unexpected plays. This was *Journey to Jerusalem*, expressing "the importance he attached to the problem of faith in a world threatened by Hitler," as Laurence Avery has suggested.[14] When Anderson first started to plan this new work, Wharton advised him about an obscure New York State law that prohibited anyone from representing "The Deity" on the stage. There was some apprehension that the law might be used to prevent *Journey to Jerusalem* from going into production, even though no one could be sure that "The Deity" applied to the boy Jesus. After the Playwrights Company threshed this matter out at several meetings, Anderson concluded that the prestige of the company plus his own good reputation would suffice to pull him through.[15] But he also took the precaution of changing his hero's name to Jeshua, and Mary's to Miriam. The story that finally reached the stage is about Jesus, at age twelve, going with his parents to the Temple at Jerusalem for the Passover celebra-tion. While there he makes the electrifying discovery that he is the long-expected Messiah forecast in a dream of his in which he saw himself as a military conqueror at the head of a victorious army. But Ishmael convinces him that he will not defeat his enemies; that, instead, he will suffer horribly and die young. On the youth's head lies an enormous unasked-for burden that shakes the soul to its foundations.[16] *Journey to Jerusalem* is not notably dramatic but succeeds in retelling a familiar story in a satisfying manner.

In the stage production the boy Sidney Lumet gave an ethereal portrayal of Jeshua, but Arlene Francis was not a felicitous choice for the role of Miriam.[17] The work ran for only seventeen performances. Though it was a commercial failure on Broadway, the Playwrights Company felt that there still might be a market for it as a film version for schools, churches, and educational or literary organizations around the country, where the cost for the individual patron could be kept low. Accordingly, for one of the presentations at the National Theatre, sound equipment and special lights were brought in and cameras were positioned at about the center of the fourth row, and onto film went the entire production. Unfortunately, the story as recorded on film by the relatively static cameras was a huge disappointment. "The dialogue seemed dull," noted one source. "The acting appeared most amateurish in the worst connotation of that word. All the artistry of the stage technicians was completely lost. The audience soon grew weary of the limitations placed on the actors' movements and the scenic background."[18]

Not long before the German parachute invasion of Crete next year, Anderson had his one-act piece of fantasy propaganda, *The Miracle of the Danube*, broadcast over the CBS radio network. Burgess Meredith was the narrator; Paul Muni read the part of Captain Cassell. Christ returns to earth, this time as a supernatural stranger with a face right out of a picture by Giotto; he haunts Cassell, a German officer in charge of the transport and execution of political prisoners, and effects in him a miraculous change of heart.[19]

It is not surprising that all Anderson's dramas about spiritual faith—*Key Largo, Journey to Jerusalem, The Miracle of the Danube, Joan of Lorraine*— arrived huddled together in the stressful wartime period when man's colossal inhumanity to man seemed to make Anderson's old code of individualism irrelevant and ineffectual. Because he was the author of these documents of faith, was he necessarily the atheist that Hesper says he often claimed to be?[20] It's as if he had said, "Yes, I'm an atheist, thank God!" All throughout his manhood Anderson was a pilgrim in quest of a spiritual certitude he had lost as religion in his youth and now longed for with all his heart as something never to be regained. His literary mentor Matthew Arnold, who was likewise the son of a stern and forceful father who had tried to drill into him too the traditional Christian beliefs, posed the sad problem well in the forlorn lines, "Wandering between two worlds, one dead,/The other powerless to be born,/With nowhere to rest my head."[21]

The next war play, *Candle in the Wind* (1941), also had its propaganda value but was a better play and enjoyed a profitable run on Broadway, at least partly owing to the skill of Helen Hayes in the leading role. In the story, famous American actress Madeline Guest, marooned in Paris just after France is invaded, plots to free her French boyfriend, Raoul St. Cloud, from his Nazi oppressors. She succeeds, he goes to England, but now she is herself trapped in France.[22] The author's red-headed neighbor Lotte Lenya took the role of Cissie.

On the morning of December 7, 1941, when the Japanese made their bombing attack on Pearl Harbor, the apple-cheeked editor (later, publisher) William M. Sloane, who lived down the road from Anderson, telephoned his house, and Mab answered. Boiling with excitement, Sloane told her about the disaster and asked whether he might come down to talk with her husband. But Mab seemed oblivious to what that shattering raid in the Pacific meant and apparently thought that she had more troubles of her own in the immediate household. "He's not here," she told Sloane. And without responding at all to the news he had spouted, she complained, "And Hesper's throwing up. But come on down."

That afternoon Sloane met with Mab and Quentin. By this time she must have comprehended the enormity of the attack because she rose to the occasion admirably: The three of them organized that very afternoon what was to become known as the North Clarkstown Civilian Defense Committee.[23] Later, Anderson, the Weills, Mrs. Julie Sloane (wife of the editor), and others joined it. Mab, with her quick, bright ways and talent for organizing, was soon elected head of Civilian Defense for Rockland County. Among her other patriotic endeavors, she served in the Red Cross War Relief Fund drive and also completed a course of study in aircraft recognition so that she could be an aircraft observer. Her husband headed the airplane spotters in his district, and in the company of Kurt Weill spent one night a week in a tower at Pomona watching for aircraft.[24] From then on, when news arrived of some war crisis or invasion or Allied victory, the neighborhood people usually gathered spontaneously at the Anderson house to talk things over and share coffee.

Anderson's acquaintances must have been amused and surprised when they opened *The New York Times* in the fall of 1942 and read Sergeant Lloyd Shearer's article called "Pertaining to Local Color." According to this article, Anderson had gone to Fort Bragg, North Carolina, where he spent the night in an army barrack, and in the morning a sergeant kicked him in the buttocks by mistake as he lay snoring on a cot. The article reported that the playwright awoke with a roar but fled back to Fayetteville when he was threatened with prosecution for trespassing.[25]

Anderson actually did journey to Fort Bragg for a five-day visit, but his stay there was not quite that violent. He had arrived early in March with the proper papers in hand from the War Department entitling him to visit that place,[26] and he reported to the office of the post commander, Brigadier General Edwin P. Parker, Jr. Thus began one of the most stimulating experiences Anderson was ever to know. If he hadn't gone to Fort Bragg, he might not have written one of the most successful of all his plays; a soldier there might not have become an overnight celebrity; and seven-year-old Hesper almost certainly would not have met that soldier and then spent the next dozen years or more adoring the man.[27]

At the time Anderson arrived at Fort Bragg, America was deeply discouraged by the Japanese conquests in the Pacific, and the Philippines were about to fall. In addition, a more personal loss had come to the playwright in the preceding November when a favorite nephew of his, Staff Sergeant Lee Chambers (son of Dan and Lela), was killed in the crash of an army bomber near Findlay, Ohio. This was the first of two of the Chambers sons to perish during the war.[28] Naturally, Max couldn't help wondering what dangers awaited his own son Alan, who was in the service as stage manager and first sergeant of the spectacularly successful "This is the Army" entertainment company, a Broadway revue by Irving Berlin, which he would take to service personnel at military bases around the world. Terence would soon enter the Army Air Corps.

After meeting the general, a pleasant man about his age, Anderson went over to the gigantic Field Artillery Replacement Center (FARC), a veritable city with a rotating population of at least a hundred thousand, where one Private First Class Marion Hargrove was to be his guide during the visit.[29] Apparently it was in the battery street by the barracks that Anderson first saw the tall, lean Hargrove, who was being good-naturedly needled by two of his fellow soldiers about the money he had already borrowed from them to date his red-headed girlfriend in New York. As the playwright drew near, Hargrove began negotiating in his Southern accent for still another loan for the same purpose. He was already so far into debt to his friends that he had allowed them to become his "creditors union" by giving them his paycheck each month and in return receiving from them only such small amounts of cash as he absolutely required.[30] Because these young men were to prove singularly useful to Anderson in stimulating his imagination, now is a good time to describe them a little. They were all specialists and headquarters personnel. All of them turned up in some form in his next big play.

Hargrove, twenty-two, was born in Mount Olive, North Carolina, the eldest of seven children in a middle-class household. He had attended high school in Charlotte and went to college briefly, but formal education could not keep up with his impatience and knack for learning on his own.[31] As "wise as a young serpent" is the way Anderson later described him.[32] Before getting drafted he had a desk job on the *Charlotte* (N.C.) *News;* he wrote nowadays a funny "In the Army" column for the same paper and was usually on the alert for the same kind of local color that the playwright was.

One of the men kidding Hargrove was his fellow clerk, a large, red-complexioned, shaggy-haired Irishman from New York, Private Thomas J. Mulvehill. The other negotiator and member of the "creditors union" was John A. Bushemi, a hyperactive news photographer from the *Gary* (Ind.) *Post-Tribune.* Two years later, while covering the invasion of Eniwetok as a combat photographer for *Yank,* an Army weekly, Bushemi would be killed by a Japanese mortar shell.[33] These three men represented the staff of the FARC public relations office. Another member of the group was Hargrove's old basic-training crony Maurice Sher, from Columbus, Ohio, now a mess sergeant at one of the training batteries.

As Hargrove recalls, Anderson was "so remarkably (and astonishingly) congenial and charming that everyone regarded himself a valuable volunteer research assistant." He goes on to say that all these soldiers were "very young [median age: twenty-five], and very busy, and in no position to be pessimistic about anything"; they were "bright, and quick, unusually articulate, and very funny."

Although the dramatist arrived pessimistic about the course of the war, more especially about his nephew's death, he was delighted by the humor he saw all around him and was "visibly inspirited" by his tour at Fort Bragg: He saw the reception center, the firing range, the service clubs, the artillery guns, the mess halls, the dayrooms, the motor pools, and in consequence was "reassured about the future of the war and the materials he had already put together for his play."[34] During evenings he occupied a room at the top of a neon sign at the Hotel Lafayette. Although he attended a stage entertainment one night with General and Mrs. Parker, Anderson usually preferred the company of enlisted men, often seen among that khaki-clad multitude wearing a tan, double-breasted suit (always pressed), a striking green tie, and smoked glasses.

He spent Saturday afternoon loafing in the Replacement Center with Hargrove and Bushemi. Sher soon joined the trio. Then Anderson ate supper with them, watched them indulge in horseplay for an hour or so, and went back into Fayetteville, where they all ended up in his hotel room for what Hargrove called a "bull session" that lasted until about eleven. In this highly informal and congenial setting the author plied them with questions about military life.

One of the many soldiers he met was Private Lloyd Shearer, from the main post public relations office, who on the side free-lanced articles for magazines as well as did a column for several newspapers. At that period Shearer had the reputation of shoveling such prodigious quantities of fictitious and hyperbolic information into his articles about Army life, in some of which the playwright figures, that today a researcher needs some kind of divining rod to locate the facts. His article "Pertaining to Local Color," summarized earlier, is a sample of his art.[35]

Anderson called up Shearer and asked whether they might be able to arrange a trip together, along with Bushemi and Hargrove, to the nearby university town of Chapel Hill. Accordingly, on Sunday morning Shearer drove all of them in a GI station wagon to the outskirts of Chapel Hill, where they had a pleasant lunch at the house of Paul Green, who had been a student at the University of North Carolina under Professor Frederick Koch. Koch, by the way, was still teaching there. And he was conspicuously present that evening when Anderson and Green paid a visit to an informal gathering of drama students.

"The gathering was small," says Hargrove, who is said to have a near-photographic memory, "and so was Koch: a brisk, cheerful, Mr. Chips type who always wore a salt-and-pepper Norfolk jacket and carried a pipe. He made an inordinate amount of fuss over Max, and Max did the usual inordinate amount of squirming under it, and the talk was mostly about Rodgers and Hart and the usual deplorable state of the American theater—Max speaking only when pressed, and Paul not at all, and Koch more than compensating for both. At length (considerable length), Koch brought up 'that marvelous peroration in *Winterset*' and suggested that 'perhaps Max would be kind enough' to recite it to the group. Max went pale with shock, and said that he couldn't remember the thing. 'Can *you* remember the thing?' he said to Green, in exactly the tone he would have used for 'Did *you* steal the man's watch?' Green shook his head nervously but with great sincerity. It turned out that nobody there could remember That Marvelous Peroration—except, of course, Prof. Koch, who proceeded to recite it himself, *andante cantabile*. He made it all right from 'Oh, Miriamne' down to 'yet is my heart' or thereabouts—and suddenly froze, unable to remember what came next. Green sat looking out the window, and Max's look was a bland compassion rotten with insincerity, and the group as a whole just blankly waited, and, you might say, in all those turning lights he found no clue. Just as it was getting time for someone to change the subject (and anyone else in Koch's position would have died), it suddenly came back to him, and he finished off the piece to warm and genuine applause. Even Anderson was impressed.

"Driving back, it was quite late—probably somewhere around eleven—before we got back as far as Bragg, and it seemed foolish for Max to be taken the rest of the way to Fayetteville simply to be picked up in a few hours and brought back to the fort. I suggested (or somebody suggested) that he spend the night in our barracks in Headquarters Battery. He could take Bushemi's bunk, between Bishop's and mine in the corner of the squadroom, so as not to be bothered; there were always a couple of spare bunks, belonging to men on furlough, and Bush could take one of those. That would not only give Max at least an extra hour of sleep, but would also expose him to the eloquent and blasphemous language of a citizen soldiery roused out of its bed in the morning. Max was delighted by the idea, and that's the way we did it, and Shearer continued back to the Main Post.

"Mulvehill must have come in about the same time that we did. Our fourth man, Bishop, was still out when the rest of us turned in; I think he spent his weekends at home in Washington, a town on the coast.

"The part of Army life that we had forgotten in the plan was the daily routine of getting Bushemi out of his bunk for reveille in the morning. The others, usually Bishop and I, were obliged to shout at him, and revile and threaten him, and sometimes Bishop had in desperation actually tipped him out of his sack onto the floor. Neither of us actually liked all this, because it always seemed to make Bushemi uncharacteristically truculent, but it was necessary. We had to have him not only up but awake—at least, sufficiently awake to get into his shoes, his cap and his overcoat, and get into formation out there in the cold and dark, and answer to his name at roll call as if fully clothed.

"At six o'clock on the morning of Monday, March 9, the whistle blew. I would imagine that at that moment Max came wide awake under his blanket and began making mental notes of all the rich potential dialogue around him. Within a few minutes the loudest and most abusive of the language was being beamed in his own direction—routinely, by Don Bishop. When this was followed by a slight, routine jiggling of the metal cot, and Bishop's routine threat to dump him bodily out of it, Max sat up in bed. 'Oh, *hi*, Max,' said Bishop. 'Didn't know *you* were here.' " But in all the confusion the real Bushemi slept on undisturbed, nobody remembering to wake him up for reveille.[36]

But pity the harmless, sensitive, well-meaning, well-fed Corporal Bishop. Imagine how aghast he was two days after the barracks episode when he read in the *Fort Bragg Post* that he, Bishop, had actually "placed a foot just below the waistline of the shrouded form and gave a hearty shove. . . ." Two days after that, the *Fayetteville Observer* magnified the incident to a "kick in the pants." Then *Time* magazine in its March 30 issue carried a blurb showing him bellowing to the playwright, "Get the hell out of there boy!" Next came the *Charlotte Observer* article written by Shearer, who could make a dragon out of the innocent Bishop if anybody could: " 'Get the hell up, Bushemi!' he shouted, all the while giving Anderson boot after boot in the upper extremity of the thigh. An enraged bull . . . Anderson whirled around emitting a grunt of agonized pain. The soldier, Corporal Don Bishop, took one look at Anderson and ran like hell." Shearer then promoted Bishop to a sergeant and let him rampage in *The New York Times* too.[37]

One day Hargrove, Sher, and Mulvehill went into town to have lunch with Anderson at the Prince Charles Hotel. While they talked, Sher brought up the subject of Hargrove's articles about Army life in the *Charlotte News* and mentioned that Meyer Berger on *The New York Times* had liked them enough to think they belonged in a book.[38] Anderson soon got a chance to look at them and was so impressed that he sent off a letter to William M. Sloane, at Henry Holt & Company, recommending them for publication. The volume, he said, "might get published as a soldier diary for prospective soldiers, and parents whose sons are about to take the plunge. The writing is amusing and imaginative, yet the author sticks to reality enough to give a fairly accurate notion of what it's like to be inducted."[39] When he went home he took copies of Hargrove's column with him to give to Sloane, who also grew excited about them. Anderson furnished a foreword, and later that year *See Here, Private Hargrove* emerged as a best seller. Later it became a motion picture.

After his return home Anderson, no doubt as an expression of gratitude for what the tall young soldier had done for him, and wanting to get him some extra leave time, wrote to General Parker and asked him to send Hargrove up for a few days to help him write a skit about barracks life that could be used in one of the camp programs. This was only a ploy, of course, for Anderson himself soon wrote unaided the playlet called *From Reveille to Breakfast,* which dealt with soldiers in a Fort Bragg barracks. Whether the piece was ever performed is not known.[40] Nevertheless, Hargrove did get up to New City that year. And little Hesper, about as isolated from young men outside the family as was Shakespeare's Miranda on the magic island, immediately developed a "crush" on this charming soldier that was to last for many, many years. Meanwhile, Max Anderson wrote his big war play.

The name *The Eve of St. Mark* as well as the theme of the play echo Anderson's reading of the John Keats poem.[41] In the legend, which Keats employed, we learn that if a virgin were to wait at the church door on St. Mark's Eve, she would have the apocalyptic experience of seeing walk past her all those parishioners who are to die that year; and if her lover should chance to be among that fated procession, he will turn and gaze at her, maybe speak. Anderson's modification of this material will be apparent as we examine the story in the play. Quizz West, a virtuous farm boy in the army, happens to meet in New York the girl Janet from his own region, he falls in love with her, and when he goes on furlough again he presents her to his folks. The innocence of the young lovers, while affecting, is almost embarrassing to behold. But of equal if not greater interest are the funny scenes of military life, realistically recorded, such as the barracks and the restaurant, where figures the golden-tongued soldier Francis Marion.

Before West can consummate his love, he is sent to a remote Pacific island about to be overrun by the Japanese. Now enters the Keatsian touch: Two dream scenes occur in Act II where the nominal hero, West, communicates in spirit with his girlfriend and his mother, asking them for help in making a life-or-death decision. He wants to know whether to make an honorable escape by boat to safety, or stay on and engage the enemy in a hopeless rearguard action. He learns that he alone must bear the burden of deciding. In electing to stay behind and fight—rather than retreat, as McCloud does in *Key Largo*—West shows the author's own newfound commitment to democracy.[42]

But this was not the end of Hargrove in the life of Max Anderson.

While *The Eve of St. Mark* was in rehearsal at the Belasco Theatre, Hargrove, now a corporal, went up with his cronies Shearer and Bushemi and talked with the cast, who were surprised to confront the real-life models for the people they were portraying.[43] Anderson had put into the play such characters as Private Thomas Mulveroy, Private Shevlin, Private Buscemi, and what may well be the real hero, Private Francis Marion, all of them readily identifiable with their counterparts at Fort Bragg. But the originals were not surprised at all, because he had told them in Fayetteville he was going to put them into a play—nor were they resentful about it then or later, especially since they all ended up in a blaze of glory in the second act. He had written to Hargrove, "[In *The Eve of St. Mark*] I hope you don't recognize yourself in a decadent Southern gentleman whose main charm is an attempt to reproduce some of your more antic humor. I adopted only your most libelous aspects, so you can sue me."[44]

The Rainbow Grill, where he had drunk beer with his soldier friends, may have furnished the model for The Moonbow Restaurant in the play. The fictional Army barracks crackles with the kind of pungent, roughhouse humor that Anderson had been collecting at Fort Bragg and possibly from the pages of *See Here, Private Hargrove*.[45] Some details about farm life came from the family of Ethel and Ralph Chambers,[46] but the people in the farm scenes were modeled after the family of Lela and Dan Chambers. In her letters to him Lela related incidents that he used in his dramatization.[47] Lee Chambers was the prototype for Quizz West; the play, accordingly, is dedicated to his memory.

Various strong differences exist between *What Price Glory* and *The Eve of St. Mark*, coming eighteen years later. The tone of the latter shows no cynicism about Allied military leaders and their aims in the war; all is honest-to-goodness patriotism related with unblushing sincerity. True, there are passages where Marion jauntily asks whether he and his comrades are willing to die to save the world from tyranny, but we know that he has already made up his mind to do so; it's just that he finds it manly to cover his patriotic soul with a tough-minded front. In this late work there is much more interest in physical sex, too, a feature that will turn up several times in Anderson's writings in the 1940s and 1950s. No doubt most readers today would object to the unalloyed purity of conduct and sentiment of these nonprofessional soldiers and object even more to the patriotically overdone ending when Quizz' brothers, inspired by his sacrifice, announce that they are going to join the armed forces to carry on the fight. But the play was written for a particular time and place in history and can best be appreciated by those who recall the idealistic fervor of Americans during the dark days after Pearl Harbor, when a proud nation of over 130 million, injured but wrathful, rose as one for battle and bravely prepared for long and costly sacrifices— whatever it took to win. The play was perfectly in tune with that spirit, as witness this fan letter from the young Robert Graeme Smith, of Wallington, Pennsylvania:

Dear Mr. Anderson,

I saw the Eve of St. Mark. It got me. It tore my heart out and made me admit something to myself.

You see, I had a brother who made some decisions and finally made his last one in the south Pacific. He was a hell of a lot like Quizz and I bawled my eyes out. But for the first time since it happened I felt proud and sort of glad. . . . I want to thank you for this.

I'm in the Marine Corps Reserve and I go on active duty in 60 days. I'm glad because I'm just old enough. I've wanted to go and I couldn't quite tell why. I know part of the reason is the urge to be a hero. Yet, I know this isn't all for I know a lot of heros don't come back and I want to come back. I've hoped that my reason was fine and good but I couldn't find what it was. Something somewhere in your play told me that it was a good reason. A good enough one to die for and I don't want to die.

Anderson never answered this letter.[48]

Anderson wanted *The Eve of St. Mark* to tour the "provinces" before making its debut in New York, and in that way avoid getting it killed off by the professional newspaper critics before it had a chance to succeed on its own with the public at large. Accordingly, he told Dr. Lee Norvelle, of the National Theatre Conference (an amateur organization), to show the play all around the country but to keep it far away from the metropolitan area of New York. Even Boston and Washington were too close. He felt that he had written in *The Eve of St. Mark* his best work in years, partly because he had had in mind the whole country for his intended audience and not just the relatively sophisticated and worldly crowd of Broadway first-nighters.[49]

The fact is, he didn't trust the judgment of the critics anymore; he had had a honeymoon with them back in the 1930s, having then no serious quarrel about the manner in which they treated his work,[50] but since that time a succession of bad reviews, declining creativity, and changed conditions in the Broadway theater combined to alter his opinion. According to him, these blasé, pained souls called newspaper critics trudged to the theater merely because they had to and yet, sad to say, they wielded the power of life and death over any new play put on in New York. Moreover, critics and authors cannot decide on questions of artistic merit; only audiences and readers can do that.

As a believer in a democratic theater he had wholehearted faith in the taste of the general public, because he realized that, down through the centuries, the critics had almost invariably been mistaken in their estimate of contemporary writers until gradually the public set them straight. Critics had praised Lord Byron, Sir Walter Scott, Thomas Campbell, "Monk" Lewis, and James Russell Lowell, whereas they ignored or laughed at William Blake, Percy Bysshe Shelley, John Keats, Emily Brontë, and Henry David Thoreau.[51]

In addition, there were much higher production costs on Broadway, costs that had a great deal to do with whether a deserving but modest earner were ever put on, even by the Playwrights Company. The edge went more and more to the money winner. Back in the 1923-27 period, when Anderson was first getting started, one could produce a nonmusical in New York for as little as $10,000;[52] by 1938, the figure had shot up to $25,000, the amount established then by the Playwrights Company as reasonable.[53] This escalation of costs continued at an alarming rate in the 1940s.[54] Consequently, Anderson had ample reason to be apprehensive about the enormous influence of a few critics in this highly risky market, where half of all plays do not earn a profit.

But out in the provinces, *The Eve of St. Mark* enjoyed a successful tour of twenty-eight weeks; audiences were warmly responsive to its genuine and timely qualities. It had more than a hundred amateur productions in America and played in numerous military camps. John Wharton was astonished that his colleague, who had earned himself a lasting place in the world's dramatic literature with his portraits of kings and queens, could also move audiences with his scenes of ordinary country folk.[55] When the play finally opened in Washington, D.C., the reception was so favorable that Anderson and the cast were invited to a White House reception and tea. Later the cast gave a command performance in the National Theatre before an audience consisting of Mrs. Franklin D. Roosevelt, Mrs. Harry Hopkins, and other visitors from the Executive Mansion. And when the work moved at last to the Cort Theatre in New York for what became a long run, the dreaded critics that Anderson had thought were tigers turned out to be purring pussycats.

John Mason Brown, long acquainted with Anderson's career, wrote that the play as a whole "speaks to the heart irresistibly even when the head says 'no.' . . . its major source of strength lies in the fact that it is so quiveringly near just now to everyone's mail and to each day's reading in our newspapers. This agonizing proximity to reality endows *The Eve of St. Mark* with a strength which at present is impossible to withstand. . . . It is hard to see how any American could remain unaffected in its presence." Brown's only negative remark was that the poetic dream scenes should have been blue-penciled[56]—the very part that Anderson himself esteemed, because he felt that the material required an exaltation that only poetry could provide.[57] Stark Young in *The New Republic* admired Anderson for the very thing that some of today's critics, like Jordan Y. Miller, find excessive fault with, namely a fearlessness in displaying sentiment and of accepting the goodness and idealism of the American way of life.[58] How critical sensibility can change when the nation is no longer engaged in all-out war!

So much had Anderson come to dread critics during recent years that he had gotten into the habit of not reading reviews of his own works anymore. To avoid some of the hurt he expected when *The Eve of St. Mark* reached New York, he took the further precaution of not going to the première. But he did ask a friend how it went, and the reply was, " 'Marvelously . . . The audience wouldn't leave the theater. They just sat there and applauded.

There could have been 10 more curtain calls.' " Still, Anderson was not easily convinced by this that New Yorkers still loved him. He had seen better days. " 'Did they stand up in their seats and cheer?' Anderson asked. The friend admitted they didn't. 'They did for *What Price Glory,*' Anderson said sadly."[59] *What Price Glory!*—always that shining morning fare invited comparison with the latest and best he could do.

He sold the film rights to Twentieth Century-Fox for $300,000 but quickly became enmeshed in tax problems. At that time the courts had not yet decided whether the Internal Revenue Service would declare the sale of a play's motion-picture rights as ordinary income or a capital gain; if the former, the tax would be much greater. Anderson's lawyer, Howard Reinheimer, gave him some questionable advice: Report the income as a capital gain but, just to be on the safe side, put enough into savings to cover the tax debt if the courts should rule that it was ordinary income. (Reinheimer should have known his client better than to expect that anything would be saved.) The upshot was that Anderson did not save the required sum. When the earnings were finally declared ordinary income, he owed the IRS over $100,000, which he couldn't pay all at once. The most he could pay was a fifth. For the rest of his life he was to worry and fret under this dark cloud.[60]

As said earlier, he disapproved of F.D.R. because, despite the latter's good intentions, the New Deal signified to Anderson too much control over the individual's actions and a reduction of freedom. Anderson continued to believe that under any conditions except wartime, government was the natural enemy of the average citizen; we recall that in *Knickerbocker Holiday* he had defined government as "A group of men organized to sell protection to the inhabitants of a limited area at monopolistic prices." No doubt this is why, for instance, he still refused to apply for a Social Security number. The exigencies of total war had compelled him to reach a truce with his own democratic government, but the old rebel was far from succumbing to any mushy sentimentalism or chauvinism that told him to relinquish any more basic human freedoms than he absolutely had to in helping defeat the common enemy. "The only way the little man can be free," he lamented, "is to keep the big boys—government, industry, labor; executive, legislative, judicial—scrapping among themselves. Then he can escape between their legs."

He has supported Wendell Willkie for President in 1940, believing him to be "the first unbossed and completely honest man to be nominated for the presidency since Wilson."[61] Even though Willkie lost the election, Anderson did not abandon him, as so often happens to losers in political races, for we find Anderson in January 1943 serving on a program with Willkie at the Astor Hotel and speaking about the need to fight censorship and uphold freedom.[62] If the reader thinks that it's easy in America to fight censorship and uphold freedom, he has either been asleep or blissfully ignorant of what goes on in tent revivals, PTA teas, knife-and-fork club confabulations, and Babbitt-ridden lodges and chambers of commerce.

And opposition can emanate even from the ranks of overly zealous professional authors, as Anderson was dismayed to learn. When Russel Crouse and Clifton Fadiman of the Authors League of America formulated a letter to President Roosevelt supporting the creation of the Office of War Information, they wanted Anderson's endorsement, but he wisely refused. He wrote to them: "The people of a democracy should never ask their government to do all their thinking for them, even in time of war." He was afraid that the bureau that Crouse and Fadiman wanted would soon be dictating to America's citizens and its allies what they would say and write. But Roosevelt went ahead and created the OWI, with Elmer Davis as its top watchdog, and from the start the bureau struck many freedom-guarding people as being more interested in censorship and propaganda than in dispensing objective information.[63] Anderson would have firsthand proof of this bias before long.

He left for Washington, D.C., the day after the Astor address and there arranged passage to England to garner material for another war play. Robert E. Sherwood, now installed as director of the overseas branch of the OWI, got permission for him to travel abroad in the guise of a news correspondent. While waiting to sail he toured Fort Eustis and Fort Monroe in Virginia and Camp Butner in North Carolina, searching for whatever he could use for still another play, this one about Negroes in the armed forces, but he never got around to writing it.[64]

On March 23, 1943, he left New York on the neutral Portuguese ship *Pinto,* embarked on the most dangerous journey of his life; after having conceived a half-dozen war plays, he was at last going to see some battlefronts. Plenty of action awaited him in England, whose cities and military bases were being pounded nightly by Luftwaffe bombers. London, where he was to stay much of the time, was a prime target for such attacks. And his voyage there and back was fraught with danger because the sea-lanes of the Atlantic were unsafe, even for neutral ships like the *Pinto:* U-boats sank many a ship under conditions where identification was poor and sometimes machine-gunned the survivors in the lifeboats. But the *Pinto* made it safely to Lisbon via the Azores; from Lisbon he flew to London, braving the skies that were being contested daily by dueling Spitfires and Messerschmitts.

All but one of the following letters that Anderson wrote on that three-month odyssey went to Mab; the other one went to Hesper. They were composed under hurried and sometimes dangerous conditions, their contents carefully guarded to pass the censor, but they are, nevertheless, among the most exciting that we have from him. They capture well the sense of a titanic struggle in which history is being made, the intoxicating immediacy of wartime stress, the heroism of the British (especially) under the aerial Blitz, the displacement and confusion and bustle of people on the move, the deprivations of battlefront living, the soldiers' constant longing for home, and some of the personalities (for example, Sergeants Peter Hromchak and Simeon Snider) who, we suspect, found their way into *Storm Operation.* One gets the impression that the soldiers he met on this trip were far more representative of the real army than was the case with Hargrove and his all-too-literate gang at Fort Bragg. Also, it is a measure of the crisis he felt in Britain that, for the sake of the war effort (and extra money—*always* needed), he put aside all considerations of pride and spent a lot of time working on propaganda films while he gradually collected materials for his next play.

London, Apr. 14— . . . We're at the Claridge—which is tres expensif. Got on a plane yesterday morning and flew six hours over the ocean, landing at Bristol. Crossing England was a delight—it was so green, so well cultivated, so somehow gentle.—Today I must get my food card and a hair-cut and see Beaumont and go to the American Embassy, hoping for news of you there. For nothing arrived in Lisbon. . . .[65]

The Claridge, Apr. 15—Darling, I begin to get terribly lonely! Just no news at all since that one cable in the Azores. But I got the O.W.I. to send you a notice that I had arrived. Maybe I'll get some word from you tomorrow. They say any cable that the censor finds suspicious or that sounds as if it were sent by a new arrival is held about ten days.—At last—your cable came!

Apr. 16—That passage was interrupted by a call from Willy Wyler,[66] who invited me to go out to the coast—in the middle of the night—to see the beginning and end of a sweep over the continent.[67] Said yes— we started at 1:30 A.M.—drove till four, got a few hours sleep, got up early, saw the planes start, waited about nervously all day till they began to come back. The colonel in command was going crazy because more than half were overdue—when they began to come in. Some landed at other airports but they all got home safely. A friend of Wyler's was killed in another sweep today, however.—There go the air-raid sirens—the Germans are coming! I will not go to a shelter. I'd rather stay here.

Well, it was a real air raid, but it's over. Gabby [Gabriel Pascal][68] and I sat talking through it—and then put the lights out to look out the window. It was bright moonlight—but with clouds. Plenty of bombs and ack-ack.

Today Gabby organized his new film company—with the greatest financier in England[69]—really—and is again sound financially. They are making me a director of the company.—Would you like to live in England for a while? Everybody seems to want me to stay here. They seem to think I could earn a living, too. But I guess I'd want to get back. Gabby's idea is to get you over here as a scenario writer.

Saturday, April 17—I've been sort of holding on to this letter hoping there was some way to get it into a quicker mail service than is likely if one simply drops it in a box. But so far I haven't found any such thing—and maybe I'll just end up mailing it and trusting that it gets through fairly quick. Today—or rather this afternoon—I'm quiet here and alone for the first time. Gabby has gone for the weekend. So perhaps I can get something said that would explain my quandary to you. It's quite unlikely that my play [*The Eve of St. Mark*] will go on. It must have an American cast, and there's no chance of getting one here—or bringing one over. Or small chance. Now I'm planning to go to North Africa because I don't think I'll find material for a play in England. However, I do have material for a picture—about the survivors—and Gabby wants me to do that right now and have it ready to be the first picture he makes here. Also he promises to get you over here to help me with the scenario, as I said.[70] I don't believe I'd be happy here for long, but at the moment we'd be nearer the center of things than we are in New York. . . . This is really a war front, here in London. One finds that out on a first inspection. . . . and the spirit of the people is so wonderful that one feels honored to be a member of the English speaking fraternity. . . .

Sunday, Apr. 18—Darling, I guess I'll have to mail this soon, or it will grow out of all bounds. Somehow or other I'll put it in the mail tomorrow. . . . Today I went out to Keats' house in Hampstead, with Garretson, Wyler and the Editor of The Stars & Stripes—who is called Llewellyn—a major, as is Wyler.[71] It was very nice to see the house and garden again, uninjured in the midst of a pretty badly bombed London—though the caretaker told us there had been three firebombs on the roof and the house was nearly lost at one time. We drove down to the bombed area below St. Pauls—and that's really something devastated. But somehow London goes right on, and quite confidently now.

Midnight—I had dinner with Wyler—and food here, by the way, is a bit scanty and without much variety. It's good for me, though. After dinner Wyler took me to see some people with whom he was to play gin rummy. Among them was Ellen Drew, who was supposed to play the girl in my play.[72] She is married to Major Bartlett, whom I had met in Hollywood and also in Washington.—Let me confirm now a few things about scarcities here. If you come over you should bring plenty of stockings, for you will get none here. Bring or send some candy. There is no fruit here except once in a while rhubarb—if that's fruit. Bring a supply of vitamins.

I have just worked out in my mind a story about merchant marine survivors which I think will make a good picture. It would even make a play, but if Gabby wants a picture immediately I may write it for him and earn some pounds to live on. . . .

I've talked now with a lot of men who have been here nearly a year—leaving wives and children in America. They are all pretty unhappy about it. Not so much because of the distance as because the difficulty of communication magnifies the distance. It's so hard to get a word through quickly. One feels really cut off. I feel it already myself— and even though I'm seeing and experiencing the most exciting things I could hope for here there's always an ache in me that keeps wishing for home and you and Hesper. And it will get worse—and not better. In all this dislocation of the world, and in the storm of violent death we feel round us here, it's the women and children at home the men cling to. Wyler showed me the pictures of his children with such pride. Victor[73] was so happy to hear even bare reports of Anne and the children. I know now that the pain at one's heart can become overwhelming.

[Note on side of page:] 1:30 A.M.—There's just been another air raid by moonlight—guns going off all around. A small raid—nobody pays attention.

Hotel Claridge
London
April 26 [1943]

It's so hard to write when one doesn't know how soon the letter will go or when it will be delivered. Such a barrier has been raised that one feels really cut off. That broadcast to America which I made last night I did largely because I hoped you might be able to tune in on the short-wave, and we could have at least a one-way conversation. But things go so slowly I'm not even sure you got my cable about the broadcast and not at all sure your short-wave set could pick the thing up even if you knew about it. If you did hear it you caught up on a lot of my activities which would take a long time to describe, like the visit to the bomber station, the waiting around for messages, the attitude of London civilians and all that. . . My diary, which I've kept so far, is a great help—if I didn't have it everything would be blurred. And, darling, please be patient with me if I tell dull things—I begin to feel the way all the men over here seem to—that I just must get into some kind of personal touch with home—that I can't say anything very real because it's so far—and yet I must let you know how I get along. . . .

. . . Tuesday I was reading Wyler's script for his air picture,[74] and saw Brewster Morgan—had dinner with him, in fact. Wednesday, I got a cable from you saying you would like to live in England if I could arrange it. I did my best to do so by finishing the synopsis of a picture about torpedoing survivors and turning it over to Gabby. If that is done Gabby says Arthur Rank can get you over here as my assistant. . . . On that day too I had lunch with Russell Lane, who has put on all my plays out in Madison, Wisc., and is now with the Red Cross here. He wanted the army to put on *St. Mark* here—and since a commercial production seems impossible I gave him permission to go ahead.[75] He went to Gen. Rogers at once, and Rogers wants to do it in London, in one of the regular theatres, with soldier actors and for soldiers. It would be a non-profit making venture, as I said in my cable to you today. And I like that much better than the first plan. I don't want to be offering a war play to the English for money. I'd rather give it to them. They've earned all we can give. Russell Lane, by the way, turned out to be the greatest Anderson fan I've ever encountered—really considers me the great American playwright—which, as I told him, came to me as a new idea.

On Thursday I wrote the 15 minute broadcast which you may have heard me deliver last night—and appeared on another broadcast—a sort of Information Please. On Friday I tried to cable you some flowers because it was Shakespeare's birthday—but it was also Good Friday, so the shops were all closed. Had dinner with Terence Rattigan, who wrote *Flare Path,* still running here,[76] and the script of Wyler's picture.

On Saturday Garretson and Chaffee, two fellows from the Bureau of Economic Warfare, got on a train with me to go to Oxford and Stratford. We walked all over Oxford that day and that night slept in students' rooms that hadn't been altered since the founding of the University. Pretty bleak and monastic. Went on to Stratford next day. It was closed up tight as a cartridge—on Easter Sunday—but we managed to get into nearly all the places I wanted to see. Trinity Church, where the bard is buried, is really a beauty. Built in 1220, or there abouts [sic]. And there's the tomb of the great man in the chancel, like you've always heard tell, and his bust, and

"Good friend, for Jesus' sake forebear"

cut into the flag where his bones lie—and his daughter and his son-in-law buried beside him. He was really a laird in his own country. Only the Shakespeares and their kin lie in that chancel! All the others lie in lesser ground, or outside the church. And this was not because he was a great poet but because he owned the tithes of Stratford, having acquired them by purchase. The bust is most disappointing. As much so as folk say. But the church is a thing of beauty. The birthplace looks quite authentic—and the Nash house, where his son-in-law lived. The Avon is a tiny little river.

Came back to London to make that broadcast—which was at 2 A.M. Monday morning here—and at 8 P.M. Sunday evening in New City. In consequence I missed a lot of sleep and slept late this morning. This evening I went to dine with a Rev. Mr. Spencer and his family. I met him when Herbert Agar asked me to make a speech[77]—and it turned out that I was to speak at a Federation of Churches—or something like that—and Spencer and I agreed that some other bloke might be a better choice.

Tomorrow night I'm having dinner with Victor again—and the night after that with Capt. Dan Selko, a friend of Kenneth's—who also works in the B.E.W. Thursday Brewster Morgan wants me to go to the theatre with him. The theatre, here, begins at 6 P.M. and ends about nine. People have dinner after the theatre. This is because of raids, blackouts, etc. But the theatres are all jammed. Everything goes.

[London]
May 6, 1943
. . . Darling, I've never in my life talked to so many interesting people

and seen so many interesting things in such a short space of time. Since I came to London there's been a constant flow of things to do and see, till I've been almost bewildered. . . . This week-end I'd like very much to look at a fighter field and talk to some of the pilots. They're the boys who drive the raiders away every time they try to reach London. But Wyler wants me to go with him to live with the bomber pilots and since I've promised to write that continuity for him—I'm doing that.

Last night I had dinner with Michael Redgrave, who is playing in *A Month in the Country,* and Manning Whiley, who has just closed a long run in *Rain.* Whiley wants to put on *The Wingless Victory* here in September, and Redgrave is to direct it. Miss Rotha, who played the lead in *Rain* for 13 months, wants to play Oparre. In fact she's so mad about the part she's turned down other things just on the chance of my allowing her to do it. I think they'll do a good job. I'm going to do some re-writing for them. The sets are brilliantly designed—really romantic and beautiful, judging by the drawings.[78]

. . . By the way, I've written a new scene for the London production of *St. Mark.*[79] Maybe I'll include a copy in this letter and you can get Victor to put it in the New York production if it's still worth while [sic]. It's a dream scene that takes the place of the two dream scenes already there. Or it could be put in place of the scene with the girl.

. . . Gabby told me this afternoon that I could have any amount I wanted as an advance on the life-boat story. It seems I *could* make a living here. And I'd like to write a play to go on in England first. But if you can't come I'll feel like going home as soon as I've seen North Africa. . . .

Saturday, May 8—7:30 A.M.

I kept this last night, after all, because I found I could mail it this morning. Last night I made a speech—on the American theatre, not very good, but I got to know some people out of it and it was passable. Got home so late I didn't write any more. This morning the paper announces the capture of Bizerte and Tunis[80]—so now I don't know whether I'll go to Africa at all. It may be too late to get a notion of what it was like—and so far I've heard nothing from the powers that be concerning permission.

Wyler is not going to the bomber field today as he planned, but Major Jack Whitney is, and it seems I'm going with him.

. . . These last days I've been so really dated up that I've had to hurry from one thing to another—but it's all so fascinating I can't bear to turn down any chance. This morning I was wakened by the air raid sirens, so there must have been German planes about. I heard no bombs, however, only some distant ack-ack guns.

This next letter in the flow of mail from Maxwell Anderson was addressed to Hesper:

[London]
May 11 [1943]

I've had three letters from you and it's beginning to be high time you got at least one from me. It's hard work to write letters but it's lots of fun to get them. Imagine me sitting in a small hotel room with nothing in it but a couple of tables and a couple of beds—one I sleep in and the other is covered with books—and I'm just sitting here trying to remember what you look like while I write you a letter.

Let me tell you a story I heard about two gunners in a B17—a Flying Fortress. There are ten men in the crew. Pilot, co-pilot, navigator, bombardier, radio man, two waist gunners, one tail gunner, one under-turret gunner and one engineer. They fly so high and it gets so cold up there that they have to wear electrically heated clothes. Otherwise they would freeze solid. And there's no air to speak of up there so they have to wear oxygen masks constantly. If the oxygen mask comes off and the man doesn't get it back on quickly he loses consciousness— and pretty soon he smothers. Well, once a Fortress was in a battle up there and one of the waist gunners was wounded and fell down and his mask came off. The other gunner grabbed the walkie-oxygen tank and went over to the wounded man and gave him a few whiffs, and he came to. But then the second gunner had passed out from lack of oxygen, and the first one, the wounded one, gave the other a few whiffs. He came to and by that time the wounded one was out again. They went on like that, giving each other drinks of oxygen, till they were out of the battle and somebody noticed them and dragged them over to their own masks where they could breathe again. That isn't a very funny story but it's one of the best I've heard about the war.

. . . I went down to the British Museum today because I wanted to see the Elgin Marbles again. They are Greek statues that Keats wrote about. But the Museum is closed now.[81]

Mother tells me that you've been learning some poems. . . . I'm glad you're learning to skip rope. If you ever want to be a prize-fighter that will be invaluable.

The particular military operation that Anderson finally selected as the background for his next play was "Torch," which had begun in the preceding November, when 107,000 American and British troops, most of them as yet unbloodied in combat, swept into North Africa from the beaches and air to close the trap from the west on General Erwin Rommel's vaunted Afrika Korps while Sir Bernard Montgomery with his "desert rats" closed in from the east. In January the Russians had reaped a tremendous victory at Stalingrad; in February the Americans had conquered Guadalcanal. It was clear that the tide of war was turning. Now the Allied hopes in the West hung upon the outcome of those swirling battles in the desert as the pincers began to close on Tunisia. Anderson feared that the whole campaign would be over before he could get to the scene himself. But delay followed delay, and at last he arrived there about two weeks after the last German and Italian resistance collapsed. Over 250,000 prisoners were taken.

The remaining letters quoted here are addressed to Mab.

> 76 Rue Gallioni, Algiers
> Aboulker residence
> May 30, 1943

... When the permission to go to Africa finally came through from the army things didn't pause.[82] I could have left Sunday night, but had a few things to do—among them the continuity for Wyler's film—so I picked Tuesday. Monday I spent writing the continuity, Tuesday I moved everything to South Molton St. and in the evening took a train to the airport. It was a sleeper and when I got to the station Wednesday morning I found that I could have the day to myself—wouldn't go out till evening. Well, it just happened that I was then near the bridge that Tam o'Shanter rode across, so I went to see that and to visit the birthplace and "Alloway's auld haunted kirk"—which was a ruin when the poem was written and still is.[83] That evening at ten o'clock we climbed on board, thirteen of us, and set out for the south. There were no sleeping accommodations, of course, and the toilet facilities were public and meager. There was considerable quiet fun over the fact that you had to move a certain French officer's feet every time you wanted to (as the British officers say) "splash your boots." A general was with us. He held out till the middle of the night—then his aide borrowed my flashlight and escorted him to the facilities. The French officer who slept so near the drains never woke up throughout all this. He had the only good bed—a packed up rubber boat—and he slept soundly. I stretched out on three aluminum "bucket-seats" and slept a little between one and four with somebody quietly kicking me in the face from time to time. It was an eleven hour trip, and we descended at nine in the morning at Marrakech, somewhere in No. Africa. No food en route except a cheese sandwich and a cup of water. There were many memorable things about that trip. I have never seen such cloud formations or such sunset effects as we got that first evening—as we flew over Ireland. Then the next morning we flew over clouds for a long time after sunrise—just white fleece rolling below us forever—and when it parted we caught a glimpse of blue sea far below. But— happening to look down one time I saw—not blue sea, but African fields—purple, yellow, red, burned brown mostly, like Southern California; and obviously merging into desert. The further south we went the more desert-like things became. No towns through this region, only occasional 'dobe houses, red or brown clay, with walls about them of the same material—blistering hot in the midst of a great blistered area. At nine we came down at the Marrakech air-port and finally got onto a bus and drove a blistering hot way into a town on the edge of the Sahara. Really an oasis place. Seven of us were put in one room in the Casino (evidently the French had intended to make this place into a sort of Agua Caliente) where I got a few minutes sleep, then woke up to see as much of the place as we'd have time for before leaving. Drove about in a native rig—horses and an ancient contraption—with some fellow passengers, saw the bazaar, the native market, the Sultan's palace, now deserted, and then managed to wangle a room in a hotel along with Jim Cook, a War Shipping Board man. The filth, the poverty, the disease, the below stairs humanity of the place were quite sickening, and of course there was no water for baths, or toilet paper, nothing really ready for civilized occupation. How these people live! I've seen them picking over garbage pails in the alleys in Algiers, but Marrakech was a step beneath anything one quite believes. A sort of bad dream. It's hard to imagine applying democracy to such a population. Yet the workmanship on the sultan's palace—who had 365 wives—was really incredibly beautiful. . . .

. . . Thursday night I slept at the *La Mamounia,* an elegant hotel on the edge of the decline and fall of civilization [in Marrakech], and Friday morning we began a series of hops in the general direction of Algiers. Fez, Casablanca, Oran, then here. It took all day, and at seven in the evening Jim Cook and I had just managed to get a billet from the army and a lieutenant had lent us two cots and two blankets to set up in a room which was empty for the night. We had decided to go without dinner because it was too late to get into the officers' mess, but then a sergeant came upstairs and told us we were invited to eat with the family who owned the house. It's a well-to-do family of many brothers and brothers-in-law, French and Jewish and very happy. They took us in at once, gave us an excellent meal and plied us with wine and brandy. The family name seems to be Aboulker, and they've given up the top floor of their city home to American and British soldiers. The billeting office had sent us here, and now we've slept two nights on those borrowed army cots with no pillows and no mosquito-netting. We're near the top of a hill here, and a long way from the city, which makes transportation a difficulty. The view of the Mediterranean which we get on the way up and down is worth a lot of trouble, though, and the city is so crowded that we're lucky to have cots at all. Army officers are often reduced to sleeping on the floor. They say Algiers was built as a city of 250,000—and it now contains 500,000 civilians, to say nothing of the soldiers. And there must be 200,000 of them.

. . . [Y]esterday Cook and I went down to the junior officers' mess with Captains Porter and Hill and Lieutenant Schlanger, who are bil-leted on this floor also.—Along with many others, British and Ameri-can. There was no water in the morning, but I had been warned by Schlanger that there might not be, so I had saved a quart in an empty Johnny Walker bottle. We came up the hill, shaved with that quart of water, and set out in the heat to locate our offices. I found O. H. P. Garrett, head of the OWI in Algiers,[84] and had lunch with a few of the OWI men in their own mess. When I tried to send you a message saying I was here I met with a blank refusal, both from the Red Cross—which I finally located—and from my own office. . . . At any rate this zone is entirely military and no private messages get out. I can write a letter and that's all.

. . . [C. D. Jackson, the OWI head in Africa[85]] suggested that I meet Commander Butcher, Eisenhower's aide,[86] and ask him for anything I wanted in the way of contacts, etc. It's been suggested that I might visit some of the rest camps where the soldiers who were in the thick of the fighting go to recuperate. . . . Captain Hill and Capt. Potter, who live here, were in some of the scrimmages and Potter had his whole battery killed around him, escaping alone; also last night Cook and I had dinner with some enlisted men in a signal and communications group. I made friends with the top sergeant, who is a Keats enthusiast, and intend to see him again. He and his buddies drove us through a corner of the native quarter of Algiers—it seems there was a picture that used it for a background—and then we came home. A long talk with Potter about his experiences in the war, and then bed—or cot—after midnight. . . .

Thursday, P.M.,
June 3 [1943]

. . . Now I must try to remember, for myself as well as for you, what's been happening so far. My first impressions were just a North African blur—made up of dust, heat, sunshine, crowded streets, military cars dashing up and down, ships in harbor, veiled women, more dust, more heat, delay, crowded offices, lifts that won't work, ten men in one billet, mosquitoes, no water in the taps, no baths, cold water shaves in water saved in a Johnny Walker bottle, French officers, British officers, American officers, salutes, Moorish castles taken over for supply depots, California sunshine, Scotch and English accents, crowded buses, paper francs, misdirections, desperate attempts at French, getting lost, walking miles in the heat to get money changed, trying to locate the American consulate, dinner with American soldiers at their stand-up mess, officers' mess, stories of fighting, stories of narrow escapes, a supply sergeant and a top sergeant who have adopted me as their special care,[87] frustration in outer offices, dirty clothes, no water, no laundry, Moslems on street cars, dirty Arab boys with and without shoe-shine boxes, officers yelling "Alley!" at same, the Kasbah, the native market, dirty Arabs in black, dirty Arabs in white, dirty white veils, never, by any chance, anything clean, except the officers' uniforms on that day when they first put on their summer tans. I saw General Eisenhower on that day,[88] and he was really clean and cool. I could go on with these impressions and add soldiers in knickers, 8th Army boys, so tanned they look like natives, horrible drinks in native cafes while one talks to soldiers of the 8th and 1st Armies, drivers honking down narrow twisting streets while the natives move casually out of the way, atabrine pills supplied by the 1st sergeant, mosquito netting supplied by the supply sgt, who stole it from the navy,[89] French chatter everywhere, Arab chatter, a plethora of money in the army, nothing to buy in the stores, a corporal named Alfred, in charge of this billet, who polishes my shoes, which are white with dust, and talks longingly about dairy-farming in up-state New York—a great longing on the part of all the boys to go home, to get out of this obnoxious Arabian place, a general hatred of John L. Lewis, a general feeling that the miners should get in the army once and find out what it's like.[90]

. . . Had dinner with Sergt. Simeon Snider and 1st Sgt. Peter Hrom-chak, at their mess. They drove me home in the weapons carrier. Next morning [Tuesday] I went to see [Colonel] Phillips again. We had a chat and then he said, "Gen. Eisenhower will see you this morning if you want to go up." I went and talked half an hour with the C. in C., who is most enthusiastic about what I'm trying to write about. He suggested some material for the story. I had lunch with Snider in his mess at the Palais [illegible]. Tuesday evening I had dinner in a native restaurant with my sergeants. Yesterday—Wednesday—I was all day with Commander Butcher—Col. Gault, Col. Torrance—who dictated a partial history of the N.A. campaign to me—and in the eve. I had dinner with the sgts. again. . . .

Sunday, June 6 [1943] or thereabout

. . . Friday I saw Marshal Tedder and he gave me a history of the strategy in the Mediterranean—especially from the point of view of an airman.[91] Saturday I talked a long while with Capt. Ruwct, who led a company at the time of the landing. Today I drove out to the beach with Sgts Hromchak and Snider—and Capt Head. Had dinner with the sergeants. Found that I'm to get my tickets tomorrow and leave Tues. for Casablanca. Lt. Col. Phil. Cockane is in Casablanca—and I hope to see him there. I'm beginning to know my way around this place a bit, but I'm very happy to get out of it. . . .

Friday night—I forgot to say—we had a considerable raid here—and I've never seen such fire-works as the anti-air fire put up. The whole sky was illuminated with patterns made by the tracer bullets.

Oh, darling—I'm so weary of traveling about. I want to see you and home.

Casablanca, June 9

Darling—I'm now in Casablanca—and without my luggage—all because of my own foolishness, I suppose. . . . my luggage has gone on to Marrakech. . . . I'm in the officers' quarters of the American Merchant Seaman's Club—and I've been lent pajamas and have bought myself a razor and a clean shirt. Also I've just been bitten by a mosquito, so I'd better close up and get ready for bed. . . .

June 11 [1943], Friday

. . . The sleeping that first night [in Casablanca] was rather hectic here—because the seamen have a way of getting a bit tight and noisy

and I was in a room with a lot of them. Last night was better.—
Yesterday I got up at six and got all shaved and scoured. It was my first
real bath in Africa. Then I went out . . . to the airport and was lucky
enough to get there just as Lt. Tector was arriving back from Marrakech. And the lad was as good as his word. He had taken the trouble to
hunt up my luggage, get [it] on his plane and bring it back here. The
pilots on these courier planes are really wonderful fellows. Only my
officer's coat was missing. . . . Then I started out to get my passage on
the ship—and found that I had to go to several places—among them
army headquarters. Going there I ran into the C.O. of this post and
area—and he took me to lunch along with several officers. One of them
was going out to the prison camp here—full [of] Germans and Italians,
and offered to take me along. I went with him—it was Maj. Maguire—
and met Major Morgan who went with us. The camp was huge. I'll have
to tell you about that later. Anyway Maguire offered to help me with
the passage, and this morning I went to his office and found that he had
collected all the official signatures necessary except the consul's. I
went and got that myself. It remains for me to see a certain Lt. Smith
who allocates space on ships. That I'll do later this afternoon. Meanwhile I have just had lunch with Maguire and Woodhouse and Kaplin and a
French officer who also helped with my ticket and who told us his
story of his escape from France. It was unbelievable and hair-raising.
His name is Jean de Bretauil.

Let me come back now to that cable of yours. On the day before I
was to leave Algiers I was sick. The reason was merely that I hadn't
eaten any candy for a long time and was [un?]used to sugar. . . . one
thing I didn't need at all—a bar of Baby Ruth. It was awful stuff, but was
rather starved for sweets, I guess, for I ate it, and almost instantly got
one of those attacks of indigestion. That was Monday afternoon. I ate
nothing that night and nothing all the next day—just lay in bed. . . . 1st
Sgt. Peter Hromchak came over in the evening bringing a can of pears
and about 8 that night I felt good enough to eat some of them. Next
morning Hromchak and his supply sergeant, Simeon Snider, came over
with the weapons carrier and drove me to the airport in style, carrying
my luggage and saying goodbye with as much affection as if I had been
their own papa. I got along really well with the enlisted men. Anyway I
found or made a lot of good friends among them in Algiers. Here I've
had to concentrate on officers because that passage is my first concern. . . . Tomorrow I intend to start visiting men in hospital, among

them, I hope, some German and Italian prisoners. I hear such conflicting reports about them I'd like to find out a bit for myself. . . .

Sunday, June 13 [1943]

. . . Last night the heat was the worst so far and the mosquitoes really got me. Tonight I've been promised a netting over my cot. If I don't come home with malaria it'll be just good luck. Thirty per cent of the population is said by the medics to be infected. . . .

Today is the day I might get a call to come on board. . . . I know the voyage will seem long and not too safe, but it's the last lap of the journey home and I can't keep my mind off it. I understand how these boys look back at their homes now. They want only one thing—to get this war over so they can go home. And of course the end is coming nearer. Pantelleria capitulated day before yesterday—and Lampedusa has now surrendered.[92] The way is being cleared for an assault on the mainland somewhere. . . .

Wednesday, June 16 [1943]

Went on board at 6 on Monday, watched them loading. . . . Cabin with Weston Haynes, naval photographer. Took on a lot of wounded, some wounded prisoners. Many able-bodied prisoners. Italians wait on our tables very happily.

Thursday, June 17 [1943]

Darling—I'm sitting here at the moment in a life-jacket, awaiting instructions. They're holding "Abandon Ship" drill. . . . Weston Haynes, the Assoc. Press photographer, is asleep in his chair. This morning I went around with him while he took pictures of wounded Americans and we also went in among the German prisoners, but they were eating and very crowded, so no pictures were taken there. . . .

Saturday, June 19 [1943]

Darling—Yesterday I did a lot of exploring about the boat with my photographer room-mate. Saw the galleys and the hospital quarters and the prison quarters. Saw the German officers heiling and shaking hands on the after-deck. When we sailed there was a great shortage of help in the galley and the dining-room. Now that has all been solved by the Italian prisoners. They are all happy and smiling about going to America and they bring you coffee with an eager willingness that would earn fabulous tips ashore.—The Germans, however, are moody and surly, are not trusted out of rifle range, and are not even asked if they wish to help.—Yesterday at 4:30 we were being followed by a submarine, according to one of the officers, but we ran away from it. Our course is far south. Flying fish skitter away from our bow like flights of little birds or grasshoppers.

> Sunday, June 20 [1943]
> ...We're steaming through sub-tropical ocean, with flying fish spraying out from the bows on both sides. . . . My guess is that we're in the Caribbean, somewhere south of Cuba, at the moment. . . .

> Tues., June 22 [1943]
> ... [T]o the best of my observation this wonderful old ship turned north. It's a beautiful job of shipbuilding, this vessel, and gives me great respect for American ship designers. Yesterday I talked much to sailors, wounded men and flyers. We bought a gallon of ice-cream and consumed it. First since leaving home. . . .

The ship carrying Max docked at Boston about noon on Saturday, June 26.[93]

In the course of Anderson's trip to North Africa—a visit facilitated by the United States War Department in return for his submitting the resulting script to them for approval—he made a point of getting to know the soldiers and the women attached to the battlefront, and he could not help but see the deteriorating moral values occasioned in these people by the war. He had planned for *Storm Operation*—whose title General Eisenhower allegedly suggested to him at Algiers[94]—to be essentially a work of deluxe propaganda entertainment. As he wrote in a letter to the general, the play would be useful "in interpreting between the battlefront and our homes"; for "the great problem of the civilian nowadays," he explained, "is to understand the men and women who have borne the heat and burden and death and wounds of this war. . . ."[95]

The text of *Storm Operation* that he sent to the War Department before making certain revisions shows that he tried to render an inspiring albeit frankly honest and realistic picture of the multinational relationships among the Allied personnel in North Africa. Against a background of desert warfare, the Australian nurse Thomasina Grey and the American Sergeant Peter Moldau, both former lovers, chance to meet again in a tent in Tunisia; and amid the flurry of setting up military equipment and facilities for the campaign underway, their old romance blossoms like a lily pad opening in a pool of sharks. One conflict in this human relationship is represented in the camp by the nurse's latest lover, Captain Sutton, a married Englishman; another conflict is her unwillingness to wed Sergeant Moldau because of the insecurities of wartime. As outlined thus far, the plot ought to remind us at least faintly of *What Price Glory:* a captain-sergeant squabble over who gets into bed with the foreign woman. (Sutton has been sleeping with her of late.) But there the similarity ends. The love triangle has for background the funny public relations and technical feats of Sergeant Simeon who, on the side, has his own love problem in the form of an Arab girl he has bought. The enlisted men's constant interest in sex shows up in their speech, full of *muck* and *mucking*—euphemisms that the War Department could hardly object to, but it did object to the unmarried American nurse Kathryn Byrne getting pregnant, an American soldier kicking a Moslem at prayer, and English and American soldiers abusing German prisoners of war. Getting back to the main story, true love finds a path to the heart of Nurse Grey, whereupon she decides to stop playing around with Captain Sutton and to marry Sergeant Moldau. There is a melodramatic late scene in which the three principals are gathered in a tent, and Captain Sutton, who had studied for the Church in the days before he reached adultery, pulls out his *Book of Common Prayer* and chivalrously performs a marriage ceremony for Grey and Moldau. Though German fighter planes roar in with machine guns strafing the camp and the lights go out and sensible people duck for cover, Sutton and the two lovers stand bravely throughout the rite—as if to defy war to take asunder what God was joining in holy matrimony.[96]

This version of the *Storm Operation* script sent to General Alexander D. Surles, director of public relations in the War Department, immediately ran into snags that must have confirmed just about everything Anderson had ever feared about government censorship. The stuffy Surles in his long telegram of reply demanded that the playwright get the nurse Kathryn Byrne unpregnant again, take out the part where the American soldier kicks the Moslem along with the part showing the mistreatment of German prisoners, and make over the character of Nurse Grey so that she is not so disillusioned and so concupiscent with the British officer, Sutton. Surles showed a glimmer of sense, however, when he referred the characterization of naughty Nurse Grey to an acknowledged playwright, Robert E. Sherwood, of the Office of War Information, who was to check with Australian and British authorities to learn whether *they* might be offended by her.

Anderson had complicated things for himself not only by agreeing in advance to submit to the War Department rulings but also by rushing ahead with a tryout run at the Maryland Theatre in Baltimore. So much was he a man of his word, and so determined was he to serve the best interests of his country (at least as the War Department interpreted them), that he had no choice but to comply with the censorship. Accordingly, he wrote Surles a conciliatory letter, though it must have galled him to do so.[97] But what must have crushed him—and it certainly spelled the ruin of the play—was the letter of instructions he got from his friend Sherwood, now turned anesthetized bureaucrat, who told him to delete Nurse Grey's admission that she and Sutton were sleeping together. Simply state that they love each other. Omit also her statement that she had done a lot of bed hopping among the patients during her service in the hospital. Please keep in mind, Sherwood warned his friend, that wartime audiences get emotionally involved in a way quite different from what it is like in peacetime. Undoubtedly the allusion to Grey's promiscuity would cause audiences to get a distorted view of the whole play.[98]

This was the same carefree Sherwood who had put adultery into his own plays *The Road to Rome* and *Reunion in Vienna;* some kept women into *This is New York, Acropolis,* and *Idiot's Delight;* and a street walker into *Waterloo Bridge.* When he had portrayed a pregnant, unmarried girl in *There Shall Be No Night,* whose setting is Finland during World War II, he certainly did not first clear matters with the Finns! The disturbing fact is that Sherwood, for all his patriotism and other good qualities, simply did not have Elmer Rice's courage as an administrator to resist unwarranted censorship. It would be grossly misleading, however, to leave the reader with the impression that this incident damaged in any way the friendship between these two playwrights; they apparently continued to be the best of friends. No doubt Anderson thought that Sherwood was simply carrying out an unpleasant duty.

Having eviscerated *Storm Operation* to please the censors—deleted "the more forceful and characterizing depictions of North Africans . . .," as Dr. Avery so aptly words what happened[99]—and in general made the Allied personnel rather genteel, Anderson had the humiliating experience of seeing this long-prepared-for work fail in New York after just twenty-three performances. The serious reviews were all negative. As one might expect, theatergoers found Nurse Grey unbelievable even though she is the most important figure in the play.[100] To a large extent, this was the price that Anderson paid for serving so loyally the interests of his country.

At about the same time *Storm Operation* made its appearance on the stage, he released a documentary one-acter called *Letter to Jackie,* which was inspired by a letter that Commander John J. Shea had written to his little son on the eve of the father's departure for the Pacific, where he sank to his death on the aircraft carrier *Wasp.* The Lunchtime Follies, a branch of the

Stage Door Canteen, acted this play for the edification of men and women war-production workers during their noon breaks in the factories.[101] The playlet served its purpose but added nothing to his stature as a dramatist. In general it can be said that as he grew year by year more admirable as a citizen and a patriot, he diminished as a writer.

One of Anderson's more pleasant friendships in the Playwrights Company was with Samuel Behrman, whose letters to members of the company and to Mrs. Robert E. Sherwood are sometimes delightfully lighthearted and witty. Once, when he was running for reelection to the presidency, he received from Mrs. Sherwood (a stockholder) what must have been a gently reproving but courteous letter about his record as president for earning them money, and he replied to her in ironic jocosity that *he,* and not his vagrant colleagues, was responsible for eliciting moneymaking works like *Abe Lincoln in Illinois* and *The Eve of St. Mark;* that she, so innocent about matters of high finance and the principles of sound money, must be a dreamy soul who likes to meander around shoeless in fields of asphodel; that he wrote his second financial report in such an incandescence of ecstatic creativity that later he couldn't understand the report himself, but that trivial shortcoming didn't provoke *him* to scribble a thoughtless letter to himself criticizing his performance; that because her husband was now a poor civil servant, she probably had to sneak into obscure eateries for her meals; and he concluded with the gracious proposal that she allow him to take her out to some elegant and expensive restaurant, where he can explain over candlelight the principles of sound money. He signed with "S. N. (Net Worth) Behrman."[102] A little later he sent out a mock letter to fellow members of the company announcing his awareness that there were forces attempting to block his reelection. And Behrman such a financially skillful president, too! Therefore, he is submitting in his defense a "pitiless analysis" of each of the other members, one of which might be his successor, pointing out their fiscal irresponsibility. With a fine exuberance he ticks off each man, telling them that, for instance, Max Anderson, noted for believing that authors should not have any money, has every now and then uncontrollable creative seizures in consequence of which he ends up with large sums of money that embarrass and startle him. If you elect Anderson, he tells them, you may well end up living "in a lean-to on Walden Pond."[103]

Here is Anderson's reply, written after the votes were counted:

An Open Letter to THE PLAYWRIGHTS' COMPANY:
The greatest need of The Playwrights' Company at present is a vigorous and vehement opposition to President S. N. (synonym mad) Behr-

man, recently re-elected for a third term and obviously campaigning
for a fourth. In his mad reach for power, we can be certain that he will
let nothing stand in his way. This may be our last opportunity to speak
freely. At the last Playwrights' session, President B. remarked to me that
if I dared lift a voice against his candidacy, my words would be torn
from their context and twisted in such a way as to destroy me. "I rely,"
said the power-swollen President, "on your inexperience in political
chicane, your noble nature and your innate decency. I shall destroy
you." Gentlemen, this is our President. I tremble for our democratic
principles. *Every argument used by Behrman in favor of a third term
is equally applicable to a fourth, a fifth, a sixth!* Is there to be a
Behrman dynasty?

Mr. Behrman scoffs at the idealistic records of possible opponents
and chooses to stand on the McKinley platform. He boasts of his lifelong adherence to the principles of sound money, acquired, evidently,
during the campaign of 1896. Any deviation from devotion to sound
money he regards as Bryanism. He has made it plain that while he runs
the company, it will have only one goal—the acquisition of hard cash.
Yet, by his own standards, he has signally failed. It was he who pre-
vented the company from buying a theatre,[104] and he boasts of this at a
time when theatres are at a premium and every theatre in the city has
doubled in value. The Playwrights' Company was organized with a
capital of $100,000. That sum is now reduced, according to the audi-
tors' latest figures, to $59,782.03. And this sum, dwindled and inade-
quate, is available only in depreciated currency.

We have been brought to this by Mr. Behrman's fanatical adherence
to a nineteenth century financial doctrine first promulgated by the
notorious Mark Hanna—the Pennsylvania boss responsible for the
imitation marble columns in the capital at Harrisburg, paid for by the
voters, of course, at the cost of real marble.

I hesitate to dwell upon the inroads made into Behrman's higher
nature by his crude monetary interpretation of the world. But I must,
in justice, point out that he spoke only mildly against Mr. Sherwood's
removal to Washington in a close election year.[105] Shortly thereafter,
Mr. B. quietly maneuvered himself into a dictatorial position among the
voting stockholders and took advantage of Sherwood's absence to
write a play for the Lunts.[106] It is to be noted that, though other
members of the company have their ups and downs, Mr. Behrman is
always unobtrusively solvent. Where he gets his money is beginning to
puzzle some of his colleagues not so blessed as he with an eye to the

main chance. Perhaps it will be remembered that Mr. B., alone among us, has been known to show irritation at the presence of auditors in the outer office. "What are these people doing here?" he has been heard to mutter. It is a short step from Mark Hanna to Teapot Dome. Who was it who inaugurated the custom (now followed by others in self defense) of dipping into the petty cash for taxi fares and charging lunches to the company? Gentlemen, without vision, the people perish. And Mr. Behrman visualizes nothing beyond the dollar—the pre-Spanish War issue of the dollar.

MAXWELL ANDERSON[107]

In 1944 Anderson did not complete a single full-length play although, during this interim, he was beginning the long preparation of what would finally become *Joan of Lorraine*. It must have been an altogether lean year for him financially, inasmuch as the Playwrights Company, in which he owned stock, did not produce any works at all save for the abortive *Storm Operation*. Apparently there were no film-writing assignments either. On May 8 of the next year, he listened with what must have been enormous pleasure to President Truman's radio broadcast of the Allied victory in Europe. Three months later, his diary recorded that the neighbors held a spontaneous evening party at his house to celebrate the news of the Japanese surrender; also that he listened on radio to the formal ceremony of that surrender when it took place aboard the battleship *Missouri* in Tokyo Bay.[108]

Now aged fifty-six and with much of his youthful exuberance gone, and with no more need to write plays to help the war effort (one of the supreme causes in his life now gone), and with production costs on Broadway so high as to discourage quality plays that did not at the same time stand to win a mass audience, and with *Storm Operation* to live down, he must have wondered how many more productive years he had left. Drama critic Louis Kronenberger published an article in *Commentary* magazine where he listed what he considered the basic reasons for the decline of the present theater, and among them were "a lack of discipline, of aspiration, of maturity, not to speak of talent,"[109] which article prompted Anderson to fire off a letter of reply to him. Anderson had another diagnosis entirely for the malaise, and we cannot help but conclude that he had been looking at his own plight most carefully in reaching that diagnosis:

For the first time in our history the majority of thinking people have come up against a crippling lack of faith. There is no faith, political, religious, social or personal, that remains unshaken nowadays. . . . Now a good play cannot be written except out of conviction—for or against—and when convictions wobble the theatre wobbles. No matter what his other equipment may be, if a dramatist has no faith he cannot fashion a play. The era of good playwriting is an era of confidence—usually, in retrospect, mistaken—confidence that runs through playwrights, audiences, actors and the whole structure of society. Every play, even a farce or a mystery or a comedy of manners, must uphold or attack some standard of loyalty or behavior. But we are beginning to wonder whether there are standards based on anything firmer than a desire to survive. We are edging toward that frame of mind which has meant the end of a good many epochs of the theatre—to say nothing of civilizations. And it's likely that there has never been such a general disintegration of beliefs and morals as now. Men and women, one and all, are in the unfortunate position of having to live by unprovable, improbable and generally nonsensical propositions which their busy, logical brains are constantly attacking and bringing to the ground. And when logic has won, and the man—or the civilization—is entirely cynical—then the man or civilization is ready for the eternal junk-pile. Novels and poems don't necessarily die at such a time. Novels can be made out of pure gossip; and poems can be made out of pure despair. But a play cannot exist without some kind of affirmation.

And then he alluded to the awesomely enormous power of the atomic bombs recently dropped on Nagasaki and Hiroshima:

The fission of the atom adds to our confusion, of course. With unlimited power in a few hands, it grows doubtful that democracy can operate much longer, and democracy—a faith that the people will somehow feel and find their way, even though blindfold[ed]—was about all we had left to cling to. Only the insensitive and the fanatics remain unconfused at present—and they don't write good plays.[110]

His anger at the New York critics reached a boil when they responded to his first play of the postwar era, *Truckline Cafe.* This is a fairly insipid melodrama about the problems that ex-servicemen have with their wives after the demoralizing experiences of the war. Like *White Desert,* the work probes into the subject of sexual infidelity, which he would revert to again in 1947 with his short story "West Coast, Night."[111] The two cuckolded husbands in the play seem to represent the warring positions of the author on the subject of whether to forgive the adulterous wife: the ex-serviceman Mort, having fathered an illegitimate child during his escape from a Nazi prison, doesn't have much to complain about when he discovers that his wife had given him up for dead and begun cohabiting with another man; he easily forgives her and enters into a promising reconciliation. Sage finds out that his wife has been using cabin No. 5 nearby for her trysts with his buddy, and he kills her in a fit of anger. But in this dramatized sermon on the values of marriage, true love, and forgiveness of sins, the action is too static, the parallel plotting too obvious and too dependent upon coincidence, and the device of using a motherless child to bring Mort and his wife back together is on the level of a soap opera.[112]

The other members of the Playwrights Company tried to dissuade Anderson from staging this new work, but he was adamant; he with his experience among the troops in wartime knew that marriage was the chief casualty when couples are separated indefinitely and grow desperate for sex. He managed to recruit the directing-producing team of Elia Kazan and Harold Clurman for a coproduction deal with the Playwrights Company. Wharton is usually gentle when he speaks of Anderson's weaker endeavors, but Wharton notes in his memoir that the play had the marks of failure beginning with its first opening, in Baltimore. After the opening, business manager Victor Samrock had coffee with the lawyer, at which time Samrock stared gloomily at his drink and said, "You know, I bet even the coffee was bad at the Truckline Cafe!"[113] A superb young unknown actor named Marlon Brando, in the role of Sage, stole the show and gave it the only signs of vitality during its thirteen-day run at the Belasco Theatre in New York. There is no need here to quote from the unanimously bad morning-after notices following the Broadway première; the titles alone must have churned Anderson's stomach: "Anderson in *Truckline Cafe* Writes an Agony Column"; " *Truckline Cafe* Is a Hopelessly Jumbled Play, Its Author Badly off Form"; "Maxwell Anderson Hits His Low with a Dreadful *Truckline Cafe*"; and "*Truckline Cafe* a Confused Study of Post-War Period."[114]

In response to these reviews, Kazan and Clurman placed an ad in *The New York Times* announcing their intention of closing the play during the week but that they first wanted to get some things off their chest. They charged that the critics were strangling the New York stage because they were steadily aggrandizing powers which they had neither the taste nor the training to exercise; and that their domination effectively excluded any informed opposition.[115] Then Anderson in an ad in the *New York Herald Tribune* blasted the critics with a violence hitherto unheard from his pen: "The public is far better qualified to judge plays than the men who write reviews for the dailies," he warmed to his subject; then fulminated: "It is an insult to our theatre that there should be so many incompetents and irresponsibles among them. There are still a few critics who know their job and respect it, but of late years all plays are passed on largely by a sort of Jukes family of journalism who bring to the theatre nothing but their own hopelessness, recklessness and despair."[116]

Behrman, finding that he too was having trouble winning favor again with theatergoers, resigned from the Playwrights Company in June and went back to having Lawrence Langner and the Theatre Guild produce his works. His was the first resignation from the company, although a most friendly resignation, and Anderson felt deeply the departure of his friend.[117] The loss was counterbalanced somewhat by Kurt Weill's election to membership next month.[118] In this year holding so much disappointment for him, Anderson was happy to accept an invitation from Columbia University to receive a Doctor of Letters degree. Quentin had been a professor there for several years, and Terence now studied there as an undergraduate.[119]

As said earlier, extensive revisions in one of his scripts did not ordinarily bring marked improvement, but *Joan of Lorraine* is a notable exception to the rule. He worked longer on this play than on any other one. The story of Joan of Arc is told as a parable of the need of modern man for a faith like Joan's. The setting for the play is strikingly original: a Broadway stage where a director (Masters) is rehearsing his cast for a drama about the historical Joan. Harassed with problems of production, he realizes that he must make certain minor compromises if he is ever to open the show. But the idealistic leading lady (Mary Grey) balks at the manner in which the author is rewriting the script to show that Joan is willing to compromise with the evil Dauphin in order to carry out the commands of her "voices." The real Joan wouldn't do that! she objects. The director (who is a persona for Anderson) tells her that Joan *had* to enlist the help of some bad but influential people in order to achieve her goals; that this is the only practical and true-to-life method available; that, for example, even to get their idealistic play going, he (Masters) had to bail out the crooked theater renter and use black-market materials to make their set. After their lunch break Mary balks again on the issue of whether Joan would shut her eyes to the corruption around her. Finally, she learns from enacting the new dialogue for the trial scene that Masters is right; for though Joan weakens so far as to recant during her trial, the "voices" come to her again, she regains her faith and is now strong enough to face her execution. Despite little concessions, Joan never lost her soul.[120]

Joan of Lorraine is a dramatized version of the message in Anderson's essay "Compromise and Keeping the Faith," which he wrote just two months after the play was first published. In the essay he tells us that in many areas of endeavor the practitioner is at some point faced with the unpleasant need to make adjustments to practical conditions in the world—even unsavory ones—if he is to stand a chance of getting his work or idea accepted. Anderson has chiefly in mind a play for the theater, but he says the same rule applies to statesmanship, journalism, mathematics, philosophy, medicine, music, and other fields—wherever one is tempted to compromise in order to achieve something worthwhile. An adjustment in trivial or inessential matters is all right, he tells us, but do not compromise the "essential soul" or "dream" of a play, for instance, or else it may be better not to produce the play at all![121]

Almost anyone who reads Anderson's *Joan* will try to compare it with George Bernard Shaw's famous *Saint Joan,* from which it differs radically. Anderson's heroine hears "voices" of divine inspiration; she is a feminine, modest, shy, and home-loving creature who in following a martial life goes counter to her natural impulses; in the battle scenes she cries over the death of fallen troops from both sides. The Joan in Shaw's drama also hears "voices" but she says they originate in her head as common sense; she is so witty as to expose her trial judges as the arrant fools they are; as a hoyden yearning for combat—finding inaction to be "dull! dull! dull!"—she is not deterred by the thought that thousands may die in the coming battles. Another big difference in the two stage pieces is that Shaw's judges are represented as reasonable, even if benighted, men, some of whom actually try to save Joan's body and soul; but in Anderson's drama they are vindictive and cruel, evil and bigoted, just as history has painted them.

In an unpublished note Anderson pointed out what he thought was the chief distinction between his treatment and that of the Irishman, whom he otherwise practically worshipped:

> Shaw wrote a whole play about Joan without once touching on her real problem. He took up the institutions of her time—the medieval church and feudalism—and discussed them brilliantly. He indicated that if those institutions had only been wisely managed Joan would have come out all right. But Joan's problem was not one of survival. It was one of belief. And that problem is not even posed in Shaw's play.
>
> For Joan's problem was the problem of the whole modern world—of every one of us—the problem of faith. Of what we're to believe in—and how we can justify what we believe—not to others, maybe, but to ourselves. We have to believe in something, as everybody tells us nowadays. We have to have a faith, but sometimes it looks as if no faith would bear critical analysis. So we're caught between two impossibilities—we have to believe in something—and we can't honestly say we accept any faith, belief, dictum, or even point of view.... [Joan] wasn't afraid of death. She was afraid of nothing except being untrue to herself or her

voices. And when the very foundations of her faith were attacked and she had to find a way to defend them, she found it.[122]

His colleagues in the Playwrights Company liked the script, but they were surprised to hear him say that he was going to get Ingrid Bergman for his leading lady. Owing to her success in such films as *Intermezzo* and *For Whom the Bell Tolls,* Miss Bergman was one of the most sought-after stars in Hollywood, where with her statuesque beauty and astonishingly sensitive acting she could earn a fortune in a matter of weeks; why should she drop all that to risk a Broadway run?

But Mab told him that if he wanted Miss Bergman for the part, then he ought to insist on getting her. So he flew out to Hollywood, obtained the star's telephone number, and called her. The foreign Miss Bergman had only barely heard of Anderson before but was so impressed by his audacity that she agreed to look at the script; he delivered it personally; and the next day she called *him,* greatly enthusiastic over what he had written, and said she had a special affinity for the role, moreover had always wanted to play Joan of Arc. Though Hollywood people then advised her against doing his play, she drove out to the beach with him and talked business and ended up signing contracts. There was only one hitch: She was contracted to perform in two films after the one she was currently in; that would entail a year's delay. Could he wait? He agreed.[123] But during the summer after V-Day she found time to make a tour of Allied military camps in Germany, where she enacted scenes from the play, at which time she always told her appreciative soldier audiences, "This is from Maxwell Anderson's play that I am going to do sometime. Don't forget!"[124]

Before it opened at the Alvin Theatre on November 18, 1946, Anderson took the precaution of denying his supposed enemies the newspaper and magazine critics their usual free tickets for opening night and, instead, sent them tickets for performances much later; in so doing he hoped to allow the public to discover on its own the merits of his work before the critics poisoned the wells. The critics, however, trooped to opening night *anyway* and wrote rave notices[125] for what was one of the most original and heartfelt documents of faith in the modern theater. Each night saw a packed house. In Wharton's opinion, only the fact that Miss Bergman had limited her engagement kept *Joan* from going on past 199 performances before closing.[126]

With her considerable talent she contributed to but could not guarantee the success of the play which, as it happened, was a quality piece in its own right. Nevertheless, Anderson's works are such that sometimes they require outstanding acting talent to bring out their full values as dramatic literature.

Next year saw him in Hollywood writing the script for a film based on the historical Joan of Arc, tentatively called *Joan of Lorraine*. This was the only time that he ever consented to do the film script for one of his own plays; and if Miss Bergman had not been selected for the star role, he might have declined his assignment. Here was one of the finest writers of the age creating a story for one of the finest acting talents; surely the film would have to be outstanding! Sad to say, he was to learn all over again how right he was in "Cut Is the Branch That Might Have Grown Full Straight," namely that the scenarist has pitifully little control over the finished product. According to what Alan Anderson told me, Miss Bergman was not content to be just an actress; she and her acting coach, Ruth Roberts, and others made the mistake of rewriting the Maxwell Anderson script so that it would be, as they thought, more historically accurate and therefore better; and to this end they introduced for the trial scene literal translations of the Old French (which did not sound well in modern English). By means of such interference they helped make the dialogue dull and the figure of Joan a plaster saint. Seeing that his judgment was being overruled and his art bastardized, he suddenly left Hollywood without notice and headed home by car with his wife and daughter. He took a route calculated to baffle and infuriate the producer and director and agents and Miss Bergman herself if they tried to intercept him with messages along the way (which they did). Apparently, the bastardized rewrite was not going well.

Anderson made a nostalgic visit to Whittier College—his first since leaving there under duress in 1918—and on the long drive home via North Dakota he revisited for the first time those scenes of his youth, Minnewaukan and Grand Forks. He who disliked traveling and sight-seeing took a leisurely two weeks to cross the nation and ignored with a quiet smile of vengeance the frantic telephone calls and telegrams waiting for him at each hostel. In the 1930s he seems to have been coldly indifferent to what Hollywood did to his finely woven script once he was through, but of late, now that the Broadway critics had been giving him a trouncing, he waxed more and more resentful toward all forms of what he considered outside interference in the packaging of his art.

Hesper tells in her "Someone Else" what happened when the trio finally reached home. The night the car entered the driveway in New City the kitchen telephone was ringing away for him—a call from an anxious Miss Bergman—and Hesper hung around to listen to the explosion that she knew was coming: Anderson entered, picked up the receiver, listened for a moment, and shouted in a way fit to start an avalanche on South Mountain, "You big, dumb, goddamn Swede!"

Soon he got word that film producer Walter Wanger intended to change the name *Joan of Lorraine* to the prosaic *Joan of Arc*—whereupon, as Anderson's diary notes, he immediately "saw red."[127]

True to his expectations, the film was wretched. Critics assailed it right and left.

Meanwhile, Anderson's reputation abroad as a playwright was in full flower. He was popular on the European continent, especially in the Mediterranean countries and in Scandinavia. As of the date of this writing, *Joan of Lorraine* has been seen in Denmark, Finland, Holland, Italy, Poland, Portugal, Romania, Sweden, Switzerland, and Yugoslavia, as well as in Central and South America. *Winterset* appears to have been about equally attractive to foreign audiences, with productions in Denmark, England, Finland, Germany, Hungary, Italy, Norway, Poland, and Sweden. Of all places, Sweden has seen the greatest variety of Anderson works on the stage; England and Scotland very few, probably because the British do not take kindly to the way he had transformed the lives of their monarchs—as if Shakespeare had not taken liberties with them also![128]

Greece was another country eager to see *Joan*. Greek publisher Theodore Kritas arranged for it to be presented in the fall of 1947 in Athens; and Basil Vlavianos, head of that country's newspaper *National Herald*, invited the distinguished American to be his guest during production. That November Max and Mab left New York on the liner *Queen Elizabeth* for a voyage to Athens via London. He played the tourist among the ruins on the Acropolis and traveled around the country, taking special note of the government's military campaigns against the Communist insurgents in the North, who were making hit-and-run forays from across the borders in Albania and Yugoslavia. So convinced was he that Greece was in a life-and-death struggle against the red tide of Communism that he cabled back to the *New York Herald Tribune* a series of five articles on the subject, only two of which got published in the New York paper; the Paris or International edition carried two others; and the fifth, on the subject of drama among the Greek populace, never reached print.[129]

Having lately pored over Dr. Arnold Toynbee's *A Study of History*—in Anderson's words "the most complete and erudite of all the attempts to set down a record of men and civilization on this planet"[130]—which credits the well-being of any civilization to its ability to respond successfully to human and environmental challenges, he saw Soviet Communism as *the* great challenge facing the Western democracies. Consequently, in these newspaper dispatches Anderson stressed that, since democracy was very much alive in Hellas notwithstanding the strong-arm tactics of the government, America was justified in supporting Greece in its struggle against the guerrillas lest that country become another Soviet satellite.[131] (In March of that year, President Harry Truman had promulgated the "Truman Doctrine," which provided Greece with military and economic aid to the tune of $300 million, which was to prove crucial in liquidating the Communist bands.) Before Anderson left the country he promised Kritas that he would someday compose a drama about Athens.[132] And he would keep that promise.

In early December the *Mauretania* departed from Southampton and took him on the voyage back to New York. During that passage Mrs. Dorothy Hammerstein, wife of songwriter Oscar Hammerstein II, kept praising to Anderson the merits of a certain new novel, one written with lyrical simplicity about the ordeal of South African blacks uprooted from the security of their tribal life and plunged into the big city maelstrom of temptation and crime. The playwright simply had to dramatize it! she declared.

The novel was *Cry, the Beloved Country,* to be published by Scribner's on February 2 of the following year. This was Alan Paton's first novel. At the time in question, he was the principal of a South African reformatory for delinquent boys and was currently on a tour of penal and correctional institutions in various countries, including the United States.[133] Mrs. Hammerstein had apparently learned about this book, which was to be the basis of one of Anderson's noblest and most beautiful adaptations for the stage, through some unknown third party in London or Sweden, places where Paton had preceded her by several weeks. Anderson grew enthusiastic also, and upon his return to New City discussed with Kurt Weill the possibility of making *Cry, the Beloved Country* into a tragic musical.[134] At a party on March 1, 1948, Mrs. Hammerstein at last gave Anderson a copy of the book.[135]

After planning with Weill how to adapt the novel, Anderson returned to a play that he had been working on and finished the first draft: this was *Anne of the Thousand Days,* set in one of his favorite backgrounds, the Elizabethan era, and treating of the doomed Anne Boleyn; the third and final published member of his Tudor verse trilogy. But excellent as it is, this lusty and gripping tragedy has somehow not received the critical attention it deserves. *Anne* deals with sexual passion in conflict with power politics in the lives of King Henry VIII (the "Sexual Everyman," as the author calls him[136]) and his mistress-turned-wife until the royal adulterer himself finally charges her with adultery and has her beheaded in 1536.[137]

Needless to say, Anderson took some liberties with history, but his spectacle of Henry and Anne—the ogre luring and pressuring the initially innocent woman deeper and yet deeper into the web of evil until she is likewise corrupted by the temptations of power and becomes his partner in crime—is absorbing enough to make the theatergoer leave his nitpicking and

wonder why so many other modern playwrights seem amateurs by comparison. Alone among Anderson's Tudor works this one illustrates his growing
attention to the commanding role that physical sex plays in human behavior.

The first Broadway production, featuring Joyce Redman and Rex Harrison,
began in December 1948 and ran for 288 performances and a 10-week tour.
The dramatist had every reason to be happy with the writing, the cast, the
acting, and the reviews that poured in. But dampening his happiness came
news that Francis Hackett, a former colleague of his on *The New Republic,*
had brought a lawsuit against him claiming plagiarism from three of his
works: a biography, *Henry the Eighth* (1929), a novel, *Queen Anne Boleyn*
(1939), and a play, *Anne Boleyn,* finished in 1942 but neither produced nor
published.[138] The astonished and incensed Anderson struck back with a
$100,000 libel suit and adduced evidence from his diary—excerpts from it
appeared in the *New York Herald Tribune*[139]—that traced the development
of *Anne* from its earliest beginnings to its final shape as an independent and
original entity. Unlike Hackett, we are told, he conveyed the entire action as
happening within the minds of the principal characters.

He finally agreed to pay the other man a dollar; they then dropped their
charges against each other.[140] Such are the facts. But what we *don't* read in
the records of this foolish case is what damage all this bad publicity did to
Anderson's nerves and peace of mind.

Soon after he finished reading the novel that Mrs. Hammerstein had given
him, he wrote to Alan Paton: "I hope to convey to you, at so great a distance,
something of the emotion with which I read 'Cry, the Beloved Country' and
which many Americans must feel now as they read it. For years I've wanted
to write something which would state the position and perhaps illuminate
the tragedy of our own negroes [sic]." In the letter he asked permission to
do an adaptation with Weill. He proposed to retain the dialogue and plot of
the original, and buttress these by means of a chorus—a distinct innovation
for him—which would unite the large number of scenes and provide comment for the action, just as Paton in his own voice had commented in the
descriptive and philosophical sections of his book. He would have to convert
some of the material into verse, and Weill would lift out some of the lyric
prose and set it to music. "It would be our task," Anderson continued, ". . . to
translate into stage form, without dulling its edge or losing its poetry, this
extraordinarily moving tale of lost men clinging to odds and ends of faith in
the darkness of our modern earth. For the breaking of the tribe [an omni-
present wrong demoralizing and destroying the blacks, according to Paton]
is only a symbol of the breaking of all tribes and all the old ways and
beliefs."[141] Of course, to Paton, the tribal breakdown was not only a symbol;

it was also a fact of life that he had seen evidenced every day in numerous delinquent youths at the reformatory.

Weill had long wanted to write music for a Greek-style chorus, was delighted with this new project, and in the beginning planned for this to be the only music, but before very long the script acquired a few songs for the actors themselves to deliver. Not less than three songs came from *Ulysses Africanus,* another Negro musical that Anderson and Weill had completed a few years earlier but couldn't get produced, and one of these, "Lost in the Stars," gave the play its title. Originally, Anderson had placed at the end this song of man's alienation from God, but, evidently deciding to close on an optimistic note, he replaced it with the somewhat more hopeful "Thousands of Miles."[142] Taken altogether, the final score contained surprisingly little African or even American-African coloration: absent are Southern spirituals; and even the tom-tom beat, though present, is not at all like the one indigenous to jazz; at most there are just hints of these traditions. Weill evidently figured that to reach the heart of a mostly white and liberal theater audience he would have to forego using any local color that Negro music might provide.[143]

In order to understand why Anderson in his present state of development was drawn so forcibly to the novel in the first place, and why he surpassed Paton in laying special stress on the theme of brotherhood, we must go back to the voyage on the *Mauretania* for the answer. The playwright and his wife had gotten acquainted not only with the Hammersteins but also with a Dr. and Mrs. Everett Clinchy. Dr. Clinchy was at once a Presbyterian minister and the president of the National Conference of Christians and Jews. The three couples played chess together and discussed the gloomy likelihood of further world wars made all the more imminent by the Soviet Union, by declining religious faith, and by new and more frightful weapons. Before these couples separated, Dr. Clinchy proposed that back in New York they get together some representatives of the theater who might discuss means whereby that institution could, in Anderson's words, "lead men toward some kind of amicable adjustment that would avoid these recurrent and expanding disasters we've so far lived through." Consequently, several such meetings took place; at one of them spoke Arnold Toynbee, at which time the others in the group tried to nail him down on what *he* thought the theater could do to help prevent such disasters. "There is nothing that can save us except brotherhood," Toynbee informed them. "Brotherhood, amity, tolerance, understanding—understanding that crosses all the boundaries—this is the great need."[144] There is no question at all that Toynbee deeply colored Anderson's thinking.

The Playwrights Company, however, did not exactly keep pace with the nobility of this idea. As usual, the economic pressures of putting a play on the Broadway stage meant that even among these liberal-minded men there would be some trade-offs. The company sought out an inexpensive musical director, kept the orchestra small (12 instrumentalists), and budgeted the production for $90,000—a modest figure for a musical in 1949. They made the mistake of renting for their purpose the Music Box, whose rather limited seating would keep the weekly overhead too close to the weekly gross earnings.[145]

About the only suitable Negro singing actor for the role of the Reverend Kumalo was Paul Robeson, the man whom Anderson had originally selected for the lead in *Ulysses Africanus* but who had turned it down because of its condescending attitude toward the Negro. Robeson was again unavailable; and, besides that, his increasingly active Communist stance would have irked Anderson. Instead, Todd Duncan took the role, a man who had played the lead in another Negro musical, *Porgy and Bess;* he was charming but he was not able to project the massive strength of the Paton/Anderson hero.[146]

Government officials in South Africa were so outraged over *Cry, the Beloved Country,* with its implicit challenge to apartheid, that they made it unnecessarily difficult for Paton to get away to attend the Broadway première. When he arrived in the United States he had but "3 sixpenny pieces" about him. Anderson greeted him at Idlewild Airport, invited him to be a guest at his house, and undertook to get him an advance royalty payment.[147]

Though critical reviews had lauded the new work, and the National Conference of Christians and Jews honored Anderson with its coveted Brotherhood Award for his contribution in this very play, within three months the Music Box ceased to be filled each night. Anderson, already staggering under his huge debt to the IRS, had invested $12,500 in this show; Weill, $3,000; this money was in addition to their original investments as members of the Playwrights Company. So they had much to lose. Nor could they count this time on recouping possible losses with a lucrative sale to a film company, for Paton had already disposed of the novel's film rights to England's Alexander Korda.[148] Victor Samrock, business manager for the company, had warned early that racial hatred would create rough going for this particular musical. Attendance dropped off so much that the profit margin began to worry the management. Then it was found that they could schedule *Lost in the Stars* for limited engagements in Los Angeles and San Francisco during the summer and thereby stand to make a profit after all; the hitch was that the show would have to close for the summer in New York and might not reopen. The plan is said to have made the authors furious: They went to press agent Fields and to Samrock and demanded that they explain why attendance was dropping so much and why it couldn't be raised. According to Wharton, "Max became more and more irascible and Kurt more and more excitable." Fields feared that the composer would have a heart attack—a foreboding of what was to happen the next year.[149] Anderson and Weill were experiencing one of those seemingly impossible but more and more common situations on Broadway, a play that runs reasonably well by prewar standards but still does not earn enough to repay the tremendous cost of production; nor would this play ever do so, even with its eventual run of 281 performances in New York and a 14-week tour. It was no longer enough that a play be good or even excellent; it ought to run seemingly forever and pack the house every night, a necessity calculated to drive many a serious author like Anderson to despair.

The touring company ran into unexpected problems on the road. Black actors could not always get accommodations in "white hotels." In Baltimore the players were begged by the local NAACP branch and the Committee on Non-Segregation in Baltimore Theatres not to act in the Ford Theatre, which was then segregated. The company was faced with a dilemma in wanting to carry this play to as wide an audience as possible, and yet how could it in good conscience put on a show in a segregated theater? Duncan asked that they cancel the engagement. They did. But in St. Louis they consented to act in the segregated American Theatre—and were picketed. At the time the musical closed in Chicago, Anderson forwarded to the cast a telegram which read, "I believe we were engaged in a great cause together, that we benefited that cause extraordinarily and that our country will be a better place in which to live because of what we were trying to do."[150]

The Reverend William L. Anderson and his family, about 1891 or 1892. *Top, left to right:* Rev. Anderson, Maxwell, Premma. *Bottom, left to right:* Ethel, Lela

Maxwell Anderson's house of birth, Atlantic, Pennsylvania, after it was moved down the road to a neighboring farm.

Hallie Loomis, *standing at left,* when she was about ten, close to the time when Max first met her. She gave her name to the Hallies in his plays and the novel.

Anderson's childhood home at 112 Cumberland Street, Harrisburg, Pennsylvania.

Anderson, at about the time he was attending the University of North Dakota

Margaret E. Haskett, who became the first Mrs. Maxwell Anderson

Max and Margaret, probably during his newspaper days

The Haskett house at Bottineau, North Dakota, as it stands today

The old farmhouse on South Mountain Road, New City, New York, as it used to be when they first moved in, with Anderson's son Quentin shoveling show.

The farmhouse about 1934, after reconstruction and additions had been made. *(Lawrence Anderson)* .

The New House on South Mountain Road. The first structure is in the center. The new addition was added in 1935.

he second Mrs. Anderson, Mab Maynard, *ft*, as a child, with her mother, Anna Higger, nd her sister, Libbe.

Mab, at the time of their marriage.

In 1936, the Andersons lived in the house at the right, 323 West 112th Street, New York City. St. John the Divine Cathedral is in the background. *(Lawrence Anderson)*

Maxwell Anderson's cabin in the woods as it looked in 1978. It was moved to his son Terence's front yard.

Hester and her father in the summer of 1940

Marion Hargrove (shown in 1942) and his buddies were the models for Anderson's characters in *The Eve of St. Mark*.

Max and Mab in March 1943

Anderson, Rouben Mamoulian, and Kurt Weill, rehearsing for *Lost in the Stars. (Florence Vandamm)*

Mab's grave, *far right,* at Mt. Repose Cemetery. Margaret's ashes are buried here, too. Kurt Weill's grave is at back, right.

Anderson in 1943, about to voyage to England as a "news correspondent"

Anderson with his brothers at the New House, about 1949. *Left,* the youngest brother, Lawrence. *Right,* John Kenneth. *(Lawrence Anderson)*

Gilda Hazard, Anderson's last wife, was known as Gilda Oakleaf on stage.

In Hollywood for the movies, she called herself Gilda Storm.

An aerial view of Anderson's house at Stamford, Connecticut

Max and Gilda at home in Stamford

A never-before-published photograph of Anderson, during the 1950s.

The last picture of Maxwell Anderson, taken by the seawall at Stamford.

8

STORM ON SOUTH MOUNTAIN ROAD

I n the spring of 1950, while he was in the midst of writing the musical *Raft on the River* (an adaptation from *Adventures of Huckleberry Finn*), Anderson's dear friend Kurt Weill came down with a severe cold which kept him in bed at Brook House for a few days. Anderson turned up at his bedside to confer with him about their newest joint venture. On March 2 Weill recovered sufficiently to go downstairs to celebrate his fiftieth birthday with the playwright and Hesper, now a teenager. He suffered a relapse a few days later. And on the night of March 16 Weill suddenly felt a pain in his chest and a pressure about his heart. Anderson found him a specialist who diagnosed coronary thrombosis, and the stricken little composer ended up in Flower-Fifth Avenue Hospital in New York City. Again there was a brief recovery, enough for him to continue composing songs in his head for the musical; even the doctor thought he would be getting better. On the afternoon of April 3, however, the Andersons' telephone rang with a call from Lotte Lenya at the hospital: They should come immediately. They found her standing outside the composer's room.

"I think this is the end," she said.[1]

Within just a few minutes Weill passed away.

Two days later, at the lovely Mount Repose Cemetery, at Haverstraw along-

side the historic Hudson, Anderson read a graveside eulogy over the body of
his friend. He said:

> For a number of years it has been my privilege to have a very great
> man as my friend and neighbor. I have loved him more than any other
> man I knew. And I think he had more to give to his age than any other
> man I knew.
> I wish, of course, that he had been lucky enough to have a little more
> time for his work. I could wish the times in which he lived had been
> less troubled. But these things were as they were—and Kurt managed
> to make thousands of beautiful things during the short and troubled
> time he had. He made so many beautiful things that he will be remem-
> bered and loved by many not yet born.[2]

The death of Weill had a long and stunning effect on Maxwell Anderson.
He wrote in his diary five days later, "A sad sad day—over broken plans and
lives."[3] Somehow he could not get their *Raft on the River* in shape for
production, despite later assistance from Irving Berlin.[4] It is not entirely
coincidental that with the passing of Weill—whom Anderson considered the
"only indisputable genius" he had ever known—Anderson's own creativity
with stage drama began to decline more than ever. No doubt increasing age
hastened this process.

After Weill's death, Anderson turned his attention to finishing the first
draft of what was for him a bold venture, a novel. As his diary indicates, he
considered the novel so shocking that he would have to sign *Morning Winter and Night* with a pen name, in this instance John Nairne Michaelson.[5] He
extracted those pages showing sexual activity and allowed Hesper to read
the others, from which she got the distinct impression, based on the anecdotes he had told her over the years about his childhood sweetheart Hallie
Loomis, that the story was a *roman à clef* derived from the experiences of
his youth.[6]

Mab was aghast when *she* read it. And furious!—not just because the book
seemed to her so dirty but also because the explicitly drawn sexual things
that happened to the boy Jamie in the story really had happened to Max
Anderson, she thought, and here he was about to publish it all to the world.
When Anderson took the novel down the road to try out on Lenya, she liked
it, but she also believed that scenes in it were right out of Anderson's life.[7]
After Mab typed the novel, her husband took it again down the road, to
William Sloane, who now had his own publishing company, and this man

told him that the story was "probably unprintable,"[8] but he liked it anyway and wanted it. Of course, there would have to be changes. Mab and Lenya both proposed softening some passages.

The narrative in *Morning Winter and Night* is told through the memory of an aging Western man who makes a nostalgic visit to the village of Devon, Ohio, where as a twelve-year-old he had spent the winter on the farm of his grandmother. The Westerner feels a compulsion to recall that long-ago adventure in order to learn his own identity and how he got to be what he is. As the boy Jamie he lives in a small farmhouse with his Grandmother Ellen Stewart and her elderly boyfriend, Fowler, who occupies a shed at the back whenever he is not away on a hunting trip. Jamie's boyhood companion in the neighborhood is Alden Harsh. The hero develops a platonic relationship with the light-haired and blue-eyed Hallie Haviland, a schoolmate, who is to him all that is purely fine, but while she is away for the Christmas holidays he clumsily tries to rape the village "bad girl," Madie Tatum. The much-more-experienced Madie, however, takes over and seduces him. In one of the more explicitly described scenes in the story, he accidentally discovers Hallie and her aggressive older brother on the verge of committing their latest act of incest together. After that, when Hallie offers her body to Jamie one night, he cannot rouse himself to consummate his love for her: He is unmanned by the knowledge that she, his beautiful angel, has all along been wallowing in incest.

On the novel's last page, the grown-up Jamie, thinking back on these events, agonizes about the "unspeakable thing," "this horrible secret, this thing that bites into your mind and makes you flush with shame in the darkness when you are old." He cites a number of shameful mistakes that are possible to us, all of them sexual in nature, the likes of which we all supposedly commit at some time and then go around concealing. None of the offenses consist of sexual intercourse plain and simple, but of abuses and perversions of sex. At this juncture we remind ourselves of Henry VIII's soliloquy in *Anne of the Thousand Days* when he speaks of a load that every man carries around with him full of dark secrets that he hides from the world.[9]

But getting back to the novel, much of the surface background depicted here is demonstrably a blend of fact and fiction. To a large extent Anderson patterned his village of Devon, including the farm of Jamie's grandmother, after Atlantic, Pennsylvania, where he had wintered at the farm of Grandmother Shepard. The time periods are identical: the winter of 1899-1900. The grandmothers' houses are much the same, including the furnishings and even the woodshed attached at the back. It is surely no coincidence that

Stewart was Grandmother Shepard's maiden name; moreover, that both women have blue eyes and yellow hair. The name Jamie is patently a takeoff on Max's first name, James. The boys' ages differ by no more than a year. Jamie sleeps in an attic just as Max did, and likewise attends a country school nearby. Like Mr. Shepard, Fowler chews tobacco and sleeps in the woodshed and dies rather soon. The name Alden Harsh is surely taken from Alden Harshman, who lived west of the Shepards on the dirt road fronting the house. And the Haviland family is perhaps suggested by the one that lived east of the Shepards on the road (but there were no girls). The Stewart farm reminds us of the other one in that there are willows, apple trees, a spring, and a hollow. Somewhere in the neighborhood is a Blair's store too.

But the differences are almost as numerous. Grandmother Shepard had no lover, and Mr. Shepard was no hunter (unlike Fowler). No Madie Tatum lived in the neighborhood. Hallie Haviland gets her features and first name and adorableness from Hallie Loomis, who belonged in a later period of Max's life, when he was in Jefferson, Ohio. The North Star, which Jamie sees from the attic, could not be seen from the attic of the Shepard house, which was laid out east and west. Unlike Jamie, Max was not gravely ill at his grandmother's place. Furthermore, unlike the case in the story, no grave lay in the hollow at Atlantic.[10]

After being revised and getting a new ending, *Morning Winter and Night* was published on April 3, 1952, and priced at three dollars. Only the immediate family, Lenya, and Sloane and his wife knew the real identity of John Nairne Michaelson: Such a veil of secrecy hung over the authorship that it was not until twenty-five years later that the general public, including some close relatives, learned that he had written this book. Most of the reviews of this beautifully honest and sensitive childhood idyll ranged from sympathetic to enthusiastic, but sales were disappointingly small.[11] The book might have sold better had he used his own name.

For a long time before his novel was written, Max wanted to compose a play about Socrates, but Mab resisted. "I won't let him," she said. "I just think that anything in togas on Broadway would be laughed off the stage."[12] But there was his promise to Kritas to consider. And so, during the period 1950-51 he wrote his *Barefoot in Athens* and had it staged in the Martin Beck Theatre on October 31, 1951. Based mainly if not exclusively upon Xenophon's *Memorabilia* and Plato's dialogues, the play interprets the final months of Socrates, commencing at the time of the Peloponnesian War in the house of the destitute philosopher—props rather than sets representing the place—and ending in the prison cell where he awaits his death by hemlock. Anderson gives his hero several human attributes, such as a relaxed conviviality, a taste for the erotic (as in Plato), and the quaint practice of going barefoot,[13] although he consents to don sandals sometimes in order to spare his child embarrassment. Next to Socrates the most vivid and amiable of all the characters is the comic king of Sparta, Pausanias, who insists on being called "Stupid," although he is far from being so; he endears himself to us because, against his will, he learns to admire the old gadfly and offers to break him out of prison. Xantippe, depicted in tradition as a shrew, is in this drama a loving and most devoted wife who has become disagreeable only because of grinding poverty.

Just after having completed an early draft of *Barefoot,* Anderson read Karl R. Popper's *The Open Society and Its Enemies,* which is decidedly anti-Plato as well as anti-Communist, and then revised his work under the influence of what he had found in Popper.[14] The preface seemingly owed still more to that influence. What he gained from his reading was a conviction that Socrates' criticism of Athenian society was a "democratic one, and indeed of the kind that is the very life of a democracy" (Popper's words).[15] Such was his evident compulsion to make the reader draw a useful lesson from the preface (and by that we mean a political lesson) that Anderson took the liberty of identifying Sparta—the archenemy of Athens—as a completely Communist state and Athens as a completely democratic state.[16] And, as said earlier, he seriously undermined his ideological message by allowing Socrates to be convicted by a so-called democratic jury. Moreover, Pausanias, a Communist as defined in the preface, makes genuine offers to help the philosopher and likewise Xantippe when she becomes a widow. Anderson has simply made over history to suit his artistic—and in this case, political— purposes, Socrates becoming his mouthpiece just as surely as he had been Plato's mouthpiece. For example, the fondness for democracy that Anderson attributes to his hero is found in neither Plato nor Zenophon.[17]

There is still another line of thinking that dominates the drama, and this is contained in Anderson's unpublished "Notes for *Barefoot in Athens,*" where he enunciates a paradox which we can readily apply to the achievement of Socrates, that relentless inquirer into all things. It is this: By examining the basis of morality too closely, one can destroy such morality; and faith cannot withstand examination either; but freedom exists *only* when one is allowed to examine these things unhindered by external restrictions and restraints.[18] Anderson was never to resolve this paradox.

The fact is, given his political leanings at the time of writing, it was most difficult for him to admit that democracy had any drawbacks at all. It was the time of the House Un-American Activities Committee hearings, of the famous

Joseph McCarthy "witch-hunt" hearings in the United States Senate, when many sober-minded and patriotic citizens believed beyond question that Communists had infiltrated branches of the federal government and were active in subversion. Hollywood went so far as to blacklist actors, scriptwriters, and others who were suspected of being Reds or "fellow travelers"—or who refused to inform on suspects. Thanks to a recklessly assembled book called *Red Channels,* which purportedly listed the activities of all pro-Communist workers in radio and TV, some careers were suddenly curtailed or ruined in the aftermath of firings and blacklistings.

In this atmosphere of suspicion and fear, Anderson surprised the other members of the Playwrights Company by taking the view that any American member of the Communist Party was a criminal dedicated to overthrowing the government by force. He quarreled with Elmer Rice by refusing to go along with a proposal by the Dramatists Guild that it defend any member listed in *Red Channels.*[19]

Because of the way Xantippe was depicted, Mab detested *Barefoot in Athens* so much that she did not attend the opening tryout in Baltimore. She claimed that her husband stole from her mouth every word of the woman's dialogue.[20] By now there existed between Mab and her husband a deep alienation of feeling, as subsequent events will make clear.

Barefoot in Athens lasted for only twenty-nine performances, a failure that cost the Playwrights Company seventy thousand dollars.[21] Critics like Brooks Atkinson, John Gassner, Walter Kerr, and George Jean Nathan placed much of the blame on the directing and acting; and Alan Anderson, the play's director, admits that he did not require enough rewriting. "Dad and I liked each other too much to work together that closely," he concludes.[22] The playwright, nevertheless, laid the blame on Brooks Atkinson, whom he considered so powerful in the tiny circle of daily critics that no play had a chance without his support.

In his review, John Mason Brown was disappointed that Anderson did not represent Socrates in the death scene as the great man and moving philosopher that we read about in Plato but "a loving father, a loyal Athenian, an ardent democrat, and a sentimental husband"; that the playwright made the mistake of having his hero die at dawn rather than at the more poetically (and historically?) accurate sunset; that the curtain comes down before the philosopher actually dies; and that he spends most of his time in that scene with Xantippe rather than with his followers.[23] But Anderson clearly wanted to stress the human being and the patriot—the very aspects that Plato and the historians tend to gloss over.

It remained for a much later commentator, Mabel Bailey, to point out the main difficulty in accepting the version of Socrates found in *Barefoot in Athens*. The hero there is strangely unwilling to admit, being a staunch democrat, that the Athenian court that convicted him is a prime target of the corruption of power in a democratically selected body. Though they can abuse that power, though they can try to escape moral responsibility by citing their superiority in numbers, "might does not make right in a democracy any more than in a monarchy or a dictatorship," Bailey urges. Power can corrupt a group just as surely as it can an individual. In the plays completed before he had become a conservative—*Elizabeth the Queen, Masque of Kings, Both Your Houses*—Anderson had freely used the theme that power corrupts, but now, wanting desperately "to keep a free people believing in themselves and in their institutions," he would not permit his story to reveal the truth about that calamitous miscarriage of justice.[24]

He was so bitter about the critical reception of *Barefoot* that he threatened to resign from the company, to put on no more plays while that wasp Brooks Atkinson was still around, but Sherwood and Rice prevailed upon him to reconsider. Anderson lamented to Sherwood that "the kind of theatre I have always written my plays for is gone or going. I have no hope that it will be resuscitated. . . . It begins to seem to me that what's wanted in New York is quick flash stuff, with plenty of shock or sex, and vapid musicals. That sort of thing was always wanted, of course, but it wasn't honored the way it is now."[25] The theater *was* changing, and at sixty-two he had changed a lot also. But Anderson decided not to resign after all.

A gloomy period for him. And things would shortly get much worse.

Mab Maynard went a little wild when she started to work in New York City. For years she had nagged her husband to let her take a job, but he steadfastly refused.[26] But they needed money. It was hard for this essentially ambitious woman[27] to be in any way restricted to a domestic role and meanwhile have to watch her aging husband crushed like Laocoön in the coils of a monstrous tax debt and suffer further numbing defeats at the box office. Anyway, she was bored. Bored from having to spend her considerable energies in social and civic groups almost exclusively. Bored, too, with typing her husband's plays and yet having little or no perceptible control over the entire operation from origins to opening night. With her organizational background and her work with Anderson on his plays, however, she aspired to be an editor—maybe for that latest technological brainchild, TV— and as such able to do something to relieve the family finances. At last he consented to her plan. And so it was, in 1951 or shortly before that, she landed a position as adapter of TV plays for a program called "Celanese

Theatre of the Air," which won the Peabody Prize. This was during the so-called Golden Age of television, when it was fairly common in America to find original and quality video drama that was as yet unspoiled by the relentless domination of the advertisers in selecting program material and structuring it to fit the interruptions of ever longer and more numerous commercials. Mab seemed passingly competent at her work and had a modest degree of success.[28] She took up the habit of staying overnight and sometimes for weekends at the Hotel Dorset apartment that Anderson rented by the year, earned a bit of money but not enough to make much of a difference in the tax debt, and no doubt enjoyed her newly won independence. But with independence came temptation.[29]

Now in her mid-forties, still attractive, she began menopause and suffered the anxiety, nervousness, and depression that state can cause, but her condition was complicated by a deterioration of the mind whose exact nature is difficult to identify at this time except that, as Hesper writes, it must have been "manic-depressive" and definitely had a strong suicidal bent.[30] Various family sources attribute some of her anxiety to money matters, especiaily the huge income-tax bill.[31]

It was early during her work in New York that she became attached to young Jerry Stagg from the William Morris agency. He was a husky TV executive involved in putting together "Celanese Theatre"; a bright, sensual, very witty man; Jewish like herself; one who could be elegant and sophisticated when required; and also attractive to women.[32] Now that her youth and beauty were taking flight and she realized that she and Max had no more passionate love for each other, she must have seen in Stagg her chance—maybe her last—to snatch some bright passion before the dark and cold closed in. Gilda Hazard, who knew Stagg well—she lived in the same town house and was a friend of him and his wife, Maxine—recalls that Miss Maynard was definitely the aggressor in this affair; moreover, that Stagg or his wife had told her this was not the first time Mab had been unfaithful to Anderson.[33]

Meanwhile, Anderson, haunted in his private life as well as in his dramas by the overwhelming need to find faith and certainty in a world on whose increasingly slippery surface it seemed difficult to find a toehold, was quite oblivious to what his spouse was doing in beds away from home. Even though he remained faithful, the speed of subsequent developments in his new love life strongly suggests that his love for Mab had by this time lost all or most of its zest and he was sticking by her mainly out of habit, or gratitude, or concern for her mental health, or some combination of these. Probably he was unwilling to admit even to himself that she was in any way to blame for his recurring low spirits. For a long time he had not been paying much attention to her sexually, an omission that led her to the mistake of thinking him impotent.[34] Alienation developed the more readily because they had slept in separate rooms ever since the days when little Hesper insisted on climbing in with him at night, whereupon he found the visits less disturbing to Mab if he moved out of the room.[35] And, besides that, he often had trouble sleeping at night and found it convenient to occupy another room, where he would wake up to take a Seconal capsule and then read or work until the sedative took effect.[36]

Sometime in the sultry month of July 1952 occurred that jolting incident at home which utterly destroyed Anderson's relationship with Mab and plunged him into such a morass of despondency that it was a long time before he became active in the theater again.[37] He had returned home from one of his moneymaking raids on Hollywood. He picked up one of the telephones in the house to make a call and heard Mab saying to a man on the other end of the line, "Oh, darling, darling!"[38] Hers was the note of unmistakable passion. What happened immediately after that is suggested in the corresponding passage in their neighbor Bessie Breuer's novel *Take Care of My Roses*, which was modeled closely upon the major personalities and incidents in the Anderson ménage during this tempestuous period.[39] Alma Salter, the adulterous wife, tells her housekeeper about the confrontation she had had with her husband, Mr. Salter:

> He rushed in to me, where I was replacing the telephone, and grabbed my hand, and shouted. I went limp all over, and sat down on the bed and he continued to rant and shout. "You're evil, evil . . ." He went on and on, "I should shoot you and him, and then myself."
>
> You know I kept thinking, this can't be real, in astonishment thinking, this is like an old-fashioned melodrama, but he raved on.
>
> "If I can't kill you I should kill myself, as a man of honor . . . a man whose honor has been soiled."[40]

Most likely Anderson identified his rival's voice immediately, for he had had the Staggs out to his house for weekends;[41] and once he and Stagg had gone together to the Hotel Shelton in Boston to see if they could interest Eugene O'Neill in a TV series that the Playwrights Company was planning.[42]

The first thing Mab is supposed to have said to her justly outraged husband was, "What're you carrying on about? So everybody's having an affair! Lenya's having an affair, Bunny's having an affair; why are you getting hysterical? What makes you so different?" Exasperated with her, he went down the road to talk with his friend Milton Caniff, who was Bunny's husband.[43] What he said or learned at the Caniffs is not reported, but he soon heard from his house-keeper, Martha Stamper, the neighborhood clearinghouse for gossip, that she had suspected back in June that Mab was carrying on an affair in Bunny Caniff's apartment. And she was convinced, based on a long talk she had had with Mab, that his restless companion of many years would have left him soon regardless, because she wasn't happy with him.[44]

All indications are that he himself had been faithful to her from the start. Admittedly, her being almost sixteen years his junior had naturally put a strain on the relationship; stories of the old husband getting cuckolded by the young wife are legion. Suddenly in his eyes she was loathsome like a two-headed toad, this woman whom he had treated as his wife for almost twenty years, whose expensive whims he had pampered over and over until, partly for this reason, he·was now deep in financial trouble. And her deceit mocked all his yearnings for spiritual certainty in a world where values seemed to be shifting constantly. Almost immediately he packed up some things and moved into New York City, where he was to live for several months until Hollywood lured him away to do a scenario.

Friends and relatives went to him and tried to effect a reconciliation, but he would have nothing of it. He *couldn't*. It was a matter of old-fashioned manly honor born of a tradition stretching back to times immemorial, sub-scribed to in much of the great literature of the world, even in the Bible of his father; a residue, maybe, from the strict Baptist teachings he had heard as a child, but it was something that Lotte Lenya with her Continental laissez-faire view of marital relations couldn't accept at all. Weill had often been unfaithful to her, she was positive, but she knew that he would always come back, and he did. Their attachment ran so deep that it could withstand an occasional fling. One must be patient, Lenya told Anderson, for over the years a person's tastes inevitably change some; no one wears the same suit for a lifetime, even if the fabric's made of the finest silk. So what if Mab had sampled victuals at another table? He had done it himself when he was much younger—remember? Oh, it will all blow over if he would only give the woman a second chance and take her back. This Stagg infatuation will pass away.[45] "But I've been cuckolded! I've been cuckolded!" was his anguished refrain,[46] and it was clear to any listener that manly pride was at stake. To those who recalled what he had done to Margaret, it seemed simply that the shoe was now on the other foot. Even so, he no doubt realized far better than they did how irrational Miss Maynard had become in the past few years; and the situation was still more complicated than that for him because, as we shall see presently, a new love interest was developing in his life. Nevertheless, Mab's faithlessness was beyond question the hammer blow that ripped them apart for good.

In a similar crisis in *White Desert* he implies that the husband is wrong in not taking the fallen wife back to his bosom. And in *Truckline Cafe* he has the mutually unfaithful pair forgive each other and start to rebuild their shattered marriage. In his writings, therefore, he tried to be tolerant. But what he wanted to do in a real-life situation when he wrote those things as compared with what he *could* do when the burden actually lay on him in all its immensity were not the same thing. Leo Tolstoy in *War and Peace* furnishes us with an excellent illustration of the dilemma:

"I say, do you remember our discussion in Petersburg?" asked Pierre, "about . . ."

"Yes," returned Prince Andrew hastily. "I said that a fallen woman should be forgiven, but I didn't say I could forgive her. I can't."[47]

The chronology of events in Mab's life from the crisis date in July 1952 until the following March is unclear, mainly because some of the key letters and all of the Anderson diary for this period are unavailable to the public. But from my interviews with knowledgeable Anderson family members and friends, together with my correspondence with these people, the following account emerges.

Max's departure for New York City aggravated Mab's mental breakdown, throwing her into fits of anger and depression. Her weight started sliding below a hundred pounds, and she looked drawn and exhausted. As Hesper revealed in an answer to my questionnaire, her mother told her that she had offered to crawl on her hands and knees to Anderson for forgiveness—Mab was highly melodramatic when relating such woes to other people—but he coldly refused, saying that he "rotted" some inside each time that he looked at her. At card games held some nights with Bunny and Lenya, her two closest friends, she opened up the infidelity-and-rejection theme so often and with such vehemence that they began to lose patience with her; she even said more than once that she planned to kill herself, whereupon they delegated to themselves the responsibility of shoring up her spirits as best they could. With prophetic irony, people behind her back began to call her Madame Bovary. Her repentance, if any, was short-lived. The affair continued. In answering my questionnaire Hesper reveals that one night, when Mab drove her prized Cadillac into the city, presumably for another tryst with Stagg, the crushed husband (he continued to make visits) sat on Hesper's bed and asked her whether she wanted to go through her mother's stocking bag with him to find her diaphragm.[48]

Actually, her attraction to Stagg had begun long before she began working

in "Celanese Theatre," long before Anderson had overheard the fateful telephone conversation. The night that Stagg's organization aired the TV version
of *Mary of Scotland,* he and his wife, Maxine, told their assistant Gilda that
they were getting out of town the very next morning because "Mab had a
crush on Jerry."[49] This sounds like a face-saving gesture on Stagg's part, now
that his wife had already discovered what was going on. The involvement
became sexual, yes, but much more than that, in spite of what some
members of the Anderson family are inclined to believe. She wrote passionate love letters to him, but these he destroyed at some unknown date lest
they survive him in an airplane crash. He in turn proposed to take her with
him to England, but nothing came of this plan.

Anderson finally persuaded Mab to see a psychiatrist, a woman known as
Dr. Catcher; Mab went there for several therapy sessions and appeared to
make some progress. The TV work with "Celanese Theatre" having been
terminated, she flew once or twice to Denver to stay briefly with her friend
Maggie Fanning; there, at least, Mab would be welcome (she must have told
herself) and could have someone to dine with regularly now that Anderson
preferred to eat alone rather than suffer seeing her face across the table. He
continued supporting her, nevertheless, just as if his personal and professional life did not lie broken about his feet.[50]

Now to backtrack a little. Just as Mab had found Stagg at "Celanese
Theatre," Anderson later found his new love, Gilda Hazard, there too, this
being in the fall of 1951, when that organization was getting ready to air
Winterset on ABC television. At that time, apparently, neither one made any
romantic overtures to the other. But there is no question that Gilda, a
production assistant there, took a romantic interest in the dramatist at or
about the time he broke up with Mab the next year. After Anderson discovered the infidelity and grew despondent, the sympathetic Gilda began
spending a great deal of time with him until she grew worried about what
effect all this might have on Mab's precarious emotional condition and
decided to flee from any further involvement with the troubles on South
Mountain Road.

Anderson's diary, which is ordinarily a detached, sparse, businesslike
record of what he was writing or negotiating, what books he was reading,
what time he rose or went to bed, or what was said on the telephone, began
to take on a tone of sad distress. There are cries of pain, as when he learned
that Gilda must now move far away: "Can't let go with me till she's sure
about Mab. God, if there's a god, and there isn't, help me!" And, "In despair
about my life & the play [*Cavalier King*?]—and the future."[51]

Soon after this, Gilda fled to California, but before that happened Mab almost surely learned about the "other woman" in his life—a discovery that would have galled her no end, for this supposedly impotent man whom she had deceived was now rejecting *her,* with a furious distaste that she was quite unprepared for, and to top it off had attracted to himself a sensitive and compassionate woman lovelier than Mab had been for a long time. Maybe in the beginning Mab had believed she could keep both lover and husband, enjoy the excitement of the one with the relative security of the other. But now the cuckold was fleeing. He was even planning to sell the house from under her. Soon she would lose the inestimable prestige of being called Mrs. Maxwell Anderson (passing that title on to another woman); Mab would also lose her entrée to stylish social and artistic circles that had fed her ego for two decades.

By November after discovering the infidelity, Anderson made up his mind to get a divorce on the basis that, in one of the states, his union would surely be recognized as a common-law marriage; the divorce would be for the protection of Hesper.[52] What he might not have realized at first was that New York State itself could not grant them any divorce for the simple reason that, as of April 29, 1933—just a few months before he and Mab had announced their "marriage"—it ceased to recognize any more common-law marriages formed in that state.[53] Whether Anderson made application elsewhere is not known. But somewhere during the legal proceedings the news would almost certainly emerge that she, Mab Maynard, had lived a lie. She could almost see the blurb in Walter Winchell's gossip column; almost see *The New York Times'* exposé captioned with "Dramatist's Mate Revealed as Kept Woman."[54]

One of those who continued to like her despite her faults, who saw her through eyes saddened by a long succession of family tragedies and a long-endured privation to match almost anything the former orphan girl had suffered, was the patient chronicler of Anderson family history, wise old Lela Chambers. As she saw it, Mab was haunted by a fear that her husband's days of material success were all over and "she couldn't face poverty or any kind of deprivation such as she had known as a child. . . . she was just too weak to face what she thought was ahead."[55]

Then began the tries at suicide. She took an overdose of sleeping pills in the Hotel Dorset apartment, called Hesper to tell her what she had done, and the daughter in turn frantically telephoned the building superintendent to have him break down the door. Another time, when Mab had swallowed an overdose of pills and lay drowsing in the bathtub, Hesper herself dragged her out. At another time it was pills and lying in the tub, at which time Anderson just happened to be around and he pulled her out; when Hesper came downstairs she found her mother dripping wet and naked on the bed, and her father, now paralyzed with shock, sitting on the edge of the bed and unable to do anything further to help. It remained for Hesper to telephone the doctor, who told her to feed Mab coffee and walk her around until he could get there. Anderson was still in a daze when Hesper poured the coffee and began to walk back and forth supporting in her arms the slender, almost hipless body of her mother; after the doctor had done his work and left, Anderson could be seen lying exhausted on his bed with a wet handkerchief spread over his eyes. There were nearly always suicide notes, one of which forecast that he would not write another play and that Hesper would not complete college.[56]

There were still more sessions with the psychiatrist. At some point in November 1952, Dr. Catcher informed Anderson that it would at last be safe for him to go to California if he kept secret his whereabouts. Apparently, if Mab knew where he was, she might follow, maybe make trouble for Gilda. We next find him in Hollywood writing another film script. He hates the place but at least Gilda is there. In the following February, Lenya writes to him that she hopes he finds in Gilda what he needs in that time of trouble, namely trust and love. She writes that Mab has gotten herself a new job; maybe something good will come of it. If only Mab will cease her furious ravings and accept the fact that he, the object of her anger, was not the one who had started all the trouble. Early next month Lenya sends another letter, this time to report that Mab refuses to sell the house—just to spite him! For nine months Lenya has been forced to listen to her melodramatic complaints; they have now grown wearisome, for Mab has an answer to everything and simply will not come to terms with her problem and end the nightmare. Another letter says the affair with Jerry continues.[57]

By this time most of Mab's friends on the road had begun to avoid her, and she was left alone in the big house with her critic from many years back, the family housekeeper, Martha, who had cooked for her beloved Margaret in the old days, starting from the time the Andersons first moved out to the farm; then she had cooked for Mab, hating her all the while; Martha practically raised all the children and shared their confidences down through the years.[58] Mab had repeatedly begged her husband to get rid of Martha but he wouldn't, for he had intense loyalties. But was this housekeeper actually visiting a witch doctor at Nyack and performing voodoo, as Hesper suggests?[59] Some parts of our story will forever remain mysterious. But it may well be that in those final horrifying days the housekeeper secretly exulted in seeing brought low and still lower the elfin woman who had had so much power over the Anderson estate, the woman who once had wronged Margaret and usurped her place.

On the Saturday evening of March 21, 1953, Lenya, now remarried to a former editor of *Harper's*, George Davis, came back from the metropolis with Bunny Caniff, at which time Lenya suggested that they drop by Mab's place to see if she were home.[60] It had been days since they had seen her at gin rummy games, she exhausted and her weight shrunken to about ninety pounds. As they drove up the long driveway to the big house they noticed that the shades were drawn in the ground-floor bedroom of the garage apartment where their friend had been used to sleeping of late. The big house itself was unused and shut up for the most part now that Anderson had gone off to California. Thinking that Mab was in the apartment with Jerry and wouldn't want to be disturbed, they left. The next morning, Lenya called the Anderson place but got no answer. Curious now, she drove back in the afternoon and parked by the apartment; and, without peeking inside, as if she suspected that the answer to her quest lay in the garage, she went directly there and opened the huge door and found in the front seat of the Cadillac what she was looking for. And feared. The windows were down. Beautifully dressed in a negligee and mink coat with her little breasts held in place by a French brassiere, her face made up carefully with expensive cosmetics so that she would look her best when found, and with a half-burned cigarette dropped on the floor of the car, lay the cold and rigid body of Mab Maynard. Dead at forty-eight. The two satin pillows she had brought out to the car to lie on were smeared with fresh makeup. Her new job had not been enough to sustain her interest in life; nor the freedom to continue her assignations with Jerry Stagg; nor the luxuries which Anderson had left her. Her attempts at looking lovely in death were mocked by the ghastly blue coloration and puffiness of the skin, thanks to carbon monoxide. (The ignition was turned on and the gasoline tank was empty.)

Julie Sloane came over and stayed with the body while Lenya telephoned Alan in the old farmhouse next door. While waiting at the car, Julie gave vent to an overwhelming feeling of sympathy for the tiny, childlike form now collapsed on the pillows: She put out her hand to touch Mab's cheek and found it icy cold.[61] On this occasion Mab evidently did not want anyone to rescue her in the nick of time, for she had telephoned no advance warning and had dismissed the servants for the weekend. There were three notes from her: one to her maid, another consisting of a will that left all her possessions to Hesper; and the last to Anderson himself, which read:

Max Dear,
    You have been right about everything. Please, please know always this has to do with me and not you.[62]

A few days earlier her younger sister, Libbe Axlrod, who lived in Miami, Florida, had had a powerful urge to talk with her and had reached her by telephone. Mab once had tried to get some expensive heart surgery done for Libbe's son but the Paris doctor, one of the few in the world who then performed the new skill, would not come to America, and the boy was too ill to move; but at least Mab had tried. The boy lived on for ten more years. She had shown many other kindnesses toward the Axlrods too. During their telephone conversation Mab asked whether their mother could get along all right if the $300 allowance being sent down there each month were stopped. Libbe answered with a "yes," for the mother was an extravagant soul, even wasteful, and didn't need the money.[63]

Anderson rushed back from California, and Hesper from her studies at the Women's College at the University of North Carolina. Someone had entrusted Burgess Meredith to fly old Mrs. Klein up from Florida to attend the funeral, and she arrived at the local airport quite hysterical about having flown there in a tiny, private plane.[64] As Hesper told this biographer, Quentin puzzled her by suggesting that they should look around for a rabbi to conduct the services. "Why?" Hesper asked. "Because," he said, "your mother was Jewish—didn't you know?—and for that reason you are too." This was actually her first news of her racial and religious background. But she was already too stunned by her mother's death to care much at the time.

The service was short and entirely nonreligious, Anderson delivering a eulogy in the living room of the New House while the coffin rested nearby. Some listeners thought his words entirely appropriate; others, especially some neighborhood women who had sided with his wife, who tolerated a liberal margin of sexual freedom in marriage, and who recalled rumors of his conduct toward his first wife, considered his words to be hypocritical for not admitting guilt on his part for what had befallen the dead woman lying in the coffin.

But what Anderson's detractors might not have known was that Mab had had suicidal tendencies dating back to her marriage with Maynard (any of several causes besides rejection could have triggered her act). Certainly it was *she* who had brought on her latest troubles by choosing another man. Moreover, her continuing assignations suggested that she was something other than the repentant wife remembered by Hesper and pitied by some sentimentalists in the neighborhood. No matter what her guilt, it was psychologically impossible for Anderson to return to her once his sense of manhood had been violated; and, actually, he didn't abandon her in any materialistic sense.

While he was making his eulogy, Hesper, still in a state of shock, fumbled her way upstairs and soon returned carrying a portrait by Henry Varnum Poor that was done of her mother as a younger woman, fresh with spring-time radiance, and placed it by the coffin so that the mourners would not get all their last impressions of Mab from the blue-lipped and puffy and badly made up face in the coffin.[65]

Bad weather delayed burial for a week. Then Mab was laid to rest in Mount Repose Cemetery, a few feet in front of the grave of Kurt Weill.

And then a curious thing happened.

Being pressed to move belongings out of the New House now that it was about to be sold, and to empty the cabin too, Anderson did what he thought at the time was practical in disposing of Margaret's long-unburied ashes. No doubt to his way of thinking he had stood watch over the dead quite long enough and now proposed to give his sentiment to Margaret's memory alone as distinct from physical remains, a sentiment far more meaningful than some ounces of mineralized calcium. And so he took the urn containing Margaret's ashes over to Mount Repose Cemetery and, in the presence of his friend Lenya, had them interred in Mab's freshly dug grave![66] He was obviously distraught from the recent tragedy at his house. When he was finished, the tombstone remained inscribed as it was—

Mab Anderson
1904-1953
Stay Well[67]

Some while back this second Mrs. Maxwell Anderson had gone with Martha to clean out the study cabin in the woods and there, to her shock, discovered on a shelf the urn—the *urn*!; and then, pale as an anemic ghost, she hurried over to see Lenya and told her everything in breathless amazement.[68] Now, ironically, the urn rested just above her corpse: the remains of two women who in their lifetimes had been bitter enemies. May they rest in peace!

Somehow, Stagg's adultery became known to his wife. But he returned to her for a reconciliation that didn't work; then followed many years of separation until his recent death. And Maxine, perhaps owing to her own marital conflict and what she had heard about the tragic events on South Mountain Road, fell into such spells of melancholy that she finally secluded herself from the world and refused to see her own children.[69]

THE LOST SPRING

Maxwell Anderson married for the final time on June 6, 1954, while he was in Cedars of Lebanon Hospital in Los Angeles, California, waiting to undergo an operation; apparently he didn't want any accident on the operating table to prevent him from winning his bride. A Methodist minister named Leo Kline performed the ceremony. The bride was Gilda Hazard,[1] so youthful-looking and luscious at forty that some people who didn't know her, like Lynn Fontanne, mistook her for a girl. She was to make him a good and loving wife during his few years left.

Like his two earlier wives, Gilda was dark-haired and short. She was born in Providence, Rhode Island, one of three children in the Romano family, on July 17, 1913. Her mother was a sweet-natured Swede born Gurlie Walberg (whose mother's name was Eklof, which translates to "Oakleaf," the name Gilda adopted for the stage); and her father was Nicholas Romano, who had immigrated to America from Benvento, Italy. In the last phase of his career, Nicholas worked as the museum art photographer for the Rhode Island School of Design.[2] Little Gilda attended various public schools in Providence.[3] She admits to having wanted to be a great ballerina and later on yearned to be a great actress. At seventeen she left for New York City, totally committed to the theater. One day she was followed through Shubert Alley to Forty-fifth Street by a strange man who quickened his pace whenever she quickened hers, and who finally stopped her with, "Pardon me, are you an actress?" He turned out to be not the mugger or masher she suspected but Brock Pemberton, who was producing a play and wanted her to read for a part. Ironically, this was the very producer who many years before had given Anderson *his* first start in the theater by accepting *White Desert!* That evening other guests at the Dancer's Club, where she was lodging, laughed at her story when she related it. Imagine—to be chased down Shubert Alley by the noted Brock Pemberton himself! But the laugh was on them the next day when she went to the producer's offices at the Little Theatre and obtained her first major role.[4]

Starting in the 1930s she was launched upon a promising career, always billed for the stage as Gilda Oakleaf, and acted in Hawthorne Hurst's *Christopher Comes Across,* her husband Lawrence Hazard's *Manhattan Medley,* Helen Claire's *Coquette,* Robert Turney's *Daughters of Atreus,* Leopold Atlas' *But for the Grace of God,* and Sir James Barrie's *A Kiss for Cinderella.* She understudied for a role in Ian Hay's *Bachelor Born* and later took on the role. This last play ran for at least two hundred performances. Being a petite lady, she was especially suited to ingenue parts. In 1933, with her brown hair grown long, she was Gilda Storm playing the role of Vesta, Jennie's teen-age daughter, in a film version of Theodore Dreiser's *Jennie Gerhardt.* Photographs in Gilda's scrapbook for that period show flawlessly regular features; an oval face capable of tender Juliet sensitivity; full, sensuous lips; and a smile so fresh and radiant as to make even stonehearted critics want to give her a hug. And her acting, too, made a favorable impression on these critics. However, Gilda's marriage in 1940 to playwright Lawrence Hazard and the birth of their children, Laurel and Craig, put a crimp into her professional career.

Anderson had been a hero to her for many years before she met him. She had read and adored his plays from a distance but, somehow, never had a chance to act in any of them; nor had she ever been to the offices of the Playwrights Producing Company.

They first met in the studio of the "Celanese Theatre" when Mab was one of the scriptwriters who were adapting *Winterset* for television. The shy Gilda, who was a friend of Jerry Stagg and an even closer friend of Stagg's wife, Maxine, worked for "Celanese" as a production assistant. When *Winterset* was being readied for the air late in 1951—and several months before he learned of Mab's affair—Max Anderson dropped into this circle and caught sight of Gilda.

"You should be playing Miriamne," he told her.[5] She found him completely charming; no doubt he felt the same way about her. By that time, Mab's mental health was going to pieces; he no longer slept with her; and a deep alienation had set in. Circumstances could not have been riper for him to get interested in Gilda. Frank Hill notes in his memoir that Anderson had a special liking for little women and that when anyone introduced such a person to him, such as at a party, he reacted with genuine interest.[6] But without exception my informants all agree that Max did not begin dating Gilda until *after* he discovered that Mab was playing around with Stagg. Even Hesper, so quick to find fault with the way he treated her mother after the affair was exposed, admits that he was faithful up to that point.[7]

Not long after that initial meeting, Gilda spent a long weekend with the Andersons in New City and, dressed in a Chinese ensemble, played poker to while away the hours, but she noticed that the couple were "barely speaking" to each other, the atmosphere being "strained and heavy." Her relationship with Mab during this visit was friendly—but not intimate. Gilda had no desire to return, she said.

Later, in a "highly emotional state," Anderson drove up to Providence to check with her on the Jerry and Mab affair but found she had no information to give him. "We all sat around consuming enormous amounts of iced tea and trying to calm him," she wrote. The three fatal words on the telephone, "Oh, darling, darling!" had so stricken him that there could never be any turning back in the hope of making a new start.

And having met Gilda was more than ample reason for not turning back. Then, in the latter part of 1952, in the weeks after he discovered Mab's liaison, he went up to Providence again, this time using the excuse that he wanted to look at Gilda's brother's sailing boat, *Triton,* but his real motive must have been to see the trim lines and fittings of another vessel. The next day they took Laurel and Craig to the beach. Not long after that, Gilda left with her family for a two-week cruise on the boat and during her absence he barraged her with love letters. It was during this period that he also wrote her a series of love poems, for example, "For Gilda" and "Evadne," published posthumously in *Notes on a Dream.*[8]

After Mab's funeral Anderson returned to Agoura, California, where he rented Elsa Lapworth's strange, cavernous, still incomplete castle and did his best to make it habitable. He started anew on the screenwriting which had been interrupted and began to collaborate with Rouben Mamoulian and Allie Wrubel on a new musical called *Devil's Hornpipe,* a modern version of the Faust legend. But none of his work went well. On November 13, 1953, he wrote to Hesper, "I get so low about my work sometimes, I don't want to go on at all. But I do, and I will."[9]

In sunny California he began to court Gilda Hazard in earnest. By December of that year he was so happy with the progress of his suit that he was able to write to Lela, ". . . I am loved, and it's something not to be lonely. I won't try to explain it, but there is a woman of great beauty and sweetness who finds me worth while [sic] still and that has pulled me through."[10] Gilda was to prove most important in rebuilding his life. His nature craved the love of woman, for did not the plays speak over and over again of the wonder of romantic love? And she was clearly desirable, even if she were encumbered with two young children who might, and indeed did, prove bothersome when he needed quiet for writing, and even if she were still not divorced. But for a long time in their relationship she did not want to marry him at all—and for a variety of reasons that included her children and the nightmare on South Mountain Road.

But she finally relented, pending her divorce from Hazard. "He's just worn me down. We're going to get married," she told Hesper.[11]

Nevertheless, as hinted earlier, the hospital bed had priority over the conjugal one. For years Anderson had been sure that he had heart trouble. On May 23—about two weeks before the marriage took place—he entered Cedars of Lebanon Hospital for an operation that he hoped would take care of this. The surgeon, however, discovered that the heart was sound but that the diaphragm over the stomach was pressing against the heart and causing the alarming symptoms that Anderson had been worrying about. The situation was fairly complicated; Anderson would have to come back soon for another operation. It was during this stay in the hospital that he got married. The need for further surgery right away caused the otherwise happy pair to put off their planned honeymoon trip (they were never to have one). Once out of the hospital he started to work on TV and film stories[12] and finished *The Masque of Queens,* a play about the aging Queen Elizabeth,[13] a work that would never be staged or published during his lifetime.

Back into the hospital he went on July 8, this time for an operation on his prostate gland, which was of immediate concern because this gland had been giving trouble to the kidneys; and it was necessary to get the kidneys in good condition before the next and final operation—the big one—on the diaphragmatic hernia.[14] (This last operation took place in Lenox Hill Hospital in New York City next February.[15])

While there in the hospital for the first operation, he entered one of his despondent moods, believing that he might never again write a successful play for Broadway. Typically, he went into a bleak period between writing plays, and also when a current play was not turning out well; and at such times things seemed to him to be in a pretty sorry mess and the world hardly a fit place to live in.[16] He was in such a mood when Gilda, with wifely shrewdness, brought to his hospital bed a copy of William March's hair-raising novel *The Bad Seed,* which with its study of hereditary evil in a little girl had been thrilling readers for about a year. Gilda's plan was to convince her bedridden husband that he could write another important play, and to prove it would adapt this very novel.[17] March's *The Bad Seed* is a fast-paced and gripping example of modern Gothic which, aside from its cold and repellent heroine and a few other things that needed changing, seemed ready-made for adaptation to the stage. Anderson, who did not often read novels, had nothing much else to do and so he read this one; and before he left Cedars of Lebanon Hospital for good on July 13 he had already decided to write a dramatic version of this "fascinating" book. A few days after he got back home he set to work on it; by August 15 he completed his final draft, wrote "curtain" at the end, and gave it to Gilda for typing.[18]

Meanwhile, the Playwrights Producing Company had rushed to obtain for him the stage rights to the novel. And then it rounded up a good cast for the fall première: Patty McCormack (Rhoda), Nancy Kelly (Christine), Henry Jones (Leroy), and Eileen Heckart (Mrs. Daigle), to mention only a few.

In the play's story, eight-year-old Rhoda Penmark, a sweetly smiling "model child" in pigtails, murders three people and gets away at the end scot-free. The audience is left wondering whether the little monster will chalk up any more crimes. *Bad Seed* reached the Forty-sixth Street Theater on Broadway in December 1954 and had a long and profitable run. This was to be Anderson's last commercially successful and satisfying play, his *salve atque vale* to the theater. It is curious that in writing this work he violated two of his celebrated rules for dramatic composition, namely that (1) the protagonist, representative of the forces of good, must win out in the end; and (2) evil must not triumph. Those critics who say that Max Anderson was handicapped by rules of his own making, was too rigid in dramaturgy, should take heed in this case. As a practical man of the theater, he knew that he had to make—and violate, if necessary—his own rules. Perhaps he remembered Emerson's dictum, "A foolish consistency is the hobgoblin of little minds. . . ."

At any rate, Gilda proved to him that he still had much of his old fire left.

As an aging man most of whose children were grown and married and who must have felt keenly the generation gap, he had trouble adjusting himself to a household containing "two head-strong children" (as he called them even before he committed himself to marriage and settled down into a two-bedroom apartment in Los Angeles)[19] who, with the high spirits of youth, stormed into the apartment each day after school and distracted him from his work. He soon found it convenient to find himself a quiet office completely away from home, but once the family moved to Stamford he found the study near the garage quiet enough for his purposes. In this marriage there was no motherly Martha around to take the children off their hands and practically raise them, and no brotherly Quentin around to be bribed into housing them next door. Laurel and Craig were eleven and eight years old, respectively, at the time of the marriage. Laurel, in particular, bore the archetypal resentment of the older child for the new stepparent—even in the old fairy tales the stepparent is in a class with the big bad wolf—and gave him black looks when he told her to do things. She was a stubborn little rebel. The situation was sad and painful to him not only because he had raised his own children by using a remarkable degree of indulgence which, as perhaps expected, didn't work in Laurel's case, but also because he naturally didn't want to disrupt that delicate probationary status held by all arriving stepparents until such time as they proved themselves on the side of the angels. As time wore on and the children grew more independent while he grew more conservative, Laurel entered that tempestuous phase of growing up that is politely called adolescence. She had been difficult to manage before the marriage began, and now her behavior at home must have seemed to him more nerve-piercing that a dentist's drill operating on Saturday night.

This same Laurel, however, grew into an extremely attractive girl; she was so fetching that whenever she stepped foot outside the front door there was likely to be a clutch of young male admirers hanging around. Anderson could not help feeling uncomfortable in having such a sexually attractive stepdaughter around the house, like dynamite with a slow fuse burning.[20] And he was helpless, too, as a responsible albeit aging stepparent who somehow had to cope with the relentless biology of growing up, the rambunctious spirits, the giddy freedom that children expect. He could recall how he and his brother Harold had rebelled in their day against the strictures of the Reverend Anderson, and how he had created for his plays many a rebel hero, and how his son Quentin had boiled with anger at the arrival of Mab in the family.

The fact is, all of his own children except Alan had had severe emotional problems, whether in youth or later on, that took them to psychiatrists; the awareness that he had somehow failed them weighed on his conscience. Out of this deep sense of domestic tragedy he told his brother Lawrence, "The worst thing you can do for your children is to leave them either fame or fortune."[21] During the interview he had had with Eugene O'Neill in the Hotel Shelton, as recounted briefly in the last chapter, the first and only meeting these two famous men ever had together, Anderson was so burdened with his problems that he made a point of trying to share them with his fellow sufferer, a man who had lost one son (Eugene, Jr.) to suicide, another (Shane) to dope addiction, and a daughter (Oona) to a marriage of which O'Neill scathingly disapproved. Barely touching on theatrical topics, Anderson directed the conversation almost exclusively to family matters. "The great tragedy," he confided to O'Neill, "is to discover that you have not armed your children for life." At hearing this the creator of *Strange Interlude* and *Long Day's Journey into Night* is said to have "nodded thoughtfully," maybe with a misery too deep for words.[22]

It's commonly believed that the children of famous writers fare poorly because such writers are too self-centered and too absorbed in the struggle of giving life to the creatures of their imagination to spare much attention for their own flesh and kin. But generalizations of this type are risky, especially in the case of Anderson. He was far from being indifferent to the risks his own children were running; the many long conversations he had with Terence and Hesper in their times of need demonstrate that he was or at least tried to be an emotionally supportive father.[23]

As for the stepchildren, Laurel's salty tongue irked him. Although he was adept at profanity, he rarely used it,[24] certainly not gratuitously. In addition, he tended to idealize his women and grew uncomfortable when they didn't observe the traditional forms of maidenly decorum. But the tables were turned now on the old archrebel, he who as a child used to delight in tormenting his starchy preacher-father by standing in the doorway when the man came home from a church service and then greeting him with a mischievous "Hell—o!"[25]

At last the parents packed her off to Rosemary Hall Boarding School to put more discipline into her studies. But then she grew homesick and ran away, but at the wrong time as it turned out, for her parents were on the road with a play. Hesper came to the rescue by offering to share her New York City apartment with the girl, and this arrangement pleased all parties concerned.[26]

Craig loved his new stepfather and they got along well together,[27] but without meaning to he "wore on . . . Max's nerves some," reported Anderson's nephew Avery Chambers, who visited there in 1958. Avery remembers that once when he was down at the beach, the boy somehow allowed a rowboat to go adrift, whereupon big Max Anderson handled the minicrisis with his usual calm and directness: He simply waded out into the sound with his shoes on and pulled the boat back in. No need to alert the police or harbor authorities.[28]

Let us now learn what had happened to Hesper. Once Mab had put an end to her long torment and lay at last in her coffin, Hesper began to slip into emotional shock. This was the first of her big losses coming upon her almost all at once. She was troubled almost certainly by her own feelings of guilt at how she had been treating her mother. Then almost immediately she lost her boyfriend, Marion Hargrove, he who had become a celebrity in 1942 with his book of reportage about American soldier life. When she was but eight, her father had brought home with him this young man—tall, amusing, golden-voiced, a knight in khaki from another world than hers and gifted with a mind of quicksilver brilliance. For Hesper, the princess of the cinderblock castle, it was infatuation at first sight. Her "Someone Else" typescript describes in frank, relentless, unpitying detail this "crush" she had for the soldier almost three times her age. The "crush" continued unabated after he married and moved into an old Dutch farmhouse across the road from Kurt Weill and became her longtime friend and mentor. For years and years she waited anxiously to grow up and become his woman. But the two never dated until she was nineteen and he was getting separated from Alison, his first wife. A poignantly brief affair ensued. Then Hargrove, who did not share in her long-delayed dream of fulfillment, lost interest and married someone else.

And now that her father had remarried, Hesper was about to lose via the new set of loyalties entailed by matrimony the very man, Maxwell Anderson, who was the closest human being to her. She who had been so dependent would now be alone as never before. For reasons too complex to explain here, even if they could be explained, she came to believe that he was partly to blame for her mother's death because he had refused to take Mab back even after she supposedly cried out to him for forgiveness.[29] No doubt he recited over and over his reasons for not returning to Mab. In an undated letter to Hesper, he defended what he had done by declaring that, like a man on the verge of drowning, he had no choice but to try to save himself; that if he had made the mistake of going back, he would have been "miserable," "a failure," "a castrated man."[30] But Hesper wouldn't accept this.

But when she had her own post-Hargrove heartaches and mailed her father the full details, he took time out not merely to offer sympathy but also to show her the perils in her way and counsel a wise course of action.[31] Very often he sent her gifts of money that he could ill afford. He was now reduced to living off an annual income of $36,000, and out of this was paying $5,000 a year so she could have the services of Dr. Geso, her New York psychiatrist.[32]

Hesper told me that once she had learned the secret that she was Jewish, she deliberately set out to spite her mother by learning all she could about that religion, and she ended up marrying a young Jewish man named Earl Levenstein. Accounts agree that he was altogether a most pleasing fellow, but the marriage failed after they had three children together. Following her divorce she went into the business of scriptwriting for motion pictures and TV, and at the present time she seems to have reached a moderate level of success. In 1972 the Mark Taper Forum in Los Angeles presented two of her full-length plays.[33] She also writes poetry.

It's appropriate here to add a few words about what happened to Maxwell Anderson's other blood children. Quentin, after working a few years as a bit actor and stage manager on Broadway, began teaching English at Columbia University. He holds a Ph.D. degree. Several of his books are about great American authors but, like the other children, he has never yet given to the world a published account of his own illustrious father. After World War II, his brother Alan turned briefly to writing, then stage-managed plays on Broadway for years, directed some plays there and elsewhere, began directing such TV shows as "Kraft Theatre" and "Studio One," and finally became a vice-president at the J. Walter Thompson advertising agency in New York, from which position he has recently retired. Terence finished college, tried a variety of jobs as a bit actor, stage manager, realtor, and teacher, and finally became a postman. In his spare time he writes poetry and plays.

Hesper, Quentin, and others report that Maxwell Anderson's new marriage was generally happy from beginning to end. To some, Gilda seemed the lady whom he by rights should have met and married long ago and thereby saved himself no end of worry and expense. After two unhappy unions he surely deserved a change. To Gilda's skills as a homemaker were joined a sensitivity to his needs as a creative artist, and she found unobtrusive ways to facilitate his work, such as by removing background distractions and buoying him up in his hours of despondency. According to Lawrence, this new sister-in-law was much less theatrical in her everyday relationships than Mab was. And far more normal and lovable.

After living at Stony Point, New York, for a year, the couple moved on July 1, 1955, into the small mansion on Shippan Point (141 Downes Avenue) in Stamford, Connecticut, which was to be Anderson's last home.[34] As usual, the cost—$56,000[35]—did not deter him in the least, even though he was still laboring under the huge tax bill that hung over him like a dark cloud. Soon he bought a 35-foot motor cruiser, which he christened *Thalassa* (Greek for *water*), so that he could take his family out on Long Island Sound for rides, and he attired happily in a captain's hat and coat.[36] Always he had yearned to live by the ocean, and now he had by night and day salt waves lapping against the seawall in his backyard, and the sounds of foghorns and sea gulls floating through his study windows while he worked. He loved the place.[37]

One day, soon after his arrival, an amusing thing happened. He drove into his newly adopted but unfamiliar city on an errand. The hours passed. At home, Gilda grew anxious about her husband, wondering if he had had an accident. After a long time he finally returned, the great man announcing sheepishly that he had simply lost his way somehow and had driven around for hours.[38]

This was a more attractive house than the cinderblock wonder that Poor had designed for him in New City; what the Stamford house lacked in uniqueness it made up for in character and taste; if anything suffered by comparison, it was the natural setting. This building was made of brick in Norman French design, with five bedrooms, four baths, a three-car garage, and chauffeur's quarters attached to the house. In addition to the other usual rooms there was a cozy study and a large, glassed-in porch where he liked to sit except on the coldest days. On a table in the far left corner of the living room Gilda placed on view some special memorabilia: his large, circular, and extremely handsome Gold Medal from the National Institute of Arts and Letters;* his smaller medal attached to a purple ribbon that announced his election to the American Academy of Arts and Letters; and his silver and ebony plaque from the National Conference of Christians and Jews. But he would not allow his portrait by Poor to be hung downstairs,[39] and consequently Gilda kept it upstairs until after his death. Using the excuse that she had to hide the nails studding the walls, she hung some handsome, framed playbills from *Barefoot in Athens, Bad Seed,* and other plays.

Anderson steeped himself in Tacitus and Suetonius[40] for *The Golden Six* (1958), which tells of the rise and fall of the Roman emperors from Augustus to Claudius and betrays the author's own pessimism about the disparity between a people's aspiration for free government and what they feel impelled to put up with and perpetuate once tyranny has set in. In this bitter story Anderson tells us of a truth that many of us have confirmed for ourselves, that government, no matter how obviously in error, is *ipso facto* self-serving and carries within its makeup a soulless momentum that is steadfastly resistant to change. No doubt his ill health contributed to the noticeable drop in dramatic quality. It had only seventeen performances in the York Playhouse. His last staged play was *The Day the Money Stopped* (1958), adapted from a comic novel by Brendan Gill and written as a potboiler in one more futile effort to pay off the tax debt. It too failed quickly. The immense energy and versatility were with him always, but nothing seemed to click anymore; his genius was failing him at last.

His life ever since his first commercial success had been spent helping his

*Only four playwrights had ever received the Gold Medal before: Augustus Thomas, Eugene O'Neill, William Gillette, and Robert E. Sherwood, in that order.

friends and relatives to enjoy the bounty of his purse; his was essentially a magnanimous soul that was happy in giving—and rarely asked for or received money in return. It's heartwarming to report that in this time of need Alan went out of his way to help his father with moneymaking schemes; there wasn't much earned this way, Alan confesses, but he was always inclined to modesty about what he was doing. As a realtor, Lawrence aided his famous brother by setting up a corporation consisting of himself, Anderson, and Gilda for the purpose of buying for investment a plot of land on Little Tor (overshadowed by the famous mountain). Two years later, on August 24, 1958, the playwright wrote him a note of thanks: "You have been an enormous help to me, and I'm happy about it for both of us." Yes, the investment paid off.

His activity in the Playwrights Producing Company became less and less important now that under Roger L. Stevens' reorganization the original Playwrights themselves were less necessary to provide new scripts and to read the scripts of outsiders; and, as if to make matters worse, their own ability to create marketable plays had taken such a nose dive that their newest member, Robert Woodruff Anderson, could not approve of any of the works they were turning out.[41] The company was now almost exclusively a firm for producing the plays of nonmembers. In short, it truly was a producing company—though not what was originally intended. Once upon a time Maxwell Anderson was the chief supplier of plays for the group, several times saving the firm from financial ruin by means of a timely moneywinner, but now he had more and more of his refused by his colleagues; and when he did manage to get one on the stage somewhere, it was almost sure to flop. Various complete but unproduced plays began to accumulate in his files, such as *Raft on the River, Adam, Lilith and Eve, The Masque of Queens, Richard and Anne,* and *Madonna and Child.*

Long before the vicissitudes of old age and declining health had weakened his creative force, why hadn't he returned to the genre that had won him the widest recognition in both critical and popular circles? The genre in which he no doubt made his greatest contribution to world theater? The choices he made for his only two play collections—*Eleven Verse Plays 1929-39* (1940) and *Four Verse Plays* (1959)—surely indicate that he recognized what his best work had been even though he believed in his heart that he had not yet wrought a single thing that would last the ages.[42] *Elizabeth the Queen, Winterset,* and *High Tor* had pointed the way for him with their skillful handling of characterization and imagery and delicate feeling; in such works he had gone far beyond the mere application of his dramatic theory, which in itself had never guaranteed success.

There are several answers to why he did not return. One is that he believed his poetry was not as good as his prose.[43] For other reasons, we must look to his enlarged scale of living and mountainous tax debt as well as to the radically changed Broadway conditions spoken of earlier; in this context we can understand why he was driven more and more to avoid the daringly experimental during his search for plays that would at once satisfy his ideals of workmanship and be box-office smashes.

Joseph Wood Krutch was for the most part correct when he opined that O'Neill surpassed his colleague in originality for the reason that he forced the stage to accommodate itself to him, whereas Anderson accommodated himself to the stage. The difference, however, is not as absolute as all that sounds, for O'Neill also on occasion had adapted traditional forms for his dramatic uses, as witness the Greek masks in *The Great God Brown,* masks and chorus in *Lazarus Laughed,* and Aeschylus' *Oresteia* trilogy in what critics often proclaim to be his masterpiece, *Mourning Becomes Electra.* Nevertheless, when it comes to graceful and harmonious dialogue, it's no secret that the author of *Winterset* far outshines his rival.[44]

Now for Anderson's own stated reasons for abandoning dramatic poetry after he had spent many years in the field. Simply put, he came to the conclusion that his was an age of prose after all. He said that "the society we live in doesn't look for the kind of speech on the stage that calls for it. If you give it to them, you have to trick them or force it down their throats—make them listen by some other device. Because the music of words is a very small part of what people are listening for now." And he added with characteristic candor: "I think my verse has been disintegrating under the pressure . . . of public opinion. They don't want it."[45] This was the reward for his faith in a democratic audience.

If he was near the end of his life sadder than usual about his art, at least none of the family seemed to notice it. From every failure he always landed on his feet like a cat and immediately set to work on the next play. There was always something hopeful in the works. Still, it is only fair to relate here what Robert Woodruff Anderson wrote to me about his colleague's state of mind. He did not know the early Anderson, hence could not make comparisons.

In many ways, a very sad man . . . at least in later life when I knew him. During that period he was having a hard time coming up with a play, and I once asked him why he didn't write more 'personally' . . . suggesting that there were many areas of his experience out of which he could write. He said words to the effect that much of his life had been sad, and he wrote to get away from it.[46]

Nor did the Cold War give him any comfort. He had long seen the menace of Soviet Communism, but too many Americans in the 1950s considered him an alarmist, especially after Senator Joseph R. McCarthy had been censured in Congress for his wild accusations that so often proved groundless. As Anderson told one news reporter, America was "so spoiled, so luxury-minded, so carefree, so devoted to the pursuit of happiness, that we have let Russia get ahead of us . . . in the armament race. If Russia gets far ahead of us with ICBMs she will probably bury us, and then proceed to take over the earth." According to him, the arms race is something America must accept for as long as Russia is in it.[47] What a far cry from the sympathy he had voiced long ago in his poem "Sic Semper," when he hailed the new Russia of 1917, where freedom would follow the Revolution!

Anderson continued his retired way of life but, as always, took pleasure in the visits of his brothers and sisters, his children and grandchildren. To Lawrence he was especially attached; and Lela was always a favorite, as his warm letters to her amply demonstrate. To his family at large he was, incidentally, not at all the somber, deadly serious, almost forbidding man that various published photographs and essays have represented him to be to the unsuspecting public. His gloom, if any, he kept discreetly under wraps, and he was both witty and charming in conversation. This fun side of him cannot be emphasized too much. Practically all the relatives interviewed for this book make a point of stressing how quietly amusing Anderson could be. Just as in former years he did not throw large parties or care to attend them, large groups made him uncomfortable unless they consisted of family and very close friends.

Once he urged the wife of Marion Hargrove, who had been invited to a White House reception, to attend despite her advanced pregnancy: "If your baby should be born there," said Anderson, "who knows—he may be the only person to be born in the White House and to wind up in a log cabin."[48]

For most of his adult years he had drunk great quantities of coffee but later grew wary that the brew would hurt him and he switched to drinking tea. He even gave up smoking, which was for him difficult because he had been an inveterate devotee of the weed for most of his adult life, but still he was not averse to joining his son Alan and others in smoking cigars sometimes, because he had the peculiar notion that cigars were relatively harmless.[49]

Until his last years, when stomach troubles came along and he began to be a little cautious about his diet, he had always been a hearty eater. He told his brother Lawrence that his ailment was probably owing to his having had to eat such a spartan diet of whole wheat bread and bananas at the University of North Dakota. There were certain dishes he liked a great deal. Alan recalls that "he would love getting hold of a good piece of salmon. . . . he had favorite cheeses and loved good fruit. . . . he became more interested in really [healthful] foods."[50] He was no ascetic, of course, but neither did he overindulge in diet or drink; and it is tempting to conclude that his upbringing in genteel poverty as a son of a Baptist minister must have had some restraining influence upon his personal luxury once his income made that luxury possible.

His muscle tone remained good even though he continued to neglect physical exercise.[51] Sometimes one could find him playing badminton with Gilda, or doing a little swimming in the Sound. Out on the side of the house he took pleasure studying the heavens through a high-powered telescope he had mounted on a tripod. Gilda says that Max knew the stars so well that if he were lost in the woods at night he could surely find his way out by taking a fix on the heavens. (References to stars occur often in his poems and plays.) Every now and then he practiced songs on the piano, some old church hymns he loved, as well as lyrics he wrote himself. By this time, Mozart had become his favorite composer, just as Mozart had been the favorite of George Bernard Shaw generations earlier.[52]

In 1955 Anderson refused an invitation to go to New York City for a University of North Dakota alumni reunion, explaining that he did not like banquets or crowds.[53] Nor did he like having to make a speech. He did, however, have warm memories of that prairie school. Indeed, no one who reads his touching poem "1908-1935," where he speaks fondly of Margaret along with Professors Koch, Squires, and Hult, can doubt the depth of his feeling; he writes there that every turn of the pathways would remind him of how even the loveliest all come to die.

In November 1958 the alumni association asked him to come out to help celebrate the school's seventy-fifth anniversary and to receive an honorary doctorate, but again he declined, pleading sickness.[54] In lieu of making the trip, he sent to the association his "Love Letter to a University," and the letter was read to the assembled alumni and then published. It is one of the most tenderly beautiful and nostalgic tributes that a former student has ever made to his school, and it is also the fullest autobiographical account that he ever wrote, brief though it is. In the letter he goes to the very heart of the problems that the sensitive student faces at a university, even today, and in so doing indicates the chief value that university experience has for devotees of the arts:

For the first time in my life I found myself among people who thought the life of the mind was more important than banking, and who respected any attempt to conquer an art form. Professor Gottfried Hult, who taught me Greek, also wrote poetry, and sometimes sold it. Professor Vernon Squires . . . made me proud that I was able to quote and tried to write in verse. I found there was a place in society even for an odd duck like me! This is perhaps the most important cultural influence a university can have. In a world given over so largely to getting, using, and keeping property, it maintains a retreat for those who are more interested in the creation of beauty or the discovery of truth than in the making of a profit.

And he concluded with the gracious note:

I wish I could be with you. Since I can't be, I'll remember you as you were then. And, still looking at the young faces in the old book [his copy of the 1911 *Dacotah*], I want to thank each of you for being there then and for being the kind of person you were when the world and the university and I were so young.[55]

Not often did he go to the theater. He was obliged to go, of course, if one of his own plays or one by another member of the Playwrights Company were on. But nothing he saw on the stage moved him quite as much as did a performance some years before when the Old Vic company put on *Oedipus Rex,* with the great Laurence Olivier in the star role, on which occasion he wrote in his diary that it was "the finest experience I have ever had in the theater."[56] When his colleague Robert Anderson lost his wife to cancer, Max Anderson wrote to him that in his own sadness he invariably found consolation in the works of the Greek playwrights.[57] So abiding was his love of the masters, most notably the classical tragedians Sophocles, Shakespeare, and Marlowe, that exceedingly little in the modern tradition drew a cheer from him. Something in those old writers comprehended and made bearable for him a mysterious universe in which he spied tragedy on every face along the road, a world of beauty threatened with atomic annihilation, a clear disparity between desert and reward, an incessant yearning for things of the spirit in the same man who has no assurance of an immortal soul or a heaven, and most bitter of all, a grave that yawns wide and waiting for all men, most of whom never quite fulfill themselves or clear up a fraction of the eternal mystery. Man is born for tragedy because man must die.

As usual his tastes in current theater were being dictated by his poetic theory as well as by an understandable partiality toward certain works by friends and colleagues in the Playwrights Company. As for contemporary plays, he considered Enid Bagnold's *The Chalk Garden* "fantastically good" and the adaptation of Shaw's *Pygmalion* called *My Fair Lady* "an exceptional musical, probably the most perfect musical, because of Shaw."[58] But we rarely hear a word of praise from him for any of those three popular figures of the post-World War II era, Arthur Miller, Edward Albee, and Tennessee Williams. "Williams' work I don't understand very well," he said. "No use posing about it, I just don't understand it."[59] Perhaps he had in mind Williams' *Cat on a Hot Tin Roof,* which the Playwrights Company had recently produced. Anderson's admission here shows only too well that as he grew older and age made him increasingly critical of passing fashions—such as emphasis on explicit sex—he was as always marching to a different drummer. This at least he could say about most of his own leading characters, that they are not men and women of low sensibility and elemental desires who yield themselves readily to their environment, but instead are delicately organized and in revolt against the inexorable tragedy of existence. They reflect and weigh, they doubt and rebel, they strive and fail—but always attended on their way by a kind of glory.

John F. Wharton in his *Life Among the Playwrights* wrote of something else that was making Anderson's own situation as a member of the Playwrights Company hard for the new generation to appreciate, and vice versa. He wrote that "the cynicism which grew up in the 1950s was replacing the idealism of the first half of the twentieth century" and that Anderson as a member of the company was one who tried to help men "clear up the confusion in their lives." These men of the Playwrights Company were:

> . . . liberals in the true sense of the word. They believed that people were capable of improvement and that perhaps the greatest feature of that improvement would be a reduction in Man's inhumanity to Man. And they expressed their beliefs in a dramatic form that anyone could understand.
>
> This point of view and this style of writing are almost unknown today (1974). Clarity of theme is no longer regarded by critics as a necessity—not even a desideratum. Praise may be heaped on an abstruse play which the author defiantly refuses to explain.[60]

One of his dreams, we are told, was to be able to read someday his beloved Shakespeare from his own copy of the First Folio itself, a book that cost in 1623, when first published, only $45, but a good copy of which today might cost well over $100,000—if any were for sale, which is highly unlikely. In all the world there are only about 238 copies, in various states of decomposition. He owned a facsimile reprint of the Folio, among the many editions of Shakespeare about the house, but an original!—Well, that was something to dream about! And thereon hangs a tale. In February 1959, a local book dealer named Mr. Keats talked him into the idea that he should now indulge himself and buy a First Folio if he wanted to and if one could be found at a suitable price. The purchase might seem to us outrageous for one in his depressed financial situation (he was paying $1,000 a month on his federal income tax bill), but what a fulfillment it would mean for a man whose greatest inspiration as a playwright had been the Olympian himself!

As Gilda recounts it, Mr. Keats telephoned Anderson that the Parke-Bernet Galleries in New York City listed in their auction catalogue an imperfect Folio whose price might be within their means. Thus informed, they went with their friend Marion Kahn to Parke-Bernet's, and Gilda recalls the delight with which Anderson received that rare book into his hands and sat looking at it while she and Marion roamed about the gallery.[61]

Came the day of the auction but he had a cold and felt that he ought to stay in bed and get some writing done.

But we can't afford the book right now, he told his wife. Let's wait and see if the next play's successful.

But Gilda told Keats to make a bid at the auction in her husband's behalf. It was a low bid, very low at $4,000, for one of the world's rarest and most treasured books. All day they waited for the dealer to telephone, but no call came, and they gave up all hope. Then at 5:30 P.M. the doorbell rang. Keats, at the door, congratulated him and put the marvelous book into Anderson's hands. That evening the playwright read to Gilda from the Folio and smiled and said that he didn't feel quite so guilty now. It was one of his greatest moments.

On his bedside that night lay the Folio and the Bible (he who had renounced his father's Church and had sworn up and down many times to Hesper that he was an atheist was especially fond of the Sermon on the Mount and Ecclesiastes). Late into the night he worked, lying in bed. At one o'clock he wrote the last entry he was ever to make in his diary: It was an imperfect Folio, he wrote, but still wonderful.[62]

The next morning, February 26, he and Gilda were in the kitchen quietly going about their tasks, he setting up a tray for his wife and himself, and she preparing the children's breakfast. Suddenly he had a stroke and fell to the floor.[63] Gilda immediately put him into the Stamford Hospital. There he regained consciousness but could not talk, though he seemed to know what people were saying around him. His right side was paralyzed, but he mustered enough strength to raise himself in bed and give Gilda a kiss.

The paralysis and other symptoms continued for two more days. On the final day, February 28, his breathing grew heavy, and the nurse told Gilda to leave the room. The clock read 7:45 P.M. While Gilda waited outside, he expired.[64] The attending physician certified the death as caused by "cerebral embolism" owing to "essential hypertension with auricular fibrillation."[65]

He was dead at seventy, gone into that "masterless night" of which he had once written in *Winterset*.

A crowd of 350 friends and relatives, associates, fellow playwrights, actors, and actresses attended the funeral service in St. Paul's Chapel at Columbia University, where his son Quentin taught in the Department of English. The Reverend Dr. John McGill Krumm, chaplain of the university, conducted the service and read from the Book of Common Prayer and quoted those lines from Ecclesiasticus in the Apocrypha which began, "Let us now praise famous men." Anderson, the complete agnostic, would have smiled at this Christian service. A succession of eulogies came from Mark Van Doren (professor of English at Columbia); Marc Connelly (actor and playwright), who mentioned Anderson's "ageless youth"[66]—something Gilda noticed in the few years they shared together; and Robert Woodruff Anderson, whose words were so affecting and appropriate that they bear repeating here at length:

> I have been spending a lot of time with Max the last two days . . . I suppose most of us have . . . thinking about what he had meant to me and the Theater . . . reading parts of his plays and essays . . . just remembering and coming again to the realization that he was that kind of man by which other men are measured.
>
> Max first touched my life importantly long before I knew him as a man [in the Playwrights Producing Company] . . . back in the mid-thirties, when he was one of the leaders of that stunning generation of playwrights who were making our drama the most exciting in the world. . . .
>
> On my graduation from the University, I don't remember what the speaker said. Something Max had written was far more important.
>
> To the young people of this country, I wish to say: if you practice an art, be proud of it, and make it proud of you. If you now hesitate on the threshold of your maturity, wondering what rewards you should seek, wondering perhaps whether there are any rewards beyond the opportunity to feed and sleep and breed, turn to the art which has moved you most readily. It may break

your heart, it may drive you half mad, it may betray you into unrealizable ambitions or blind you to mercantile opportunities with its wandering fires. But it will fill your heart before it breaks it; it will make you a person in your own right; it will open the temple doors to you and enable you to walk with those who have come nearest among men to what men may sometimes be.

I next remember Max after the war, around 1949, when he climbed the five flights of stairs to a room over the Hudson Theatre to talk to the first group of New Dramatists . . . young unproduced playwrights who gathered together once a week to learn more about playwriting.

It was my first glimpse of Max, and I was not disappointed. As always he was shy, quiet, brief in his responses . . . and with that smile, that sad, wise, kind smile which seemed to say that he accepted life as he had found it, happy, tragic, rewarding and bitter.

Sometime during the evening, Howard Lindsay, who was conducting the session, started to name some of Max's plays . . . *What Price Glory, Mary of Scotland, Both Your Houses, Elizabeth the Queen, Valley Forge* . . . and we looked at Max, who looked somewhat surprised . . . *High Tor, The Wingless Victory, The Masque of Kings, Saturday's Children, Winterset* . . . and we looked at each other and shook our heads . . . *Knickerbocker Holiday, Star-Wagon, Key Largo, Anne of the Thousand Days, Joan of Lorraine* . . . and the list went on. we smiled, smiles of wonder and admiration . . . smiles that were close to tears. . . .

Last Spring at the Theatre Guild Party, I sat at a table with Max and Gilda. And towards the end of a festive, lighthearted evening during which there had been songs and moments from Theatre Guild plays . . . suddenly, there on the stage were Helen Hayes and Helen Mencken in the last scene from *Mary of Scotland.*

It was a great moment. It was as though we had all forgotten the excitement and splendor and sweep of words and poetry . . . and we were being reminded as only the theater can remind you, so that you can say nothing, but can only stand and applaud until your hands hurt . . . When the ovation eventually was over, I looked across at Max and by a senseless bobbing of the head tried to convey how I felt . . . And he said, with that lovely air of surprise . . . "It sounded all right, didn't it?" [ellipses are Robert Anderson's own][67]

The New York Times on March 8 carried William Fields' eulogy. Fields, the mysterious and temperamental public relations man for the Playwrights Company, had known Anderson ever since the origin of that circle. Fields wrote that no one could ever be luckier than to have been called a friend by Maxwell Anderson; that as a generous and stouthearted colleague, Anderson was quite unsurpassed in the groups where Fields had observed him during the last two decades; and that those best acquainted with him were often dismayed at the "spectacular scope of his philanthropies"—which went far beyond his means. Fields went on to describe the difficult early years that the dramatist knew as a homesteader in New City, building the fires and feeding the livestock before bicycling each morning the four miles to Haverstraw station, etc. What a hardy and yet humble man! Fields concludes. And, God! What a *good* man!

Confusion reigned when it was discovered that Anderson had left not one will but three, dated 1954, 1955, and 1957, respectively; and that none of these were witnessed, as should have been the case. All were holographic, the first two drawn up in successive hospitals when he was faced with an operation. Judge John P. Keating, of the probate court in Stamford, Connecticut, rejected the last two but accepted the first one because it was of a type recognized in the state of California, where it was executed. Into this probated will, drawn up moments after he and Gilda were married in Cedars of Lebanon Hospital, Anderson could not resist tossing a jest on that solemn occasion: "This is my last will and testament written in my own hand . . . which was always bad." Gilda obtained possession of the literary estate, which included practically all royalties from the publications. The Stamford house, not part of their property at the time of the will, finally went to her too, but the government quickly put a lien on it pending payment of the long-standing tax bill. Quentin received a desk and some other incidentals; Alan a piano; Terence the cabin, some adjoining land, and the Critics Circle Award trophies; and Hesper some furniture plus the "studio" house that was built just in front of the New House on South Mountain Road.[68]

Following her husband's request, Gilda had his body cremated, and for several years she stored the ashes in a mausoleum in Hartsdale, New York, until she could find a suitable burial place away from the crowded cities and where his tomb would have the distinction it deserved. Finally she found the right place. But first she scattered some of the ashes back of the house along the seawall—because he had so loved the water—and took the remainder to the little Anderson family cemetery near Geneva, Pennsylvania, only about eight miles across the hills from tiny Atlantic, where he had been born late in the last century. The dying year, as if in sympathy, flamed in color from the surrounding woods that Saturday afternoon of October 19, 1963. In the presence of his widow; his son Quentin; his daughter, Hesper; his brother Kenneth; and his sisters Ethel and Lela, besides other relatives and friends, his urn was interred in the new section of the little cemetery that his ancestor, the second Samuel, had donated as a family burial ground.[69] Nearby were the graves of his mother and father, his Uncle Frank, and many other members of the family, some of whom had been dead generations before he had made the Anderson name shine in the annals of dramatic literature. Save for his, all the markers held obscure names of plain folk. One quaint marker in the field read "Lonely Anderson"—a grandmother on his father's side of the family. Now there was a new monument in their midst, much larger and more expensive than the rest, a block of dark, polished stone bearing the inscription "Maxwell Anderson/1888-1959" plus an epitaph of selected lines from his poem "Epilogue" in *You Who Have Dreams:*

> Children of dust astray among the stars
> Children of earth adrift upon the night
> What is there in our darkness or our light
> To linger in prose or claim a singing breath
> Save the curt history of life isled in death.[70]

Quentin delivered in his brief dedicatory address one of the most profound and apt assessments yet uttered about the man he had known as his father. He illuminated the meaning of the epitaph by saying that his father believed that "only such virtues as man could himself incarnate seemed to remain [after death]. . . . that we had nothing else to live by but these traditional virtues, by what nobility we could find and recognize and help to create in each other. . . ." And yet that Maxwell Anderson had not, despite his high aims, reached the stature of the very great writer, for the reason that he did not achieve "the kind of power Emerson described as the highest human power—deeply to color our sense of the world." But he conceded that his father's talent nevertheless took him so far as to humble the rest of us because his life had "a kind of heroic amplitude. . . . The country was bigger then, and those who sought to attain a position of mastery had farther to go." In his intellectual approach Quentin strove to recapture what is most difficult to do in Anderson's case, the magic of his personality—a personality so markedly delightful among those close to him that people interviewed for this book referred to it repeatedly. Quentin came close when he spoke of "the gentle, smiling man [not easily known] who . . . was often like a visitor—no, like a host surprised into hospitality by our sudden appearance, yet still wearing the air that his business gave him." He also spoke of his father's deep desire to be near water and how he often sought it on the coasts of the Atlantic and the Pacific. "Yet if there is one place in all the world that had been the imaginative center of his life I have little doubt that it was the spring on his grandmother's farm"; and it was therefore appropriate, Quentin added, that his ashes rest "close to the place where his being took its rise," where he "saw in the dancing waters of that spring an emblem of the bright, cold destiny of man."[71]

So apt, so perfect were these polished phrases that it seemed Professor Quentin Anderson had indeed said the last word on the subject. On the other hand, Anderson's dear Aunt Emma Harper, now gone before him, had written many years earlier a kind of epilogue whose plain rustic beauty would have pleased her illustrious nephew. Constituting the final line in her sketch of the family history that she had mailed to him, it was rough-hewn and innocent of the arts of grammar and spelling, for quite unknown to this country woman were Quentin's learning and sophistication. It ran simply:

We have wandered far but there is tender memories and our lives are like mericles in every way.

Maxwell Anderson, the native son, had come home to rest.

Meanwhile, over in East Fallowfield Township, along the narrow, unnamed road that dips and rises east from the village of Atlantic, still stood undisturbed the autumn woods where the children of the Reverend Anderson used to frolic and spin their summer dreams. And in these woods still lay the hollow with its Indian mound, and just beyond it the quiet swimming hole, rather shallow now and too cold for bathing.

But the spring had long vanished from where it once gurgled forth into the sunlight of Grandmother Shepard's yard and ran under her springhouse to cool the pans of milk and crocks of butter. Not only the spring but the springhouse and the farm dwelling too, together with its barn and the willows bending out front and the apple orchard in the back; all these had vanished like youth's bright dream, and in their place on a now treeless field stood a new bungalow. The spring had been negligently covered over by loads of dirt when a former owner filled in the boggy slope and pasture to the right of the present-day house. When Wesley Phillis, today's owner of the place, had first heard of the buried spring, he was concerned about the loss of those rumored crystal waters and tried to recover them by digging. But dig though he did, the spring eluded him. Maybe it had grown discouraged and changed its underground course, yet might someday well up into another farmer's yard in the neighborhood and delight *his* children and puzzle some thoughtful urchin about its far-off source and why it chanced to bubble forth in that place and not in some other one. Springs are as unpredictable as the arrival of genius in the world.

NOTES

About the letters to and from Maxwell Anderson: Wherever the notation "Univ. of Texas collection" alone occurs as the immediate source, that means I used the copy filed in the Humanities Research Center at the University of Texas rather than the one in Avery's published collection designated as *Letters.* Wherever I indicate neither "Univ. of Texas collection" nor *Letters,* that means I used a private source, namely the person to whom the letter was addressed, or his or her next of kin (in Anderson's case, his widow, Gilda).

CHAPTER NOTES

INTRODUCTION

1. Boston: Twayne, 1976.
2. Letter to me from Robert Woodruff Anderson, Aug. 22, 1978. This dramatist, not related to Maxwell, was a late member of The Playwrights Producing Company. He is discussed later in this book. The wives of the members must not have been socially close either. Mab, who was Maxwell's second wife, reportedly detested Elmer Rice's last wife, and vice versa. Madeline H. Sherwood, the widow of Maxwell's close friend and associate Robert Emmet Sherwood, wrote to me on Sept. 12, 1978, that she had only a slight acquaintance with Mab, and she professed to have no information of value about her to use in this book.
3. *Five Million Words Later: An Autobiography* (New York: John Day, 1970), p. 120.
4. My interview with Quentin Anderson in his apartment in New York City, May 19, 1978 (hereinafter referred to as "Quentin Anderson").
5. *Life Among the Playwrights Being Mostly the Story of the Playwrights Producing Company* (New York: Quadrangle, 1974), pp. 25-26, 81-82, et passim.
6. My interview with Hesper Anderson in her apartment at Studio City, Calif., and in other places in Los Angeles County, on Jan. 4, 5, and 8, 1980 (hereinafter referred to as "Hesper Anderson").

7. Letter to me dated Aug. 29, 1970 (Bloomington, Ind.).

8. Letter to me from John Kenneth Anderson, Feb. 10, 1980 (Olean, N.Y.). One of my several telephone conversations with Mrs. Maxwell Anderson (Gilda), who lives in Stamford, Conn.

9. *"Mister Abbott"* (New York: Random House, 1963), p. 104.

10. New York: Dodd, Mead, 1930, facing p. 68.

11. As quoted in Laurence G. Avery, *Dramatist in America: Letters of Maxwell Anderson, 1912-1958* (Chapel Hill, N.C.: University of North Carolina Press, 1977), pp. 30-31 (hereinafter called "Letters"). The extract that Barrett H. Clark makes in his *Maxwell Anderson: The Man and His Plays* (New York: Samuel French, 1933), pp. 3-4, differs slightly from the original as reproduced in *Letters*.

12. *Tribulations and Laughter: A Memoir* (London: Hamish Hamilton, 1972), p. 221.

13. This is a 34-page typescript transcribed from a tape recording made in his home at Stamford, Conn., on May 10, 1956, by Louis M. Starr of the Oral History Research Office at Columbia University, and copyrighted in 1972 by The Trustees of Columbia University. Passages from the transcript are quoted in this biography by permission. The typescript was edited in *Letters,* pp. 301-18.

14. This was read to the assembled alumni at a reunion there and later published in the *University of North Dakota Alumni Review,* Dec. 5, 1958; reprinted as "Love Letter to a University" in *North Dakota Quarterly* XXXVIII (Winter 1970), 89-90. Also found in *Letters,* pp. 288-90.

CHAPTER 1

1. "Uncle Recalls Maxwell Anderson in Childhood Days Spent Here,' *Meadville* (Pa.) *Tribune-Republican,* Apr. 11, 1945, p. 3. Uncle Frank Anderson, at that time seventy-two and quite possibly failing in memory is quoted as saying that about three years earlier he had helped Maxwel during the latter's visit locate this house which he, Frank, had helped to build. Frank was Anderson's paternal uncle.

But when I visited "Henry's Corners" in May 1978, I could not find the house in spite of having questioned neighborhood old-timers or the subject, none of whom had any recollections about it to help me Mrs. Helena Phillis Goodemote, the mother of Wesley J. Phillis, whose house now occupies the site of the Shepard one, could have helped me had I known her then. She wrote to me from Atlantic on November 20, 1978, that the Anderson house must have been moved prior to 1912, for she had arrived on the road at that time and does not remember seeing it. According to her, what happened to Grandmother Shepard's house is easier to explain. The Shepard farm was sold (in 1912) to a close neighbor, R. O. Unger (father of Mrs. Goodemote), who then rented the house for several years and afterward moved it to the Henry farm, where Mrs. Goodemote now lives, for the storage of grain. It rotted and was torn down.

2. Family tradition consistently traces the Anderson line back to Scotland—and the name *is* Scottish—even though the genealogy from the Revolutionary War backward is at this time unsupported by any documentary evidence. In the incomplete and unpublished typed record "Someone Else," by Anderson's daughter, Hesper, one reads that her father was so conscious of his Scottish ancestry that he often wore the Anderson plaid tie. This handsome pattern consists of light blue and dark green rectangular checks crossed diagonally by narrow stripes of red, yellow, white, and black. Anderson's brother Lawrence wrote to me on June 23, 1979, in response to the problem of ancestry: ". . . all Dad told me was that our ancestors were Scots." This is perhaps the best brief statement of the whole case.

Not only is the pre-Revolutionary phase of the Anderson family unknown at this time, but the Revolutionary phase itself is subject to conflicting accounts, the most dramatic sample of which came to me from Lawrence in the preceding letter. He writes half seriously, "I was brought up on the story that there were three brothers in the service of the British, and that two of them deserted to the American side. Their name was Sutton [a name Anderson employs for a British officer in *Storm Operation*], and to escape hanging as deserters they changed their names. One to Peterson—one to Anderson. The Peterson branch were able to trace and authenticate their story quite well, but the Anderson side appears to have little or no proof of their origin." Opposed to this account is the one furnished to me by Dr. Donald M. Anderson (son of Anderson's brother Kenneth and nephew to Lawrence), who wrote to me on July 26, 1979, that he had heard a story from the same source as Lawrence did and became wary when he could find no records or other evidence to support it. Dr. Anderson, who has been most active in genealogical research on his family, cites approvingly the paper by Harry Hollingsworth, "James Peterson, Sr. Alias James Sutton of Crawford

County, Pennsylvania," *The American Genealogist* LI (1975), 58-61, as giving a clear and probably true version. In his July 10, 1979, letter Dr. Anderson summarizes the Hollingsworth findings: "It seems that a James Sutton, son of Thomas Coates Sutton, deserted from the British loyalist forces in New Jersey in 1778, and fled into Pennsylvania, where he changed his name to James Peterson. Later, he moved from Washington Co. to Crawford Co., where he and his several children lived under the name of Peterson. The paper does not mention what happened to the other Suttons, but it seems probable that John Sutton, who came to the same area of Crawford Co. from New Jersey . . . was a grandson of Thomas Coates Sutton. John Sutton's granddaughter Polly became the wife of James Christy Anderson, and hence one of Anderson's ancestors. The Petersons also became related to the Andersons by marriage when a Mary Peterson married Joseph Anderson. . . . Because the written records I have seen indicate that Samuel Anderson Sr. [Max's alleged paternal forebear in America] came from Mifflin (then part of Cumberland) Co. Pa. and was there from 1776-1795, serving in the Cumberland Co. Militia from 1777-1782 . . ., I don't think he could have had any part in the Sutton-Peterson story. Also, there was no Samuel among the sons of either Thomas C. Sutton or James (Sutton) Peterson, according to the paper by Hollingsworth." Dr. Anderson goes on to say that his paternal grandfather told his father, Kenneth, that their ancestors were Scots. As Scots, they would "almost certainly not have had the name Sutton, which is an English name." I have checked the Hollingsworth paper; the Anderson genealogy published by Thomas L. Yoset, "Maxwell Anderson, Playwright," *Crawford County Genealogy* I (July 1978), 79-84; and the "Three Generations of Maxwell Anderson's Family" outlined in Avery's *Letters,* pp. 319-21, and find Dr. Anderson's interpretation of the case reasonable even though it gives no details of the Scottish origin of the first Samuel Anderson and what he was doing just before he served on the American side during the Revolutionary War.

My information about Ireland derives from an unsigned and undated two-page handwritten letter penned by some unknown, almost unlettered descendant of James C. Anderson, the playwright's grandfather, and found by Mrs. Shirley Borger among some papers thought to have belonged to her grandmother, Mina (Anderson) Johnston (the copy originating with Kenneth Anderson and furnished to me courtesy of Lela Chambers). The letter may not be completely trustworthy, but since it apparently is the only early extant family record pertaining to the first two Samuel Andersons, it deserves mention here. The letter reads in part: "Samuel Anderson came from Ireland but as the name was Scotch there is no evidence as to his nationality. he was an orange man in favor of Wm. of Orange as near as I can come to the truth he was forced to leave Ireland in order to save his life. He was a blacksmith by trade. His wife was of Irish descent. He was found dead on the side of the road and a man by the name of Cook had been with him and it was thought he had killed him. his son Samuel was born in the eastern part of this state [Pennsylvania]. his wifes name was Mary Cristy her father was a Scotchman he was a soldier in the revolution he married a Dutch woman. Samuel Anderson & Mary Cristy was the father or parents of James Anderson.... on mother's [Mrs. James Anderson's] side the men were carpenters and stone masons on fathers blacksmiths and farmers [sic]."

Of further help to me in tracing Anderson family origins in Pennsylvania is the letter to me from Dr. Anderson, dated Dec. 8, 1978, which enclosed copies of eighteenth-century land records pertaining to the first Samuel's purchase of acreages in Mifflin County, the records being filed at Lewistown (Deed Book B, p. 88) and at Harrisburg (Land Warrant No. 65 and No. 66). Also, this Dr. Anderson supplied me with copies of pages from *The People of Mifflin County Pennsylvania* by John Martin Stroup and Raymond Martin Bell, published in 1973 by the Mifflin County Historical Society, which show several male Andersons, including one Samuel, on the Cumberland County tax rolls (1767-89) and the state militia rolls (1777-82). Before 1789, Mifflin County was part of Cumberland County.

In *Maxwell Anderson* (Boston: Twayne Publishers, 1976), I dared to write that the first Samuel served in the British armed forces and based this claim upon a tradition reported to me by Lela. In the light of the latest available documentary evidence, this claim cannot be supported—but neither can it be disproved. For all we know, he may have switched sides, as so many did in that day; he was definitely on the American side from 1777 to 1782.

3. Letter from J[ohn] Martin Stroup, Mifflin County Historical Society, to Dr. Donald M. Anderson, Feb. 14, 1972, a copy of which was kindly furnished to me by the recipient via Lela Chambers.
4. The will of the second Samuel Anderson, dated Jan. 22, 1866; codicil dated Nov. 30, 1866. (Both documents are in Will Book D, pp. 245-47, at Crawford County Courthouse, Meadville, Pa.) Copies of these documents furnished to me courtesy of Dr. Donald M. Anderson. Another man who has personally helped me with Anderson genealogy is Thomas

L. Yoset. Mr. Yoset, who edits *Crawford County Genealogy,* is a professional genealogist.

During World War II, the Keystone Ordnance Works bought the ancestral estate at Geneva. Today it is an industrial park on which lies the Pittsburgh Plate Glass Company.

5. The two published genealogies of the Anderson family are Yoset's (see note No. 2 for this chapter) and Avery's (see *Letters,* pp. 319-21).

6. Anderson's only ancestor to achieve any kind of promise of which public record remains seems to be Peter Monroe Smock, b. 1874, a grandson of the second Samuel Anderson, and who reached some distinction in the West as a preacher, lecturer, newspaper editor, and lawyer.—From a letter to me Dr. Donald Anderson, Jan. 12, 1979, which included copied material from the following: "Smock, P(eter) Monroe" in *Who Was Who in America* (Chicago: Marquis' Who's Who, 1969-1973) V, 676. Also, *The Abridged Compendium of American Genealogy First Families of America . . .,* eds. Frederick A. Virkus and Albert Nelson Marquis (Boston: Genealogical Pub. Co., 1925; repr. 1968) I, 833.

7. From the 22-page set of notes that Emma Stephenson Harper sent to Maxwell Anderson around 1927 at his request. This work contains ancedotes about Perrimela's antecedents, the Stewarts (mainly) and the Stephensons, who came from Scotland via Ireland. Emma was Anderson's maternal aunt and died in 1945. There is more about her later in this book. Copy furnished to me courtesy of Lela Chambers (this copy hereinafter cited as "Emma's letters and notes").

8. Letter from Lela Chambers to me, July 5, 1978. There was still another Aunt Emma in Maxwell Anderson's life, namely his father's sister, but he did not like her.

9. Letter from Thomas L. Yoset to me, July 16, 1978, citing "Crawford County marriage license #65, copied in volume 1, p. 65."

10. Most of my information about Anderson's childhood and youth is drawn from Lela Chambers; and, indeed, it would be difficult to exaggerate the importance of this source in any accurate coverage of the Anderson family: an 11-page set of typed notes she furnished me in her letter to me dated Apr. 26, 1972 [hereinafter called "Lela Chambers' biographical notes"]; a typed, 178-page, unpublished "Life" written about herself and her family, ranging from the time of the first Samuel up to 1975; numerous letters from her to me; and the taped interview which I had with her in Olean, N.Y., on May 11, 1978. Exceptions to these sources will be noted wherever they occur.

11. Anderson's Columbia memoir, p. 1.

12. On his "Personal Information" form he submitted on Dec. 8, 1932, to the Ministers and Missionaries Board of the Northern Baptist Convention in applying for a pension, he wrote a short, testy letter—all that he was willing to supply on a four-page questionnaire. The last third reads:

> I have nothing to ad [sic] to what you already possess. Furthar [sic] than to say that I have attended School [sic] at The Academy of Meadville, also Edenboro State Normal, Allegheny College, all of Pa. [, and] Des Moines College. Took some work at Drake University, also [the word here is unclear] Theological Seminary, and had two years Under [sic] the direction of Rev. S. Griffiths.

   When I wrote to Drake University and Allegheny College for records of the Reverend Anderson's studies, I was told that no such records could be found. Des Moines College no longer exists. The copy of the form with its letter was given to me by the Reverend Arthur Yeagy, who in turn obtained it from Nancy M. Roman at The American Baptist Historical Society, Rochester, N.Y., in her letter of May 5, 1978.
13. My interview with Lawrence Anderson, Ledyard, Conn., May 18, 1978 (hereinafter referred to as "Lawrence Anderson").
14. Maxwell Anderson's letter to Louis Azrael, Nov. 1, 1938 (Univ. of Texas). Also see next note.
15. Robert Rice, "Maxwell Anderson," *PM's Sunday Picture News* II (Nov. 29, 1942), p. 24.
16. Letter to me from Gilda Anderson, Stamford, Conn., Mar. 4, 1980. Anderson's daughter, Hesper, uses even stronger language in describing the grandfather, calling him a con man and a phony.—My interview with Hesper Anderson in Studio City, Calif., Jan. 4, 5, and 8, 1980 (hereinafter referred to as "Hesper Anderson").
17. Lela Chambers' letters to me, Jan. 11 and Mar. 6, 1979.
18. Quentin Anderson. See the Reverend Anderson's letter in note No. 12 for this chapter.
19. The records of the First Baptist Church of Jefferson, Ohio, 1811-1921, filed at The Western Reserve Historical Society, Cleveland, Ohio, indicate that the Reverend Anderson was, in Jefferson, an insistent bargainer for traveling expenses and salary: One reason, maybe the only one, that he finally left Jefferson was that he tried unsuccessfully to get a $200 per annum raise. No scandal is mentioned.
20. Lawrence Anderson. The parson's professional skill is confirmed by the testimony of some of his other children and by Mr. and Mrs. J. Forest Wood, who were married by him.—From my interview with the Woods in Atlantic, Pa., May 10, 1978.

The material on prices and wages in Washington, D.C., comes from S. E. Forman, "Conditions of Living Among the Poor," *Bulletin of the Bureau of Labor,* No. 64, Washington, D.C.: U.S. Government Printing Office, May 1906.

21. Anderson's Columbia memoir, p. 1.
22. Letter from Ethel Chambers to Maxwell Anderson, June 27, 1956 (Univ. of Texas collection). Also, letter to me from Jan Christopherson, church historian of the First Baptist Church of Jamestown, N.D., postmarked Apr. 19, 1978.
23. Lawrence Anderson.
24. Robert Rice, p. 24.
25. Quentin Anderson.
26. Robert Rice, p. 24.
27. My interview with Glen Avery Chambers, Olean, N.Y., May 12, 1978 (hereinafter referred to as "Avery Chambers").
28. Frank Ernest Hill's memoir, p. 165, filed in the Oral History Research Office at Columbia University (a 611-page typescript transcribed from a tape recording made by Donald F. Shaughnessay in the Oral History Research Office in 1960 and 1961 and copyrighted by The Trustees of Columbia University in 1972). Passages from the typescript are quoted in this biography by permission.
29. Letter from Lela Chambers to me, May 8, 1972.
30. Lela Chambers' biographical notes. For a full list of the Reverend Anderson's children, see Appendix I. *Current Biography* (1942) and Robert Rice (p. 23) are wrong in stating that there were four boys and girls in the family—there were eight altogether.

In 1910, the Reverend Anderson obtained the supervisory post of General Missionary over the Baptist churches in North Dakota and moved to Grand Forks. His Church work here, as always, entailed a good deal of traveling and living away from home. In a few years, he settled in Minot; later, minus the three oldest children, who had by then married, he built a covered wagon and took his family homesteading in Montana, a farming venture that did not prove successful. Then he went back to Iowa, where he took up preaching again. In 1924, now retired, he moved to a farm which Anderson had bought for him at Hinsdale, N.Y., in which locality settled various of his married children. After his first wife died he married Josephine Fitzpatrick, but there were no children by this second union. Two years later, in 1936, he died of cancer in Lakeland. Fla.

Lela and Ethel married farmers and taught school. Lela at one time was a justice of the peace; at another, she was a specialist in the artificial insemination of cattle. Harold became a surveyor for Polk County, Iowa; Ruth married a glass blower; Kenneth entered the publishing world, managed Anderson House company, and for a long time worked in the Brookings Institute in Washington, D.C.; Lawrence went into newspaper advertising, real estate, and teaching photography.

31. Lela Chambers' biographical notes.
32. Helen Deutsch, "A Playwright and Poet," *New York Herald Tribune,* Sept. 22, 1935, p. 1.
33. Hesper Anderson. Letter to me from Gilda Anderson, Mar. 4, 1980.
34. Ethel Chambers' undated, typewritten sketch is called "Out of Dark and Bright" (from a line in Anderson's poem "Dust Remembering," which is said by Lela to commemorate Grandmother Charlotte Shepard or Aunt Emma Shepard [later married to a Harper] or both) and is filed at the Univ. of Texas. This only known copy contains in its 18 pages "Chapter 1 Atlantic" and "Chapter Two Geneva." These parts of the incomplete autobiography constitute a highly detailed and senti-mentalized description of Ethel's visits, at age six, with her family to Grandmother Shepard's at Atlantic and to Grandfather James Ander-son's at Geneva, respectively. "Footnote by Max," Anderson's handwritten, undated letter to her in response to reading the sketch, is also at this university and runs to three pages. Both the sketch and the notes were probably penned around 1956. Some of my other information about life at the Shepard's derives from Lela's biographical notes, her drawings and map done for my use, her letter to me dated July 5, 1978, and a photograph of a painting that she owns of the place.
35. John Nairne Michaelson (pseudonym for Maxwell Anderson), *Morning Winter and Night* (New York: William Sloane Associates, 1952). Published simultaneously in Toronto by George J. McLeod. See dis-cussion of the novel in Chapter 8.
36. "Footnote by Max" (see note No. 34 for this chapter).
37. Ibid.
38. Lawrence Anderson.
39. Ibid. Also, letter from Lawrence Anderson to me, Sept. 15, 1978. In a letter to Anderson, June 8, 1936, and filed at the Univ. of Texas, Uncle Frank says that he is raising "some chickens" and doing some truck gardening; he wants Anderson to send money to buy a car so that he can "get feed from the mill." By 1938 the monthly payments were arriving. But about 1942, when the property was taken over for the construction of the Keystone Ordnance plant, his dream of living on

the farm while buying it for Anderson was ended when he was forced to sell it in the interests of national. defense. He had fought off the seizure for as long as he could, and when the new owners came with bulldozers, Uncle Frank left by the front door and went down the road to Geneva and never looked back. With his meager payment for the farm he bought a small house in Meadville, where he gardened a little. Then Anderson arranged with Anderson House (which he ran jointly with his brother Kenneth) to send him $40 a month out of the playwright's earnings, and this continued until about 1954, when the old uncle died.

40. My telephone conversation with Alan Anderson, Mar. 12, 1972.
41. Hesper Anderson.
42. Letter from Lela Chambers to me, Mar. 27, 1972. Also, her biographical notes.
43. Letter from Alan Anderson to me, Jan. 15, 1972.
44. My interview with Terence Anderson in New City, N.Y., May 14, 1978 (hereinafter referred to as "Terence Anderson"). Also, Hesper Anderson.
45. "Uncle Recalls Maxwell Anderson in Childhood Days Spent Here."
46. Letter from Ethel Chambers to Max, June 27, 1956 (Univ. of Texas).
47. Letter from Gilda Anderson to me, dated Mar. 4, 1980. Earlier, during our interview, Hesper Anderson had told me about this dream.
48. *Morning Winter and Night*, pp. 19, 35.
49. "Uncle Recalls Maxwell Anderson in Childhood Days Spent Here."
50. Anderson sent her financial support in her old age. This is another example of his remarkable generosity.—Lela Chambers letter to me, Aug. 30, 1978.
51. In my coverage of the Reverend Anderson's pastorate in Jefferson, I am indebted to Mrs. Robert Kenyon, a member of the church, who sent me two letters of information and a brochure on the history of the building, Mar. 20 and Apr. 14, 1978.
52. Washington, D.C.: Anderson House, 1937.
53. Hesper Anderson's "Someone Else," pp. 59-60. Hesper's recollection also comes to me in the questionnaire she filled out and mailed to me on June 14, 1978; my telephone interview with her on May 26, 1978; and the promotion pamphlet "Morning Winter and Night/Maxwell Anderson/A Synopsis" printed by Xanadu Productions, a film company for which she wrote a scenario of the novel. The record I prepared from all this was read and corrected for me by Mrs. Hallie Loomis Craytor (Bloomington, Ind.).

Like Lela Chambers' "Life" and biographical notes (prepared for my use), and like Ethel Chambers' "Out of Dark and Bright"—all three unpublished—Hesper Anderson's sketch called "Someone Else" deals with Maxwell Anderson indirectly. But unlike them it is agonizingly subjective in many places, unsparingly frank about acquaintances and family members, and makes no pretension of being the stuff of biography. It exists as Part I of a projected two-part work and runs to seventy-nine typed pages; it focuses on her life in the Anderson household up until her break with her boyfriend (Marion Hargrove) when she was nineteen. Used judiciously, the sketch proved helpful in preparing this book.

54. Letters to me from Mrs. Hallie Loomis Craytor, of Bloomington, Ind., July 14 and 31; and Sept. 22, 1978.
55. He was thirteen, she not more than eleven at the time.
56. Maxwell Anderson's letter to Mrs. Hallie Loomis Craytor, Dec. 26, 1950. Copies sent to me, separately, by Mrs. Craytor and by Dr. Laurence Avery.
57. Letter to me from Mrs. Hallie Loomis Craytor, July 14, 1978.
58. Ibid.
59. Letter to me from Louis L'Amour, Los Angeles, Calif., Mar. 28, 1978. Born LaMoore in Jamestown, N.D., he changed his surname and became popular with dozens of cowboy novels that reportedly use accurate historical research. Louis' sister Edna (see later), who knew the Andersons far better than he did, wrote to me on Mar. 24, 1978, from Castro Valley, Calif., that all of the Andersons went through unbelievably difficult times during their moves about the Middle West—more difficult than I could imagine! As Mrs. Waldo, she became a nationally known magazine writer, lecturer, and authority on pioneer days in the Midwest with such books as *Dakota, an Informal Study of Territorial Days* (1932 and 1936) and *From Travois to Iron Trail* (1944). She also worked as a teacher, high school principal, and librarian.
60. As quoted in Helen Deutsch.
61. Letter to me from Mrs. Gertrude Hintz, office manager, New Hampton (Iowa) Community High School, Mar. 20, 1978.
62. Hesper Anderson. Letters to me from Lela Chambers, Jan. 30 and Feb. 26, 1980. Letter to me from Gilda Anderson, Mar. 4, 1980. Maxwell Anderson, "Preface," *Four Verse Plays* (New York: Harcourt, Brace & World, 1959), p. vii.
63. Anderson's Columbia memoir, pp. 4-5.

64. Letter to me from Melvin I. Orms, Zephyrhills, Fla., Apr. 19, 1978.
65. P. 24.
66. Anderson's Columbia memoir, p. 4.
67. Anderson's letter of Feb. 17, 1943, quoted in Allan G. Halline's "Maxwell Anderson's Dramatic Theory," *American Literature* XVI (May 1944), 70.
68. Laurence G. Avery, "The Maxwell Anderson Papers," *The Library Chronicle of the University of Texas* VIII (Spring 1965), 23.
69. Ruth W. Sedgwick, "Maxwell Anderson, Playwright and Poet," *The Stage Magazine* XIV (Oct. 1936), 55. Also, Maxwell Anderson, "Preface," *Four Verse Plays* (New York: Harcourt, Brace & World, 1959), p. vi.
70. Anderson's letter to actress Helen Hayes, Mar. 3, 1941 (Univ. of Texas collection). His love for Keats and Shakespeare is verified in my correspondence with Alan Anderson—for example, Alan's letter dated Nov. 23, 1970. Hesper in her interview with me said that her father often quoted Keats to her. In 1941, Anderson broadcast his 30-minute radio play "John Keats in America" over NBC radio.
71. Maxwell Anderson, "To the Editor, *Dial*," in *Letters*, pp. 10-12.
72. Anderson, "Preface," *Four Verse Plays*, p. vii.
73. Lela believes that his poem "End-All" is about Leona Kemman.
74. The following sketch of Jamestown derives mainly from letters to me from these people. subject to Lela's corrections. Louis L'Amour: letters dated Mar. 14 and 28, 1978; May 8, 1979. Edna LaMoore Waldo: letters dated Mar. 23 and 24, 1978; Apr. 5 and 13, 1978.
75. P. 5.
76. Letter to me from Frank N. Fischer, superintendent of Jamestown Public Schools, Apr. 14, 1978, accompanied by transcript of grades, list of graduates, and program for the May 28, 1908, commencement ceremonies in the Opera House.
77. Hesper Anderson.
78. Lawrence Anderson.
79. Robert Rice, p. 24.

CHAPTER 2

1. Lela Chambers' biographical notes. Maxwell Anderson, "Love Letter to a University," p. 89.

2. Louis G. Geiger and J. R. Ashton, "UND in the Era of Maxwell Anderson," *The North Dakota Quarterly* XXV (Spring 1957), 59. Geiger wrote the history of the University of North Dakota, of which chapters V and VII were adapted by Ashton for publication as this article.

3. Letter from Ethel Chambers to Maxwell Anderson, June 27, 1956 (Univ. of Texas).

4. After the first semester was over he moved to Budge Hall.—Lela Chambers' interview with me in Olean, N.Y., May 11, 1978.

5. "Love Letter to a University," p. 89.

6. "UND in the Era of Maxwell Anderson," p. 58.

7. Maxwell Anderson letter to Melvin Ruder, Jan. 31, 1939 (Univ. of Texas collection). Concerning the waiting on tables in the Commons, Thomas McGrath and Marian Points write in "Maxwell Anderson: Portrait in Pencil," *The North Dakota Quarterly* XXXIII (Winter 1965), 12, that Max quit after one day "because he could not remember the orders the diners gave him." But Lela said in her interview with me on May 11, 1978, that this is an error, that Anderson worked there quite a while, "because I used to eat at the Commons and he was there." The article by McGrath and Points, although appreciative even to the extent of being rhapsodic, contains several errors of fact. The authors clearly did no research among Anderson's relatives, many of whom were still alive at that time. In my correspondence with McGrath I learned that he had drawn several bits of information indirectly from Professor Gottfried Hult, one of Anderson's teachers there, who had died in 1950.

8. Lela Chambers' "Life."

9. "In the Days of Peg Top Trousers," *The North Dakota Quarterly* XXV (Spring 1957), 53. To this article I owe practically all my information about clothing fashions of the day.

10. Lela Chambers. Confirmed during my interview with Anderson's neighbor and friend, the worldly Lotte Lenya, widow of Kurt Weill, on May 15, 1978.

11. Lela Chambers.

12. My information on Margaret as a personality comes from a variety of sources, principally: Alan Anderson—miscellaneous letters and my personal interview with him on May 14, 1978, in New City; Lloyd R. Hamilton (son of Margaret's sister Elizabeth)—letter to me, May 12, 1978; Lela Chambers; Margaret H. Zimmer (daughter of Margaret's brother James E. Haskett)—letters to me, Apr. 21 and May 26, 1978.

13. Unsigned, "Miss Haskett Won First Prize," *The Student* (Univ. of North Dakota student newspaper, which she at one time helped to

edit), May 10, 1911, p. 1. The topic was "The Value of a Total Abstenance [sic] Life." Whatever her stand might have been, she smoked and drank a little during her married years.

14. Letter from Olive Benson, of Bottineau, N.D., to her cousins Esther Reagan and Margaret Zimmer, dated Mar. 31, 1978, and forwarded to me for my information. All of these women are related to Margaret.

The 1910 issue of the University annual *The Dacotah* shows Margaret as a member of Phi Kappa Chi. The 1912 issue does not list this membership among her credits.

15. Letter to me from Esther Reagan (daughter of Margaret's brother James E. Haskett), May 9, 1978.

16. Letter to me from Margaret H. Zimmer, Apr. 21, 1978.

17. James J. Haskett was born in Tipperary, Ireland, in 1851, and worked for a while in the woolen mills in Ontario. He died of diabetes in Bottineau, N.D., in 1920, leaving an estate valued at $30,000. Drought and rust during the years of World War I had played havoc with his wheat crops. His wife, born Elizabeth Hart in 1851, had parents who had immigrated to Canada from County Sligo, Ireland. She died at Wagner, S.D., in 1932.

Margaret's siblings were: Mary Alice (b. 1875); John Francis (b. 1876)—editor and owner of the *Bottineau Courant;* James Edmund (b. 1880)—salesman and banker; David Charles (b. 1882); Anne (b. 1883); Harry E. (b. 1886)—mechanic; Elizabeth Sarah (b. 1891); and Sylvester Ambrose (date of birth unknown).

My information on the Haskett family is taken from various and widely scattered sources: (1) letters from Lloyd R. Hamilton and Margaret H. Zimmer (see note No. 12 for this chapter); (2) letter to me from Esther Reagan (daughter of Margaret's brother James E.), May 9, 1978; (3) letter to me from Cora W. Russell, May. 24, 1978 (resident of Bottineau, N.D.); (4) letter to me from Helen Mohlberg, Mar. 12, 1978 (Bottineau high school teacher), which came with the pamphlet "Bottineau County Diamond Jubilee 1884-1959," published at Bottineau and containing valuable period photographs and bits of information on early settlers; (5) interviews with Lela Chambers and Alan H. Anderson; (6) the letter to me from Ross McNea, county judge of Bottineau County, N.D., Mar. 20, 1978, which contained copies of the death record of James J. Haskett, the Petition for Probate of Will for James Haskett, Report of Sale of Land under Power of Will for the estate of James Haskett, Final Decree in the matter of the foregoing estate, and Petition for Probate of Will for Elizabeth Haskett (deceased widow of James).

Contrary to the information supplied me at the time I wrote *Maxwell Anderson,* Margaret's middle initial was *E.* (for Ethel) and not *C.,* as some sources give it.

18. Anonymous, untitled section in *Whittier College Bulletin* XII (Aug. 1917), 8. Also, the obituary on Max titled "Maxwell Anderson, Playwright, Is Dead," *The New York Times,* Mar. 1, 1959, I, 84 (hereinafter designated as "Obituary").

19. Official transcript of Maxwell Anderson's grades at the University of North Dakota, 1908-11, sent to me courtesy of Lela Chambers.

20. Barbara Leifur, "Leading American Dramatist UND Graduate," *Dakota Student* (Univ. of North Dakota student newspaper), Mar. 7, 1956, p. 6.

21. As quoted in "Maxwell Anderson: Portrait in Pencil," p. 10. Anderson's transcript of grades shows an incomplete in Greek for the fall semester of 1909-10.

22. Quentin Anderson.

23. Letter to me from Frederick J. Brockhoff, May 6, 1978. Brockhoff is mentioned in Max's school play *The Masque of Pedagogues.*

24. "In the Days of Peg Top Trousers," p. 54. Mrs. George F. Shafer, who was a freshman at the University of North Dakota at the time that Anderson was a senior, wrote to me about Apr. 12, 1978, that Anderson did not generally mix with the other students.

25. Letter to me from Shirley D. Naismith, assoc. registrar, Univ. of North Dakota, July 20, 1978.

26. Hill's memoir, p. 165.

27. Anderson edited the 1912 issue (actually published in 1911).

28. Quoted favorably by McGrath and Points in their essay.

29. McGrath and Points, p. 12.

30. For much of my information on Dr. Gottfried E. Hult (1869-1950) and his wife, I am indebted to Dr. Donald Murray's article "Gottfried Emanuel Hult" in *The North Dakota Quarterly* XXIV (Fall 1956), 123-33. Anderson was a friend of the Hults for many years, and after he became an established playwright he tried to get his teacher's plays produced but without succeeding. Two books of poetry by Hult are *Reveries* (1909) and *Outbound* (1920). In 1933, he published a translation of Henrik Ibsen's *Peer Gynt.* His unpublished play *The White Swan,* about Dion, Tyrant of Syracuse, lies in manuscript form at the University of North Dakota.

31. From the caption under his picture in the 1912 *Dacotah*. Geiger and Ashton provide in their article a record of the courses and professors; Anderson's official transcript does not name the professors.

32. Letter to me from C. L. Robertson, Mar. 3, 1972. Hult's eccentricities were confirmed for me by Lela during our interview.

33. Maxwell Anderson's letter to John M. Gillette, Sept. 15, 1912 (*Letters*, p. 3). Gillette wrote *Constructive Rural Sociology* (1913), a pioneer work on that subject.

34. Letter to me from C. L. Robertson, Mar. 14, 1972.

35. Lela Chambers.

36. John P. Hagan, "Frederick H. Koch and North Dakota: Theatre in the Wilderness," *North Dakota Quarterly* XXXVIII (Winter 1970), 84. Frederick Henry Koch (1877-1944), born in Peoria, Ill., early wanted to be an actor, but his father opposed it. He attended Ohio Wesleyan University, Emerson School of Oratory, and Harvard, where he studied under G. P. Baker and G. L. Kittredge. He was at the University of North Dakota from 1905 until 1918, except for his one-year break to reenter Harvard for graduate work. While at North Dakota, he organized and was the prime force in the Sock and Buskin Society which, a year before he left, became the Dakota Playmakers. From 1918 until his death he continued his teaching at the University of North Carolina, where he became even more influential as a teacher of regional drama. The Forest Theatre there was dedicated to him in 1953. He edited a series of carefully designed books called *Carolina Folk-Plays*, which contained the work of his students. His Dakota years he covered in "The Dakota Playmakers: An Historical Sketch," *The Quarterly Journal of the University of North Dakota* IX (Oct. 1918), 14-21, and in "Folk-Play Making in Dakota and in Carolina," *The Playground* XVIII (Jan. 1925), 599-601. A sympathetic treatment of him is Samuel Selden and Mary Tom Sphangos' *Frederick Henry Koch: Pioneer Playmaker* (Chapel Hill: Univ. of North Carolina Library, 1954). Also, see John P. Hagan's "Frederick Henry Koch and the American Folk Theatre," Ph.D. dissertation, Indiana University, 1969.

37. Selden and Sphangos, p. 40. Koch was noted for giving readings of Dickens' *Christmas Carol*, a work that Anderson dramatized for TV in 1954.

38. Dramatization by Joseph J. Dilley and Lewis Clifton of *Martin Chuzzlewit*.

39. Hagan's article, from which I have taken much of this material, draws

upon such writings as Koch's "Towards a New Folk Theatre," *The Quarterly Journal of the University of North Dakota* XX (Spring 1930), and the unpublished "Record of the 1906 Senior Class Play Tour," n. d., in the Playmakers Scrapbook, "Dakota Playmakers" I (Univ. of North Dakota).

40. Paul Green's essay "Professor Koch as Teacher" in Selden and Sphangos, p. 91. Much the same essay appeared as "Frederick H. Koch" in Green's *Drama and the Weather* (New York: Samuel French, 1958).

   Green was a student of his later at the University of North Carolina.

   On Mar. 22, 1978, I interviewed Green and his wife, Elizabeth, at their home in Chapel Hill, N.C., at which time both of them confirmed and expanded upon details found in published accounts about Koch. Elizabeth Lay (later married to Paul) was in Koch's first playwriting class at the University of North Carolina and wrote for him the first play, *When Witches Ride,* that was produced by the Carolina Playmakers. Both Elizabeth and Paul had a long and affectionate relationship with their former teacher Koch. (Interview with Paul hereinafter referred to as "Paul Green.")

41. Hagan, p. 75, where he quotes from an unidentified speech or writing by Koch defending his scheme for promoting regional drama.

42. From Archibald Henderson's essay "Freddy Folkplay" included in the book by Selden and Sphangos, p. 86.

43. Frederick H. Koch, "Making a Regional Drama," *Bulletin of the American Library Association* XXVI (Aug. 1932), 468.

   Upon receiving the handbills of the first native plays of the Midwest from Koch, Anderson expressed to him great enthusiasm in his California letter, dated 1917.—Frederick H. Koch, "Making a Regional Drama," p. 468.

44. Selden and Sphangos, p. 6, quoting Mrs. Koch.

45. Interview with Mrs. Paul Green in Chapel Hill, N.C., May 22, 1978. *Electric* is Mrs. Green's word in describing the teacher.

46. Starting about 1914.

47. Hagan, pp. 80-83.

48. Geiger and Ashton, p. 57. Also, Helen Deutsch, "A Playwright and Poet," *New York Herald Tribune,* Sept. 22, 1935, p. 1.

   Robert H. Montgomery (b. 1889) graduated from the University of North Dakota in 1909 and from the Harvard Law School in 1912. After that he practiced law in Boston. This man years later gave Anderson the idea for the judge in *Winterset* (see the discussion of this play). Montgomery wrote *Sacco-Vanzetti: The Murder and the Myth* (1960).

49. "The Masque of Pedagogues," *North Dakota Quarterly* XXV (Spring 1957), 33-48. Complete reprint of the play with illustrations.
50. Ibid., p. 37.
51. He was promoted from instructor to assistant professor in 1907.
52. *The Masque of Pedagogues,* pp. 43, 45.
53. Selden and Sphangos, passim.
54. The title's mocking use of the word *masque* will be revived for two of his mature plays, *The Masque of Kings* and *The Masque of Queens.*
55. Walter Prichard Eaton, "He Put Poetry Back on the Stage," *New York Herald Tribune,* Jan. 28, 1934, p. 12.
56. Paul Green's review of Avery's *Dramatist in America: Letters of Maxwell Anderson, 1912-1958* in *The Chapel Hill Newspaper,* Sun., May 7, 1978, p. 4C. Also, my interview with Paul Green.
57. Copy of "Marriage License and Certificate" for Miss Margaret Haskett and Maxwell Anderson. Marriage license issued on July 31, 1911, at Bottineau, N.D., by John H. Kirk, judge of the county court, and filed on Aug. 7, 1911, in Book 6 of Marriage Records, p. 18.
58. Anderson was said to be on friendly terms with the woman later on, at which time she was a needy widow, and sent her gifts of money around 1929-30. His first check, for $250, he justified by saying that he thought he should share his sudden fortune because he had just received $3,000 a week for six weeks of work on the screenplay *All Quiet on the Western Front.* He sent more checks in the $15 to $20 range during the winter and spring. The Great Depression had just struck.—Letter to me from Lloyd R. Hamilton, May 12, 1978.
59. Letter to me from Esther Reagan, May 9, 1978. Reagan is a daughter of Margaret's brother James E. Haskett.
60. Letter to me from Kenneth Anderson, Mar. 2, 1980. Lela Chambers. Lawrence Anderson.
61. Lela Chambers.
62. Anderson's Columbia memoir, p. 8; Leifur, p. 6; Lela Chambers.
63. Lela Chambers' "Life."
64. McGrath and Points, p. 12.
65. Lela Chambers.
66. Quentin Maxwell Anderson, July 21, 1912. As a gesture of separating his own identity from that of his father, he dropped the "Maxwell" from his name after he grew up.
67. Maxwell Anderson, *You Who Have Dreams* (N.Y.: Simon and Schuster,

1925), pp. 18-22. A few of his poems appeared in *A Stanford Book of Verse 1912-1916*, The English Club of Stanford University, 1916. A posthumous collection of poems about Gilda (the third Mrs. Maxwell Anderson) is *Notes on a Dream*, edited and with introduction by Laurence G. Avery (Austin: Univ. of Texas, 1971). Journals in which his poems saw print over the years include *The Chapbook*, *The Conning Tower*, *The Freeman*, *Ladies' Home Journal*, *The Measure*, *The Nation*, *New Republic*, *New Yorker*, *Scholastic*, *Smart Set*, and *Youth*. Issues of the *Dacotah* contain some of his juvenilia.

68. R. P. Wilkins, Editor's Notes of *North Dakota Quarterly* XXXVIII (Winter 1970), 4; Philip Stevenson, "Concerning M. Anderson: A Word about the Career and Thoughts of the War Dramatist," *The New York Times*, Jan. 9, 1944, II, 1; McGrath and Points, p. 12. But Lela Chambers in her biographical notes contends: "Max said nothing about this being the reason for his leaving Minnewaukan when he and Margaret and Quentin visited us in the summer of 1913."

69. Anderson's Columbia memoir, p. 8.

70. Lela Chambers' biographical notes.

71. David Star Jordan (1851-1931) was born in Gainesville, N.Y., and educated at Cornell University, Indiana Medical College, and Butler University. His books include (short list): *Fishes of North and Middle America* (with B. W. Evermann, 4 vols., 1896); *The Human Harvest* (1907); *Evolution and Animal Life* (with V. L. Kellogg, 1907); *War's Aftermath* (1914); *Democracy and World Relations* (1918); *The Days of a Man* (autobiography, two vols., 1922); *The Trend of the American University* (1929). Anderson's friend Bruce Bliven occasionally had talks with Jordan at his home. See Bliven's memoir for the Oral History Research Office, Columbia University, 1965, as transcribed from an interview conducted by W. H. Link in 1951.

72. Hill's memoir, p. 6; Lela Chambers' "Life"; letter to me from Marianne Bahmann, library specialist, The Stanford University Libraries, Mar. 22, 1978.

73. Anderson's Columbia memoir, p. 8.

74. Letter to me from Susan R. Rosenberg, assistant archivist, The Stanford Univ. Libraries, Nov. 9, 1971.

75. Hill's memoir, p. 170. Frank Ernest Hill (1888-1969) was born in San José, California, when that region was pioneer country. Of all of Anderson's close friends, he was one of the most intimate and appreciative, even though their association began to wane after 1936. Hill far surpasses all other memorialists in the amount of space he

devotes to Anderson and shows considerable insight into his mind and character, as revealed in the memoir mentioned above. Hill taught at Illinois, Stanford (where Anderson first met him), and at Columbia; joined Anderson on the *Globe* in 1919 (see later); lived across the road from him in New City for many years; read drafts of his friend's plays and poems and offered suggestions for improvement (which usually were not adopted); worked as editor at Longmans, Green publishing company, which brought out Anderson's *Saturday's Children;* wrote radio scripts for "School of the Air" programs; and became a leader in the American Association for Adult Education. His memoir reveals him as a widely read and tolerant man with a good sense of humor and a willingness to try his hand at many types of writing (as a poet he was mediocre). His numerous books include *The Winged Horse* (1927) with Joseph Auslander; *Stone Dust* (1928); *The Winged Horse Anthology* (1929); *What is American?* (1933); *The Westward Star* (1934); *Listen and Learn* (1937); *Man-made Culture* (1938); *Educating for Health* (1939); *Training for the Job* (1940); *The Canterbury Tales* (1940), a modern English translation; *The Groups Tune In* (1940); *Radio's Listening Groups* (1941); *India* (1942); *Youth in the CCC* (1942) with Kenneth Holland; *To Meet Will Shakespeare* (1949); *King's Company* (1950); *The History of the Ford Motor Company* (1954, 1957, 1963) with Allan Nevins; *The New World of Wood* (1965); and *The Automobile* (1967).

76. Maxwell Anderson, "Incommunicable Literature," *The Dial* LXV (Nov. 2, 1918), 370.
77. *Letters,* p. 316n.
78. Hill's memoir, p. 164.
79. Maxwell Anderson, "The Scholar Too Late," *The Dial* LXVII (Sept. 20, 1919), 239-41. The date of composition is unknown, but at the time the essay was published Anderson was in New York on the *Globe.*
80. Hill's memoir, pp. 141, 152, 154, 171; *Letters,* footnotes on pp. 5, 55, 57, 316; Bruce Ormsby Bliven's memoir, pp. 13, 20, 30, 35; Robert Luthur Duffus, *The Tower of Jewels* (New York: W. W. Norton, 1960), pp. 205-9.
81. Letter to me from Susan R. Rosenberg, assistant archivist, The Stanford Univ. Libraries, Nov. 9, 1971.
82. This letter is to Mrs. Marguerite Wilkinson, New York City, Apr. 29, 1917. It reveals nothing about Anderson's precise whereabouts or activities. For some unknown reason, it was mailed from Stanford University, although he and his wife were no longer going to school

there. Perhaps they still lived in nearby Palo Alto and/or attended Dr. Gray's Round Table meetings.—*Letters*, p. 4.

83. Full title: *A Stanford Book of Verse 1912-1916*. Printed for the English Club of Stanford University, 1916. Some of Hill's poems are in this collection too.

84. Unsigned prose sketches of new teachers in *Whittier College Bulletin* XII (Aug. 1917), 8.

85. Quentin Anderson.

86. My interview with Mrs. Maxwell Anderson (Gilda) in her home at Stamford, Conn., May 17, 1978 (hereinafter referred to as "Gilda Anderson").

87. Kathryn C. Hulme, *Undiscovered Country: A Spiritual Adventure* (Boston: Little, Brown, 1966), p. 6.

88. Letter to me from Kathryn C. Hulme, Nov. 10, 1978.

89. *The Tower of Jewels*, pp. 205-9.

90. Letter to me from Carl E. S. Strem, Apr. 5, 1978. Also, *Quaker Campus* (Whittier College newspaper), Sept. 20, 1917, pp. 1, 4.

91. Letter to me from Dr. Arthur F. Camp, Apr. 26, 1978. Camp was a senior at Whittier in 1917.

92. My information about the social and political climate at Whittier College comes from a series of letters to me from Dr. Paul S. Smith, Sept. 30, 1971 (who, as later president of Whittier, had arrived there soon after the Anderson episode); from Dr. Charles W. Cooper, Oct. 4, 1971, and Feb. 1, 1972; and from Dr. Arthur F. Camp, Mar. 20 and Apr. 26, 1978. I have also consulted Cooper's *Whittier Independent College in California* (Los Angeles: The Ward Ritchie Press, 1967). The latter is the official history.

93. *Whittier College Bulletin* XII (Aug. 1917), 7, and *Quaker Campus*, Sept. 20, 1917, p. 1. These two notices do not mention that Anderson will be department head. The first news of that role comes from the published notice of his "resignation" in the *Quaker Campus*, Apr. 18, 1918, p. 1.

94. For materials relating to Max's teaching and his support of Camp, I am indebted to Cooper's *Whittier*, pp. 127-32, and to his research notes for that book, which he kindly supplied to me.

95. Cooper's taped interviews with Thomas' brother Morris Kimber, who became a professor at Whittier, and with R. C. Hunnicutt, both of these lifelong friends of his who now are dead. The tapes have been erased.—Cooper's letter to me, Feb. 1, 1972.

96. Letter to me from Carl E. S. Strem, Apr. 5, 1978.

97. Helen Deutsch, "A Playwright and Poet," *New York Herald Tribune,* Sept. 22, 1935, pp. 1, 5.

98. *Whittier Independent College in California,* pp. 130-32. In my account of the incident I have availed myself of extensive information supplied to me by Dr. Arthur F. Camp in his two letters to me, Mar. 20 and Apr. 26, 1978. His account, while not contradicting the one found in the official history, bears mainly on the personalities of the teachers and on the social and "political" life of the academic community; and much of it is given over to his private experiences as a non-political student. His arrest is not covered.

    Following overseas duty, Camp received an honorable discharge and earned a Ph.D., from the University of Washington (1923), became the head of the University of Florida's horticulture department, and published learned works; after his retirement there, the citrus industry of Florida insisted that he be made director emeritus, and he became a consultant for them.

99. *Quaker Campus,* Nov. 1, 1917, in column called "Open Forum."

100. "Head of English Department Resigns," *Quaker Campus,* Apr. 18, 1918, p. 1.

101. *New Republic* XII (Sept. 8, 1917), 169.

102. *Whittier Independent College in California,* p. 132. I am indebted to Dr. Cooper for first pointing out to me via his notes these references to Quakers.

103. Maxwell Anderson, "Incommunicable Literature."

104. Maxwell Anderson letter to Arthur Hobson Quinn, May 4 [1927], in *Letters,* p. 29.

CHAPTER 3

1. Maxwell Anderson, "Compost," in *You Who Have Dreams* (New York: Simon & Schuster, 1925), p. 62.

2. Anderson's Columbia memoir, p. 9.

3. Maxwell Anderson's letter to Fremont Older, Oct. 24, 1918 (*Letters,* p. 6). Older's book appeared as *My Own Story* (1925).

4. Barrett H. Clark, *Maxwell Anderson: The Man and His Plays* (New York: Samuel French, 1933), p. 6; Helen Deutsch, "A Playwright and Poet," *New York Herald Tribune,* Sept. 22, 1935, p. 5.

5. Anderson's Columbia memoir, p. 10.

6. I cannot accept Anderson's version in the Columbia memoir, p. 10, because the whole memoir was obviously hurried and never corrected by the playwright himself. There he said that the epidemic struck him while he was still on the *Bulletin* and that it cost him his job.

   Four other accounts, at least three of them based on personal interviews with him, and one, apparently, on a questionnaire that he answered, show that he lost the *Bulletin* post because of his controversial editorial. Of these four, only the one by Deutsch mentions the epidemic, and Deutsch says that the epidemic caused him to get fired from the *Chronicle*. All of these accounts predate the Columbia memoir by many years, and, because of the law of priority, are more likely to be true: Barrett H. Clark, *Maxwell Anderson: The Man and His Plays,* p. 6; Helen Deutsch, "A Playwright and Poet," p. 5; Ruth Woodbury Sedgwick, "Maxwell Anderson," *The Stage Magazine* XIV (Oct. 1936), 55; and Robert Rice, "Maxwell Anderson," *PM's Sunday Picture News* III (Nov. 29, 1942), 24.

7. Anderson's Columbia memoir, p. 32.

8. As quoted in Hill's memoir, p. 165.

9. Alvin Johnson, *Pioneer's Progress* (Lincoln, Nebr.; Univ. of Nebraska Press, 1960), p. 272; Anderson's Columbia memoir, p. 10. Bliven in *Five Million Words Later,* p. 120, mistakenly writes that it was the editor-in-chief, Croly, who sent Anderson the invitation. In any case, it was Johnson who initiated it.

10. Anderson's Columbia memoir, p. 10 (he says "a neighbor," but Deutsch, p. 5, reports "two spinster neighbors," and Robert Rice, p. 24, reports "two retired teachers"). Sedgwick, p. 55.

11. As quoted in Anderson's Columbia memoir, p. 18.

12. *Letters,* p. 316n.

13. *Five Million Words Later,* p. 120.

14. Alvin Johnson, pp. 271-72.

15. Hill's memoir, pp. 140, 175, 182.

16. As quoted in Hill's memoir, pp. 177, 187.

17. Ibid., pp. 177, 179, 181, 225.

18. Anderson letter to Harold Monro, editor of the British *Chapbook,* Nov. 29, 1920 (*Letters,* pp. 17-18). But after Anderson and Hill left the editorial board of *The Measure,* the other editors did publish some of Untermeyer's poems but never any by Lowell.

19. All these nine are listed in the March 1921 issue as being regular editors even though Hill, in his memoir, says there were only "seven"

to begin with. Hill omits to mention David Morton and says that Padraic Colum was invited into the group by the founding members.

20. "Thunder in the Index," *The Measure: A Journal of Poetry*, First Number (March 1921), 24-25. New York: Kraus Reprint Corporation, 1966.

21. Hill's memoir, pp. 213-14. But Hill errs where he states that the journal "went on for ten or eleven more years . . .," for it died out with the June 1926 number, making a total run of about five years. His memory is accurate where he names specific dates, but it suffers when he attempts to measure a span of years. For instance, he writes on p. 213 of his memoir that Winifred Welles died "about five years later" (than 1921), whereas she actually lived on until 1939.

22. Hill's memoir, pp. 167-68.

23. Ibid., pp. 256-57.

24. Anderson's Columbia memoir, pp. 11-12, 14-15; Robert Rice, p. 24; Sedgwick, p. 55; Deutsch, p. 2; Hill's memoir, p. 167.

25. Jane McDill Anderson, *Rocklandia: A Collection of Facts and Fancies, Legends and Ghost Stories of Rockland County Life* (Dobbs Ferry, N.Y.: Morgan & Morgan, 1977), pp. 15, 19-20. Also, Danton Walker, *Spooks Deluxe: Some Excursions into the Supernatural* (New York: Franklin Watts, 1956), pp. 164-65; and Francis Sugrue, "High Tor Sold with its Ghosts and Old House," *New York Herald Tribune*, Feb. 10, 1950, p. 21.

26. Maxwell Anderson, "Preface" to Amy Murray's *November Hereabout* (New York: Henry Holt, 1940), p. xiii. Hill's memoir, p. 268.

27. Hill's memoir, pp. 264-65.

28. My interview with Nancy Anderson (Mrs. Alan Anderson) at her home in New City, N.Y., May 15, 1979 (hereinafter referred to as "Nancy Anderson").

29. Ibid.

30. Maxwell Anderson's "Preface" to *November Hereabout*, pp. xiii-xv.

31. Maxwell Anderson, "A Confession," *The New York Times*, Dec. 5, 1954, II, 7.

32. Hill's memoir, pp. 270-71.

33. Alan Anderson letters to me, Jan. 15, 1972, and Apr. 16, 1973. I confirmed this description during my week-long visit there in May 1978.

34. Maxwell Anderson letter to Lela Chambers [Oct. 4, 1925] (*Letters*, p. 23).

35. William Fields, "Maxwell Anderson: Some Fond Memories," *The New York Times*, Mar. 8, 1959, II, 3. Lawrence Anderson. Alan Anderson's

letter to me dated Jan. 15, 1972. In later years, residents on the road went over to Mount Ivy to catch the train to New York City.

36. Alan Anderson letters to me, Jan. 15, 1972, and Apr. 16, 1973.
37. Nancy Anderson. Letter to me from Alan Anderson, Jan. 15, 1972. Carroll French died in Nov. 1971.
38. My interview with Marion Hargrove at his home in Santa Monica, Calif., Jan. 6, 1980 (hereinafter referred to as "Marion Hargrove").
39. Hesper Anderson. Henry Poor's painting of Bessie Breuer is reproduced in Peyton Boswell, Jr.'s *Varnum Poor* (New York: Hyperion Press, 1941).
40. New York: Atheneum, 1961.
41. Hesper Anderson.
42. Marion Hargrove.
43. Letter to me from Kenneth Anderson, Mar. 2, 1980.
44. As quoted in Hill's memoir, p. 272.
45. Terence Anderson.
46. Alan Anderson. Also his notes that he sent to me in his letter of Jan. 29, 1981.
47. Gilda Anderson's letter to me, Mar. 4, 1980. Gilda here is reacting against Hesper's claim during her interview with me that her father often used his money to buy love from his children.
48. Lawrence Anderson.
49. Terence Anderson.
50. Lela's "Life," pp. 50-51.
51. Hill's memoir, pp. 273, 275.
52. John Keats, *You Might as Well Live: The Life and Times of Dorothy Parker* (New York: Simon & Schuster, 1970), p. 80.
53. Hill's memoir, pp. 280-81.
54. Eunice Tietjens, *The World at My Shoulder* (New York: Macmillan, 1938), p. 258.
55. Alan Jay Lerner, *The Street Where I Live* (New York: W. W. Norton, 1978), p. 35.
56. My interview with Lotte Lenya Weill at her home in New City, N.Y., May 15, 1978 (hereinafter referred to as "Lotte Lenya").

   Kurt Weill (1900-50) was born in Dessau, Germany, the son of a cantor. He studied music first with Albert Bing; later with Engelbert Humperdinck, author of *Hansel und Gretel*; and then with Rudolph Krasselt at the Music School of Berlin. For years Weill studied the art of pure music under the guidance of Ferruccio Busoni, becoming an accomplished pianist while still a teenager. His *Frauentanz* (Woman's

Dance) was performed at the Salzburg Festival. Weill's interest in vocal expression led naturally to opera, in which medium he was to make striking innovations. In this vein he wrote *Der Protagonist* (The Protagonist); *Royal Palace,* using a libretto by Ivan Goll; and *Der Zar laesst sich photographieren* (The Czar Has His Picture Taken), using a libretto by Georg Kaiser. With Bertolt Brecht he composed his two European masterpieces *Die Dreigroschenoper* (The Threepenny Opera) and *Austeig und Fall der Stadt Mahagonny* (The Rise and Fall of the City of Mahagonny). His was an assimilative talent for combining the American idioms of jazz and popular songs with the avant-garde techniques of modern music such as polytonality, polyrhythms, and atonality. In 1933, his work having been condemned by Hitler's bootlickers and himself on the verge of arrest, he fled with his wife to France, and two years later to the United States, where he teamed with dramatists such as Paul Green to compose musicals.

His wife, Lotte Lenya, was born Karoline Blamauer in 1898 in Vienna, Austria, the daughter of a coachman and a laundress. When only six she was a dancer in a circus; later, a tightrope walker. In 1926 she married Weill. After playing the role of Jenny in her husband's *Die Dreigroschenoper* as well as starring in two other plays by him—where her singing and dancing talents attracted notice—she made her Broadway debut as Miriam in *The Eternal Road* (1937), a dramatic oratorio by Weill and based on a text by Franz Werfel. *Candle in the Wind* provided her second role. She appeared in the long-running Broadway production of *Cabaret* also. Several times she made TV appearances; she acted in a number of films such as *What* and won an Academy Award nomination for her role in *From Russia with Love.* In 1951, after Weill died, she married George Davis. For her performance in a revival of *The Threepenny Opera* she received a Tony Award in 1956. Seven years later she married Russell Detweiler. Lenya died in November 1981.

57. From Maxwell Anderson's biographical sketch about Weill on the back of the phonograph record album "Tryout," published by Heritage in 1953. This album consists of a series of "private rehearsal recordings including actual performances by Kurt Weill and Ira Gershwin. Music by Kurt Weill and lyrics by Ira Gershwin."

The only full-length, documented biography of Weill thus far is Ronald Sanders, *The Days Grow Short: The Life and Times of Kurt Weill* (New York: Holt, Rinehart & Winston, 1980). Aside from the numerous short items on the composer published in dictionaries of music and musicians as well as in encyclopedias, I found the following useful: Olin Downes' two articles in *The New York Times,* "People's Composer," Apr. 9, 1950, II, 9, and "Memorial to Weill," July 9, 1950, II, 7; also, Maxwell Anderson's "Kurt Weill," *Theatre Arts* XXXIV (Dec. 1950), 58.

58. "Tryout" (see note No. 57 for this chapter).

59. Anderson's Columbia memoir, p. 12.

60. Hill's memoir, p. 289.

61. Laurence G. Avery, *A Catalogue of the Maxwell Anderson Collection at the University of Texas* (Austin, Texas: Univ. of Texas, 1968), pp. 64-65. The unpublished manuscript is at the Univ. of Texas.

62. Maxwell Anderson letter to Mrs. F. Durand Taylor, Apr. 5, 1938 (*Letters,* p. 71).

63. Maxwell Anderson, "A Prelude to Poetry in the Theatre," preface to *Winterset* (Washington, D.C.: Anderson House, 1935), p. xi. This essay was later published as "Poetry in the Theatre" in his *Off Broadway Essays about the Theatre* (N.Y.: William Sloane Associates, 1947).

64. Maxwell Anderson, "A Confession," *The New York Times,* Dec. 4, 1954, II, 7. Hill in his memoir, pp. 289-90, devotes some space to these attempts.

65. Maxwell Anderson, "Poetry in the Theatre," p. 50.

66. Maxwell Anderson's letter to Hazel A. Reynolds, Sept. 2, 1937 (*Letters,* pp. 59-60).

67. Anderson's Columbia memoir, p. 12.

68. Hill's memoir, p. 289.

69. *Catalogue,* pp. 80-82. The manuscript exists in disarray in the Univ. of Texas collection.

70. "Off Broadway," *Off Broadway,* p. 26.

71. Anderson's Columbia memoir, p. 12; Hill's memoir, pp. 289-90; "Preface," *Four Verse Plays,* p. v.

72. George Abbott, *"Mister Abbott"* (New York: Random House, 1963), pp. 104, 113-14; Anderson's Columbia memoir, pp. 12-13. Abbott records that the payment given Anderson was $1,500.

CHAPTER 4

1. Brooks Atkinson, *Broadway,* rev. ed. (New York: Macmillan, 1974), p. 174.

2. Anderson's Columbia memoir, p. 32.

3. John Kobler, *Damned in Paradise: The Life of John Barrymore* (New York: Atheneum, 1977), pp. 130-50; Atkinson, *Broadway,* pp. 147-50; Phyllis Hartnoll, ed., *The Oxford Companion to the Theatre,* 3rd ed. (London: Oxford Univ. Press, 1950), pp. 86, 672.

4. Anderson's Columbia memoir, p. 27.

5. As quoted in Laurence Stallings, *Plumes* (New York: Harcourt, Brace, 1924), p. 348. He later wrote a script for the popular motion picture *The Big Parade* based on his story of the same name and on *Plumes.*

6. Letter from Sylvia Stallings Lowe (Mrs. William Webb Lowe) to me, Mar. 29, 1978. Sylvia is one of his two daughters by Helen. Other sources of information about Stallings: Unsigned, "'What Price Glory' and Its Authors," *The New York Times,* Sept. 14, 1924, VIII, 1-2 (Stallings, not Anderson, seems to have been the one interviewed here); *Twentieth Century Authors,* ed. Stanley J. Kunitz and Howard Haycraft (New York: H.W. Wilson, 1942), p. 1,325; *The Biographical Encyclopedia & Who's Who of the American Theatre,* ed. Walter Rigdon (New York: James H. Heineman, 1966), p. 840; *The Reader's Encyclopedia of American Literature,* ed. Max J. Herzberg (New York: Thomas Y. Crowell, 1962), p. 1,071.

7. Anderson's Columbia memoir, p. 22.

8. Letter from Alan Haskett Anderson (the playwright's son) to me, Oct. 27, 1970. Also: Unsigned, "The Pulitzer Prize Winner," *Literary Digest* CXV (May 20, 1933), 15.

9. Anderson's Columbia memoir, p. 13; "'What Price Glory' and Its Authors"; Unsigned, "How a 'Great Play' Is Written," *Current Opinion* LXXVII (Nov., 1924), 617-18; Maxwell Anderson, "A Confession," *The New York Times,* Dec. 5, 1954, II, 7; Lewis Nichols, "Talk with a Self-Critical Author," *The New York Times,* Jan. 18, 1959, II, 5; and Hill's memoir, p. 291.

10. Unsigned, "Car Kills Case, War's Original 'Captain Flagg,' " *New York Herald Tribune,* Dec. 11, 1933.

11. *Five Million Words Later,* p. 121.

12. As quoted in Anderson's Columbia memoir, p. 13.

13. Ibid., p. 21.

14. Hill's memoir, p. 291.

15. Anderson in his Columbia memoir, p. 13, calls the place a "dugout," but the published text of the play calls it a "wine cellar."

16. In his Columbia memoir, p. 13, Anderson gives full credit to Stallings

for the "dugout" part, but throughout that memoir he reveals himself as an excessively tolerant and generous person in judging others. No one ever fires him or does him an injustice ("We get more tolerant as we grow older," he once said). A much more reliable account of the play's composition occurs in "'What Price Glory' and Its Authors," which was published just a few months after the playwriting experience. This article was based on an interview with Stallings alone (his coauthor was never interviewed until the mid-1930s) and definitely speaks of the second act in Anderson's draft as being colorless and vague; also, that once Stallings had something to correct, he went to work with alacrity (p. 1). Drama critic and teacher Walter Prichard Eaton, who had studied Anderson's career and corresponded with him, wrote the following in "He Put Poetry Back on the Stage," *New York Herald Tribune,* Jan. 28, 1934, VIII, 21: "Stallings reworked the first draft to make the speech and incidents more realistic, and then the two men redrafted the whole together."

17. James Thurber, "The Years with Ross," *Atlantic Monthly* CCII (July 1958), 42. Thurber's book *The Years with Ross* was published in 1959. Also, Margaret Case Harriman, *The Vicious Circle: The Story of the Algonquin Round Table* (New York: Rinehart, 1951), p. 115. Some of my material on Woollcott comes from Samuel Hopkins Adams' *Alexander Woollcott: His Life and His World* (Freeport, N.Y.: Books for Libraries, 1970) (originally published in 1945). Margaret Case Harriman's father, Frank Case, who was proprietor of the hotel for many years, wrote a senitmental and nostalgic account of the place in *Tales of a Wayside Inn* (New York: Frederick A. Stokes, 1938) but devoted extremely little attention to Woollcott and Parker.

18. Thurber, p. 41.

19. As quoted in John Keats, *You Might as Well Live: The Life and Times of Dorothy Parker* (New York: Simon & Schuster, 1970), p. 120.

20. Thurber, p. 41.

21. As quoted in the preface to Arthur F. Kinney's *Dorothy Parker* (Boston: Twayne, 1978).

22. As quoted in Max J. Herzberg et al. (eds.), *The Reader's Encyclopedia of American Literature* (New York: Thomas Y. Crowell, 1962), p. 853.

23. Keats, p. 42.

24. Harriman, passim; Keats, passim.

25. Kinney, pp. 31-32.

26. Hesper Anderson's unpublished memoir "Someone Else," p. 28.

27. Edna Ferber, "The Curtain Rises at 8:30 Sharp," *McCall's* (Mar. 1928), 4, as quoted in Kinney, p. 32.

28. In my account I follow the report given in "'What Price Glory' and Its Authors," p. 1, rather than the one in Adams' *Alexander Woollcott,* pp. 132-33, where one reads that Woollcott had read the play in advance and actively interceded in Stallings' behalf in getting Hopkins to read the play. The report by Adams was written long after the fact, is undocumented (like the rest of the book), does not mention the *Times* article (with which it obviously conflicts), and has the meeting occur at lunchtime—probably too early. And for most of these same reasons I reject the report in Howard Teichmann's *Smart Aleck: The Wit, World and Life of Alexander Woollcott* (New York: William Morrow, 1976), pp. 132-33, which freely elaborates on what is evidently taken from Adams without consulting the *Times* article.

29. Arthur Hopkins, *To a Lonely Boy* (Garden City, N.Y.: Doubleday, Doran, 1937), p. 236.

30. Ibid., pp. 38-39.

31. Anderson's Columbia memoir, p. 20.

32. Atkinson, *Broadway,* p. 281.

33. As quoted in *To a Lonely Boy,* pp. 236-37.

34. Letter to me from Kathryn C. Hulme, Aug. 28, 1979.

35. Robert Rice, "Maxwell Anderson," *PM's Sunday Picture News* III (Nov. 29, 1942), 24.

36. *To a Lonely Boy,* p. 237.

37. Lewis Nichols, "Talk with a Self-Critical Author," *The New York Times,* Jan. 18, 1959, II, 5.

38. Herzberg, p. 1,251.

39. Review in *American Mercury* III (Nov. 1924), 372-73.

40. Anderson's Columbia memoir, pp. 29-30; John Mason Brown, *The Worlds of Robert E. Sherwood: Mirror to His Times 1896-1939* (New York: Harper & Row, 1965), pp. 163, 341.

41. Atkinson, *Broadway,* p. 281. Hesper Anderson and also Marion Hargrove, who was Maxwell's protégé during the latter part of World War II and for a short time afterward, told me versions of the story that were similar to this one.

42. Maxwell Anderson, "A Confession," *The New York Times,* Dec. 5, 1954, II, 7; Robert Rice, p. 24; Anderson's Columbia memoir, p. 18.

43. Quentin Anderson. Also, Anderson's "A Confession," p. 7.

44. Unsigned, "Wilbur Criticizes 'What Price Glory,'" *The New York Times,* Sept. 28, 1924, I, 9. Robert P. Wilkins in "Editor's Notes,"

North Dakota Quarterly XXXVIII (Winter 1970), 91, gives a good, short summary of the attempts to censor *What Price Glory.*
45. "Wilbur Criticizes 'What Price Glory,'" p. 9.
46. Unsigned, "Hayward Considers 'What Price Glory,'" *The New York Times,* Sept. 27, 1924, I, 17; Unsigned, "U.S. Prosecutor Takes No Action against War Play," *New York World,* Sept. 27, 1924.
47. Unsigned, "Hylan Acts against New Broadway Play," *The New York Times,* Sept. 24, 1924, I, 1.
48. As quoted in *To a Lonely Boy,* p. 241.
49. "Hylan Acts against New Broadway Play," I, 8; *To a Lonely Boy,* p. 237; Unsigned, "Broadway Show Chastened before Police Interfere," *The New York Times,* Sept. 25, 1924, I, 1, 6.
50. Brooks Atkinson and Albert Hirschfeld, *The Lively Years: 1920-1973* (New York: Association Press, 1973), p. 32; "Broadway Show Chastened before Police Interfere," p. 1.
51. Background in "Hayward Considers 'What Price Glory,'" p. 17.
52. Unsigned, "Censors of 'Glory' Hit from the Pulpit," *New York World,* Oct. 27, 1924, p. 28.
53. *To a Lonely Boy,* p. 241.
54. Anderson's Columbia memoir, p. 27.
55. Elmer Rice, *Minority Report: An Autobiography* (New York: Simon & Schuster, 1963), p. 106. Maxwell Anderson, "Stage Money," *Collier's* LXXIX (May 28, 1927), 30.
56. Quentin Anderson.
57. Lawrence Anderson.
58. John P. Hagan, "Frederick H. Koch and North Dakota: Theatre in the Wilderness," *North Dakota Quarterly* XXXVIII (Winter 1970), 83-84. Hagan claims to have gotten the present version from Winifred Camp. Other versions appear in Frederick H. Koch's "Making a Regional Drama," *Bulletin of the American Library Association* XXVI (Aug. 1932), 468; also, his "Towards a New Folk Theatre," *The Quarterly Journal* XX (May 1930), 167-68.
59. Paul Green.
60. Letter from Anderson's lawyer Howard E. Reinheimer to him, Mar. 3, 1931 (Univ. of Texas). Motion pictures of *What Price Glory* came out in 1926, 1936, and 1952.
61. Quentin Anderson.
62. Maxwell Anderson letter to secretary of state, state of Delaware, Apr. 5, 1934 (Univ. of Texas). His second mate, Mab, purchased stock from Pittston Company, Chicago Pneumatic Tool Co., and West

Pennsylvania Electric Co. but apparently made little if anything from these investments.

63. *To a Lonely Boy,* p. 241.

CHAPTER 5

1. Barrett H. Clark, *Maxwell Anderson: The Man and His Plays* (New York: Samuel French, 1933), p. 30.
2. Copies of *Sea-Wife* are owned by the New York Public Library, Stephen F. Austin State University, and me. The play was reportedly staged by amateurs in 1932 at the University of Minnesota, and in 1936 by Syracuse University. Probably the reason Anderson never published the work was that he intended to revise it (but never did).—Letter from Anderson's secretary Alfred C. Sturt to some unknown person, Mar. 3, 1937 (Univ. of Texas collection).
3. Nina N. Selivanova (Valley Cottage, N.Y.), "Folklore: Rockland County," New York State Writer's Project, 1938, pp. 28-30. From a duplicate copy filed in The Nyack Library, Nyack, N.Y. In *Sea-Wife* are other names possibly suggested by people among Anderson's family and acquaintances: Margaret, Kenneth, Dan (Dan Chambers married Lela Blanch Anderson), and Hallie (see "Hallie Loomis" in Chapter 1).
4. Maxwell Anderson letter to John F. Wharton (May 1949) (*Letters,* p. 234).
5. Kenneth Anderson letter to me, Feb. 10, 1980.
6. Ibid.
7. Kenneth Anderson's letter to me, Mar. 2, 1980. Lawrence Anderson's letter to me, May 2, 1980.
8. Quentin and Terence Anderson.
9. Miscellaneous postal cards sent by Mr. and Mrs. Maxwell Anderson to their children in 1926 (correspondence owned by Alan Anderson). Also, letter to Margaret from Kenneth, July 28, 1926 (Univ. of Texas collection).
10. Carbon copy of letter to Kenneth from Margaret, July 17 (1926 or 1927). Her address is: Times Square Hotel, New York City.—From Univ. of Texas collection.
11. Anderson's Columbia memoir, p. 23.

12. Maxwell Anderson, *Saturday's Children* (New York: Longmans, Green, 1927), pp. 80, 107-8 (Act II).
13. Alan Anderson successfully directed *Saturday's Children* in the Houston Playhouse during the early 1950s.—Questionnaire sent to me from him, Nov. 23, 1970.
14. Letter to me from Kenneth Anderson, Mar. 2, 1980.
15. Paul Green. This impression was confirmed in all the interviews I had with Anderson's relatives and acquaintances.
16. Some of my dates for tracing Mab's life come from a penciled chronology left by her on four small pieces of Hotel Dorset memo paper stuck inside a 1953 notebook kept by her. There is no doubt that the writing is hers. The chronology opens with her marriage to Charles Maynard in 1923, followed by her first meeting with Anderson in 1927, and ends with the production of *Winterset* in the fall of 1935. Very likely all this was written down during her final months alive, when she was living in the city and doing television work. Like the doomed Anne Boleyn in *Anne of the Thousand Days,* she seems to be reviewing her troubled married life; unlike Anne, she identifies herself closely with her husband's artistic achievements. (Hereinafter cited as "Mab's Hotel Dorset chronology").
17. Letter to me from Mrs. Phoebe Brand Carnovsky (Easton, Conn.), Jan. 29, 1979. This is the wife of Morris Carnovsky, the Shakespearean actor.
18. The original, unacted version has Ellen turn off the gas at the end and respond gratefully to Welles' call. But neither version seems to have been published, even though it is listed opposite the title page of *Both Your Houses* (Samuel French edition of 1933) as among the author's published works. The play is synopsized in Burns Mantle's *The Best Plays of 1928-1929* (New York: Dodd, Mead, 1929). Both versions of the text are in the University of Texas collection.
19. Lela Chambers. Much of my information on Mab's physical appearance comes from the questionnaire that Hesper filled out and mailed to me in her letter of June 14, 1978; from numerous photographs; also, from my interview with her.
20. Official copy of birth registration, Palais de Justice, Court House, Montreal, Canada. The date and parentage agree with Hesper's records. The transcript of her school record at Ohio State University lists an "H" as the middle initial, but the birth record lists only "Gertrude Higger."
21. Most of my information about Mab's early life derives from a series of

letters to me from her sister Libbe Higger Axlrod (Coral Gables, Fla.), Sept. 26, Oct. 10, Nov. 15, and Dec. 4, 1978; Jan. 21, 1979; Mar. 21 and Apr. 7, 1980.

Also, I make use of a three-page, handwritten, untitled, and undated biographical account written by Mab and filed at the University of Texas, telling about her early poverty, a trip she supposedly made to Portland, Oreg. (Libbe says the trip is fictional), and the embarrassing affair in Montreal. The account is incomplete.

Additional information comes from interviews with Mr. and Mrs. Alan Anderson, Mr. and Mrs. Terence Anderson, and Hesper Anderson. Also, a letter from the relative Doris Higger to Mab Maynard, Feb. 15, 1941, filed in Hesper's strongbox. Exceptions to these sources will be noted wherever they occur.

22. In compliance with the request of my main informant, Mrs. Libbe Higger Axlrod, I do not disclose the full details.

23. "Someone Else," p. 36.

24. Official transcript of Gertrude H. Higger's grades from Alvin C. Whyte, Office of Registrar, Records and Scheduling, Ohio State Univ., Dec. 14, 1978.

25. Mab's obituary, *The New York Times*, Mar. 23, 1953.

26. Kenneth Anderson's letter to me, Mar. 2, 1980. Nancy Anderson.

27. In her application for a French visa, c. 1940s, she listed her maiden name as "Maynard," and this was long after her divorce from Maynard. And in her "Certificate of Literacy" granted for voting purposes at New City in 1942 we read that she calls herself "Gertrude M. Anderson."—From documents in Hesper's strongbox.

28. Hesper and Nancy Anderson.

29. Hesper Anderson.

30. Avery Chambers.

31. Nancy Anderson.

32. S. N. Behrman, "Playwright's Company," *People in a Diary: A Memoir* (Boston: Little, Brown, 1972), p. 221.

33. News about this affair comes from my interview with Mrs. Julie Sloane (New City, N.Y.), May 14, 1978, whose husband, William M. Sloane, had published several Anderson books. The Sloanes, however, never knew Margaret, because they arrived in the neighborhood long after she died. Julie's recollections owe something to reports from the longtime servant in the Anderson household, Margaret Stamper. Some news reached me via my interview with Martha (Meg) Anderson, who is Quentin's divorced wife. Meg knew Margaret.

During his interview with me, Terence Anderson was confident that his father had informed his mother of the affair while it was going on, which openness parallels how Harvie Salter treated his wife, Ellen, in the *roman a clef* novel *Take Care of My Roses*.

34. Lawrence Anderson letter to me, Sept. 15, 1978. Gilda Anderson letter to me, Mar. 4, 1980. Hesper Anderson's "Someone Else," pp. 8-9. Martha later married a Jackson.

35. Kenneth Anderson letter to me, Mar. 2, 1980. Quentin Anderson.

36. Kenneth Anderson letters to me, Feb. 10 and Mar. 2, 1980. Alan interprets Margaret's remark as reflecting her hurt and despondency arising from the intrigue between his father and Mab, whereas Kenneth interprets it as reflecting her fear of entering menopause.

37. Maxwell Anderson, "Off Broadway," *Off Broadway Essays about the Theatre* (New York: William Sloane Associates, 1947), p. 22. This essay was originally titled "The Basis of Artistic Creation in Literature" and was delivered as a lecture at Rutgers University in 1942.

38. For *Gods of the Lightning* Anderson had teamed up with his neighbor Harold Hickerson to embody in a thinly disguised form the recent internationally publicized trial of Nicola Sacco and Bartolomeo Vanzetti; the result was the closest Anderson ever came to pure propaganda. Of all the famous legal cases in United States' history, only the Scopes "monkey" trial of 1925 comes close to rivaling it as a *cause celebre*. Boston, near which the Sacco-Vanzetti trial had taken place and where passions still ran high, was incensed at the prospect of seeing *Gods of the Lightning* on the stage there. John M. Case, chief of Boston's Licensing Division, ruled that the text was practically "anarchistic and treasonable" because of its inflammatory attack on the government officials of Massachusetts, hence he denied a license for its presentation. After the play was shown at the Little Theatre in New York City, starting in October 1928, the critic of the conservative paper *The New York Times* called it cruelly disturbing. The play lasted only twenty-nine performances in New York.

Taken purely as dramatic literature, this work is certainly not a good one. It was written too close to the events dramatized; all runs to one-sidedness and extremism. Here if anywhere in the early corpus we can see Anderson as the socialist radical. The characters are not well developed, only the ideas are.

Vanzetti is changed into Dante Capraro, the humane and gentle anarchist; Sacco is much transformed into the native-born IWW militant James Macready; and Madeiros (the convicted criminal who exonerated the immigrants) becomes the fatalistic and bleak-minded restaurant owner Suvorin—whose lines, we suspect, carry the burden of Anderson's own bitter feelings at the time. When Capraro and Macready are put on the witness stand, they each level indictments against a corrupt capitalistic society. In the legal system used against them we see such incredible abuses as the foreman of the jury standing up in the jury box and accusing Macready, the crooked district attorney blackmailing witnesses to get false testimony from them, and the thick-witted judge bent on a conviction delivering unfair rulings to aid the prosecution. All is justice perverted and innocence maligned. Left-wing commentators like Anita Block have praised *Gods of the Lightning* for its proletarian message, but most later commentators see this work as inferior art and too much in the socialist vein of what Clifford Odets would soon be doing.

39. Alan and Terence Anderson. Terence, whose dating I use, puts the year at 1928; Alan puts it within a year or two after his mother's death, which would mean 1932 or 1933.

40. Quentin Anderson. Also, various other family members.

41. Terence Anderson.

42. "Sexy" is a word that Alan and several other men reportedly used in describing Mab.—Hesper Anderson.

43. Avery Chambers.

44. Hesper Anderson.

45. Mab's Hotel Dorset chronology.

46. Owned by Hesper Anderson.

47. Anderson's Columbia memoir, p. 23. *Letters,* pp. xliii, 33-34.

48. Anderson's Columbia memoir, p. 22. Maxwell Anderson letter to Theresa Helburn, Oct. 16, 1929 (*Letters,* p. 31). *Elizabeth the Queen* was published in New York by Longmans, Green in 1930.

49. From Lord Acton's famous letter to Bishop Mandell Creighton, Apr. 5, 1887.

50. In both *Elizabeth the Queen* (1930) and *Mary of Scotland* (1933) Elizabeth is a principal figure. She also occurs in the completed but unacted and unpublished *Masque of Queens* (written in 1954), where she is an old woman leading an empty life now that she cannot have normal human relationships and is unable to exert any effective control over the course of history. She has a stroke at the end. As in the case of *Richard and Anne* (written in 1955), this work exists in manuscript form at the University of Texas.

51. *Mary of Scotland,* p. 151 (Act III).

52. *Anne of the Thousand Days* as published in *Theatre Arts* XXXIII (June 1949), p. 79 (Act II, Scene 2). Originally published by William Sloane in 1948.

53. *Richard and Anne* as summarized in *Letters,* pp. 75-76.

54. Maxwell Anderson, "Compromising and Keeping the Faith," *Off Broadway,* pp. 74-80.

55. Most of the following material about the first stage production derives from Maurice Zolotow's *Stagestruck: The Romance of Alfred Lunt and Lynn Fontanne* (New York: Harcourt, Brace & World, 1965), pp. 177-79; Lawrence Langner's *The Magic Curtain* (New York: E. P. Dutton, 1951), p. 252; and Roy S. Wadau's *Vintage Years of the Theatre Guild 1928-1939* (Cleveland, Ohio: Case Western Reserve Univ., 1972), pp. 98-99, 101.

56. Mab's Hotel Dorset chronology.

57. Letter to me from Phoebe Brand Carnovsky (Easton, Conn.), Jan. 29, 1979.

58. John F. Wharton, pp. 91-92; "Lunt," *The Oxford Companion to the Theatre,* 3rd ed., ed. Phyllis Hartnoll (London: Oxford Univ. Press, 1967), pp. 589-90.

59. Letter to me from Lynn Fontanne (Genessee Depot, Wisc.), Aug. 21, 1975. Incidentally, some of the information that she supplied to Zolotow's book *Stagestruck* for its section on Anderson's love life is grossly inaccurate. We read there that Anderson is supposed to be an old man who philanders with teenage girls (p. 179), whereas Anderson was actually no more than thirty-nine when he first met Mab, the first "young girl," and she was close to twenty-three. The second "young girl" was Gilda Hazard, who was not "sixteen or seventeen" at the time she began her relationship with Anderson but close to thirty-nine! The claim that he ever as a grown man chased teenage girls has no foundation in fact, as attested by his longtime friend and business partner John F. Wharton, who wrote a clarification to me on Aug. 22, 1975. When I wrote to Miss Fontanne asking her to discuss certain details about the girl-chasing matter, she admitted that she didn't know anything about Mab and didn't like Anderson.—From her letter (see above).

60. As quoted in Lawrence Langer's *The Magic Curtain,* p. 252.

61. Zolotow, *Stagestruck,* p. 179.

62. Theresa Helburn, *A Wayward Quest: The Autobiography of Theresa Helburn* (Boston: Little, Brown, 1960), pp. 240-41.

63. Questionnaire filled out by Alan Anderson and mailed to me with his letter of Oct. 27, 1970.

64. Wadau, *Vintage Years,* p. 101.

65. Stark Young, "Elizabeth," *New Republic* LXV (Nov. 19, 1930), 19.

66. Alan Anderson.

67. Quentin Anderson.

68. Lawrence Anderson letter to me, May 2, 1980. Lawrence Anderson.

69. Alan Anderson; also his notes to me in his letter of Jan. 29, 1981. Lawrence Anderson. Kenneth Anderson letter to me, Feb. 10, 1980. Lela Chambers letter to me, Jan. 30, 1980.

70. Terence Anderson.

71. Anonymous, "Death of Mrs. Maxwell Anderson," *The New York Times,* Feb. 27, 1931, p. 23. She died on the 26th. *Letters,* p. xliii, lists the cause of death as "blood clot." Alan calls it a "stroke."

72. Hesper Anderson.

73. *Lord Hervey's Memoirs,* ed. Romney Sedgwick (New York: Macmillan, 1952), p. 247.

74. See letters by Lela Chambers and Kenneth Anderson, respectively, in note No. 69 for this chapter. Kenneth gets his information directly from Margaret's unidentified lady friend in the death car.

75. Alan's reaction comes from his interview with me; Terence's from my interview with his longtime neighbor Mrs. Julie Sloane (widow of publisher William M. Sloane), who quotes the Anderson family governess Martha, who was serving with the Andersons at the time Margaret died.

76. Meg Anderson.

77. Anderson's confession is quoted from the letter sent to me by Gilda Anderson, Mar. 6, 1979. The short poem (unpublished) is handwritten on the back of a mailing envelope that is stamped "May 13, 1958" (Univ. of Texas collection). Gilda, too, believes that the poem refers to Margaret.

78. Alan and Terence Anderson.

79. Letter to me from Lloyd R. Hamilton (Fontana, Calif.), May 12, 1978. Lloyd is a son of Margaret's little sister Elizabeth.

80. As mentioned in the letter to me from Margaret H. Zimmer (Birmingham, Mich.), Apr. 21, 1978. Mrs. Zimmer is a daughter of James E. Haskett.

81. These ran May through October. The last item was "The Strange History of Pedro Martinez of Taos," Vol. XXIV, pp. 230-42.—*Letters,* p. xliv.

82. As quoted in Margaret H. Zimmer's letter to me, May 26, 1978.
83. Kenneth Anderson's letter to me, Mar. 2, 1980.
84. Quentin Anderson.
85. During his interview with me, Paul Green said that Mab had acted as a "member of the crowd" in *The House of Connelly.*
86. Harold Clurman in his *The Fervent Years: The Story of the Group Theatre and the Thirties* (New York: Alfred A. Knopf, 1945), p. 37. On this same page Clurman states that Anderson submitted to him that summer a verse play about the Russian Revolution—surely *The Princess Renegade*—though he didn't care for it and told Anderson so. But Clurman must be in error about the year, for Avery in his *Catalogue* says the play was written in 1932. It was also copyrighted in 1932 but never published or produced.
87. *Letters,* p. xliv. First produced on Mar. 9, 1932, at the Forty-eighth Street Theatre, New York. It ran for thirteen performances.
88. Maxwell Anderson, "Poetry in the Theatre," *Off Broadway,* p. 47.

CHAPTER 6

1. *Letters,* p. 39n. Mab's Hotel Dorset chronology.
2. Helen Hayes and Lewis Funke, *A Gift for Joy* (Philadelphia, Pa.: M. Evans, 1965), p. 127.
3. "The Essence of Tragedy" in *The Essence of Tragedy and Other Footnotes and Papers* (Washington, D.C.: Anderson House, 1939); and "By Way of Preface: The Theatre as Religion," *The New York Times,* Oct. 26, 1941, drama section, pp. 1, 3. This second work was originally Anderson's Founders Day Address that he delivered at Carnegie Institute in 1937; after its newspaper publication it became "The Basis of Artistic Creation in Literature" for *The Bases of Artistic Creation,* by Maxwell Anderson, Rhys Carpenter, Roy Harris et al. (New Brunswick, N.J.: Rutgers Univ. Press, 1942); and then "Off Broadway" in *Off Broadway Essays about the Theatre* (N.Y.: William Sloane Associates, 1947).
4. Allan G. Halline, "Maxwell Anderson's Dramatic Theory," *American Literature* XVI (May 1944), 64.
5. "Off Broadway," pp. 22-28, 33.
6. Hill's memoir, p. 421.

7. "The Essence of Tragedy," pp. 6-8.

8. See Arthur Miller's essay "Tragedy and the Common Man."

9. Letter to me from Phoebe Brand Carnovsky (Easton, Conn.), Jan. 29, 1979.

10. *Men in White* opened in New York on Sept. 26, 1933. Hesper Anderson was born Aug. 12, 1934.—From Mab Maynard's letter to Lela Chambers, Nov. 12, 1934 (copy of letter furnished me by Lela Chambers). Birth date verified elsewhere, for example, by Hesper Anderson.

11. Maxwell Anderson letter to Gertrude Anthony (Mab Maynard) (late July 1933) in *Letters,* pp. 39-40. Alan Anderson wrote to me on Jan. 7, 1979: ". . . his affair with Mab started in secrecy while my mother was alive and their relationship was so far advanced by the time mother died and they were free to 'go public' that there was nothing Dad had to prove to Mab or she to him. They were together for good, they thought."

12. Lawrence Anderson letter to me, Sept. 15, 1978.

13. Lela Chambers letter to me, June 24, 1978. Lela's "Life," p. 115.

14. Alan, Terence, and Quentin Anderson.

15. Terence and Quentin Anderson. "Someone Else," p. 57. It was Avery Chambers who first told me about the nonmarriage. He assumed that the knowledge was family-wide.

16. My interview with Mrs. Terence Anderson (Lulu), New City, N.Y., May 15, 1978. Hesper Anderson.

17. Kenneth Anderson; also, Kenneth's letter to me, June 8, 1978. When I sent Hesper a questionnaire covering this subject of marriage, she replied enigmatically on June 14, 1978, that she knew the answer but, in compliance with her mother's last request, she would not divulge it. During my *tête-à-tête* and telephone interviews with her she expressed serious doubts that her parents had married; and she writes as much in "Someone Else," p. 8. Her half brother Alan reports that she had told him of her *certainty* that no wedding had taken place.—Alan's letter to me, Jan. 7, 1979.

18. Gilda Anderson letter to me, Oct. 10, 1978. I checked with all the relatives, friends, and acquaintances who would cooperate with me, and I checked with bureaus of vital statistics in all those states where Anderson was known to have lived or visited during 1932-33, but I invariably received negative responses. Dr. Avery was also frustrated in his search for a legal marriage record.

When I wrote to Anderson's close friend and neighbor Milton Caniff about the marriage question, he replied that I had a serious problem! He said he was most willing to cooperate but there were troublesome aspects about the case, for example, people still alive who would be affected. Then, being evasive but still wanting to point out the answer by means of an illustration, he told me a brief anecdote about a writer who was trying to do a book on John Ringling, the famous circus man, whose wife was cousin to Caniff's mother. Women in the Ringling family refused to tell the writer anything, for reason that Ringling had never married the woman he lived with. On that note Caniff broke off his letter and did not respond to my further appeals for information.— Letter to me from Milton Caniff (Palm Springs, Calif., Sept. 3, 1978).

19. Alan Anderson letter to me, Jan. 7, 1979.
20. Lela's "Life," pp. 76-77, 115.
21. Elmer Rice, *Minority Report: An Autobiography* (New York: Simon & Schuster, 1963), p. 183.
22. Hesper and Gilda Anderson.
23. Quentin and Meg Anderson, "Someone Else," p. 7.
24. Lawrence Anderson letter to me, Sept. 15, 1978.
25. Nancy Anderson. Some information about the house came to me from Lela Chambers' letter, Aug. 30, 1978, and from my visit at the site.
26. Lawrence Anderson letter to me, Sept. 15, 1978.
27. Raymond T. B. Hand, "Maxwell Anderson's House," *House Beautiful* LXXVIII (Aug. 1936), 36-37, 58.
28. Hesper Anderson. See note No. 10 for this chapter.
29. Alan and Nancy Anderson. The old farmhouse, having been given to Quentin with the understanding that he marry Meg and take care of his two younger brothers, was left to Meg as a divorce settlement. When Meg put it up for sale, Alan bought it and has lived in it ever since.
30. Hesper Anderson's questionnaire sent to me, June 14, 1978. Some of the material on the flower gardens is taken from my interview with Nancy Anderson. For varieties of plants, shrubs, and trees, I rely on passages in "Someone Else" and on copies of nursery orders and receipts on file at the Univ. of Texas.
31. Nancy Anderson. Alan Anderson.
32. Letter from unidentified secretary to Mr. and Mrs. Maxwell Anderson, May 17, 1947 (Univ. of Texas).
33. Hesper and Gilda Anderson.
34. Lawrence Anderson letter to me, Sept. 15, 1978.
35. Meg Anderson.
36. "Someone Else," p. 4.
37. Ibid., pp. 35-36.
38. Meg Anderson. Most of my information on the child-parent relationship

comes from my interview with Hesper Anderson and from her "Some-one Else," a work whose accuracy I felt necessary to check with other family members; and to a lesser extent from such people as Mr. and Mrs. Alan Anderson, including Meg Anderson. Marion Hargrove provided to me in his interview some material about Mab's relationship with her husband.

39. Nancy Anderson. "Someone Else," p. 2.
40. Letter to me from Libbe Higger Axlrod, Oct. 10, 1978.
41. Nancy Anderson. Lela Chambers letter to me, May 22, 1978.
42. "Someone Else," pp. 58-59.
43. Nancy Anderson.
44. "Someone Else," p. 22.
45. Meg Anderson.
46. Hill's memoir, pp. 566-67.
47. Nancy Anderson.
48. "The Queen from Keokuk," *This Fabulous Century: The Thirties,* by the editors of Time-Life Books I (New York: Time-Life, 1969), 154. Originally published in the *New York Mirror,* Dec. 16, 1938.
49. Alan Anderson's notes and letter sent to me on Dec. 8, 1980. Nancy Anderson. "Someone Else," pp. 33-34.
50. For information about the cabin I relied on miscellaneous sources, for example, Lawrence Anderson's drawing and notes sent to me in his letter, Mar. 24, 1979; interviews with Lela Chambers, Alan Anderson, Terence Anderson, Hesper Anderson (plus her "Someone Else"); Ruth Sedgwick's "Maxwell Anderson," *The Stage Magazine* XIV (Oct. 1936), 56; and my own visit to the site and to the remains of the cabin now moved to Terence's front yard. Some sources disagree as to whether the cabin contained a cot or a built-in bunk. There was a succession of stoves and evidence that electric lights might have been used at a later period. Hesper errs in "Someone Else" where she claims that the cabin was made of logs.
51. Lawrence and Meg Anderson. Alan Anderson letter to me, Jan. 15, 1972.
52. In Anderson's letter of Mar. 15, 1948, to Alan Paton, he confesses that *Cry, the Beloved Country* was the first novel he had read in many years (*Letters,* pp. 221-22). Alan Anderson wrote to me on Oct. 27, 1970: "And of course he read a great deal—biography and history—not novels."
53. Alan Anderson. Lela Chambers. Hesper in "Someone Else" makes much ado of his lying around in there most of the year, writing only about three months; what she means by this, however, as she told me in our

interview, is that while he was lying around he was also thinking a good deal about what he was going to write.

54. Sedgwick, p. 56.

55. Laurence G. Avery, "The Maxwell Anderson Papers," *The Library Chronicle of the University of Texas* VIII (Spring 1965), 26.

56. Maxwell Anderson, "Poetry in the Theatre," *Off Broadway Essays about the Theatre* (New York: William Sloane Associates, 1947), p. 50.

57. Avery in "The Maxwell Anderson Papers," pp. 29-31, provides a good description of what Anderson did in revision.

58. Alan Anderson.

59. Lillian Anderson letter to me, June 23, 1979 (combined with her husband, Lawrence's, letter of that date).

60. Alan Anderson.

61. Hesper Anderson in "Someone Else" and during her interview with me in California asserted emphatically that her mother had an important role as editor, that nothing he wrote was published without her prior approval. The business manager of Anderson House, who was Kenneth, says that Mab was useful to her husband in some editorial capacity but he could give me no details whatsoever. The only contemporary evidence of Mab's editorship that I have uncovered is a letter cited in *Catalogue,* p. 111, written by Anderson to Homer Fickett (c. 1940) explaining that the playwright's delay in sending along a manuscript was owing to his wife's feeling that the verse was not good enough. As stated later in this book, Mab felt that some passages in *Morning Winter and Night* needed softening—but Lotte Lenya, whom he consulted, thought so too—and there is no telling how much weight Mab's opinion carried in this instance because, though he toned down some passages in this novel that she considered shocking, he still left it shocking when it went to press.

62. Letter to me from Alan Anderson, Sept. 3, 1980, where he responds vehemently to Hesper's claim (see foregoing note), i.e., that it is "sheer nonsense" to believe Mab "had any part of writing anything he [Maxwell Anderson] ever put his name to." Gilda seems to be of the same opinion, also, for she wrote to me in a questionnaire dated Mar. 6, 1979, "There was only one Master Builder."

63. Letter from Maxwell Anderson to Arthur Hobson Quinn, May 4 [1927] (*Letters,* p. 29).

64. Letter from Maxwell Anderson to Elmer Rice, Apr. 20, 1956 (*Letters,* p. 280).

65. Avery, "The Maxwell Anderson Papers," p. 31.

66. Maxwell Anderson letter to Mrs. Florence B. Hult, Nov. 12, 1938 (*Letters,* p. 78).

67. Avery, "The Maxwell Anderson Papers," p. 30.

68. Maxwell Anderson letter to Dorothy Thompson, Sept. 8, 1940 (*Catalogue,* p. 128). When Elmer Rice proposed in 1938 that the Playwrights Producing Company form a repertory company to train actors and in other ways raise the level of the American theater, Anderson was similarly unenthusiastic—as were the other members of the company.—From Albert C. Gordon's Ph.D. dissertation "A Critical Study of the History and Development of The Playwrights Producing Company" (Tulane Univ., 1965), pp. 73-76, citing Rice's memorandum in Box 7 of the company's papers at the State Historical Society of Wisconsin, Madison, Wisc.

69. Further examples: In a letter to Paul Muni he disclosed that he had tried to interest Muni in a play about Napoleon, but the actor had rejected the project, whereupon Anderson announced that he would search about for some subject that would interest him. (Eventually, Muni starred in *Key Largo.*) He planned the never-finished *Duquesnes* for the Lunts. Next year he tried to interest Paul Robeson in a yet-to-be-written musical called *Aneas Africanus,* but Robeson turned him down, saying that he didn't want to help perpetuate the Uncle Tom stereotype implicit in the role of Aneas. Once Anderson had completed his *Joan of Lorraine* script, he went to the Hotel Bel-Air in Los Angeles to meet Ingrid Bergman and sign her to play the title role. For another piece, *Lilith and Eve,* he wanted Rex Harrison as his star. For his *Cytherea* he planned to use Helen Hayes, but he never got around to finishing it.—From Maxwell Anderson letters to Paul Muni (Dec. 31, 1938), to Guthrie McClintic (Mar. 5, 1938), and to Paul Robeson (Mar. 3, 1939) as included in *Letters;* the unsigned "Playwright Tells Why He Wrote 'Joan' and How He Signed His Star," *The New York Times,* Dec. 1, 1946, II, 3; miscellaneous Anderson letters to Bergman filed at the Univ. of Texas; and *Catalogue,* pp. 138-39.

70. *The New York Times,* Dec. 5, 1954, II, 7.

71. The figures for most early sales are not available, but he sold *Joan of Lorraine* for $250,000, *Bad Seed* for $300,000, and *The Eve of St. Mark* for $300,000. In these particular transactions he received only 60 percent of the selling price after subtracting the author's agent's 6½ percent and the negotiator's 3½ percent, the amount remaining going to the Playwrights Producing Company—from whose dividends he earned still more money.

72. "Someone Else," pp. 48-51.
73. Paul Green.
74. Maxwell Anderson, "'Cut is the Branch that Might Have Grown Full Straight,'" *Off Broadway*, pp. 67-73.
75. Maxwell Anderson letter to Mrs. Harriet Keehn, Apr. 21, 1934 (*Letters*, p. 48). Mrs. Keehn, employed by the Library of Congress, had volunteered to assist him in doing research for *Valley Forge*.
76. Letters from Maxwell Anderson to John C. Fitzpatrick, former archivist at Library of Congress, Mar. 12 [1934] and Mar. 16, 1934 (*Letters*, pp. 46-48 plus Avery's notes on p. 47).
77. Samuel Blaine Shirk in his *The Characterizations of George Washington in American Drama since 1875* (Easton, Pa.: J. S. Correll, 1949) is wrong where he assumes that Martha spent Jan. 1778 at Valley Forge, and that for this reason the Mrs. Morris incident is most unlikely. The incident is most unlikely for another reason entirely. Actually, Martha first arrived in early Feb., for which see James Thomas Flexner, *George Washington in the American Revolution, c. 1775-1783* (Boston: Little, Brown, 1968); also, Douglas Southall Freeman, *Washington*, abridged by Richard Harwell from the seven-vol. *George Washington* (New York: Scribner, 1968).
78. Produced at the Royale Theatre in New York City, Mar. 6, 1933. It ran for 120 performances. Published by Anderson House in 1934.
79. *Catalogue*, p. 24.
80. Maxwell Anderson letter to Walter Prichard Eaton, Feb. 9, 1934 (*Letters*, p. 45).
81. Walter Prichard Eaton, "He Put Poetry Back on the Stage," *New York Herald Tribune*, Jan. 28, 1934, VIII, 21.
82. Maxwell Anderson letter to Walter Prichard Eaton, Feb. 9, 1934 (*Letters*, pp. 45-46, and Avery's note No. 1 on p. 46).
83. As quoted in Anderson's Columbia memoir, p. 28. Letter from Gertrude (Mab) Anderson to Martin Maloney, Nov. 25, 1938 (Univ. of Texas collection).
84. Helen Deutsch, "When Drama and Poetry Wed, Was It to Last Forever After?" *New York Herald Tribune*, May 31, 1936, p. 1. But see Brooks Atkinson's review of *Mary of Scotland* in *The New York Times*, Dec. 3, 1933, IX, 1, where it appears that he might have had some influence on Anderson's decision to write *Winterset*.
85. *Catalogue*, p. 24.
86. *Winterset* in *Eleven Verse Plays*, p. 129 (Act III).
87. Deutsch, "When Drama and Poetry Wed . . .," p. 2. At the presentation

of the Drama Critics Circle Award on Apr. 5, 1936, Brooks Atkinson read a letter from Eugene O'Neill praising the group for selecting Anderson's " 'splendid contribution . . . to what is finest in the American theatre.' "—O'Neill's letter appeared in *The New York Times*, Apr. 5, 1936. *Winterset* had a first run of 179 performances in the Martin Beck Theatre and then was revived. Shortly later, an inferior motion picture was made from it, starring Burgess Meredith, that converted the story into melodrama.

88. *Winterset* in *Eleven Verse Plays,* p. 133 (Act III).
89. Letter from Frederick H. Koch to Maxwell Anderson, Nov. 3, 1937 (Univ. of Texas collection).
90. *High Tor* (Washington, D.C.: Anderson House, 1937). This edition contains drawings by Henry Varnum Poor. Anderson accepted the Drama Critics Circle Award on Apr. 1, 1937.
91. Unsigned, "Mounting High Tor," *The New York Times,* Feb. 14, 1937, X, 2. The writer of this article supplies no exact date for the climb, but one can easily calculate it from other information given there and in the *Catalogue.* The writer almost certainly was William Fields, a friend of Anderson as well as the press representative for the Playwrights Company.
92. Terence Anderson.
93. The beacon no longer stands on the mountain.
94. Barrett H. Clark and George Freedley, *A History of Modern Drama* (New York: D. Appleton-Century, 1947), p. 697.
95. *High Tor* in *Eleven Verse Plays,* p. 105 (Act II, Scene 2).
96. Some ways in which Van Van Dorn resembles Thoreau include (1) a dislike of routine or conventional employment; (2) pride in being able to earn enough for his annual support by working only a few weeks in the year; (3) ability to make the land completely sustain him; (4) unhappy experience at working in a factory—see Thoreau's stint in the family pencil factory; (5) belief that no one should sacrifice the best days of one's life so that he can earn money to retire on later; (6) many skills, especially manual ones; (7) interest in Indian legends; (8) admiration for the natural beauty of the wilderness; (9) love for wild animals; (10) dislike for government; (11) scorn for unnecessary travel (a trait Max shared); (12) contentment in a cabin life as a bachelor—until Judith arrives; (13) solitary existence; (14) dwelling alongside a body of water; (15) departure from that dwelling place while one is still young.

When I asked Lela during the interview in Olean, N.Y., whether

Anderson had read and talked about Thoreau, she immediately responded: "Yes, he did. I can remember when we studied—one of the teachers in New Hampton high school was very fond of Thoreau, and I remember when she taught that course, that's one thing that we [Max and she] did discuss. We were both interested in him."

97. Letters to me from Alan Anderson, Jan. 15, 1972, and Apr. 24, 1974.
98. Letters to me from Alan Anderson, Apr. 24, 1974, and Jan. 1, 1975; also, letter to me from Kenneth Anderson, July 28, 1980. I had queried the Anderson relatives because of a statement made by Danton Walker in his undocumented *Spooks Deluxe: Some Excursions into the Supernatural* (New York: Franklin Watts, 1956), p. 166. There Walker writes that Max Anderson neither knew Van Orden nor climbed his mountain before writing the drama. Both Alan and Terence are openly scornful of what Walker had said!
99. Letter to me from Quentin Anderson, May 17, 1971. Also, my interviews with him and his brother Alan.
100. As quoted in "Mounting High Tor," X, 2.
101. Unsigned, "Elmer Van Orden, 79, Is Dead; High Tor Owner Inspired Play," *New York Herald Tribune,* Feb. 20, 1942.
102. Quote and other information about the ghost come from Danton Walker, pp. 166-67; supplemented by Jane McDill Anderson, *Rocklandia,* p. 60. In her letter to me, Sept. 4, 1979, from Nyack, N.Y., this Mrs. Anderson said that she had gotten the tale from her friend Hume Dixon (now dead) and then told it to Danton Walker.

In addition to "Mounting High Tor," I used these other *Times* articles about Van Orden and sometimes his mountain: "Neighbors Honor Owner of High Tor," June 16, 1939, I, 25; "The Savior of High Tor," June 17, 1939, I, 14; Charles Grutzner, "Look-Out Park on High Tor," Aug. 5, 1956, II, 25. *New York Herald Tribune* articles include "Elmer Van Orden, 79, Is Dead; High Tor Owner Inspired Play," Feb. 20, 1942; "Hudson Society Buys High Tor for Park Use," Feb. 17, 1943; Francis Sugrue, "High Tor Sold with Its Ghosts and Old House," Feb. 10, 1950, (refers to sale of house and of the land surrounding but not including the summit, which was already donated for park use). And from the *Nyack* (N.Y.) *Journal News:* "High Tor Land Is Bought by River Group," Feb. 17, 1943; "Palisades Park System Takes Title to High Tor . . .," Apr. 14, 1943. Also, booklet titled "Palisades Interstate Park 1900-1960" (n. d.) issued by Palisades Interstate Park Commission, Bear Mountain, N.Y.

CBS television presented on Mar. 10, 1956, a musical version of

High Tor, with text and librettos by Anderson and music by Arthur Schwartz. Bing Crosby, Everett Sloane, and Julie Andrews sang the following songs: "Living One Day at a Time," "When You're in Love," "Sad Is the Life of the Sailor's Wife," "A Little Love, A Little While," "John Barleycorn," and "Once Upon a Long Ago." Decca published this music in a phonograph recording.

103. *Letters,* p. xlviii.

104. *The Feast of Ortolans* was published in *The Stage Magazine* XV (Jan. 1938), 71-78.

105. "A Confession," p. 7. *The Star-Wagon* was produced at the Empire Theatre in New York City, on Sept. 29, 1937. It ran for 223 performances.

106. Lawrence Anderson notes written to me on Sept. 15, 1978; also, my interview with him. Alan Anderson letter to me, Jan. 15, 1972. Meg Anderson.

107. *The Star-Wagon* (Washington, D.C.: Anderson House, 1937), p. 73 (Act II, Scene 2).

108. Alan Anderson letters to me, Nov. 23, 1970, and Jan. 15, 1972. He says that Stephen is a composite.

109. The mink ranch fiasco is covered in Stanley Oliver's letter to Maxwell Anderson, Aug. 12, 1937; Mab's letter to Carl C. Marcum (Suffern, N.Y.), Oct. 15, 1940; and a series of letters from Dorothy Elizabeth (Beth) to Maxwell Anderson in July, Sept., Nov., and Dec. 1946, and in Apr. and June 1947 (Univ. of Texas collection). Also, interviews with Lawrence, Quentin, Alan, and Nancy Anderson. In addition, Lela's "Life," p. 102.

110. The most extended published study of this company is John F. Wharton's *Life Among the Playwrights: Being Mostly the Story of the Playwrights Producing Company, Inc.* (New York: Quadrangle, 1974). It is popularized and for the most part undocumented but based on numerous records that Wharton had kept in his role as lawyer for the firm. Anderson published two articles about this remarkable organization: "About the Playwrights' Company," *The Stage Magazine* XVI (Dec. 1938), 16-17, and "The Playwrights' Birthday," *The New York Times,* Oct. 10, 1948, II, 3. His friend S. N. Behrman wrote a chapter titled "Playwrights Company" in his *People in a Diary: A Memoir* (Boston: Little, Brown, 1972), pp. 212-28. (The book came out in England under the title *Tribulations and Laughter: A Memoir.*) Elmer Rice provides some coverage in his *Minority Report: An Autobiography* (New York: Simon & Schuster, 1963) in the chapter called "Fellow-

ship," pp. 374-95. Also, see Jack Alton Hensley, "The Playwrights' Company," masters thesis (Univ. of Wisc., 1952), based on some interviews with company members; Clyde Harold Bassett, "The Playwrights' Producing Company, Inc., 1938-1960," Ph.D. dissertation (Univ. of Wisc., 1965); Albert Claude Gordon, "A Critical Study of the History and Development of the Playwrights' Producing Company," Ph.D. dissertation (Tulane Univ., 1965); and Kay Irene Johnson, "Playwrights as Patriots: A History of the Playwrights Producing Company, 1938-1960," Ph.D. dissertation (Univ. of Wisc., 1974). These dissertations were based partly on a study of the company papers on file at the Wisconsin Center for Film and Theatre Research, housed in the State Historical Society of Wisconsin, Madison, Wisc.

111. *Life Among the Playwrights,* p. 10.
112. Scott Meredith, *George S. Kaufman and His Friends* (Garden City, N.Y.: Doubleday, 1974), p. 390. *Minority Report,* p. 180.
113. As quoted from Rice's remarks in *Life Among the Playwrights,* pp. 9-10.
114. Scott Meredith, pp. 393-94. *Life Among the Playwrights,* p. 16.
115. Theresa Helburn, *A Wayward Quest: The Autobiography of Theresa Helburn* (Boston: Little, Brown, 1960), pp. 310-11.
116. J. A. Hensley, pp. 13-14. A. C. Gordon, pp. 18-21. The New Playwrights are discussed also in John Gassner, *Masters of the Drama* (New York: Random House, 1954) and in Elmer Rice's *The Living Theatre* (New York: Harper & Brothers, 1959).
117. *Minority Report,* pp. 374-75.
118. *Life Among the Playwrights,* p. 98.
119. Allan Lewis, *American Plays and Playwrights of the Contemporary Theatre* (New York: Crown Publishers, 1965), p. 134.
120. Donald Heiney and Lenthiel H. Downs, *Recent American Literature after 1930* (Woodbury, N.Y.: Barron's Educational Series, 1974), p. 302.
121. "Behrman, S(amuel) N(athaniel)," *Modern World Drama: An Encyclopedia,* ed. Myron Matlaw (New York: E. P. Dutton, 1972), p. 72.
122. In addition to the works already cited, Behrman is discussed in Bernard Dukore, ed. et al., "S. N. Behrman," *McGraw-Hill Encyclopedia of World Drama* I (New York: McGraw-Hill, 1972); Joseph Wood Krutch, *The American Drama since 1918,* rev. ed. (New York: George Braziller, 1957); Arthur Hobson Quinn, *A History of the American Drama from the Civil War to the Present Day,* rev. ed. (New York: Appleton-Century-Crofts, 1936); Gerald Rabkin, *Drama and Commitment Politics in the American Theatre of the Thirties* (Bloomington, Ind.: Ind. Univ. Press, 1964); and Gerald Weales, *American Drama*

since World War II (New York: Harcourt, Brace & World, 1962).

123. *Life Among the Playwrights,* pp. 67, 69-71.

124. Ibid., pp. 74-75. Studies of Howard occur in "Sidney Howard," *McGraw-Hill Encyclopedia of World Drama* II; Donald Heiney, *Recent American Literature* (Woodbury, N.Y.: Barron's Educational Series, 1958); Krutch; and Quinn.

125. *Life Among the Playwrights,* p. 97.

126. Ibid., pp. 5, 52. Book-length studies of Rice are: Frank Durham, *Elmer Rice* (New York: Twayne, 1970) and Robert Hogan, *The Independence of Elmer Rice* (Carbondale and Edwardsville, Ill.: Southern Ill. Univ. Press, 1965). Shorter studies include "Elmer Rice," *McGraw-Hill* Encyclopedia of World Drama III; Jean Gould, "Elmer Rice," *Modern American Playwrights* (New York: Dodd, Mead, 1966); Donald Heiney, *Recent American Literature;* Krutch; Lewis; Quinn; Rabkin; and Weales. Rice died in 1967.

127. Walter J. Meserve, *Robert E. Sherwood: Reluctant Moralist* (New York: Pegasus, 1970), p. ix.

128. In addition to Meserve's *Robert E. Sherwood . . .,* the book-length studies of this playwright include John Mason Brown's *The Worlds of Robert E. Sherwood: Mirror to His Times 1896–1939* (New York: Harper & Row, 1962) and the posthumous volume *The Ordeal of a Playwright: Robert E. Sherwood and the Challenge of War* (New York: Harper & Row, 1970); also, R. Baird Shuman's *Robert E. Sherwood* (New York: Twayne, 1964). Shorter studies are "Robert E. Sherwood," *McGraw-Hill Encyclopedia of World Drama* IV; S. N. Behrman, "Old Monotonous," *The New Yorker* XVI (June 1, 1940), 33-36, 40-41, and (June 8, 1940), 23-26, 28, 30, 33; Gould; Heiney, *Recent American Literature;* Krutch. Sherwood died in 1955.

129. From the dust jacket of *Life Among the Playwrights.*

130. *Minority Report,* p. 375.

131. In John F. Wharton's letter to me, Sept. 4, 1975, he said "ten." I accept "eleven," as given in *Life Among the Playwrights,* because of the law of priority—memory can slip with age. His book about the company contains a short sketch of his life. Additional information taken from the dust jacket.

132. Unsigned, "The Lives of John F. Wharton," *Fortune* XXXIII (May 1946), 192, 194.

133. A. C. Gordon, pp. 46-47.

134. *Life Among the Playwrights,* p. 28. *Minority Report,* p. 376.

135. Wharton in *Life Among the Playwrights,* pp. 28-29, is not clear

about the whole financial arrangement, and the Basic Agreement which he reprints in the appendix is difficult for the layman to interpret. Good interpretations occur in C. H. Bassett, pp. 4-5, and in K. I. Johnson, p. 60, but there are slight discrepancies between these two accounts with respect to the distribution of net profits. I have accepted Bassett's figures. In addition to net profits from the company, the playwright with a show running received 10 percent of the gross weekly box-office receipts. And if he sold a play to the movies or radio or television, he got over 50 percent of the sale price.

136. From the Basic Agreement in *Life Among the Playwrights,* p. 270.
137. J.A. Hensley, pp. 39, 55.
138. *Minority Report,* p. 377.
139. *Life Among the Playwrights,* p. 27.
140. Maxwell Anderson, "Author Looks Back over Ten Years and Concludes that the Hopes of His Company Have Been Fulfilled," *The New York Times,* Oct. 10, 1948, II, 3. In this article Anderson quotes some things he had published in "About the Playwrights' Company," *The Stage Magazine* XVI (Dec. 1938), 17.
141. Anderson, "A Confession," p. 7.
142. Maxwell Anderson letter to Robert E. Sherwood [Mar. 8, 1938], *Letters,* p. 70.
143. As quoted in Ronald Sanders, *The Days Grow Short: The Life and Music of Kurt Weill* (New York: Holt, Rinehart and Winston, 1980), p. 271, who in turn took the quotations from William Field's blurb in a souvenir program of *Knickerbocker Holiday* filed in the Univ. of Texas collection.
144. Unsigned, "Dutch in the Forties," *The New York Times,* Sept. 25, 1938, IX, 1.
145. Joshua Logan, *My Up and Down, In and Out Life* (New York: Delacorte Press, 1976), p. 129. Ronald Sanders, p. 272.
146. My interview with Mrs. Lotte Lenya at her home in New City, N.Y., May 15, 1978.
147. Alan Anderson.
148. As quoted in Logan, p. 129; the material about the recognition scene coming from pp. 133-34. Richard Charles Rodgers (b. 1902), musical composer, and Lorenz Milton Hart (1895-1943), lyricist, were extremely popular then for their collaborations. Rodgers later collaborated successfully with Oscar Hammerstein II.
149. Ronald Sanders, p. 274.
150. *Life Among the Playwrights,* p. 40.

151. As quoted in Joshua Logan, p. 130. Walter Huston recalled the California get-together in his article "There's No Place Like Broadway Be It Ever So Noisy," *The Stage Magazine* XV (Oct. 1938), 22-26.
152. As quoted in Ronald Sanders, pp. 275-76. This roughly corresponds with what Lotte Lenya told me during my interview. Also, Naomi Jolles, "Hitler Hates Weill's Songs," *New York Post,* Oct. 20, 1943, p. 43.
153. Lotte Lenya, Naomi Jolles, p. 43.
154. Joshua Logan, p. 131. Quotation same as found in Logan.
155. Anderson, "A Confession," p. 7.
156. *Minority Report,* p. 383. Lotte Lenya.
157. Maxwell Anderson, *Knickerbocker Holiday* (Washington, D.C.: Anderson House, 1938).
158. *Minority Report,* p. 380.
159. Joshua Logan, p. 132.
160. Unsigned, "Roosevelt at Operetta, Laughs at Sallies of 'Peter Stuyvesant' Twitting Government," *The New York Times,* Oct. 16, 1938, I, 3. President Roosevelt's telegram to Hitler and Benes received front-page notice in *The New York Times,* Sept. 26, 1938.
161. Joshua Logan, p. 133.
162. "A condensed version of *Knickerbocker Holiday,* starring Walter Huston in his Stuyvesant role, was produced for radio in 1939 by the Theatre Guild on the Air; this was recorded, and a limited number of copies has long been in existence. In about 1976 a producer called Joey Discs in Lawton, Maryland, issued a simulated stereo edition of this recording (Joey-7243), which could be found in record stores for a brief time. This, of course, is one of several discs that reproduce Huston's splendid rendition of 'September Song': it includes six of the show's other numbers besides. . . . One should also mention Bing Crosby's 78 rpm recording of the 'September Song' (Decca 23754, 10"), which helped make it famous."—Ronald Sanders, p. 447.
163. Lela's "Life," p. 52.
164. *Letters,* pp. 22n, 127. Anderson letter to Lela and Dan Chambers, Aug. 17, 1942. Lela Chambers. Letters from Avery (who was at Drake University) to Anderson, Sept. 21, 1940; June 11, 1941 (Univ. of Texas collection).
165. *Letters,* p. 22n. Anderson Columbia memoir, p. 20.
166. Undated letters (c. 1940) from Anderson to Ethel Chambers (Hinsdale, N.Y.). Anderson letter to Ralph and Ethel Chambers, Oct. 15, 1940 (*Catalogue,* p. 109).

167. Kenneth Anderson letter to Maxwell Anderson, Jan. 19, 1940 (Univ. of Texas collection).
168. Kenneth Anderson.
169. Letters from James E. Haskett to Maxwell Anderson: one letter dated May 10, 1934; another undated (Univ. of Texas collection). Maxwell Anderson letter to his secretary Alfred Sturt, Jan. 18, 1935 (Univ. of Texas collection).
170. Letter from Libbe Higger Axlrod to me, Oct. 10, 1978. "Someone Else," p. 36.
171. Mrs. Julie Sloane.
172. "Someone Else," p. 12.
173. Alan, Nancy, Meg, and Quentin Anderson.
174. Maxwell Anderson letter to Margery Bailey, Apr. 9, 1936 (*Letters*, p. 55, 59n). In his letter of [Nov. 25, 1936] to her he set down a set of rules characteristic of his own technique:

> Play structure is much more important that playwriting, even in a poetic play. Look well to the emotional stress at the end of the second act, and take care that this stress emerges from the characters in the situation, not from the situation alone. Read Aristotle on the "recognition scene," the most important point in any dramatic structure. Avoid the imitation of verse mannerisms from another age, avoid archaisms, save rarely for historical color. Write the living language, even though in verse; try for limpidity, clarity of meaning and, above all, accuracy of metaphor. The accurate metaphor, instantly recognizable, is the test of good poetry for the stage. Use words carefully. Remember that every word you write is magnified by ten diameters when spoken on the stage. Never choose a soft or sentimental subject for poetic treatment. The more beauty and ornament your style carries, the sturdier must be the skeleton of plot and thinking underneath. Spend three times the effort planning your play which you will require to write it.—From *Letters*, p. 58.

175. Maxwell Anderson letter to Margery Bailey [Nov. 25, 1936] (*Letters*, pp. 57n, 58).

CHAPTER 7

1. *Letters,* p. 1; *Catalogue,* p. 64.
2. Kay I. Johnson in "Playwrights as Patriots . . .," p. 120, writes without offering supporting evidence, that Sherwood probably wrote both speeches. Excerpts from both were printed in the unsigned "Benefit Performance for German Refugees," *The New York Times,* Nov. 21, 1938, I, 4; also in Avery's article "Maxwell Anderson and *Both Your Houses*" (see note No. 4 for this chapter).
3. Entry for Sept. 21, 1938, as reprinted in Brown's *The Worlds of Robert E. Sherwood,* p. 384.
4. Laurence G. Avery, "Maxwell Anderson and *Both Your Houses,*" *North Dakota Quarterly* XXXVIII (Winter 1970), 21. The typescript speech is in the Anderson collection at the Univ. of Texas.
5. Brown, *The Worlds of Robert E. Sherwood,* p. 385.
6. Maxwell Anderson letter to Kate Klugston, Nov. 13, 1939 (Univ. of Texas collection).
7. At the Ethel Barrymore Theatre on Nov. 27, 1939. It had a run of 105 performances, starring Paul Muni in the lead role. John Steinbeck wrote to Maxwell Anderson that audiences in Oslo, Norway, greeted *Key Largo* with considerable enthusiasm when he (Steinbeck) was there.—From Steinbeck's letter [c. Nov. 29, 1946] (Univ. of Texas collection).
8. Maxwell Anderson, "Whatever Hope We Have," *Off Broadway Essays about the Theatre,* p. 38. This work was the Founders Day Address that he delivered at Carnegie Institute in 1937.
9. *Letters,* p. li, where Avery alludes to a Maxwell Anderson letter to Collier Young, June 30, 1939.
10. Maxwell Anderson letter to Brooks Atkinson, Aug. 21, 1939 (*Letters,* pp. 90-91).
11. Avery, "Maxwell Anderson and *Both Your Houses,*" p. 24.
12. *Letters,* p. li; *Catalogue,* p. 23.
13. Walter Johnson, *The Battle against Isolation* (New York: Da Capo Press, 1973), pp. 85-87, 97. *Life Among the Playwrights,* pp. 108-10.
14. *Catalogue,* p. 36.
15. Ibid. Also, *Life Among the Playwrights,* p. 112.
16. Maxwell Anderson, *Journey to Jerusalem* (Washington, D.C.: Anderson House, 1940).

17. *Life Among the Playwrights,* p. 112.
18. Edward A. Wright, *A Primer for Playgoers* (Englewood Cliffs, N.J.: Prentice-Hall, 1958), pp. 203-4.
19. First published in *The Free Company Presents: A Collection of Plays about the Meaning of America* (New York: Dodd, Mead, 1941), pp. 239-67. Reprinted in *The Best Short Plays,* ed. Margaret Mayorga (Boston: Beacon Press, 1957), pp. 115-30.
20. "Someone Else," p. 19.
21. "Stanzas from the Grande Chartreuse."
22. *Candle in the Wind* came out in 1941 under the imprint of Anderson House.
23. Julie Sloane.
24. From Howard Whitman's "Art Defense Post Raked by Poetry," published in an unidentified regional newspaper on Aug. 14, 1943. Also: Unsigned, "To Cut Civil Defense Work or Not to Cut it is the Literary Question up Rockland Way" from an unidentified regional newspaper c. Aug. 1943. Clippings forwarded to me by Julie Sloane. Robert Rice, p. 25. Maxwell Anderson letter to Viola Paradise, Feb. 28, 1942 (Univ. of Texas collection).
25. Sgt. Lloyd Shearer, "Pertaining to Local Color," *The New York Times,* Oct. 4, 1942, VIII, 1. Error: Bushemi was still a private then.
26. Contrary to what Avery writes in *Letters,* p. liii, Anderson arrived at Fort Bragg in March rather than in February 1942; almost certainly it was during the first week of the month, probably Wednesday, March 4. He spent five days there, left Fayetteville, N.C., the following Monday or Tuesday, and arrived back in New City by Wednesday, March 11. During the spring, Anderson visited at least two war camps, including Fort Bragg and Camp Butner, N.C.—*Letters,* p. liii.
27. "Someone Else," pp. 64-78.
28. Lela's "Life," p. 131. Photocopy of p. 6 from Olean, N.Y. *Clark Angle,* a trade paper, forwarded to me courtesy of Lela Chambers. Unsigned, "Dead Soldier 'Lives' Again in Play Nephew Becomes Anderson's Model," *Buffalo Evening News,* Oct. [14], 1942—From copy of news clipping supplied to me courtesy of Lela Chambers. Lee Chambers, who inspired the play, died Nov. 1, 1941. And on May 31, 1944, his brother Lt. Keith M. Chambers was reported killed in action over Italy (he was a pilot).
29. Maxwell Anderson, "Foreword" to Marion Hargrove's *See Here, Private Hargrove* (New York: Henry Holt, 1942), pp. ix-xi. Marion Lawton Hargrove was born on Oct. 13, 1919. In addition to the book named

above, he wrote *Something's Got to Give* (1948), which satirizes the radio industry; and *The Girl He Left Behind* (1956), which is an entertaining account of draftees. He wrote to me on Nov. 6, 1980, that Anderson's "Foreword" to *See Here, Private Hargrove* is a "playful and open adaptation of material in the book itself."

30. Hargrove's letter to me dated June 20, 1978. Also, letter to me from Thomas James Montgomery Mulvehill (Arlington, Va.), Oct. 31, 1978.

31. Letter to me from Hargrove, Sept. 8, 1980.

32. Quote occurs in letter from Maxwell Anderson to William M. Sloane [March 1942]. Copy of the letter given to me by Hargrove, who in turn received it from Mrs. Julie Sloane. No doubt the quote is a paraphrase of Christ's injunction to his disciples in Matthew 10:16, "Behold, I send you forth as sheep in the midst of wolves: Be ye therefore as wise as serpents, and harmless as doves."

33. Hargrove's letter to me, June 20, 1978. I first learned of Bushemi's death, which occurred in Feb. 1944, by chancing upon a news clipping that I found among the Playwrights Producing Company papers at the State Historical Society of Wisconsin.

34. Marion Hargrove letter to me, June 20, 1978. Unless otherwise indicated, materials that I use for the Fort Bragg experience came from the letters and other papers that Hargrove kindly furnished to me.

35. Ibid.

36. Ibid. Plus Hargrove's letter to me, dated Aug. 9, 1978. Details of how the men usually got Bushemi out of his bunk are described in *See Here, Private Hargrove*, pp. 150-53. This book is factual reportage.

37. Quoted and summarized from Marion Hargrove's "Poor Sergeant Donald Bishop Is Broken on the Wheel of Fortune," which appeared in *The Charlotte* (N.C.) *News* [Apr.], 1942.—Copy furnished to me courtesy of Marion Hargrove.

38. Letter to me from Thomas James Montgomery Mulvehill, Oct. 31, 1978.

39. Maxwell Anderson letter to William M. Sloane [Mar. 1942]. In 1946, Sloane founded the publishing company known as William Sloane Associates.

40. A 10-page, typed carbon copy is in the Univ. of Texas collection. Never published. Anderson's letter to General Edwin P. Parker is dated Mar. 11, 1942 (*Letters*, p. 120). In a note on p. 120 of *Letters* we read that Hargrove assisted in the composition of "From Reveille to Breakfast," but Hargrove denies having any part of it.—Marion Hargrove's letter to me, Oct. 6, 1980.

41. In Anderson's letter to Hesper—May 11 [1943]—he reminds her of the time that she was "learning 'The Eve of St. Mark.' " On that same page in *Letters* (p. 158n), Laurence Avery remarks that the poem was important in the inception of *The Eve of St. Mark*.
42. Maxwell Anderson, *The Eve of St. Mark* (Washington, D.C.: Anderson House, 1942).
43. This much about the visit to New York may be safely deduced from Sgt. Lloyd Shearer's "Pertaining to Local Color."
44. Maxwell Anderson letter to Marion Hargrove, May 15, 1942 (letter owned by Hargrove; he excerpted the passage for me). Robert Rice, who interviewed Anderson, wrote in his article that the drama was based on real people.
45. In "The Maxwell Anderson Papers," Avery writes (p. 23) that letters from Hargrove and Mulvehill to Anderson show personalities matching their counterparts in *The Eve of St. Mark*. The idea of the "Holding Company" found in Anderson's "Foreword" to Hargrove's book turns up in the book per se as well as in the play.

    After the war, Hargrove became a scriptwriter for motion pictures and television and now makes his home in Santa Monica, Calif. Shearer became editor of the Sunday newspaper supplement "Parade" and now lives in Los Angeles. Sher became owner and operator of the Maramor restaurant in Columbus, O.; at present, he is a stockbroker in Santa Monica, Calif.
46. Alan Anderson letter to me, May 5, 1973.
47. *Catalogue,* p. 39.
48. Typed letter in the Playwrights Producing Company papers at the State Historical Society of Wisconsin, box 45. The letter was written on Apr. 11, 1943 (year mistyped as 1942). R. Graeme Smith served as a first lieutenant in the U.S. Marine Corps, after the war became an attorney with the firm of Alcorn, Bakewell, and Smith of Hartford, Conn., and to the end of his life was deeply involved with theater and the academic community. Permission to reprint his letter is granted by his widow, Mrs. Ellen Smith (Hartford, Conn.).
49. Maxwell Anderson letter to Dr. Lee Norvelle, June 22, 1942 (*Letters,* pp. 122-24). Dr. Norvelle, of the Speech and Theatre Department at Indiana University, would become president of the National Theater Conference later that year. This conference had been formed in 1932 to "encourage the development of the noncommercial theater in America, [and] was seeking production rights to new plays by established playwrights in an effort to break the hold of Broadway

on new play production. Paul Green, current president of the NTC, and Norvelle had begun the effort by negotiating with Anderson for the rights to his next play, *The Eve of St. Mark*."—Avery's note, *Letters*, p. 124. No doubt Anderson's trip to Chapel Hill in 1942 had such negotiations as its purpose.

50. Maxwell Anderson letter to John Mason Brown [Oct. 1937] (*Letters*, pp. 60-62).

51. Maxwell Anderson, "More Thoughts about Dramatic Critics," *New York Herald Tribune*, Oct. 10, 1948.

52. Ibid. Also, Anderson's "Stage Money," p. 24.

53. *Minority Report*, pp. 376, 380. The cost of producing *Knickerbocker Holiday* that year was $60,000, however, because it was a musical play—and that genre costs more.

54. By 1950, a costume play with multiple settings was to cost about $100,000; and a lavish musical, $250,000.—Glen Hughes, *A History of the American Theatre 1700–1950* (New York: Samuel French, 1951), p. 484. By 1959, the year of Anderson's death, the cost for a one-set play was commonly $100,000, and for a musical close to $500,000.— Howard Taubman, *The Making of the American Theatre* (New York: Coward McCann, 1965), p. 289.

55. *Life Among the Playwrights,* p. 124.

56. "The Eve of St. Mark is a Very Moving Play," *New York World-Telegram,* Oct. 8, 1942.

57. Robert Rice, p. 25.

58. Stark Young, "War Theatre," *New Republic* CVII (Oct. 26, 1942), 546. Jordan Y. Miller, "Maxwell Anderson: Gifted Technician," *The Thirties: Fiction, Poetry, Drama,* ed. Warren French (Deland, Fla.: Everett Edwards, 1967), p. 191.

59. Robert Rice, p. 24. Anderson, however, did see at least one of the later Broadway productions; this was in the company of Dr. Lee Norvelle. —Norvelle's letter to me, Jan. 18, 1973.

60. Maxwell Anderson's diary entry for Feb. 17, 1950. *Life Among the Playwrights,* pp. 124-25. Terence Anderson. Maxwell Anderson letter to Lawrence Anderson, Nov. 28, 1956.

61. This as well as the next preceding quote taken from Robert Rice, p. 26.

62. *Letters,* p. liv. Speech reported in *New York Herald Tribune,* Jan. 13, 1943, p. 1.

63. Maxwell Anderson letter to Russel Crouse and Clifton Fadiman, Mar. 29, 1942 (*Letters,* p. 121 and note).

64. *Letters,* pp. liv, lv, 128, 129n. Photographs from the overseas trip

show him wearing the distinctive uniform of an army officer minus the insignia of rank.

65. This letter of Apr. 14, 1943 was written in journal form on continuous sheets along with those letters dated 15th, 16th, 17th, and 18th. Anderson employed this method because it was impossible to send mail regularly. Note: All letters reproduced here from the trip derive from the published Avery collection.

66. William Wyler (b. 1902), an American movie director, was at that time a major in the U.S. Army making documentary war films.—From Avery's note.

67. Heavy American bombers began to operate out of England starting in Aug. 1942, and by the time Anderson made his visit the AAF and the RAF were assaulting Germany day and night. The Americans, committed to high-altitude precision bombing, took the risk of using the daylight hours for their flights and counted on their massed armament to fend off enemy fighter interception over the target. But the practice of going by day proved too costly, just as the British had warned (for example, the AAF lost 153 aircraft in one week in October 1943), whereupon they discontinued such daylight raids until the P-51 Mustang fighter appeared. The Mustang, with its long-range flying capability, could escort bombers far into Germany.—C. L. Sulzberger et al. (eds.), *The American Heritage Picture History of World War II* (New York: American Heritage, 1966), p. 423.

68. Gabriel Pascal (1894-1954). Hungarian director-producer who went to England in the 1930s and filmed several George Bernard Shaw plays. Now he was going back to England to prepare war documentaries.—From Avery's note.

69. This was J. Arthur Rank (b. 1888), a magnate who directed about a hundred companies in America and Great Britain. These included motion-picture companies.—From Avery's note.

70. Neither Mab nor Hesper joined him.

71. Albert Henry Garretson (b. 1910), who had formerly taught law at Colgate University, was presently in the Economic Warfare Division of the American Embassy in London. After 1946 he served as a professor of law at New York University (Washington Square); also, he worked in several State Department and United Nations posts. Ensley Llewellyn edited the military paper *Stars and Stripes.*—From Avery's note.

72. Ellen Drew (b. 1915). American actress, mainly known for her motion-picture roles.—From Avery's note.

73. Victor A. Rapport (b. 1903). A former sociology professor, he was

then a major in the U.S. Army based in London. Later he became a dean at Wayne State University in Detroit.—From Avery's note.

74. Avery identifies the "air picture" as perhaps *The Memphis Belle,* released by Paramount Pictures in 1944.

75. The U.S. Army produced the play under Russell Lane's direction in 1943 at the Scala Theatre in London, with free admission to Allied service personnel and the civilians who accompanied them. It ran from July 4 into December (*Letters,* p. 297).

76. Terence [Mervyn] Rattigan (b. 1911), English playwright and author of some of the most popular comedies of the era. *Flare Path* is a war play. At the time Anderson met him he was serving with the RAF.

77. Herbert S. Agar (b. 1897), special assistant to the U.S. Ambassador in London. Agar was an American journalist who had won the Pulitzer Prize for his book *People's Choice* (1933).—Avery's note.

78. Bernard Delfort produced *The Wingless Victory* at the Phoenix Theatre in London on Sept. 8, 1943, with Michael Redgrave directing. Viennese Wanda Rotha played Oparre; her husband, Manning Whiley, played Nathaniel McQuestion. *A Month in the Country* is Emlyn Williams' adaptation of a novel by Turgenev. *Rain,* first produced in 1922, was written by John Colton and Clemence Randolph and based on W. Somerset Maugham's short story "Miss Thompson."—From Avery's note.

79. Reprinted in *Letters,* pp. 297-98.

80. On May 7, 1943, the British First Army under Gen. Harold L. R. Alexander entered Tunis, and the U.S. II Corps entered Bizerte, together trapping three Axis divisions; within a few days all organized enemy resistance stopped in North Africa. The big victories at Tunis and Bizerte marked the end of the German and Italian occupation of North Africa and prepared the way for the Allied invasion of Sicily later that year.

81. "For one of its periodic cleanings."—Avery's note.

82. This is the first of fourteen letters that Anderson wrote in journal form to Mab. In this first entry, dated Sunday, May 30, he summarizes his trip to Algiers from London. On Tuesday evening, May 25, he had left London by train and arrived in Alloway, Scotland, the following morning. That evening he left Alloway by plane and arrived the following morning at Marrakech, Morocco, where he stayed the day and night. On Friday, May 28, he took a flight to Algiers, stopping

along the way at Fez and Casablanca in Morocco, and at Oran, Algeria.—From Avery's note.

83. Mail censorship caused him to be vague about his movements, but this visit was to Alloway, Scotland, the birthplace of Robert Burns. The quoted line is from Burns' "Tam o'Shanter."—From Avery's note.

84. Oliver H. P. Garrett (1898-1952), who had been a newspaperman before the war. He wrote such film scripts as *A Farewell to Arms, Moby Dick* and *A Duel in the Sun,* and he won an Academy Award for his 1934 *Manhattan Melodrama.* Garrett early attacked the Nazis in his play *Waltz in Goose Step* (1938).—From Avery's note.

85. Charles Douglas Jackson (1902-64) had been assistant to the U.S. Ambassador to Turkey, 1942-43; during the period 1943-45 he had various government jobs, including one in the Office of War Information. In 1952-53 he was President Eisenhower's special assistant; in 1954 the U.S. delegate to the Ninth U.N. General Assembly.—From Avery's note.

86. Harry Cecil Butcher (b. 1901) was prior to the war an agricultural expert and CBS radio executive. He became a naval aide to General Eisenhower in 1943. In his book *My Three Years with Eisenhower* (1946) he tells of his association.—From Avery's note.

87. Sergeant Simeon Snider and First Sergeant Peter Hromchak.—From Avery's note.

88. The visit occurred on Tuesday morning, June 1, 1943, and is recorded in the ledger containing the manuscript of *Storm Operation.* In Avery's words, "The interview shows Eisenhower's enthusiasm for Anglo-American cooperation and Anderson's intention to make the interplay of diverse cultures his theme."—*Catalogue,* p. 41.

89. Atabrine is a synthetic antimalarial drug used in lieu of the quinine that was scarce during the war. The netting came from Sergeant Simeon Snider, the pills from Sergeant Peter Hromchak.—From Avery's note.

90. John L. Lewis (1880-1969), the president of the United Mine Workers, threatened to have his men strike if they did not get a pay increase that exceeded the wage/price control figure set by the government. In May and June 1943, some locals in the UMW did strike, and it took direct orders from President Roosevelt to send them back to work.—From Avery's note.

91. Air Marshal Arthur W. (Lord) Tedder (1891-1967) had been commander of the English RAF in the Middle East since the war began and was now deputy supreme commander of the Allied forces under Eisenhower.

92. On June 11, 1943, the Allies captured the Italian-held island of Pantelleria, about halfway between Tunisia and Sicily. Lampedusa, south of Sicily, surrendered the following day. The fall of these islands was preliminary to the invasion of Sicily.

93. *Letters,* p. 178n.

94. Lewis Nichols' review in *The New York Times,* Jan. 12, 1944, II, 28. Also, Rosamond Gilder's review in *Theatre Arts* XXVIII (Mar. 1944), 133.

95. Maxwell Anderson letter to General Dwight D. Eisenhower [Nov. 1943] (*Letters,* pp. 184-85). Anderson enclosed a copy of the *Storm Operation* script—the as yet uncensored one.

96. The manuscript version, filed at the University of Texas, is described in *Catalogue,* pp. 40-41, and in *Letters,* pp. 186-87n. The published play came out in 1944 under the imprint of Anderson House and differs from the manuscript version in several ways, such as including Act II, Scene 2, and an epilogue.

97. Maxwell Anderson letter to Alexander D. Surles, Dec. 7, 1943 (*Letters,* pp. 186-87n).

98. *Catalogue,* p. 42. The Sherwood letter was dated Dec. 7, 1943.

99. *Catalogue,* p. 41.

100. Wharton blames the out-of-town failure of *Storm Operation* on the play's young and naïve and inexperienced director, and on a "dull" cast. But when the company found a new and better director and made changes in the script and cast, the play still fared poorly with audiences.—*Life Among the Playwrights,* p. 130.

101. Maxwell Anderson, "Letter to Jackie," *The Best One-Act Plays of 1943,* ed. Margaret G. Mayorga (New York: Dodd, Mead, 1944), pp. 3, 5-7.

102. Typed copy of S. N. Behrman letter to Mrs. Robert E. Sherwood, Sept. 17, 1943, in box 6 of the Playwrights Company papers filed at the State Historical Society of Wisconsin.

103. Typed copy of S.N. Behrman letter to "Members of the Playwrights' Company," Oct. 14, 1943, in box 6 of the Playwrights Company papers filed at the State Historical Society of Wisconsin. Reprinted in *Life Among the Playwrights,* pp. 102-5.

"After discussion of the aforesaid statement, Mr. Wharton moved the re-election of Mr. Behrman by acclamation. Mr. Anderson stated that he thoroughly disapproved of Mr. Behrman's fiscal policy but on the basis of his literary ability he would second the motion. Mr. Rice gave up any effort to resist, and the election was carried."—*Life Among the Playwrights,* p. 105.

104. A proposal made by Elmer Rice, who once owned the Belasco Theatre. —From the S. N. Behrman letter cited in the preceding note. Incidentally, Anderson spells the company's name with an apostrophe, but the official name does not use an apostrophe.
105. Sherwood, in addition to being head of the Overseas Branch of OWI, had become an assistant to President Roosevelt (as a speechwriter) at the time when *he* was running for a third term.—*Letters*, p. 184n.
106. The Lunts were favorite choices for Sherwood; they had starred in *Reunion in Vienna, Idiot's Delight*, and *There Shall Be No Night*. They starred in Behrman's *The Pirate* during the recent season.—*Letters*, p. 184n.
107. Dated Oct. 21, 1943, [New City].—*Letters*, pp. 182-83.
108. *Letters*, p. lvii.
109. As quoted by Maxwell Anderson in his letter to Louis Kronenberger, Nov. 21, 1945 (*Letters*, p. 203).
110. Ibid., pp. 203-4. Kronenberger's article was "The Decline of the Theater," *Commentary* I [Nov. 1945], 47-51.
111. Summarized in *Catalogue*, pp. 98-99. The story was never published.
112. *Truckline Cafe* was never published. Martha Cox in her *Maxwell Anderson Bibliography* (Charlottesville, Va.: Bibliographical Society, Univ. of Virginia, 1958), p. 4, writes that the play was probably published (for it was listed in *Cumulative Book Index* under the imprint of Dodd, Mead in 1946) but then withdrawn. The only copy that she and I have been able to locate is the typescript in the Library & Museum of the Performing Arts, New York Public Library.
113. As quoted in *Life Among the Playwrights*, p. 133.
114. Rascoe Burton, *New York World-Telegram;* Ward Morehouse, *New York Sun;* John Chapman, *New York Daily News;* and Vernon Rice, *New York Post*. All reviews are dated Feb. 28, 1946.
115. *The New York Times*, Mar. 1, 1946, p. 17; Mar 7, 1946, p. 31. The war with the critics is summarized in "Cafe Brawl," *Time* XXXXVII (Mar. 11, 1946), 86; also, "Producer Bites Critic," *Newsweek* XXVII (Mar. 11, 1946), 82.
116. *Life Among the Playwrights*, p. 134. Anderson's ad appeared in *The New York Times* on Mar. 4, 1946, under the heading "To the Theatre Public."
117. Maxwell Anderson letter to S. N. Behrman, Aug. 1, 1946 (*Letters*, p. 206, plus note). The resignation took place June 14.
118. *Life Among the Playwrights*, p. 151.
119. Maxwell Anderson letter to Frank D. Fackenthal, acting president of

Columbia University, Mar. 8, 1946. Anderson received the Doctor of Letters degree on June 4. (*Letters,* pp. 204-5, plus notes).

120. Maxwell Anderson, *Joan of Lorraine* (Washington, D.C.: Anderson House, 1946). The first version of the play, *The Warrior's Return,* was begun about late summer of 1944; then followed a second version called *A Girl from Lorraine;* and finally *Joan of Lorraine,* which was completed Nov. 22, 1944.—From *Catalogue.*

121. Essay written March 10-12, 1947. Published in *Off Broadway.*

122. Penciled, two-page, undated note [c. 1944] by Maxwell Anderson in a red leather notebook in the Univ. of Texas collection.

123. Maxwell Anderson, "Playwright Tells Why He Wrote 'Joan' and How He Signed His Star," *The New York Times,* Dec. 1, 1946, II, 3. Burns Mantle, *The Best Plays of 1946-47* (New York: Dodd, Mead, 1947), pp. 120-21. Garson Kanin, *Hollywood* (New York: Viking, 1974), pp. 205-6.

124. As quoted in Burns Mantle, *The Best Plays of 1946-47,* pp. 120-21. Ingrid Bergman's letter to Maxwell Anderson, July 15, 1945 (written in German).—Univ. of Texas collection.

125. See Anderson's letter "To the New York Newspaper and Magazine Critics" (accompanied by tickets to them) [Sept. 15, 1946] in *Letters,* pp. 209-12, plus notes.

126. *Life Among the Playwrights,* p. 148.

127. *Letters,* p. lx, quoting from the diary entry of Sept. 14, 1947.

128. From a list of Maxwell Anderson overseas productions supplied to Mrs. Maxwell Anderson (Gilda) by the Harold Freedman Brandt & Brandt Dramatic Department, Inc., New York City, Oct. 1, 1980. Copy sent to me courtesy of Gilda. Hensley thesis, pp. 106-7, which draws upon interviews at the Playwrights Producing Company. *Life Among the Playwrights,* pp. 81-82.

129. The two articles on Greece published in the American edition were: "An American Observer in Greece," Nov. 28, 1947, p. 26; and "The Plight of the Greek People" Dec. 1, 1947, p. 22. The Paris or International edition carried "Freedom in Greece," Nov. 25, 1947, and "The Conflict in Greece," Nov. 27, 1947.—*Letters,* p. 220n.

130. From his acceptance speech for the Brotherhood Award given by the National Conference of Christians and Jews in honor of *Lost in the Stars;* speech reprinted in *Letters,* pp. 298-301.

131. CBS foreign correspondent George Polk attacked him for whitewashing what Polk considered a repressive and corrupt Greek government, but the playwright defended himself in "An American

Playwright Looks at Greece," *New York Herald Tribune*, Jan. 18, 1948, II, 7.—Reprinted in *Letters*, pp. 218-20.

132. Maxwell Anderson letter to the Playwrights Company, Sept. 5, 1950 (*Letters*, pp. 245-46). He left Southampton on Dec. 9, 1947, and reached New York on Dec. 15, 1947.—*Letters*, p. 301n.

133. Alan Stewart Paton was born in Pietermaritzburg, Natal, on Jan. 11, 1903. He attended Pietermaritzburg College, after which he taught school for eleven years; and from 1935 to 1948 he served as principal of the Diepkloof Reformatory (near Johannesburg, scene of events in his famous novel). He is said to have written two novels which he threw away before beginning *Cry, the Beloved Country* (1948). A second novel was *Too Late the Phalarope* (1953). He coauthored *South Africa in Transition* (1956); then followed his collection of short stories, *Tales from a Troubled Land* (1961); his biography of Jan Hendrik Hofmeyr (1964); and his book of essays, *The Long View* (1968). After his first book appeared, he retired from Diepkloof and became active in South African politics, challenging the racial theory of white supremacy. *Towards the Mountain: An Autobiography* came out in 1980.

134. Avery, "Maxwell Anderson and *Both Your Houses*," p. 18n. *The Days Grow Short*, p. 376.

135. "Maxwell Anderson and *Both Your Houses*," p. 19n; *Letters*, p. 301n; both these draw from the Anderson diary.

136. Maxwell Anderson, "How a Play Gets Written: Diary Retraces the Steps," *New York Herald Tribune*, Aug. 21, 1949, V, 1-2.

137. Maxwell Anderson, *Anne of the Thousand Days* (New York: William Sloane Associates, 1948).

138. Maxwell Anderson letter to John Wharton [May 1949].—From pp. 232-38, plus notes in *Letters*.

139. See note No. 136 for this chapter.

140. *Letters*, p. 240n. *Catalogue*, p. 131. Other details about the suit appear in "Maxwell Anderson Files Libel Action," *Publisher's Weekly* (June 4, 1949), p. 2,301. Also, Anderson's letter to John Wharton (May 1949). Back in the 1920s an Orrie Lashin sued Anderson for using in *Saturday's Children* "atmosphere and background" that he had allegedly taken from a play by her. But, according to him, he was the one who had given her the plot of that play to start with; she failed to do a creditable job of writing the work; he got her permission to write the play himself and came up with *Saturday's Children*. To soothe her

feelings he gave her $1,000.—Maxwell Anderson's letter to his lawyer, Samuel J. Silverman, June 9, 1949 (*Letters,* p. 239).

141. Maxwell Anderson's letter to Alan Paton, Mar. 15, 1948 (*Letters,* p. 221-22).

142. Avery, "Maxwell Anderson and *Both Your Houses,*" p. 19n.

143. *The Days Grow Short,* pp. 380-81. Sanders' material about the genesis of the play derives from miscellaneous sources, some of which I have cited elsewhere, plus Maxwell Anderson's "Assembling the Parts of a Musical Play," *New York Herald Tribune,* Oct. 30, 1949; Harry Gilroy's "Written in the Stars," *The New York Times,* Oct. 30, 1949; and telephone interview with the play's director, Rouben Mamoulian.

144. As quoted in Anderson's acceptance speech for the Brotherhood Award (*Letters,* pp. 299-300).

145. *The Days Grow Short,* p. 391.

146. *Life Among the Playwrights,* pp. 191-92. *The Days Grow Short,* pp. 379-80.

147. *Letters,* p. lxiii, quoting from Anderson's diary entry of Oct. 11, 1949.

148. *The Days Grow Short,* p. 391.

149. As quoted in *Life Among the Playwrights,* p. 192.

150. As quoted in Kay I. Johnson, "Playwrights as Patriots," p. 439. Other materials taken from pp. 437-39. *Lost in the Stars* was published by William Sloane Associates in 1949.

CHAPTER 8

1. As quoted in *The Days Grow Short,* p. 394.

2. Ibid., pp. 394-95, said to be taken from a typescript on file at the University of Texas. Much of my information about Weill's decline and death comes from Ronald Sanders' biography, which in turn draws from Anderson's diary, Feb. through Apr. 1950; from *The New York Times* obituary of Apr. 4, 1950; and from interviews with Alan Anderson and Rouben Mamoulian, who was a theatrical director and colleague of Weill and Anderson. Some of the pertinent diary entries are summarized on p. lxiv of *Letters.* Lotte Lenya, in her corrections to this chapter, which she mailed to me in her letter of Dec. 7, 1980, has her husband laid up with a cold, whereas Sanders calls it

"psoriasis." I also used the unsigned "Kurt Weill is Buried" article in *The New York Times,* Apr. 6, 1950, I, 29.

Throughout this chapter and the next one I make use of my own photocopies of many diary entries running from Nov. 28, 1949, through Dec. 31, 1951; and Oct. 20, 1952, through Nov. 8, 1952.

The extant Anderson diaries (all unpublished, and some of them restricted by order of Mrs. Maxwell Anderson) begin with 1945. In a letter to their attorney, Reinheimer, Mab wrote that the diaries covering the end of 1943 and all of 1944 have been lost.

3. *Letters,* p. lxiv.
4. Ibid., p. lxv, as drawing from diary.
5. Maxwell Anderson's diary entry, Jan. 6, 1950.
6. Hesper Anderson.
7. Lotte Lenya.
8. Maxwell Anderson's diary entry, May 14, 1950.
9. As printed in *Theatre Arts* XXXIII (June 1949), 82 (Act II, Scene 4).
10. Taken from a detailed list of comparisons and contrasts noted by Lela Chambers in her letter to me, July 5, 1978. She wrote that *Morning Winter and Night* has "aspects of being both [fantasy and autobiography] for I can place many of the names and places and people as being real, but there are others that do not correspond [with the time period] or [with] the persons who seem to have been involved or for some other reason simply do not fit." Like Gilda, she doubts that the sexual adventures happened to Anderson; Hesper holds the contrary view. Lela adds that the village in the novel may owe its name, if nothing else, to an actual Devon, a village about seven miles from New Hampton, Iowa, where the Reverend Anderson once preached.
11. John Nairne Michaelson (pseudonym for Maxwell Anderson), *Morning Winter and Night* (New York: William Sloane Associates, 1952). Published simultaneously in Toronto by George J. McLeod. In the William Sloane edition it sold only 1,491 copies.—Letter to me from Naomi Cutner, of William Morrow & Co., Inc., Publishers, Mar. 3, 1978. It was reprinted in paperbound form in New York by Berkley Books; and, in the late 1970s, it was reissued under Anderson's name (for the first time) in a limited and unauthorized edition by Xanadu Productions, a film company that was preparing a motion picture based on the book and using a scenario written by Hesper Anderson.
12. Julie Sloane recalling Mab's remark to her.
13. "That Socrates went barefooted is based on passages in the *Phaedrus*

and *Symposium* of Plato . . . [but] Xenophon [in *Memorabilia*] puts sandals on Socrates."—Jackson K. Hershbell, "The Socrates and Plato of Maxwell Anderson," *North Dakota Quarterly* XXXVIII (Winter 1970), 55.

14. *Catalogue,* p. 139.
15. Karl R. Popper, *The Open Society and Its Enemies,* 5th ed. (Princeton, N.J., 1966), I, 189. The passage quoted is typical of what is found in the 1943 and 1950 editions.
16. Hershbell, pp. 49-51.
17. Ibid., pp. 56-58.
18. Box 22 of papers of the Playwrights Producing Company at the State Historical Society of Wisconsin. The paper is excerpted in Kay I. Johnson's dissertation. Also, Anderson's diary entry for Apr. 4, 1951, carries this idea.—*Letters,* p. lxv.
19. *Life Among the Playwrights,* pp. 207-13.
20. Kenneth Anderson letters to me, June 8, 1978, and Mar. 2, 1980. During the play's first production, in New York, Lotte Lenya played Xantippe; Barry Jones, Socrates; George Mathews, Pausanias. "In November, 1966 . . . *Barefoot in Athens* was presented on NBC television network's 'Hall of Fame.' The distinguished British actor Peter Ustinov played the leading role of Socrates."—Hershbell, p. 45.
21. Maxwell Anderson letter to Dr. Jackson Toby, Nov. 30, 1951 *(Letters,* p. 252).
22. Questionnaire sent to me with Alan Anderson's letter of Nov. 23, 1970. He writes there that he stage-managed some of his father's plays, at which times father and son worked together quite harmoniously because their functions were quite different.
23. John Mason Brown, "Socrates Without Plato," *Saturday Review of Literature* XXXIV (Nov. 24, 1951), 28.
24. Mabel Driscoll Bailey, *Maxwell Anderson: The Playwright as Prophet* (London: Abelard-Schuman, 1957), p. 96.
25. Maxwell Anderson's letter to Robert E. Sherwood, Nov. 29, 1951; also, his letter to Victor Samrock, Nov. 20, 1951; both of these as found in *Letters,* pp. 250-51 and 252n.
26. Hesper Anderson.
27. Lotte Lenya.
28. Alan Anderson.
29. Details about her restlessness at home and her work in TV come mostly from family sources, especially my interviews with Mr. and Mrs.

Alan Anderson, with Hesper, and with Lawrence. Also, some details from Lotte Lenya, her confidante.

30. Questionnaire filled out by Hesper Anderson and mailed to me in her envelope postmarked June 14, 1978.

31. Anderson's diary entry for May 6, 1951, notes that tax problems are destroying her emotional health and that she "says life is hopeless."— As quoted in *Letters*, p. lxvi.

32. Gilda Anderson in questionnaire sent to me with her letter dated Mar. 4, 1980. Hesper Anderson.

33. From the questionnaire (see preceding note) that Gilda had sent to me. "Someone Else" (p. 22) at once hints and discounts the possibility that her mother had numerous affairs previous to the one with Stagg. But Mr. and Mrs. Alan Anderson as well as Lotte Lenya told me they doubted the existence of any earlier ones. Gilda Hazard later married Anderson.

34. Lotte Lenya.

35. Hesper Anderson.

36. Gilda Anderson in the questionnaire she sent to me with her letter of Mar. 6, 1979.

37. Maxwell Anderson's letter to Archer Milton Huntington, Mar. 29, 1953 *(Letters,* pp. 260-61). Details of this affair were furnished to me by many familial sources, the best one from outside the family being Lotte Lenya, who with Bunny Caniff were two of Mab's closest acquaintances.

38. As quoted from Gilda Anderson's letter to me, Oct. 10, 1978.

39. New York: Atheneum, 1961. Although the reviewers were unaware of the real-life basis of the story, Anderson's immediate relatives and neighbors certainly caught on, and at least a half dozen told me that as a biographer I ought to read this book. Bessie Breuer's stories are typically done in an experimental style and consist of, it is said, thinly veiled accounts of real people and events known to her, and *Take Care of My Roses* is no exception. Breuer admitted in a letter to Mr. and Mrs. Alan Anderson (undated but penned soon after the book came out) that she had used a topic close to the lives of the Andersons but had invented numerous incidents to enliven the story. Her story, however, remains flaccid and tedious; its main interest lies in conveying a surprisingly accurate record of Mab Maynard's last days.

Take Care of My Roses tells about Mrs. Alma Salter trying unsuccessfully to rebuild her marriage with her novelist-husband, twenty-five years her senior, and ending up killing herself by leaping off a cliff. The setting is the recent past; the area much like New City. Many years before the story opens, the selfish and predatory and ambitious Alma, working at that time as a stenographer to support her husband's voice lessons, destroys the lovely marriage that Harvie Salter has with his first wife, the sweet and forgiving Ellen. This Ellen has allowed her bed-hopping husband unrestricted freedom to "experience life." Once the adultery begins, Harvie dutifully informs Ellen about it. Finally, Ellen cannot bear the burden of this knowledge any longer and dies of a broken heart.

No doubt this novel drew upon and in turn colored the memories of a few of my informants among the Anderson circle. Accordingly, I was wary of accepting as factual those things in the novel that were not at the same time clearly verified in external accounts where the novel's influence was not obvious.

The portrait of Mab, as Alma, is startlingly detailed and accurate, as many sources agree. But Breuer's known resentment toward and envy of Anderson shows up in the cold, withdrawn figure of Harvie, a man who has difficulty establishing warm human relationships. Furthermore, speaking through her mouthpiece Ida—a vastly whitewashed version of Martha Stamper—the author finds him culpable for not putting up with his wife's infidelity now that he had been inconstant toward Ellen. Other portraits include Dolly Engisch (Lotte Lenya), Via (combination of Hesper and Quentin), Beryl (Gilda Hazard), George Mills (Jerry Stagg), and Josepha (the Catholic Ukrainian washerwoman Teppi).

40. *Take Care of My Roses,* pp. 103-4.
41. Julie Sloane.
42. Louis Sheaffer, *O'Neill Son and Artist* (Boston: Little, Brown, 1973), p. 660. The time was spring in 1951.
43. Hesper Anderson.
44. Anderson's diary entries, Oct. 20 and 21, 1952.
45. Lotte Lenya.
46. Alan Anderson. Lotte Lenya.
47. Trans. Louise and Aylmer Maude (Chicago: Encyclopedia Britannica, 1952), p. 339.
48. Questionnaire sent to me by Hesper Anderson with her letter of June 14, 1978. Hesper Anderson. Lotte Lenya. Lawrence Anderson.
49. Gilda Anderson letter to me, Oct. 10, 1978. Also, the questionnaire sent to me with her letter of Mar. 4, 1980.
50. Contrary to Hesper Anderson's claim during the interview with me

when she said that her father "abandoned" Mab in some general way. He continued to support Hesper, too, on a generous scale long after the mother died and the girl reached maturity and married. He even paid the rent for her husband, Earle Levenstein.—Maxwell Anderson letter to Earle Levenstein, Feb. 14, 1959 (Univ. of Texas collection).

51. Anderson's diary entries, Nov. 8 and Oct. 30, 1952, respectively.
52. *Letters,* p. lxvi. Gilda Anderson. Hesper Anderson.
53. Chapter 606 of the Laws of 1933, which became effective on Apr. 29, 1933.—Copy of new law sent to me, along with interpretation, in the letter from Louis J. Lefkowitz, attorney general for state of New York (Albany, N.Y.), Dec. 6, 1978.
54. Hesper Anderson.
55. Lela Chambers letter to me, Feb. 25, 1979.
56. Hesper Anderson. The attempted suicides are confirmed in familial accounts, but no two people are able to agree on any exact number, nor are they able to give exact dates. Gilda Anderson told me that one instance occurred at the New House even before she became involved with Maxwell Anderson.
57. From Lotte Lenya letters to Maxwell Anderson. The first two are dated Feb. 11 and Mar. 4, 1953. The third (date unknown but about early 1953) has been misplaced or lost.
58. Mr. and Mrs. Alan Anderson. Hesper Anderson. Julie Sloane.
59. Hesper Anderson. She told me that Bessie Breuer in *Take Care of My Roses* took great liberty in transforming the housekeeper, Martha Stamper, into her fictional counterpart, Ida. Both Hesper and Gilda Anderson testify to the unsavory aspects of Martha.
60. Most of my information on the discovery of the body comes from interviews with Lotte Lenya, Julie Sloane, and Mr. and Mrs. Alan Anderson; to a lesser extent from Hesper Anderson and the obituaries in the *New York Daily Mirror, The New York Times,* and *Newsweek* and *Time* magazines.
61. Julie Sloane.
62. Gilda Anderson letter to me, Mar. 6, 1979. Hesper Anderson.
63. Letter to me from Mrs. Libbe Axlrod, Oct. 10, 1978.
64. Quentin Anderson.
65. Lotte Lenya. Julie Sloane.
66. Lotte Lenya. The double burial was confirmed by letter to me from the secretary-treasurer of Mount Repose Cemetery, Hilliary Hunt, and dated July 3, 1978. Quentin Anderson wrote to me that there is simply

no truth to the rumor that one of the Anderson sons subsequently moved the ashes to the father's grave at Geneva, Pa.

67. Refrain from the line of a song in *Lost in the Stars.*
68. Lotte Lenya.
69. Gilda Anderson letter to me, Aug. 2, 1978.

CHAPTER 9

1. Copy of "Certificate of Marriage" for James Maxwell Anderson and Gilda Hazard, from County Recorder, Los Angeles, Calif. Filed June 9, 1954. She had married writer Lawrence Hazard in Las Vegas, Nevada, in 1940, and divorced him in Los Angeles, Calif., in 1953. For her children by this first marriage, see note No. 28 for this chapter.
2. Nicholas Romano (b. 1887) married Gurlie Walberg in 1910 in America and they had the children Gilda, Hilda, and Ovid (all three of whom are alive at the time of this writing). From 1906 to 1917 he worked for an M. L. Buffington, but from 1917 to 1926 Romano was self-employed as a photographer; from 1926 until his death in 1953 he was the "Museum Photographer" for the Rhode Island School of Design. His surviving widow still lives in Providence, R.I.—Letter to me from Mrs. Risa Gilpin, librarian, Rhode Island School of Design, Aug. 17, 1978.
3. Arnold Street School (1918-20); Ives Street School (1920-22); East Manning School (1922-23); and John Howland School (1923-28), where she graduated from the ninth grade.—Letter to me from Robert Ricci, assistant superintendent, Department of Public Schools, Providence, R.I., Aug. 10, 1978. Gilda appears to have continued her education privately.
4. Letter from Gilda Anderson to me, Oct. 10, 1978.
5. As quoted in the foregoing letter. Also, Gilda Anderson.
6. Hill's memoir.
7. Hesper Anderson.
8. Edited and with introduction by Laurence G. Avery (Austin, Tex.: (Univ. of Texas Press, 1971).
9. Univ. of Texas collection.
10. Dec. 14, 1953 (*Letters,* p. 263).
11. Hesper's words as quoted in Nancy Anderson.

12. Maxwell Anderson letter to Hesper Anderson, June 29, 1954 (Univ. of Texas collection).
13. *Letters,* p. lxviii; *Catalogue,* pp. 73-74.
14. Maxwell Anderson, letter to Hesper Anderson, July 8, 1954 (Univ. of Texas collection).
15. *Letters,* p. lxviii.
16. Quentin Anderson.
17. Gilda Anderson.
18. Maxwell Anderson letter to Hesper Anderson, Aug. 15, 1954 (Univ. of Texas collection).
19. Maxwell Anderson letter to Hesper Anderson, Apr. 15, 1954 (Univ. of Texas collection).
20. Alan Anderson. Hesper Anderson.
21. Lawrence Anderson. Gilda Anderson.
22. Sheaffer, *O'Neill Son and Artist,* p. 660.
23. Gilda Anderson letter to me, Mar. 4, 1980. Among the Maxwell Anderson correspondence filed at the University of Texas are many tender and solicitous letters sent to Hesper.
24. Gilda Anderson. Lawrence Anderson.
25. Hesper Anderson.
26. Maxwell Anderson letter to Hesper Anderson, Mar. 20, 1958 (Univ. of Texas collection). Letter to me from Anderson's stepdaughter, Mrs. Laurel Hon (Redding, Conn.), Apr. 14, 1980; also, letter to me from Gilda Anderson, Mar. 4, 1980.
27. Letter to me from Gilda Anderson, Mar. 4, 1980. Glen Avery Chambers.
28. Glen Avery Chambers. Laurel was born in Los Angeles, Calif., Oct. 14, 1942. She married a Jack Hon and bore him two children; then they divorced. She now works as a certified private airplane pilot. Lawrence Craig was born Nov. 16, 1945. At the time of this writing, he and his wife, Monika, work at Phoenix Films in New York City. Laurel and Craig Hazard later adopted the surname "Anderson."—From one of my 1982 telephone interviews with Gilda Anderson; also, Thomas L. Yoset, "Maxwell Anderson, The Playwright," *Crawford County Genealogy* (Crawford County [Penn.] Genealogical Society) I (July 1978), 80.
29. Letter from Hesper Anderson to me, in the form of my questionnaire, which she filled out and mailed on June 14, 1978.
30. Univ. of Texas collection.
31. Maxwell Anderson letters to Hesper Anderson: undated [c. 1953], referring to her boyfriend Jim; Feb. 14, Apr. 21, July 8, and July 13,

(esp.), 1954—all these from Univ. of Texas collection. Hesper Anderson. See note No. 23 for this chapter.

32. Maxwell Anderson letter to Hesper Anderson, Feb. 15, 1956 (Univ. of Texas collection).

33. Unsigned, "Morning Winter and Night/Maxwell Anderson/A Synopsis," an undated promotional brochure printed by Xanadu Productions, Inc. (Hollywood, Calif.), headed by David Peters and Ross Berria. The planned film was never completed.

34. Gilda Anderson.

35. Letter from Gilda Anderson to me, Oct. 10, 1978. In it she corrected the price of $75,000 given in the unsigned article "Playwright Buys Home," *The New York Times,* July 24, 1955, VIII, 2.

36. Alan Anderson. Gilda Anderson's letter to me, June 15, 1979.

37. Gilda Anderson.

38. Ibid.

39. Ibid.

40. Maxwell Anderson letter to John F. Wharton, Apr. 22, 1957 (*Letters,* p. 286).

41. John F. Wharton, *Life Among the Playwrights,* p. 237.

42. Lewis Nichols, "Talk with a Self-Critical Author," *The New York Times,* Jan. 18, 1959, II, 5. Also, Anderson's letter to Lela, Mar. 26, 1956 (*Letters,* p. 277).

43. Robert Rice, p. 25.

44. "An American Drama," *Literary History of the United States: History,* ed. Robert E. Spiller et al., 3rd ed., rev. (New York: Macmillan, 1963), p. 1,323.

45. Anderson's Columbia memoir.

46. Letter dated July 16, 1978.

47. Robert Markowitz, "Anderson Believed America is Growing Wiser with Age," *The New York Times,* Mar. 4, 1959.

48. As quoted in Leonard Lyons, "The Lyons Den" column, *Buffalo Evening News,* Mar. 26, 1959.

49. Alan Anderson.

50. Lawrence Anderson. Alan Anderson.

51. Quentin Anderson.

52. Gilda Anderson.

53. Letter from J. Lloyd Stone to me, Mar. 20, 1978. In 1955 Stone was executive vice president of the UND Alumni Association.

54. *Letters,* pp. 1xx, 290n. The poem "1908-1935" was published in the *Grand Forks Herald,* June 11, 1935. Professor Frederick Koch, to

whom the poem was dedicated, delivered the commencement address at UND that June. Anderson, though invited to the commencement, did not attend.

55. Letter written Nov. 3, 1958. First published in *University of North Dakota Alumni Review* (Dec. 5, 1958). Reprinted in *North Dakota Quarterly* XXXVIII (Winter 1970), 89-90; also, in *Letters,* pp. 288-90.

56. Diary entry for May 22, 1946, as reported in *Letters,* p. lviii, and in Avery's "The Maxwell Anderson Papers,"p. 26.

57. Robert Woodruff Anderson letter to me, Aug. 22, 1978.

58. Anderson's Columbia memoir, p. 30.

59. Ibid., pp. 30-31.

60. New York: Quadrangle, 1974, pp. 261, 263.

61. Letter from Gilda Anderson to me, Oct. 10, 1978.

62. Gilda Anderson, "Make Your Dream Come True," *National Sunday Magazine* (Oct. 25, 1959), p. 2. Hesper Anderson. Quentin Anderson.

63. Gilda Anderson's letter to me, Jan. 23, 1982, verifying the factual accuracy of details in Hesper Anderson's poem about the death. The poem is titled "For One Alone."

64. Gilda Anderson.

65. From a copy of the Certificate of Death filed with the Connecticut State Department of Health, Bureau of Vital Statistics, Stamford, Conn.

66. Unsigned, "Anderson's Rites Held at Columbia," *The New York Times,* Mar. 2, 1959.

67. Quoted in Wharton's *Life Among the Playwrights,* pp. 257-59. The passage beginning "To the young people of this country . . ." is taken from Maxwell Anderson's "Whatever Hope We Have" essay in *Off Broadway Essays about the Theatre,* pp. 45-46. Robert W. Anderson's eulogy is reprinted here with his permission.

68. From copies of unsigned newspaper clippings furnished to me by Lela Chambers: "Maxwell Anderson's Will, Handwritten, Is Accepted" (Stamford, Conn., Sept. 28 [1959]), and "Playwright's Wife Gets Back Love-Letter Wills" (Stamford, Conn. [1959]); also from the announcement of the California will in *The New York Times,* Sept. 29, 1959, I, 36. In addition, interviews with Alan, Quentin, Terence, and Hesper Anderson.

69. Unsigned, "Rites Held for Greenwood Township Son," *The Meadville* (Pa.) *Tribune,* Oct. 21, 1963. An error: Anderson never at any time lived in Greenwood Township, but in East Fallowfield Township, just west of there.

70. This follows the original except that *stars* was substituted for *suns* at the end of the first line, commas and the final question mark were

dropped, and the third and fourth lines of the original were dropped too, perhaps because of their revolutionary and anarchistic flavor: "Who have shaken the pageants of old gods and thrones,/And know them crushed and dead and lost to sight." The poem was written in the 1920s, or slightly earlier, when Anderson entertained socialistic ideas and when he was more than pleased to learn of the successful Russian revolution.

71. From the three-page, typewritten, signed copy of Quentin's memorial address, supplied to me courtesy of Lela Chambers.

APPENDIXES

APPENDIX I

Family of Maxwell Anderson

Paternal great-great-grandfather
Samuel Anderson (?-c. 1811). Said to be born in Scotland.
Paternal great-grandparents
Samuel Anderson (c. 1784-1871).
Mary Christy, called Polly (1787-1873).
Paternal grandparents
James Christy Anderson (1817-1906).
Mary W. Sutton, called Polly (1824-1908).
Maternal grandparents
William Robert Stephenson (1816-1869). Scottish descent.
Charlotte Martin Stewart (c. 1832-1905). Irish and Scottish descent.
By Stephenson she had two children, Charlotte and Emma; after her
husband's death she married William Shepard c. 1875. Shepard died
in 1899.
Parents
William Lincoln Anderson (1863-1936). Also called Linc. After his first
wife died, he married Josephine (Sullivan) Fitzpatrick in 1934.
Charlotte Perrimela Stephenson (1867-1934). Also called Premma.

Wives

Margaret Ethel Haskett (1886-1931). Married Anderson in 1911.

Gertrude (Mab) Maynard née Higger (1904-1953).

Gilda Hazard née Romano (1913-   ). Married Anderson in 1954.

Children

By Margaret Ethel Haskett:

Quentin Maxwell (1912-   ). Married Margaret Elizabeth Pickett in 1933; divorced in 1946. Their child: Martha Haskett, b. 1942. Married Thelma Ehrlich in 1947, by whom he had these children: Abraham Bruce, b. 1954; Maxwell Lincoln, b. 1956.

Alan Haskett (1917-   ). Married Nancy Swan in 1941. Children: Alan Haskett, b. 1943; James Maxwell, b. 1946; and Douglas Dix, b. 1948.

Terence (1921-   ). Married Anastasia (Lulu) Sadowsky in 1949. Children: Robert, b. 1950; Duncan, b. 1955.

By Gertrude (Mab) Maynard:

Hesper (1934-   ). Married Earle Levenstein in 1955. Children: Kenneth, b. 1957; John, b. 1959; Catherine, b. 1960.

Stepchildren

By Gilda Hazard:

Laurel (1942-   ). Married Jack Hon. Divorced. Children: two.

Lawrence Craig (1945-   ).

Brothers and sisters

Ethel Mae (1887-1980). Married Ralph G. Chambers in 1911. Children: Ralph Raimond, b. 1912; Charles Anderson, b. 1915; Dorothy, b. 1917; Mary, b. 1920.

Lela Blanch (1891-   ). Married Daniel H. Chambers in 1913. Children: Lee Daniel, b. 1915; Keith Maxwell, b. 1919; Glen Avery, b. 1920; Ralph Gordon, b. 1923.

Harold Alfred (1895-   ). Married Lillian Marie Stewart in 1921. Children: Jean Marie, b. 1925; Barbara Jane, b. 1932; Beverly June, b. 1932.

Ruth Virginia (1898-1972). Married Earl Patterson in 1916. After his death she married William B. Duffy in 1927.

John Kenneth (1902-   ). Married Alice Morgan in 1926. Children: Donald Morgan, b. 1930; Janet Alice, b. 1934.

Dorothy Elizabeth (1902-62). Married Luke Coulson in 1919; married Stanley A. Oliver; married Wilbur Babb. Child by Coulson: Lucy May, b. 1920.

Lawrence (1913-   ). Married Lillian Peterson in 1936. Children: Lynn, b. 1943; Gary, b. 1958.

APPENDIX II

Maxwell Anderson's Addresses While Not Traveling
or Writing Motion Picture Scripts

1888-91	Atlantic, Pa. Born Dec. 15, 1888.
1891	Andover, Ohio
1892	Richmond Center, Ohio
1892-94	Townville, Pa.
1895-96	Edinboro, Pa.
1896-97	McKeesport, Pa.
1897-98	New Brighton, Pa.
1899-1901	112 Cumberland St., Harrisburg. Pa. Spent summer of 1899 and the following winter at his grandmother's farm in Atlantic, Pa.
1902	Jefferson, Ohio
1903	Algona, Iowa
1904-7	New Hampton, Iowa
1907	Jamestown, N.D.
1908-11	Grand Forks, N.D. Attended University of North Dakota.
1911-13	Minnewaukan, N.D.
1913-14	Stanford, Calif. Attended Leland Stanford University.
1914-17	Palo Alto, Calif.
1917-18	Whittier, Calif.
1918	San Francisco, Calif.
1918-21	New York, N.Y.
1921-52	New City, N.Y.

Lives summers in old farmhouse at 170 S. Mountain Road; the rest of the year, until the mid-1930s, in New York City at these successive addresses:

70 Perry St. (until about 1924)
171 W. Twelfth St. (beginning about 1924)
323 W. 112th St. (bought about 1926)

In the mid-1930s builds and moves into the large New House next door to the old farmhouse; remains there until he learns of Mab's infidelity.

1952-53	Apartment in New York City, probably in Hotel Dorset
1954-55	Stony Point, N.Y.
1955-59	141 Downes Ave., Stamford, Conn.

APPENDIX III

Productions by The Playwrights Producing Company, Inc.

Play	Author	N.Y.C. opening
Abe Lincoln in Illinois	Robert E. Sherwood	Oct. 15, 1938
Knickerbocker Holiday	Maxwell Anderson	Oct. 19, 1938
American Landscape*	Robert Rice	Dec. 3, 1938
No Time for Comedy	S. N. Behrman	Apr. 17, 1939
Madam, Will You Walk*	Sidney Howard	none
Key Largo	Maxwell Anderson	Nov. 27, 1939
Two on an Island*	Elmer Rice	Jan. 20, 1940
There Shall Be No Night	Robert E. Sherwood	Apr. 29, 1940
Journey to Jerusalem*	Maxwell Anderson	Oct. 10, 1940
Flight to the West	Elmer Rice	Dec. 30, 1940
The Talley Method*	S. N. Behrman	Feb. 24, 1941
Candle in the Wind*	Maxwell Anderson	Oct. 22, 1941
The Eve of St. Mark	Maxwell Anderson	Oct. 7, 1942
The Pirate	S. N. Behrman	Nov. 25, 1942
The Patriots	Sidney Kingsley	Jan. 29, 1943
A New Life*	Elmer Rice	Sept. 15, 1943
Storm Operation*	Maxwell Anderson	Jan. 11, 1944
The Rugged Path*	Robert E. Sherwood	Nov. 10, 1945
Dream Girl	Elmer Rice	Dec. 14, 1945
Truckline Cafe*	Maxwell Anderson	Feb. 27, 1946
Joan of Lorraine	Maxwell Anderson	Nov. 18, 1946
Street Scene	Elmer Rice	Jan. 9, 1947
Anne of the Thousand Days	Maxwell Anderson	Dec. 8, 1948
The Smile of the World*	Garson Kanin	Jan. 12, 1949
Lost in the Stars	Maxwell Anderson	Oct. 30, 1949
Darkness at Noon	Sidney Kingsley	Jan. 13, 1951
Not for Children*	Elmer Rice	Feb. 13, 1951
The Fourposter	Jan de Hartog	Oct. 24, 1951
Barefoot in Athens*	Maxwell Anderson	Oct. 31, 1951
The Grand Tour*	Elmer Rice	Dec. 10, 1951
Mr. Pickwick*	Stanley Young	Sept. 15, 1952
The Emperor's Clothes*	George Tabori	Feb. 9, 1953

*Indicates that the play ran for less than 100 performances in the first New York presentation but may have gone on tour later.

Tea and Sympathy	Robert W. Anderson	Sept. 30, 1953
Sabrina Fair	Samuel Taylor	Nov. 11, 1953
In the Summer House*	Jane Bowles	Dec. 29, 1953
The Winner*	Elmer Rice	Feb. 17, 1954
Ondine	Jean Giraudoux	Feb. 18, 1954
All Summer Long*	Robert Anderson	Sept. 23, 1954
The Traveling Lady*	Horton Foote	Oct. 27, 1954
The Bad Seed	Maxwell Anderson	Dec. 8, 1954
Cat on a Hot Tin Roof	Tennessee Williams	Mar. 24, 1955
Once Upon a Tailor*	Baruch Lumet	May 23, 1955
Tiger at the Gates	Jean Giraudoux	Oct. 3, 1955
A Quiet Place*	Julian Claman	none
The Ponder Heart	Joseph Fields and Jerome Chodorov	Jan. 4, 1956
The Lovers*	Leslie Stevens	May 10, 1956
Build with One Hand*	Joseph Kramm	none
Small War on Murray Hill*	Robert E. Sherwood	Jan. 3, 1957
The Saturday Night Kid*	Jack Dunphy	none
Time Remembered	Jean Anouilh	Nov. 12, 1957
Nude with Violin*	Noel Coward	Nov. 14, 1957
The Rope Dancers	Morton Wishengrad	Nov. 20, 1954
The Country Wife*	William Wycherley	Nov. 27, 1957
Summer of the 17th Doll*	Ray Lawler	Jan. 22, 1958
Present Laughter*	Noel Coward	Jan. 31, 1958
Howie*	Phoebe Ephron	Sept. 17, 1958
A Handful of Fire*	N. Richard Nash	Oct. 1, 1958
The Pleasure of His Company	Samuel Taylor and Cornelia Otis Skinner	Oct. 22, 1958
Edwin Booth*	Milton Geiger	Nov. 24, 1958
Cue for Passion*	Elmer Rice	Nov. 25, 1958
The Gazebo	Alex Coppel	Dec. 12, 1958
Listen to the Mocking Bird*	Edward Chodorov	none
Look after Lulu*	Noel Coward	Mar. 3, 1959
Juno*	Joseph Stein	Mar. 9, 1959
Cheri*	Anita Loos	Oct. 12, 1959
Flowering Cherry*	Robert Bolt	Oct. 21, 1959
Five Finger Exercise	Peter Shaffer	Dec. 2, 1959
Silent Night, Lonely Night	Robert W. Anderson	Dec. 3, 1959
Motel*	Thom. W. Phipps	none
The Best Man	Gore Vidal	Mar. 31, 1960

Plays in which the company shared an indirect interest:

Miss Liberty	Robert E. Sherwood	July 15, 1949
Second Threshold	Philip Barry	Jan. 2, 1951

BIBLIOGRAPHY

Primary Sources

1. Published Plays (collections) (chronologically listed)
Three American Plays (in collaboration with Lawrence Stallings). New York: Harcourt, Brace, 1926. Contains *What Price Glory, First Flight,* and *The Buccaneer.*
Gods of the Lightning and Outside Looking In. New York: Longmans, Green, 1928 (*Gods* written in collaboration with Harold Hickerson).
Eleven Verse Plays, 1929-1939. New York: Harcourt, Brace, 1940. Contains *Elizabeth the Queen, Night over Taos, Mary of Scotland, Valley Forge, Winterset, The Wingless Victory, High Tor, The Masque of Kings, The Feast of Ortolans, Second Overture,* and *Key Largo.*
Four Verse Plays. New York: Harcourt, Brace, 1959. Contains *Elizabeth the Queen, Mary of Scotland, High Tor,* and *Winterset.*

2. Individual Published Plays (chronologically listed)
Saturday's Children. New York: Longmans, Green, 1927.
Elizabeth the Queen. New York: Longmans, Green, 1930.
Night over Taos. New York: Samuel French, 1932.
Mary of Scotland. Washington, D.C.: Anderson House, 1933.

Both Your Houses. New York: Samuel French, 1933.

Valley Forge. Washington, D.C.: Anderson House, 1934.

Winterset. Washington, D.C.: Anderson House, 1935.

Masque of Kings, The. Washington, D.C.: Anderson House, 1936.

Wingless Victory, The. Washington, D.C.: Anderson House, 1936.

Star-Wagon, The. Washington, D.C.: Anderson House, 1937.

High Tor. Washington, D.C.: Anderson House, 1937.

"Feast of Ortolans, The," *The Stage Magazine* XV (Jan. 1938), 71-78.

"Second Overture," *The Stage Magazine* XV (Mar. 1938), 41-45.

Knickerbocker Holiday: A Musical Comedy in Two Acts. Washington, D.C.: Anderson House, 1938 (in collaboration with Kurt Weill).

Key Largo. Washington, D.C.: Anderson House, 1939.

Journey to Jerusalem. Washington, D.C.: Anderson House, 1940.

Miracle of the Danube, The, in *The Free Company Presents.* Comp. James Boyd. New York: Dodd, Mead, 1941.

Candle in the Wind. Washington, D.C.: Anderson House, 1941.

Eve of St. Mark, The. Washington, D.C.: Anderson House, 1942.

Your Navy, in *This is War!* New York: Dodd, Mead, 1942.

Storm Operation. Washington, D.C.: Anderson House, 1944.

Letter to Jackie, in *Best Short Plays, 1943-1944.* Ed. M. G. Mayorga. New York: Dodd, Mead, 1945.

Truckline Cafe. New York: Dodd, Mead, 1946. Martha Cox in her *Maxwell Anderson Bibliography* writes that this play probably was published (it was listed in *Cumulative Book Index*) but then withdrawn. Neither she nor I have been able to find a copy other than the typescript in the Library & Museum of the Performing Arts at the New York Public Library.

Joan of Lorraine. Washington, D.C.: Anderson House, 1946.

Joan of Arc. (Screen version of *Joan of Lorraine,* in collaboration with Andrew Solt) New York: William Sloane Associates, 1948.

Anne of the Thousand Days. New York: William Sloane Associates, 1948.

Lost in the Stars. New York: William Sloane Associates, 1949 (in collaboration with Kurt Weill).

Barefoot in Athens. New York: William Sloane Associates, 1951.

Bad Seed. New York: Dodd, Mead, 1955.

Masque of Pedagogues, The, in *North Dakota Quarterly* XXV (Spring 1957), 33-48.

Golden Six, The. New York: Dramatists Play Service, 1961.

3. Unpublished but Complete Plays (date in parentheses indicates year or years written) (chronologically listed)

Meeting in Africa. (?) ms., Univ. of Texas.

Benvenuto. (1922) ms., Univ. of Texas.

White Desert. (1923) ms., Univ. of Texas.

Sea-Wife. (1924) ms., Univ. of Texas; typescript at Library & Museum of Performing Arts at New York Public Library.

Hell on Wheels. (c. 1926) ms., Univ. of Texas. Also, *Hell on Wheels* (a musical play) with music by Jack Niles (c. 1928) at Library of Congress.

Chicot the King. (1926) ms., Univ. of Texas and Library of Congress.

Gypsy. (1927) ms., Univ. of Texas; Library & Museum of Performing Arts at New York Public Library; condensed version published in *The Best Plays of 1928-29.* Typescript at Library of Congress.

Marriage Recipe, The. Carbon copies of typescript (1929) at Library of Congress and Univ. of Texas. One-act play based on material in *Saturday's Children.*

Princess Renegade, The. (1932) ms., Univ. of Texas.

Bastion Saint-Gervais, The. (1938) ms., Univ. of Texas. Radio play related to *Key Largo.*

Ulysses Africanus. (1939-45) ms., Univ. of Texas.

Greeks Remember Marathon, The. (1944) radio play.

Adam, Lilith and Eve. (1950) ms., Univ. of Texas.

Raft on the River (also titled *River Chanty*). (1950) ms., Univ. of Texas.

Cavalier King. (1952) ms., Univ. of Texas.

Masque of Queens, The. (1954) ms., Univ. of Texas.

Christmas Carol, The. (1954) ms., Univ. of Texas. Television play.

Richard and Anne. (1955) ms., Univ. of Texas.

Madonna and Child. (1956) ms., Univ. of Texas.

Day the Money Stopped, The. (1957) ms., Univ. of Texas.

4. Books of Poems

A Stanford Book of Verse 1912-1916. The English Club of Stanford University, 1916. Some of these poems are Anderson's.

Notes on a Dream. Edited and with introduction by Laurence G. Avery. Austin, Tex.: Univ. of Texas Press, 1971.

You Who Have Dreams. New York: Simon & Schuster, 1925.

5. Fiction

"Battle of Gibraltar, The." *Collier's* LXXXV (May 10, 1930), 26, 31, 36, 38.

Morning Winter and Night (published under pseudonym of John Nairne

Michaelson). New York: William Sloane Associates, 1952. Also published in 1952 by George J. McLeod at Toronto, Canada. It was also reprinted in paperbound form in New York by Berkley Books. Late in the 1970s, it was reissued in a limited and unauthorized paperbound edition—this time under Anderson's own name—by Xanadu Productions, a film company that was once preparing a motion picture based on the book.

"West Coast, Night." Unpublished. Written in 1947. The ms. is at Univ. of Texas.

6. Books of Criticism

Essence of Tragedy and Other Footnotes and Papers, The. Washington, D.C.: Anderson House, 1939.

Off Broadway: Essays about the Theatre. New York: William Sloane Associates, 1947.

7. Individual Essays, Articles, and Reviews

"A Confession," *The New York Times,* Dec. 5, 1954, II, 7.

"A Dramatist's Playbill," *New York Herald Tribune,* Sept. 19, 1943.

"A Foreword by the Playwright." In *Maxwell Anderson Festival* (pamphlet dated Sept. 29, 1958, and issued by Dakota Playmakers of Univ. of North Dakota in announcing presentation of two Anderson plays in Oct. 1958).

"A Prelude to Poetry in the Theatre." Preface to *Winterset.* Washington, D.C.: Anderson House, 1935, pp. v-xi.

"About the Playwrights' Company," *The Stage Magazine* XVI (Dec. 1938), 17.

"An Age of Hired Men," *The Freeman* II (Sept. 22, 1920), 31-32.

"An American Observer in Greece," *New York Herald Tribune,* Nov. 28, 1947, p. 26.

"An American Playwright Looks at Greece," *New York Herald Tribune,* Jan. 18, 1948, II, 7. Reprinted in Avery's *Letters,* pp. 218-20.

"An Open Letter to Writers of Verse," *The Measure: A Journal of Poetry* 2 (Apr. 1921), 17-19.

"Anderson Calls Drama Critics 'Jukes Family,' " *New York Herald Tribune,* Mar. 4, 1946.

"Arts as Motive Power, The," *The New York Times,* Oct. 17, 1937, XI, 1. Reprinted in *Essays Annual, 1938,* ed. Erich A. Walter. New York: Appleton-Century, 1939, pp. 212-19.

"Assembling the Parts of a Musical Play," *New York Herald Tribune*, Oct. 30, 1949, V, 13.

"Author Looks Back over Ten Years and Concludes that the Hopes of His Company Have Been Fulfilled," *The New York Times*, Oct. 10, 1948, II, 3.

"Basis of Artistic Creation, The," in *The Bases of Artistic Creation*. New Brunswick, N.J.: Rutgers Univ. Press, 1942 (various essays by Anderson, Roy Harris, Rhys Carpenter, et al.).

"Blue Pencil, The," *New Republic* XVII (Dec. 14, 1918), 192-94.

"By Way of Preface: The Theatre as Religion," *The New York Times*, Oct. 26, 1941, drama section, pp. 1, 3 (version of "Off Broadway").

"Conflict in Greece, The," *New York Herald Tribune* (Paris Edition), Nov. 27, 1947.

"Critical Mr. Anderson," *New York World*, Mar. 9, 1934, 6E.

"Curtains—Iron and Asbestos," *The New York Times*, Feb. 16, 1958, II, 3.

"Democracy's Temple," *Saturday Review of Literature* XXXII (Aug. 6, 1949), 135.

Flag Day Pageant. Educational Radio Script and Transcription Exchange. U.S. Office of Education (c. 1944). Written for the Writer's War Board. Library of Congress.

"Foreword." *See Here, Private Hargrove*, by Marion Hargrove. New York: Henry Holt, 1942, pp. ix-xi.

"Freedom in Greece," *New York Herald Tribune* (Paris Edition), Nov. 25, 1947.

"Friendly Advice," *The Freeman* I (Mar. 17, 1920), II (letter).

"Further Prejudiced Words on Amy Lowell," *The Measure: A Journal of Poetry* 8 (Oct. 1921), 18.

"Get Mad, America!" *The New York Times*, Feb. 22, 1942, I, 8.

Guaranteed Life, The. Irvington-on-Hudson, New York: Foundation for Economic Education (c. 1950), Pp. 10. Library of Congress.

"How a Play Gets Written: Diary Retraces the Steps," *New York Herald Tribune*, Aug. 21, 1949, V, 1-2.

"How Storm Operation Grew," *National Theatre Conference Bulletin* VI (Jan. 1944), 21-26.

"How Will It Be Done Again?" *The Freeman* II (Sept. 15, 1920), 9-10.

"Incommunicable Literature," *The Dial* LXVI (Nov. 2, 1918), 370.

"Journey to Jerusalem," *The New York Times*, Sept. 29, 1940, IX, 1, 2.

"Kurt Weill," *Theatre Arts* XXXIV (Dec. 1950), 58.

"Looking back at Synge," *The Measure: A Journal of Poetry* 4 (June 1921), 20-21.

"Love Letter to a University," *North Dakota Quarterly* XXXVIII (Winter 1970), 89-90. Reprinted from *University of North Dakota Alumni Review* (Dec. 5, 1958) (letter written Nov. 3, 1958).

Maxwell Anderson interview. Transcribed from a tape-recorded interview conducted by Louis M. Starr, May 10, 1956, at Anderson's home: 141 Downes Ave., Stamford, Connecticut. Oral History Research Office, Columbia University; 34-page typescript. Edited version in Avery's *Letters,* pp. 301-18.

"Menace of World War III," *The New York Times,* Mar. 8, 1948.

"Mighty Critics, The," *The New York Times,* Feb. 16, 1947, II, 1-2.

"Modern Casuists," *The Freeman* I (Aug. 25, 1920), 565.

"More Thoughts about Dramatic Critics," *New York Herald Tribune,* Oct. 10, 1948.

"Notes for Barefoot in Athens." Box 22, papers of The Playwrights Producing Company, Wisconsin State Historical Society, Madison, Wisc.

"Notes for a New Play," *PM* (Jan. 9, 1944), IV, n.p.

"Notes on Socrates," *The New York Times,* Oct. 28, 1951, II, 1-3.

"On Government, Being a Brief Preface to the Politics of 'Knickerbocker Holiday,'" *The New York Times,* Nov. 13, 1938, IX, 1.

"One Future for American Poetry," *The Dial* LXVI (May 31, 1919), 568-69.

"Playwright Tells Why He Wrote 'Joan' and How He Signed His Star," *The New York Times,* Dec. 1, 1946, II, 3.

"Playwrights' Birthday, The," *The New York Times,* Oct. 10, 1948, II, 3.

"Plight of the Greek People, The," *New York Herald Tribune,* Dec. 1, 1947, p. 22.

"Preface." *Four Verse Plays.* New York: Harcourt, Brace & World, 1959, pp. v-viii.

"Preface." *November Hearabout,* by Amy Murray. New York: Henry Holt, 1940, pp. xiii-xv.

"Prelude to Dramatic Poetry," *The New York Times,* Oct. 6, 1935, XI, 1, 3.

Review. *The Blood Red Dawn,* by Charles Caldwell Dobie. *The Freeman* I (Aug. 11, 1920), 525-26.

———. *Dramatic Legends and Other Poems,* by Padraic Colum. *The Measure: A Journal of Poetry* 22 (Dec. 1922), 17-18.

———. *Hymen,* by H[ilda] D[oolittle]. *The Measure: A Journal of Poetry* 14 (Apr. 1922), 18.

———. "Irish History in Little." *The Measure: A Journal of Poetry* 15 (May 1922), 17-18.

———. *The Keats Memorial Volume* (no editor listed). *The Measure: A Journal of Poetry* 10 (Dec. 1921), 17.

———. *Legends*, by Amy Lowell. *The Measure: A Journal of Poetry* 6 (Aug. 1921), 17-18.

———. *Nets to Catch the Wind*, by Elinor Wylie. *The Measure: A Journal of Poetry* 11 (Jan. 1922), 18.

———. *Punch: The Immortal Liar*, by Conrad Aiken. *The Measure: A Journal of Poetry* 3 (May 1921), 25-26.

———. *Rio Grande*, by Harvey Fergusson. *The Nation* CXXXVII (Aug. 16, 1933), 190-91.

———. *Second April*, by Edna St. Vincent Millay. *The Measure: A Journal of Poetry* 7 (Sept. 1921), 17.

———. *Slabs of the Sunburnt West*, by Carl Sandburg. *The Measure: A Journal of Poetry* 17 (July 1922), 15-16.

———. "Word-Craft," *The Measure: A Journal of Poetry* 18 (Aug. 1922), 16.

"Revolution and the Drama, The," *The Freeman* I (July 14, 1920), 425-26.

"Robert Sherwood," *Theatre Arts* XL (Feb. 1956), 26-27, 87.

"Scholar Too Late, The," *The Dial* LXVII (Sept. 20, 1919), 239-41.

"Socrates and His Gospel." Preface to *Barefoot in Athens*. New York: William Sloane Associates, 1951, pp. vii-xvi.

"Stage Money," *Collier's* LXXIX (May 28, 1927), 24, 30.

"Summons from Valley Forge," *New York Times Magazine* (Feb. 22, 1942), p. 8.

"Thunder in the Index," *The Measure: A Journal of Poetry* 1 (Mar. 1921), 23-25.

"To the Theatre Public," *The New York Times*, Mar. 4, 1946.

Secondary Sources

Abbott, George. *"Mister Abbott."* New York: Random House, 1963.

Adams, Samuel Hopkins. *Alexander Woollcott: His Life and His World*. Freeport, N.Y.: Books for Libraries Press, 1946.

Allison, Tempe E. "The Pasadena Summer Festival," *Players Magazine* XVI (Oct. 1939), 9-10, 20.

Anderson, Gilda. "Make Your Dreams Come True," *National Sunday Magazine* in *Buffalo Evening News*, Oct. 24, 1959, p. 5.

Anderson, Hesper. "Someone Else," Part I. Unpublished 77 pp. typescript written c. 1973.

Anderson, Jane McDill. *Rocklandia: A Collection of Facts and Fancies, Legends and Ghost Stories of Rockland County Life.* Illustrations by Don Lynch. Dobbs Ferry, N.Y.: Morgan & Morgan, 1977.

Atkinson, Brooks. *Broadway.* New York: Macmillan, 1974.

Avery, Laurence G. *A Catalogue of the Maxwell Anderson Collection at the University of Texas.* Austin: University of Texas Press, 1968.

———. ed. *Dramatist in America: Letters of Maxwell Anderson, 1912-1958.* Chapel Hill, N.C.: University of North Carolina Press, 1977.

———. "Maxwell Anderson: A Changing Attitude toward Love," *Modern Drama* X (Dec. 1967), 241-48.

———. "Maxwell Anderson and *Both Your Houses,*" *North Dakota Quarterly,* XXXVIII (Winter 1970), 5-24.

———. "The Maxwell Anderson Papers," *The Library Chronicle of the University of Texas* VIII (Spring 1965), 21-33.

Bailey, Mabel Driscoll. *Maxwell Anderson: The Playwright as Prophet.* New York: Abelard-Schuman, 1957.

Baker's Biographical Dictionary of Musicians, ed. Nicolas Slonimsky, 6th ed. New York: Schirmer Books, 1978.

Bassett, Clyde Harold. "The Playwrights' Producing Company, Inc., 1938-1960." Ph.D. dissertation, Univ. of Wisconsin, 1965.

Behrman, S. N. "Old Monotonous," *The New Yorker* XVI (June 1, 1940), 33-36, 40-41; and (June 8, 1940), 23-26, 28, 30, 33.

———. *People in a Diary: A Memoir.* Boston: Little, Brown, 1972 (published in London as *Tribulations and Laughter: A Memoir*).

———. *The Suspended Drawing Room.* New York: Stein and Day, 1965.

Biographical Dictionary & Who's Who of the American Theatre, ed. Walter Rigdon. New York: James H. Heineman, 1966.

Bliven, Bruce Ormsby. *Five Million Words Later: An Autobiography.* New York: John Day, 1970.

———. "Reminiscences of Bruce Ormsby Bliven." Oral History Research Office. Columbia University, 1965.

Block, Anita. *The Changing World in Plays and Theatre.* Boston: Little, Brown, 1939.

Boswell, Peyton, Jr. *Varnum Poor.* New York: Hyperion Press, 1941.

Breuer, Bessie. *Take Care of My Roses.* New York: Atheneum, 1961.

Brockett, Oscar G., and Findlay, Robert R. *Century of Innovation*. Englewood Cliffs, N.J.: Prentice-Hall, 1973.

Brown, Harold. "Queen 'Mab' Rules Roost in Adapting Plays for 'Celanese Theater,' " *New York Herald Tribune*, Mar. 9, 1952.

Brown, John Mason. "The Eve of St. Mark is a Very Moving Play," *New York World-Telegram*, Oct. 8, 1942.

———. "Socrates without Plato," *Saturday Review of Literature* XXXIV (Nov. 24, 1951), 26-28.

———. *The Ordeal of a Playwright: Robert E. Sherwood and the Challenge of War*. New York: Harper & Row, 1970.

———. *The Worlds of Robert E. Sherwood: Mirror to His Times, 1896–1939*. New York: Harper & Row, 1965.

Carmer, Carl. "Maxwell Anderson: Poet & Champion," *Theatre Arts* XVII (June 1933), 437-46.

Case, Frank. *Tales of a Wayside Inn*. New York: Frederick A. Stokes, 1938.

Chambers, Ethel. "Out of Dark and Bright." Incomplete autobiography containing "Chapter 1 Atlantic" and "Chapter 2 Geneva." 18 pp., typewritten. Unpublished.

Chambers, Lela B. "Lela Chambers' biographical notes." 11 pp., typewritten, unpublished; prepared for the use of Dr. Alfred S. Shivers.

———. "Life." 178 pp., typewritten, unpublished. Written 1960-75.

Chapman, John. "Maxwell Anderson Hits His Low with a Dreadful 'Truckline Cafe,' " *New York Daily News*, Feb. 28, 1946.

Clark, Barrett, H. *An Hour of American Drama*. Philadelphia: J. B. Lippincott, 1930.

———. *Maxwell Anderson: The Man and His Plays*. New York: Samuel French, 1933.

———. and Freedley, George. *A History of Modern Drama*. New York: D. Appleton-Century, 1947.

Clurman, Harold. *The Fervent Years: The Story of the Group Theatre and the Thirties*. New York: Alfred A. Knopf, 1945.

The Columbia Encyclopedia. Ed. William Bridgewater and Seymour Kurtz, 3rd. ed. New York: Columbia University Press, 1967.

Cooper, Charles W. *Whittier: Independent College in California*. Los Angeles: Ward Ritchie Press, 1967.

Covington, W. P. III. "A Maxwell Anderson Bibliography with Annotations." M.A. thesis, Univ. of North Carolina, 1950.

Cox, Martha. *Maxwell Anderson Bibliography*. Bibliographical Society. Charlottesville, Va.: Univ. of Virginia, 1958.

Deutsch, Helen. "A Playwright and Poet," *New York Herald Tribune*, Sept. 22, 1935, 1, 5.

————. "When Drama and Poetry Wed, Was It to Last Forever After?" *New York Herald Tribune*, May 31, 1936.

Downes, Olin. "Memorial to Weill," *The New York Times*, July 9, 1950, II, 7.

————. "People's Composer," *The New York Times*, Apr. 9, 1950, II, 9.

Duffus, Robert Luther. "The Reminiscences of Robert Luther Duffus." Transcript of interview with Wendell H. Link during Jan. and Feb. 1951. Oral History Research Office, Columbia University.

————. *The Tower of Jewels: Memories of San Francisco*. New York: W. W. Norton, 1960.

Durham, Frank. *Elmer Rice*. New York: Twayne, 1970.

Eaton, Walter Prichard. "He Put Poetry back on the Stage," *New York Herald Tribune*, Jan. 28, 1934, pp. 12-13, 21.

Engel, Lehman. *This Bright Day: An Autobiography*. New York: Macmillan, 1974.

Fields, William. "Maxwell Anderson: Some Fond Memories," *The New York Times*, Mar. 8, 1959, II, 3.

Flexner, James Thomas. *George Washington in the American Revolution, c. 1775-1783*. Boston: Little, Brown, 1968.

Forman, S. E. "Conditions of Living among the Poor." Bulletin No. 64 of the Bureau of Labor. Washington, D.C.: U.S. Government Printing Office, May 1906.

Freeman, Douglas Southall. *Washington*, abr. Richard Harwell from the seven-volume *George Washington*. New York: Charles Scribner's, 1968.

Gassner, John. *Masters of the Drama*. New York: Random House, 1954.

Geiger, Louis G., and Ashton, J. R. "UND in the Era of Maxwell Anderson," *The North Dakota Quarterly* XXV (Spring 1957), 55-60.

Gilbert, Vedder M. "The Career of Maxwell Anderson: A Check List of Books and Articles," *Modern Drama* II (Feb. 1960), 386-94.

Gilder, Rosamond. Review of *Storm Operation* in *Theatre Arts* XXVIII (Mar. 1944), 133.

Gordon, Albert Claude. "A Critical Study of the History and Development of the Playwrights' Producing Company." Ph.D. dissertation, Tulane Univ., 1965.

Gray, David. "Anderson at Stanford," *Prompter* IV, 3 (Mar. 1938), 7. (Palo Alto Community Players, Palo Alto, Calif.).

Green, Paul. "Frederick H. Koch," *Drama and the Weather.* New York: Samuel French, 1958, pp. 162-65.

_____. Review of Laurence Avery's *Dramatist in America* in *Chapel Hill Newspaper,* May 7, 1978, 4C.

Grove's Dictionary of Music and Musicians, ed. Eric Blom, 5th ed. New York: St. Martin's Press, 1955, IX.

Grutzner, Charles. "Look-Out Park on High Tor," *The New York Times,* Aug. 5, 1956, II, 25.

Hagan, John P. "Frederick Henry Koch and the American Folk Theatre." Ph.D. dissertation, Indiana Univ., 1969.

_____. "Frederick H. Koch and North Dakota: Theatre in the Wilderness," *North Dakota Quarterly* XXXVIII (Winter 1970), 75-87.

Halline, Alan G. "Maxwell Anderson's Dramatic Theory," *American Literature* XVI (May 1944), 63-81.

Hand, Raymond T. B. "Maxwell Anderson's House," *House Beautiful* LXXVIII (Aug. 1936), 36-37.

Hargrove, Marion. "Mr. Maxwell Anderson, Legendary Genius, Refuses to Act the Part," *Charlotte* (N.C.) *News* [Mar. 9, 1942].

_____. "Poor Sergeant Donald Bishop Is Broken on the Wheel of Fortune," *Charlotte* (N.C.) *News* [Apr. 1942].

_____. *See Here, Private Hargrove.* New York: Henry Holt, 1942.

Harriman, Margaret Case. *The Vicious Circle: The Story of the Algonquin Round Table.* New York: Rinehart, 1951.

Hayes, Helen, and Funke, Lewis. *A Gift for Joy.* New York: M. Evans, 1965.

Heiney, Donald, and Downs, Lenthiel H. *Recent American Literature after 1930.* Woodbury, N.Y.: Barron's Educational Series, 1974.

Helburn, Theresa. *A Wayward Quest: The Autobiography of Theresa Helburn.* Boston: Little, Brown, 1960.

Hensley, Jack Alton. "The Playwrights Company." Masters thesis, Univ. of Wisconsin, 1952 (the only thesis or dissertation based on interviews with Playwrights Company members).

Hershbell, Jackson K. "The Socrates and Plato of Maxwell Anderson," *North Dakota Quarterly* XXXVIII (Winter 1970), 45-59.

Hill, Frank Ernest. "Reminiscences of Frank Ernest Hill." Transcript from interviews conducted by Dr. Donald F. Shaughnessay, 1960, 1961. Oral History Research Office, Columbia University.

Hollingsworth, Harry. "A Man without a Country: James Peterson, Sr., alias James Sutton of Crawford County, Pennsylvania," *The American Genealogist* LI (July 1975), 158-61.

Hopkins, Arthur. *To a Lonely Boy*. Garden City, New York: Doubleday, Doran, 1937.

Housman, John. *Run-Through: A Memoir*. New York: Simon & Schuster, 1972.

Hoyt, Edwin Palmer. *Alexander Woollcott: The Man Who Came to Dinner; a Biography*. Philadelphia: Chilton Books, 1973.

Hughes, Glenn. *A History of the American Theatre 1700–1950*. New York: Samuel French, 1951.

Hulme, Kathryn C. *Undiscovered Country: A Spiritual Adventure*. Boston: Little, Brown, 1966.

Huston, Walter. "There's No Place Like Broadway Be It Ever So Noisy," *The Stage Magazine* XV (Oct. 1938), 22-26.

Johnson, Alvin. *Pioneer's Progress*. Lincoln, Nebr.: Univ. of Nebraska Press, 1960.

Johnson, Kay Irene. "Playwrights as Patriots: A History of the Playwrights Producing Company, 1938-1960." Ph.D. dissertation, Univ. of Wisconsin, 1974.

Johnson, Walter. *The Battle against Isolation*. New York: Da Capo Press, 1973.

Jolles, Naomi. "Hitler Hates Weill's Songs," *New York Post*, Oct. 20, 1943, p. 43.

Kanin, Garson. *Hollywood*. New York: Viking, 1974.

Keats, John. *You Might as Well Live: The Life and Times of Dorothy Parker*. New York: Simon & Schuster, 1970.

Kinney, Arthur F. *Dorothy Parker*. Boston: Twayne, 1978.

Klink, William, ed. *Maxwell Anderson and S. N. Behrman: A Reference Guide*. Boston: G. K. Hall, 1977.

Kobler, John. *Damned in Paradise: The Life of John Barrymore*. New York: Atheneum, 1977.

Koch, Frederick H. "The Dakota Playmakers: An Historical Sketch," *The Quarterly Journal of the University of North Dakota* IX (Oct. 1918), 14-21.

———. "Folk-Playmaking in Dakota and in Carolina," *The Playground* XVIII (Jan. 1925), 599-601.

———. "Making a Regional Drama," *Bulletin of the American Library Association* XXVI (Aug. 1932), 466-73.

———. "Towards a New Folk Theatre," *The Quarterly Journal of the University of North Dakota* XX (Spring 1930), 166-75.

Kronenberger, Louis. "The Decline of the Theater," *Commentary* I (Nov. 1945), 47-51.

Krutch, Joseph Wood. "An American Drama," *Literary History of the United States: History.* Ed. Robert E. Spiller, 3rd ed., rev. New York: Macmillan, 1963, pp. 1,320-23.

_____. *The American Drama since 1918,* rev. ed. New York: George Braziller, 1957.

Langner, Lawrence. *The Magic Curtain.* New York: E. P. Dutton, 1951.

Lawson, John H. *Theory and Technique of Playwriting and Screenwriting.* New York: G. P. Putnam's Sons, 1949.

Lee, Henry G. "Maxwell Anderson's Impact on the Theatre," *North Dakota Quarterly* XXV (Spring 1957), 49-52.

Leifur, Barbara. "Leading American Dramatist UND Graduate," *Dakota Student* (Univ. of North Dakota student newspaper), Mar. 7, 1956, p. 6.

Lerner, Alan Jay. *The Street Where I Live.* New York: W. W. Norton, 1978.

Lewis, Allan. *American Playwrights of the Contemporary Theatre.* New York: Crown, 1965.

Logan, Joshua. *Josh: My Up and Down, In and Out Life.* New York: Delacorte, 1976.

_____. *Movie Stars, Real People and Me.* New York: Delacorte, 1978.

Lord Hervey's Memoirs, ed. Romney Sedgwick. New York: Macmillan, 1952.

McGrath, Thomas, and Points, Marian. "Maxwell Anderson: Portrait in Pencil," *The North Dakota Quarterly* XXXIII (Winter 1965), 10-13.

McGraw-Hill Encyclopedia of World Drama, vols. I-IV. Edited by Bernard Dukore et al. New York: McGraw-Hill, 1972.

Maney, Richard. *Fanfare.* New York: Harper & Brothers, 1957.

Mantle, Burns. *American Playwrights of Today.* New York: Dodd, Mead, 1930.

_____. *The Best Plays of 1928-1929.* New York: Dodd, Mead, 1929.

_____. *The Best Plays of 1946-1947.* New York: Dodd, Mead, 1947.

Markowitz, Robert. "Anderson Believed America is Growing Wiser with Age," *The New York Times,* Mar. 4, 1959.

Meredith, Scott. *George S. Kaufman and His Friends.* Garden City, N.Y.: Doubleday, 1974.

Miller, Jordan Y. "Maxwell Anderson: Gifted Technician," *The Thirties: Fiction, Poetry, Drama,* ed. Warren French. Deland, Fla.: Everett Edwards, 1967.

Modern World Drama: An Encyclopedia, ed. Myron Matlaw. New York: E. P. Dutton, 1972.

Moody, Richard, ed. *Dramas from the American Theatre, 1782-1909.* Cleveland, Ohio: World, 1966.

Murray, Donald. "Gottfried Emanuel Hult," *The North Dakota Quarterly* XXIV (Fall 1956), 123-33.

Nichols, Lewis. "Talk with a Self-Critical Author," *The New York Times,* Jan. 18, 1959, II, 5.

Oxford Companion to the Theatre, The, 3rd ed., ed. Phyllis Hartnoll. London: Oxford University Press, 1950.

Popper, Karl R. *The Open Society and Its Enemies,* 5th ed. Princeton, New Jersey: Princeton Univ., 1966.

Quinn, Arthur Hobson. *A History of the American Drama from the Civil War to the Present Day,* rev. ed. New York: Appleton-Century-Crofts, 1936.

Rabkin, Gerald. *Drama and Commitment Politics in the American Theatre of the Thirties.* Bloomington, Ind.: Indiana Univ. Press, 1964.

Reader's Encyclopedia of American Literature, ed. Max J. Herzberg. New York: Thomas Y. Crowell, 1962.

Rice, Elmer. *The Living Theatre.* New York: Harper & Brothers, 1959.

––––––. *Minority Report: An Autobiography.* New York: Simon & Schuster, 1963.

Rice, Patrick J. "Maxwell Anderson and the Eternal Dream," *Catholic World* CLXXVII (Aug. 1953), 364-70.

Rice, Robert. "Maxwell Anderson," *PM's Sunday Picture News* III (Nov. 29, 1942), 23-27.

Robertson, C. L. "In the Days of Peg-Top Trousers," *The North Dakota Quarterly* XXV (Spring 1957), 52-54.

Sampley, Arthur M. "Theory and Practice in Maxwell Anderson's Poetic Tragedies," *College English* V (May 1944), 412-18.

Sanders, Ronald. *The Days Grow Short: The Life and Times of Kurt Weill.* New York: Holt, Rinehart & Winston, 1980.

Sedgwick, Ruth Woodbury. "Maxwell Anderson," *The Stage Magazine* XIV (Oct. 1936), 54-56.

Selden, Samuel, and Sphangos, Mary Tom. *Frederick Henry Koch: Pioneer Playmaker.* Chapel Hill, N.C.: Univ. of North Carolina Library, 1954.

Selivanova, Nina N. *Folklore: Rockland County.* Unpublished typescript, New York State Writers' Project, 1938. Copy in The Nyack Library, Nyack, N.Y.

Sheaffer, Louis. *O'Neill: Son and Artist.* Boston: Little, Brown, 1973.

Shearer, Sgt. Lloyd. "Pertaining to Local Color," *The New York Times,* Oct. 4, 1942, VIII, 1.

Sherwood, Robert E. "'White Desert' to 'Bad Seed,'" *Theatre Arts* XXXIX (Mar. 1955), 28-29, 93.

Shirk, Samuel Blaine. *The Characterizations of George Washington in American Drama since 1875.* Easton Pa.: J. S. Correll, 1949.

Shivers, Alfred S. *Maxwell Anderson.* Boston: Twayne, 1976.

Shuman, R. Baird. *Robert E. Sherwood.* New York: Twayne, 1964.

Snyder, Louis L. *The War: A Concise History 1939–1945.* New York: Simon & Schuster, 1960.

Stallings, Lawrence. *Plumes.* New York: Harcourt, Brace, 1924.

Stevenson, Philip. "Concerning M. Anderson: A Word about the Career and Thoughts of the War Dramatist," *The New York Times,* Jan. 9, 1944, II, 1.

_____. "Maxwell Anderson, Thursday's Child," *New Theatre* III (Sept. 1936), 5-7, 25-27.

Sugrue, Francis. "High Tor Sold With Its Ghost and Old House," *New York Herald Tribune,* Feb. 10, 1950.

Sulzberger, C. L., et al., eds. *The American Heritage Picture History of World War II.* New York: American Heritage, 1966.

Tanselle, G. Thomas. "Additions to the Bibliography of Maxwell Anderson," *Papers of the Bibliographical Society of America* LVII (First Quarter 1963), 90-91.

Taubman, Howard. *The Making of the American Theatre.* New York: Coward McCann, 1965.

Taylor, William E. "Maxwell Anderson: Traditionalist in a Theatre of Change," *Modern American Drama: Essays in Criticism.* Deland, Fla.: Everett Edwards, 1968, pp. 47-57.

Teichmann, Howard. *Smart Aleck: The Wit, World and life of Alexander Woollcott.* New York: William Morrow, 1976.

Thurber, James. "The Years with Ross," *Atlantic Monthly* CCII (July 1958), 40-45.

Tietjens, Eunice. *The World at My Shoulder.* New York: Macmillan, 1938.

Twentieth Century Authors, eds. Stanley J. Kunitz and Howard Haycraft. New York: H. W. Wilson, 1942.

Unsigned. "Anderson Files Action against Francis Hackett," *Publisher's Weekly* CLV (June 4, 1949), 2,301.

_____. "Anderson's Rites Held at Columbia," *The New York Times,* Mar. 4, 1959.

_____. "Benefit Performance for German Refugees," *The New York Times,* Nov. 21, 1938, I, 4.

_____. "Boston Protects Itself," *Nation* CXXVII (Dec. 5, 1928), 593.

_____. "Broadway Shows Chastened before Police Interfere," *The New York Times,* Sept. 25, 1924, I, 1, 6.

_____. "Cafe Brawl," *Time* XXXXVII (Mar. 11, 1946), 86.

_____. "Car Kills Case, War's Original 'Captain Flagg,' " *New York Herald Tribune*, Dec. 11, 1933.

_____. "Censors of 'Glory' Hit from the Pulpit," *New York World*, Oct. 27, 1924, I, 28.

_____. "Dead Solider 'Lives' again in Play: Nephew Becomes Anderson's Model," *Buffalo Evening News*, Oct. [14], 1942.

_____. "Dramatist and Poet," *The New York Times*, Mar. 2, 1959.

_____. "Elmer Van Orden, 79, Is Dead; High Tor Owner Inspired Play," *New York Herald Tribune*, Feb. 20, 1942.

_____. Gertrude (Mab) Maynard's obituaries; *The New York Times*, Mar. 23, 1953; *New York Daily Mirror*, Mar. 23, 1953; *Time* XLI (Mar. 30, 1953), 82; *Newsweek* XLI (Mar. 30, 1953), 70.

_____. "Hayward Considers What Price Glory," *The New York Times*, Sept. 27, 1924, I, 17.

_____. "High Tor Land is Bought by River Group," *Nyack*, (N.Y.) *Journal-News*, Feb. 17, 1943.

_____. "How a 'Great Play' Is Written," *Current Opinion* LXXVII (Nov. 1924), 617-18.

_____. "Hudson River Society Buys High Tor for Park Use," *New York Herald Tribune*, Feb. 17, 1943.

_____. "Hylan Acts against New Broadway Play," *The New York Times*, Sept. 24, 1924, I, 1.

_____. "Kurt Weill is Buried," *The New York Times*, Apr. 6, 1950, I, 29.

_____. "The Lives of John F. Wharton," *Fortune* XXXIII (May 1946), 192, 194.

_____. "Many New Faculty Members are Appointed this Year," *The Quaker Campus* (Whittier College student newspaper), Sept. 20, 1917, p. 1.

_____. "Maxwell Anderson," *Current Biography* III, (Nov. 1942), 18-21.

_____. Maxwell Anderson's obituaries: "Maxwell Anderson, Playwright, is Dead," *The New York Times*, Mar. 1, 1959, I, 1, 84; *Time* LXXIII (Mar. 9, 1959), 84; *Newsweek* LIII (Mar. 9, 1959), 82.

_____. "Miss Haskett Won First Prize," *The Student* (Univ. of North Dakota student newspaper), May 10, 1911, p. 1.

_____. "Mounting High Tor," *The New York Times*, Feb. 14, 1937, X, 2.

_____. "Neighbors Honor Owner of High Tor," *The New York Times*, June 16, 1939, I, 25.

_____. "Palisades Interstate Park 1900-1960" (n. d.), booklet by Palisades Interstate Park Commission, Bear Mountain, N.Y.

_____. "Palisades Park System Takes Title to High Tor . . .," *Nyack* (N.Y.) *Journal-News,* Apr. 14, 1943.

_____. "Playwright in Serious Condition," *Olean* (N.Y.) *Herald,* Feb. 27, 1959.

_____. "Producer Bites Critic," *Newsweek* XXVII (Mar. 11, 1946), 82.

_____. "The Pulitzer Prize Drama Winner," *Literary Digest* CXV (May 20, 1933), 15.

_____. "The Queen from Keokuk," *This Fabulous Century: The Thirties.* Editors of Time-Life Books. New York: Time-Life, 1969, IV, 154.

_____. "Rites Held for Greenwood Township Native Son," *Meadville* (Pa.) *Tribune,* Oct. 21, 1963.

_____. "The Savior of High Tor," *The New York Times,* June 17, 1939, I, 14.

_____. "U.S. Prosecutor Takes No Action against War Play," *New York World,* Sept. 27, 1924.

_____. " 'What Price Glory' and Its Authors," *The New York Times,* Sept. 14, 1924, VIII, 1.

_____. "Wilbur Criticizes 'What Price Glory,' " *The New York Times,* Sept. 28, 1924, I, 9.

Wadeau, Roy S. *Vintage Years of the Theatre Guild 1928–1939.* Cleveland, Ohio: Case Western Reserve Univ., 1972.

Walker, Danton. *Spooks Deluxe: Some Excursions into the Supernatural.* New York: Franklin Watts, 1956.

Wall, Vincent. "Maxwell Anderson: The Last Anarchist," *American Drama and its Critics: A Collection of Criticial Essays.* Chicago: Univ. of Chicago Press, 1965.

Watts, Harold H. "Maxwell Anderson: The Tragedy of Attrition," *College English* IV (Jan. 1943), 220-30.

Weales, Gerald. *American Drama since World War II.* New York: Harcourt, Brace & World, 1962.

Wharton, John F. *Life Among the Playwrights: Being Mostly the Story of the Playwrights Producing Company.* New York: Quadrangle, 1974.

Wilkins, Robert P. "Editor's Notes," *North Dakota Quarterly* XXXVIII (Winter, 1970) 4, 91-92.

Wright, Edward A. *A Primer for Playgoers: An Introduction to the Understanding and Appreciation of Cinema—Stage—Television.* Englewood Cliffs, N.J.: Prentice-Hall, 1958.

Yoset, Thomas L. "Maxwell Anderson, the Playwright," *Crawford County Genealogy* I (July 1978), 79-84. This is one of the two published genealogies of the Anderson family, the other one being found in Avery's *Letters.*

Young, Stark. "Elizabeth," *The New Republic* LXV (Nov. 19, 1930), 19.

———. "War Theatre," *The New Republic* CVII (Oct. 26, 1942), 546.

Zolotow, Maurice. *Stagestruck: The Romance of Alfred Lunt and Lynn Fontanne.* New York: Harcourt, Brace & World, 1965.

INDEX

Eve of St. Mark), 194
Muni, Paul, 187
Murray, Amy, 71
Music Box Theater (N.Y.C.), 230
Mussolini, Benito, 166
My Fair Lady, 266

Nathan, George Jean, 96, 177, 238
National Conference of Christians and
    Jews, 229, 230, 260
National Herald (Greek newspaper),
    226
National Theatre (N.Y.C.), 187
Nation, The, 52
Natwick, Mildred, 155
Nazimova, Alla, 60, 86
Neustadt, Baron and Baronin
    (characters in *Masque of Kings*),
    155
New Brighton, Pa., 6, 10, 18
New City, N.Y., 67 *et seq.*
New Deal administration, 172, 175,
    198
New Dramatists, 269
New Hampton, Ia., 6, 24-27
New Republic, The, 51, 56, 60, 61, 67,
    74, 164, 197, 227, 228
New Yorker, 62, 89, 91
New York Evening Post, 63
New York Evening Sun, The, 90, 92, 96
New York Herald Tribune, 52, 62, 221,
    226, 228
New York Law School, 165
New York Times, The, 51, 62, 86, 91,
    121, 186, 188, 193, 221, 245, 269
New York Trap Rock Company, 152
New York Tribune, 62
New York World, 62, 67, 70, 72, 81,
    83, 88, 89 *et passim*
Nicholl, Louise Townsend, 63
Nichols, Anne *(Abie's Irish Rose),* 86,
    160
Nietzsche, Friedrich, 183, 184
Niggli, Josephina *(Mexican Village),* 45

North Clarkstown Civilian Defense
    Committee, 188
Norvelle, Lee, ix, 196
No Time for Comedy, 163, 171
November Hereabout, 71
Nun's Story, The, 52

Oakleaf, Gilda, *See* Gilda Anderson
O'Brien, Edmond, 155
O'Casey, Sean, xix, 81, 142
Odets, Clifford, 123
Oedipus Rex, 265
Office of War Information, 199
O. Henry, 61
Oklahoma Red (character in *Outside
    Looking In*), 104
Older, Fremont, 51, 59
Oliver, Stanley, 157-58
Olivier, Laurence, 265
Olsen, Nancy, 78
O'Neil, George, 63
O'Neill, Eugene Gladstone, xvii-xviii, 68,
    77, 86, 94, 101, 120, 142, 147,
    149, 160, 162, 241, 256
    et passim
O'Neill, Eugene, Jr., 256
O'Neill, Oona, 256
O'Neill, Shane, 256
On Trial, 100, 165
Oparre (character in *Wingless Victory*),
    205
Orms, Melvin I., 25
Orser, Lloyd, 157
Othello, 147, 216

Palisades Interstate Park, 155
Palmer, Lilli, 140
Palo Alto, Calif., 59
Paolo-Francesca theme, 164
Parke-Bernet galleries, 267
Parker, Brig. Gen. Edwin P., 189, 190,
    193
Parker, Dorothy, 90, 91, 144
Pasadena Playhouse, 185